Lineberger Memorial Library

Lutheran Theological Southern Seminary   Columbia, S.C.

LOEB CLASSICAL LIBRARY

FOUNDED BY JAMES LOEB 1911

EDITED BY

JEFFREY HENDERSON

ATHENAEUS

VII

LCL 345

ATHENAEUS

THE LEARNED BANQUETERS

BOOKS 13.594b–14

EDITED AND TRANSLATED BY

S. DOUGLAS OLSON

HARVARD UNIVERSITY PRESS

CAMBRIDGE, MASSACHUSETTS

LONDON, ENGLAND

2011

Copyright © 2011 by the President and Fellows
of Harvard College
All rights reserved

First published 2011

LOEB CLASSICAL LIBRARY® is a registered trademark
of the President and Fellows of Harvard College

Library of Congress Control Number 2006041321
CIP data available from the Library of Congress

ISBN 978-0-674-99673-1

*Composed in ZephGreek and ZephText by
Technologies 'N Typography, Merrimac, Massachusetts.
Printed on acid-free paper and bound by
The Maple-Vail Book Manufacturing Group*

CONTENTS

PREFACE   vii

ABBREVIATIONS   ix

THE CHARACTERS   xi

Book XIII   2

Book XIV   98

INDEX   381

Contents

PREFACE

For a general introduction to Athenaeus and *The Learned Banqueters* and to my citation conventions, see the beginning of Volumes I and III. Like all previous editors, I have tacitly added a handful of section divisions accidentally omitted from Casaubon's text.

Thanks are again due to my undergraduate students Joseph McDonald, William Blessing, Cameron Ferguson, and Debbie Sugarbaker for their many hours of reference checking, proofreading, formatting assistance, and the like. Much of the work for this volume and the one to follow was completed at the National Humanities Center, where I held a fellowship during the 2008–2009 academic year. Volume VII is dedicated to my friends in the North Carolina rock-climbing community, and in particular to Mark Daughtridge, whose constant admonitions "Abs tight!" (translated "Rely on your core strength!") and "Elbow into the wall on slopers!" (translated "Use what you have!") I have tried to apply in other areas of my life as well.

ABBREVIATIONS

Berve — H. Berve, *Das Alexanderreich auf prosopographischer Grundlage* ii *Prosopographie* (Munich, 1926)

Billows — R. A. Billows, *Antigonos the One-Eyed and the Creation of the Hellenistic State* (Berkeley, Los Angeles, and London, 1990)

Bradford — A. S. Bradford, *A Prosopography of Lacedaimonians from the Death of Alexander the Great, 323 B.C., to the Sack of Sparta by Alaric, A.D. 396* (Vestigia 27: Munich, 1977)

FGE — D. L. Page (ed.), *Further Greek Epigrams* (Cambridge, 1981)

FGrH — F. Jacoby (ed.), *Die Fragmente der Griechischen Historiker* (Leiden, 1923–69)

FHG — C. and T. Müller, *Fragmenta Historicorum Graecorum* (5 vols.: Paris, 1841–70)

HE — A. S. F. Gow and D. L. Page (eds.), *The Greek Anthology: Hellenistic Epigrams* (Cambridge, 1965)

O'Connor — J. B. O'Connor, *Chapters in the History of Actors and Acting in Ancient Greece together with a Prosopographia Histrionum Graecorum* (Chicago, 1908)

ABBREVIATIONS

PAA J. Traill (ed.), *Persons of Ancient Athens* (Toronto, 1994–)

PMG D. L. Page (ed.), *Poetae Melici Graeci* (Oxford, 1962)

Poralla P. Poralla, *A Prosopography of Lacedaimonians from the Earliest Times to the Death of Alexander the Great (X–323 B.C.)*[2] (revised by A. S. Bradford: Chicago, 1985)

SH H. Lloyd-Jones and P. Parsons (eds.), *Supplementum Hellenisticum* (Texte und Kommentar, Band 11: Berlin and New York, 1983)

SSR G. Giannantoni, *Socratis et Socraticorum Reliquiae* (4 vols.; n.p., 1990)

Stephanis I. E. Stephanis, Διονυσιακοὶ Τεχνίται (Herakleion, 1988)

SVF J. van Arnim (ed.), *Stoicorum Veterum Fragmenta* (3 vols.; Leipzig, 1921, 1903)

TrGF B. Snell *et al.* (eds.), *Tragicorum Graecorum Fragmenta* (Göttingen, 1971–2004)

THE CHARACTERS

ATHENAEUS, the narrator; also a guest at the dinner party

TIMOCRATES, Athenaeus' interlocutor

AEMILIANUS MAURUS, grammarian (e.g. 3.126b)

ALCEIDES OF ALEXANDRIA, musician (1.1f; 4.174b)

AMOEBEUS, citharode (14.622d–e)

ARRIAN, grammarian (3.113a)

CYNULCUS, Cynic philosopher whose given name is Theodorus (e.g. 1.1d; 3.97c)

DAPHNUS OF EPHESUS, physician (e.g. 1.1e; 2.51a)

DEMOCRITUS OF NICOMEDIA, philosopher (1.1e; 3.83c)

DIONYSOCLES, physician (3.96d, 116d)

GALEN OF PERGAMUM, physician (e.g. 1.1e–f, 26c)

LARENSIUS, Roman official and also host of the party (e.g. 1.2b–3c; 2.50f)

LEONIDAS OF ELIS, grammarian (1.1d; 3.96d)

MAGNUS (e.g. 3.74c)

MASURIUS, jurist, poet, musician (e.g. 1.1c; 14.623e)

MYRTILUS OF THESSALY, grammarian (e.g. 3.83a)

PALAMEDES THE ELEATIC, lexicographer (9.379a)

CHARACTERS

PHILADELPHUS OF PTOLEMAIS, philosopher
   (1.1d)*
PLUTARCH OF ALEXANDRIA, grammarian (e.g.
   1.1c–d; 3.83b)
PONTIANUS OF NICOMEDIA, philosopher (1.1d;
   3.109b)
RUFINUS OF NICAEA, physician (1.1f)*
ULPIAN OF TYRE, grammarian and also symposiarch
   (e.g. 1.1d–e; 2.49a)
VARUS, grammarian (3.118d)
ZOILUS, grammarian (e.g. 1.1d; 7.277c)

* Neither Philadelphus nor Rufinus is said to speak anywhere in the preserved text of *The Learned Banqueters*,
and most likely some of the anonymous speeches in 1.2a–
3.73e (represented in the Epitome manuscripts only) belong to them.

THE LEARNED BANQUETERS

ΙΓ

Διαβόητος δ' ἑταίρα γέγονε καὶ ἡ Μιλησία Πλαγ-
γών· ἧς περικαλλεστάτης οὔσης ἠράσθη τις Κολοφώ-
νιος νεανίσκος, Βακχίδα ἔχων ἐρωμένην τὴν Σαμίαν.
λόγους οὖν προσενέγκαντος τοῦ νεανίσκου πρὸς αὐτὴν ἡ Πλαγγὼν ἀκούουσα τῆς Βακχίδος τὸ κάλλος
καὶ ἀποτρέψαι θέλουσα τὸν νεανίσκον τοῦ πρὸς αὐτὴν
c ἔρωτος, ὡς ἀδύνατον ἦν, ᾔτησε τῆς συνουσίας |
μισθὸν τὸν Βακχίδος ὅρμον διαβόητον ὄντα. ὁ δὲ
σφοδρῶς ἐρῶν ἠξίωσε τὴν Βακχίδα μὴ περιιδεῖν
αὐτὸν ἀπολλύμενον· καὶ ἡ Βακχὶς τὴν ὁρμὴν κατ-
ιδοῦσα τοῦ νεανίσκου ἔδωκε. Πλαγγὼν δὲ τὸ ἄζηλον
συνιδοῦσα τῆς Βακχίδος τὸν μὲν ἀπέπεμψεν ἐκείνῃ,
τῷ δὲ ὡμίλησε· καὶ τοῦ λοιποῦ φίλαι ἐγένοντο, κοινῶς
περιέπουσαι τὸν ἐραστήν. ἐφ' οἷς Ἴωνες ἀγασθέντες,
ὥς φησι Μενέτωρ ἐν τῷ Περὶ Ἀναθημάτων, Πασιφί-
λαν ἐκάλεσαν τὴν Πλαγγόνα. μαρτυρεῖ δὲ καὶ Ἀρχί-
d λοχος | περὶ αὐτῆς ἐν τούτοις·

BOOK XIII (continued)

Plangon of Miletus was also a notorious courtesan. She was extremely beautiful, and a young man from Colophon fell in love with her, even though he already had a lover from Samos named Bacchis. When the young man sent her a message, Plangon—who knew how beautiful Bacchis was supposed to be—wanted to divert his interest in herself. After this proved impossible, she asked for a well-known necklace that belonged to Bacchis as her price for sleeping with him. He was so besotted that he begged Bacchis not to let him die before her eyes, and when she saw how desperate he was, she gave it to him. Plangon recognized Bacchis' lack of jealousy and sent the necklace back to her, but still slept with the young man; after that the women were friends and treated him as the lover of them both. The Ionians were astounded by these events, according to Menetor in his *On Dedications* (*FHG* iv.452),[1] and referred to Plangon as Pasiphile ("Friendly to Everyone"). Archilochus (fr. spur. 331 West[2] = *FGE* 540–1) also offers information about her in the following passage:

---

[1] Presumably the necklace that plays a central role in the story above was one of the dedications discussed by Menetor, from whom the entire anecdote must be drawn.

συκῆ πετραίη πολλὰς βόσκουσα κορώνας
εὐήθης ξείνων δέκτρια Πασιφίλη.

ὅτι δὲ καὶ Μένανδρος ὁ ποιητὴς ἤρα Γλυκέρας κοινόν.
ἐνεμεσήθη δέ· Φιλήμονος γὰρ ἑταίρας ἐρασθέντος καὶ
χρηστὴν ταύτην ὀνομάσαντος διὰ τοῦ δράματος,
ἀντέγραψεν Μένανδρος ὡς οὐδεμιᾶς οὔσης χρηστῆς.

Ἅρπαλος δ' ὁ Μακεδὼν ὁ τῶν Ἀλεξάνδρου πολλὰ
e χρημάτων συλήσας | καὶ καταφυγὼν εἰς Ἀθήνας
ἐρασθεὶς Πυθιονίκης πολλὰ εἰς αὐτὴν κατανάλωσεν
ἑταίραν οὖσαν, καὶ ἀποθανούσῃ πολυτάλαντον μνη-
μεῖον κατεσκεύασεν· ἐκφέρων τε αὐτὴν ἐπὶ τὰς ταφάς,
ὥς φησι Ποσειδώνιος ἐν τῇ δευτέρᾳ καὶ εἰκοστῇ τῶν
Ἱστοριῶν, τεχνιτῶν τῶν ἐπισημοτάτων χορῷ μεγάλῳ
καὶ παντοίοις ὀργάνοις καὶ συμφωνίαις[1] παρέπεμπε
τὸ σῶμα. Δικαίαρχος δ' ἐν τοῖς Περὶ τῆς Εἰς Τροφωνίου Καταβάσεώς φησι· ταὐτὸ δὲ πάθοι τις ἂν ἐπὶ
f τὴν Ἀθηναίων πόλιν ἀφικνούμενος | κατὰ τὴν ἀπ'
Ἐλευσῖνος τὴν ἱερὰν ὁδὸν καλουμένην. καὶ γὰρ ἐνταῦθα καταστὰς οὗ ἂν φανῇ τὸ πρῶτον ὁ τῆς Ἀθηνᾶς
ἀφορώμενος νεὼς καὶ τὸ πόλισμα, ὄψεται παρὰ τὴν
ὁδὸν αὐτὴν ᾠκοδομημένον μνῆμα οἷον οὐχ ἕτερον
οὐδὲ σύνεγγυς οὐδέν ἐστι τῷ μεγέθει. τοῦτο δὲ τὸ μὲν
πρῶτον, ὅπερ εἰκός, ἢ Μιλτιάδου φήσειεν ⟨ἂν⟩[2] σα-

[1] συμφωνίαις Casaubon: εὐφωνίαις A
[2] add. Kaibel

> like a fig-tree among the rocks that feeds many
>   ravens,
>   good-hearted Pasiphile who receives strangers.

That the poet Menander (test. 17) was in love with Glycera is commonplace.[2] But he became angry with her; for when the poet Philemon (fr. dub. 198) fell in love with a courtesan and called her a good woman in a play, Menander responded by writing that there are no good women.

Harpalus of Macedon, who stole a large amount of Alexander's money and ran off to Athens,[3] was in love with Pythionice, who was a courtesan, and he spent a great deal of the money on her. After she died, he built her a tomb that cost many talents, and when he organized her funeral procession, according to Posidonius in Book XXII of his *History* (*FGrH* 87 F 14 = fr. 66 Edelstein–Kidd), he arranged for her body to be escorted by an enormous chorus made up of the most distinguished actors, and by instruments and musical groups of all sorts. Dicaearchus says in his *On the Descent into the Shrine of Trophonius* (fr. 21 Wehrli = fr. 81 Mirhady): The same would happen to anyone who came to Athens along the so-called Sacred Road from Eleusis. For if a person stands in the spot where the Temple of Athena and the Acropolis first become visible, he will see a tomb that has been erected directly alongside the road which is unlike any of the others and is much larger than them. Initially, as one might expect, he would be likely to say that this must certainly belong to Miltiades,

---

[2] Glycera is *PAA* 277495. For her relationship with Menander, cf. 13.585c. [3] Cf. 6.245f–6a with n.; 8.341e–2a; 13.586c with n., 595e–6b. Harpalus is Berve i #143; *PAA* 204010. Pythionice is Berve i #676; *PAA* 793690.

595 φῶς ἢ Περικλέους ἢ Κίμωνος ‖ ἤ τινος ἑτέρου τῶν
ἀγαθῶν ἀνδρῶν εἶναι, ⟨καὶ⟩[3] μάλιστα μὲν ὑπὸ τῆς
πόλεως δημοσίᾳ κατεσκευασμένον, εἰ δὲ μή, δεδο-
μένον κατασκευάσασθαι. πάλιν δ' ὅταν ἐξετάσῃ Πυθιονίκης τῆς ἑταίρας ὄν, τίνα χρὴ προσδοκίαν λαβεῖν
αὐτόν; Θεόπομπος δ' ἐν τῇ Πρὸς Ἀλέξανδρον Ἐπιστολῇ τὴν Ἁρπάλου διαβάλλων ἀκολασίαν φησίν·
ἐπίσκεψαι δὲ καὶ διάκουσον σαφῶς παρὰ τῶν ἐκ
Βαβυλῶνος ὃν τρόπον Πυθιονίκην περιέστειλεν τελευ-
τήσασαν, ἢ Βακχίδος μὲν ἦν δούλη τῆς αὐλητρίδος,
b ἐκείνη δὲ Σινώπης τῆς Θρᾴττης | τῆς ἐξ Αἰγίνης
Ἀθήναζε μετενεγκαμένης τὴν πορνείαν· ὥστε γίνεσθαι μὴ μόνον τρίδουλον, ἀλλὰ καὶ τρίπορνον αὐτήν.
ἀπὸ πλειόνων δὲ ταλάντων ἢ διακοσίων δύο μνήματα
κατεσκεύασεν αὐτῆς· ὃ καὶ πάντες ἐθαύμαζον, ὅτι τῶν
μὲν ἐν Κιλικίᾳ τελευτησάντων ὑπὲρ τῆς σῆς βασιλείας καὶ τῆς τῶν Ἑλλήνων ἐλευθερίας οὐδέπω νῦν
οὔτε ἐκεῖνος οὔτ' ἄλλος οὐδεὶς τῶν ἐπιστατῶν κεκό-
σμηκε τὸν τάφον, Πυθιονίκης δὲ τῆς ἑταίρας φανήσε-
ται τὸ μὲν Ἀθήνησι, τὸ δ' ἐν Βαβυλῶνι μνῆμα πολὺν
c ἤδη χρόνον ἐπιτετελεσμένον. | ἦν γὰρ πάντες ᾔδεσαν
ὀλίγης δαπάνης κοινὴν τοῖς βουλομένοις γιγνομένην,
ταύτης ἐτόλμησεν ὁ φίλος εἶναι σοῦ φάσκων ἱερὸν καὶ
τέμενος ἱδρύσασθαι καὶ προσαγορεῦσαι τὸν ναὸν καὶ
τὸν βωμὸν Πυθιονίκης Ἀφροδίτης, ἅμα τῆς τε παρὰ

[3] add. Kaibel

6

or Pericles, or Cimon,[4] or to some other distinguished individual, and that it was doubtless erected by the city at public expense, or failing that, that public permission must have been granted for its construction. But then, when he looks and sees that it belongs to the courtesan Pythionice, what is he supposed to think? Theopompus in his *Letter to Alexander* (*FGrH* 115 F 253) denounces Harpalus' depravity and says: Look into and carefully inquire from the people who come from Babylon about how he buried Pythionice after she died—a woman who was a slave of the pipe-girl Bacchis,[5] who herself belonged to Sinope of Thrace,[6] who transferred her whoring from Aegina to Athens, meaning that Pythionice was not just a slave three generations back but a whore three generations back as well. He spent over 200 talents building two tombs for her; this shocked everyone, given that neither he nor any other official has yet set up a marker at the burial spot of the men who died in Cilicia[7] to secure your kingdom and the freedom of the Greeks, whereas people will see that the tombs of the courtesan Pythionice, one in Athens, the other in Babylon, have long been completed. For even though everyone knew that she was available to anyone who wanted her at a minimal price, a man who claims to be your friend had the audacity to construct a temple and a sanctuary in her honor, and to refer to the temple building and the altar as belonging to Pythionice Aphrodite, both ignoring the

---

[4] Three of Athens' greatest 5th-century political leaders (*PAA* 653815, 772645, and 569795, respectively).

[5] *PAA* 261090.

[6] *PAA* 823250.

[7] A reference to the battle of Issus in 333 BCE.

θεῶν τιμωρίας καταφρονῶν καὶ τὰς σὰς τιμὰς προπη-
λακίζειν ἐπιχειρῶν. μνημονεύει τούτων καὶ Φιλήμων
ἐν Βαβυλωνίῳ·

βασίλισσ' ἔσῃ Βαβυλῶνος, ἂν οὕτω τύχῃ·
τὴν Πυθιονίκην οἶσθα καὶ τὸν Ἅρπαλον. |

d μνημονεύει δ' αὐτῆς καὶ Ἄλεξις ἐν Λυκίσκῳ. μετὰ δὲ
τὴν Πυθιονίκης τελευτὴν ὁ Ἅρπαλος Γλυκέραν μετεπέμψατο καὶ ταύτην ἑταίραν, ὡς ὁ Θεόπομπος ἱστορεῖ, φάσκων ἀπειρηκέναι τὸν Ἅρπαλον μὴ στεφανοῦν
ἑαυτόν, εἰ μή τις στεφανώσειε καὶ τὴν πόρνην. ἔστη-
σέν τε εἰκόνα χαλκῆν τῆς Γλυκέρας ἐν Ῥωσσῷ τῆς
Συρίας, οὗπερ καὶ σὲ καὶ αὐτὸν ἀνατιθέναι μέλλει.
παρέδωκέν τε αὐτῇ κατοικεῖν ἐν τοῖς βασιλείοις τοῖς
ἐν Ταρσῷ καὶ ὁρᾷ ὑπὸ τοῦ λαοῦ προσκυνουμένην καὶ
e βασίλισσαν προσαγορευομένην καὶ ταῖς ἄλλαις |
δωρεαῖς τιμωμένην, αἷς πρέπον ἦν τὴν σὴν μητέρα
καὶ τὴν σοὶ συνοικοῦσαν. συνεπιμαρτυρεῖ δὲ τούτοις
καὶ ὁ τὸν Ἀγῆνα τὸ σατυρικὸν δραμάτιον γεγραφώς,
ὅπερ ἐδίδαξεν Διονυσίων ὄντων ἐπὶ τοῦ Ὑδάσπου τοῦ
ποταμοῦ, εἴτε Πύθων ἦν ὁ Καταναῖος ἢ Βυζάντιος ἢ
καὶ αὐτὸς ὁ βασιλεύς. ἐδιδάχθη δὲ τὸ δρᾶμα ἤδη
φυγόντος τοῦ Ἁρπάλου ἐπὶ θάλατταν καὶ ἀποστάντος.
καὶ τῆς μὲν Πυθιονίκης ὡς τεθνηκυίας μέμνηται, τῆς

---

8 What follows is once again drawn direct from the *Letter
to Alexander*. The same passage of Theopompus is cited also at
13.586c. The Glycera in question is Berve i #231; *PAA* 277490.

revenge the gods might take on him and doing his best to trample in the mud the honors due to you. Philemon in *The Babylonian* (fr. 15) also refers to this situation:

> You'll be queen of Babylon, if everything works out;
> you know about Pythionice and Harpalus.

Alexis in *Lyciscus* (fr. 143) also refers to her. After Pythionice died, Harpalus sent for Glycera, who was also a courtesan, according to Theopompus (*FGrH* 115 F 254b), who claims that Harpalus refused to allow anyone to put a garland on his own head unless they also garlanded his whore.[8] In addition, he set up a bronze statue of Glycera in Syrian Rhossus, where he intends to set up statues of you and himself as well. He also gave her permission to live in the royal palace in Tarsus, and he watches as she is bowed down to by the local people, addressed as "Queen," and granted the other honors that properly belong to your mother and the woman who lives with you. Additional evidence in regard to these matters is supplied by the author of the miniature satyr play *Agen* (whether this was Python of Catana or Byzantium, or the king[9] himself), who staged it during the festival of Dionysus celebrated on the banks of the Hydaspes River. The play was put on after Harpalus had already run away to the coast and revolted. The author refers to Pythionice as dead, and to Glycera as being

[9] Alexander. Very similar language is used in regard to the authorship of the play at 13.586d (cf. 2.50f), but with no reference to the possibility that Python might be from Byzantium, an idea that probably represents confusion with a different individual (cf. 12.550e–f).

δὲ Γλυκέρας ὡς οὔσης παρ' αὐτῷ καὶ τοῖς Ἀθηναίοις
f αἰτίας γινομένης | τοῦ δωρεὰς λαμβάνειν παρὰ Ἁρ-
πάλου, λέγων ὧδε·

(Α.) ἔστιν δ' ὅπου μὲν ὁ κάλαμος πέφυχ' ὅδε
† φέτωμ' † ἄορνον, οὐξ ἀριστερᾶς δ' ὅδε
πόρνης ὁ κλεινὸς ναός, ὃν δὴ Παλλίδης
τεύξας κατέγνω διὰ τὸ πρᾶγμ' αὐτοῦ φυγήν.
ἐνταῦθα δὴ τῶν βαρβάρων τινὲς μάγοι
ὁρῶντες αὐτὸν παγκάκως διακείμενον
ἔπεισαν ὡς ἄξουσι τὴν ψυχὴν ἄνω ‖
596 τὴν Πυθιονίκης.

Παλλίδην δ' ἐνταῦθα ἐκάλεσε τὸν Ἅρπαλον. ἐν ⟨δὲ⟩[4]
τοῖς ἑξῆς τῷ κυρίῳ καλέσας αὐτόν φησιν·

(Α.) ἐκμαθεῖν δέ σου ποθῶ
μακρὰν ἀποικῶν κεῖθεν, Ἀτθίδα χθόνα
τίνες τύχαι † καλοῦσιν † ἢ πράττουσι τί.
(Β.) ὅτε μὲν ἔφασκον δοῦλον ἐκτῆσθαι βίον,
ἱκανὸν ἐδείπνουν· νῦν δὲ τὸν χέδροπα μόνον
καὶ τὸν μάραθον ἔσθουσι, πυροὺς δ' οὐ μάλα.
(Α.) καὶ μὴν ἀκούω μυριάδας τὸν Ἅρπαλον |
b αὐτοῖσι τῶν Ἀγῆνος οὐκ ἐλάττονας
σίτου διαπέμψαι καὶ πολίτην γεγονέναι.
(Β.) Γλυκέρας ὁ σῖτος οὗτος ἦν, ἔσται δ' ἴσως
αὐτοῖσιν ὀλέθρου κοὐχ ἑταίρας ἀρραβών.

[4] add. Schweighäuser

10

with Harpalus and as responsible for the Athenians receiving gifts from him, putting it as follows (Python *TrGF* 91 F 1.1–8):

> (A.) Where this reed grows there's a
> birdless [corrupt]. This structure on the left, on the other hand,
> is the famous temple of the whore, which Pallides
> built—and then condemned himself to exile for what he'd done.
> When some of the barbarian magi here
> saw the terrible state he was in,
> they convinced him they could summon up the soul
> of Pythionice.

He called Harpalus "Pallides" in this passage. But in what follows immediately after this, he refers to him by his proper name and says (Python *TrGF* 91 F 1.8–18):[10]

> (A.) Since I'm living a long way from there,
> I'm eager to learn from you what the situation
> † they call † Attica, and how they're doing.
> (B.) When they claimed they'd been reduced to slavery,
> they had enough for dinner. But now all they eat
> is beans and fennel, and no wheat at all.
> (A.) Indeed, I hear that Harpalus sent
> them 10s of 1000s of measures of grain—at least
> as much as Agen did—and became a citizen.
> (B.) This grain belonged to Glycera; maybe it'll be
> earnest money for their deaths, not the courtesan's!

---

[10] The final five verses are quoted also at 13.586d.

11

ἐνδόξους δὲ ἑταίρας καὶ ἐπὶ κάλλει διαφερούσας ἤνεγ-
κεν καὶ ἡ Ναύκρατις· Δωρίχαν τε, ἣν ἡ καλὴ Σαπφὼ
ἐρωμένην γενομένην Χαράξου τοῦ ἀδελφοῦ αὐτῆς
κατ᾽ ἐμπορίαν εἰς τὴν Ναύκρατιν ἀπαίροντος διὰ τῆς
ποιήσεως διαβάλλει ὡς πολλὰ τοῦ Χαράξου νοσφι-
c σαμένην. Ἡρόδοτος | δ᾽ αὐτὴν Ῥοδῶπιν καλεῖ, ἀγνο-
ῶν ὅτι ἑτέρα τῆς Δωρίχας ἐστὶν αὕτη, ἡ καὶ τοὺς
περιβοήτους ὀβελίσκους ἀναθεῖσα ἐν Δελφοῖς, ὧν
μέμνηται Κρατῖνος διὰ τούτων· < . . . > εἰς δὲ τὴν
Δωρίχαν τόδ᾽ ἐποίησε τοὐπίγραμμα Ποσείδιππος,
καίτοι καὶ ἐν τῇ Αἰθιοπίᾳ πολλάκις αὐτῆς μνημονεύ-
σας. ἐστὶ <δὲ>[5] τόδε·

Δωρίχα, ὀστέα μὲν σὰ πάλαι κόνις ἦν ὅ τε
    δεσμὸς
χαίτης ἥ τε μύρων ἔκπνοος ἀμπεχόνη, |
d ᾗ ποτε τὸν χαρίεντα περιστέλλουσα Χάραξον
σύγχρους ὀρθρινῶν ἥψαο κισσυβίων·
Σαπφῷαι δὲ μένουσι φίλης ἔτι καὶ μενέουσιν
ᾠδῆς αἱ λευκαὶ φθεγγόμεναι σελίδες
οὔνομα σὸν μακαριστόν, ὃ Ναύκρατις ὧδε
    φυλάξει
ἔστ᾽ ἂν ἴῃ Νείλου ναῦς ἐφ᾽ ἁλὸς πελάγη.

καὶ Ἀρχεδίκη δ᾽ ἦν ἐκ τῆς Ναυκράτεως καὶ αὐτὴ
e ἑταίρα καλή· φιλεῖ γάρ πως ἡ Ναύκρατις, | ὡς ὁ Ἡρό-
δοτός φησιν, ἐπαφροδίτους ἔχειν τὰς ἑταίρας. καὶ ἡ ἐξ

_____
[5] add. Musurus

12

Naucratis also produced famous and exceptionally beautiful courtesans, including Doriche, who was a lover of Sappho's brother Charaxus, who sailed to Naucratis on a trading journey; the lovely Sappho (fr. 254c; cf. fr. 15) abuses her in her poems for extracting a substantial amount of money from Charaxus. Herodotus (2.135.1) refers to her as Rhodopis, being unaware that this is a different person from Doriche; his Rhodopis also dedicated the well-known spits in Delphi (cf. Hdt. 2.135.4), which Cratinus (fr. 369) mentions in the following passage:[11] . . . Posidippus wrote the following epigram about Doriche and also mentioned her repeatedly in his *Ethiopia* (146 Austin–Bastianini). The epigram (*HE* 3142–9 = 122 Austin–Bastianini) runs as follows:

> Doricha, your bones have long been dust, along with the band
>> you wore in your hair, and the perfume-breathing shawl
> in which you once enfolded the graceful Charaxus,
>> flesh to flesh, and took hold of early-morning cups of wine.
> But the white columns of Sappho's lovely ode
>> still endure and will endure, proclaiming
> your blessed name, which Naucratis will preserve
>> so long as ships sail forth from the Nile into the sea.

Archedice, another beautiful courtesan, was also from Naucratis; for Naucratis somehow has a tendency, as Herodotus (2.135.5) says, to offer charming courtesans. So too

---

[11] The quotation has fallen out of the text.

Ἐρέσου δὲ τῆς <ποιητρίας ὁμώνυμος>[6] ἑταίρας Σαπφὼ
τοῦ καλοῦ Φάωνος ἐρασθεῖσα περιβόητος ἦν, ὥς φησι
Νυμφόδωρος[7] ἐν Περίπλῳ Ἀσίας. Νικαρέτη δὲ ἡ
Μεγαρὶς οὐκ ἀγεννὴς ἦν ἑταίρα, ἀλλὰ καὶ γονέων
<ἕνεκα>[8] καὶ κατὰ παιδείαν ἐπέραστος ἦν, ἠκροᾶτο δὲ
Στίλπωνος τοῦ φιλοσόφου. Βιλιστίχη δ' ἡ Ἀργεία
ἑταίρα καὶ αὐτὴ ἔνδοξος, τὸ γένος ἀπὸ τῶν Ἀτρειδῶν
σῴζουσα, ὡς οἱ τὰ Ἀργολικὰ γράψαντες ἱστοροῦσιν.

f   ἔνδοξος δ' ἐστὶν καὶ Λέαινα | ἡ ἑταίρα, Ἁρμοδίου
ἐρωμένη τοῦ τυραννοκτονήσαντος· ἥτις καὶ αἰκιζο-
μένη ὑπὸ τῶν περὶ Ἱππίαν τὸν τύραννον οὐδὲν ἐξει-
ποῦσα ἐναπέθανεν ταῖς βασάνοις. Στρατοκλῆς δ' ὁ
ῥήτωρ ἐρωμένην εἶχε τὴν ἐπικληθεῖσαν Λήμην ἑταίραν, τὴν καλουμένην Παρόραμα < . . . > διὰ τὸ καὶ δύο
δραχμῶν φοιτᾶν πρὸς τὸν βουλόμενον, ὥς φησι Γορ-
γίας ἐν τῷ Περὶ Ἑταιρῶν.

Ἐπὶ τούτοις ὁ Μυρτίλος μέλλων σιωπᾶν, ἀλλὰ
μικροῦ, ἔφη, ἄνδρες φίλοι, ἐξελαθόμην ὑμῖν εἰπεῖν
597   τήν τε Ἀντιμάχου Λυδήν, || προσέτι δὲ καὶ τὴν ὁμώνυ-
μον ταύτης ἑταίραν Λυδὴν ἣν ἠγάπα Λαμύνθιος ὁ
Μιλήσιος. ἑκάτερος γὰρ τούτων τῶν ποιητῶν, ὥς φησι

---

6 add. Kaibel   7 Νυμφόδωρος Wilamowitz: Νύμφις A
8 add. Coraes

---

12 For Sappho and Phaon, see the material collected as Sapph.
fr. 211a–b. For the "other Sappho," cf. Ael. *VH* 12.19.
13 Cf. 13.576e–f, where she is associated with Ptolemy Philadelphus.   14 *PAA* 602683. For the assassination of the Athe-

the courtesan Sappho of Eresus, who shared a name with the poetess, was notorious for being in love with the handsome Phaon, according to Nymphodorus in the *Voyage along the Coast of Asia* (*FGrH* 572 F 6).[12] Nicarete of Megara was a quite refined courtesan and was particularly attractive because of her ancestry and her education, since she had been a student of the philosopher Stilpo (fr. 156 Döring = *SSR* II O 17). The Argive courtesan Bilistiche[13] was also a notable person, who traced her ancestry back to the Atreidae, according to the authors of the *History of Argos* (*FGrH* 311 F 1). The courtesan Leaena,[14] the lover of the tyrannicide Harmodius, is also a notable person; when she was being manhandled by the henchmen of the tyrant Hippias, she told them nothing and died under torture. The orator Stratocles[15] had the courtesan named Lêmê as his lover; she was referred to as Parorama . . . because she would visit anyone who wanted her for two drachmas,[16] according to Gorgias in his *On Courtesans* (*FGrH* 351 F 1).

Although Myrtilus was about to stop speaking at this point, he said: But I nearly forgot, my friends, to mention Antimachus' Lyde to you, as well as the courtesan Lyde who shared her name (cf. Hermesian. fr. 7.41–6, p. 99 Powell, below), and whom Lamynthius of Miletus was sweet on. For both poets, according to Clearchus in his

nian tyrant Hipparchus in 514 BCE by Harmodius and Aristogiton, see 15.695a–b with n. Hippias was Hipparchus' brother.   [15] See 13.580d n. Lêmê is *PAA* 607353.

[16] *lêmê* is the crust that forms in one's eyes, while *parorama* normally means "oversight, error." But the wit is not obvious, and a second nickname has perhaps fallen out of the text.

Κλέαρχος ἐν τοῖς Ἐρωτικοῖς, τῆς βαρβάρου Λυδῆς
εἰς ἐπιθυμίαν καταστὰς ἐποίησεν ὁ μὲν ἐν ἐλεγείοις, ὁ
δ᾿ ἐν μέλει τὸ καλούμενον ποίημα Λυδήν. παρέλιπον
δὲ καὶ τὴν Μιμνέρμου αὐλητρίδα Ναννὼ καὶ τὴν
Ἑρμησιάνακτος τοῦ Κολοφωνίου Λεόντιον· ἀπὸ γὰρ
ταύτης ἐρωμένης αὐτῷ γενομένης ἔγραψεν ἐλεγειακὰ
b τρία βιβλία, | ὧν ἐν τῷ τρίτῳ κατάλογον ποιεῖται
ἐρωτικῶν, οὑτωσί πως λέγων·

οἵην μὲν φίλος υἱὸς ἀνήγαγεν Οἰάγροιο
    Ἀργιόπην Θρῆσσαν στειλάμενος κιθάρην
Ἀιδόθεν· ἔπλευσεν δὲ κακὸν καὶ ἀπειθέα χῶρον,
    ἔνθα Χάρων κοινὴν ἕλκεται εἰς ἄκατον
ψυχὰς οἰχομένων, λίμνη δ᾿ ἐπὶ μακρὸν ἀϋτεῖ
    ῥεῦμα διὲκ μεγάλων ῥυομένη δονάκων. |
c ἀλλ᾿ ἔτλη παρὰ κῦμα μονόζωστος κιθαρίζων
    Ὀρφεύς, παντοίους δ᾿ ἐξανέπεισε θεούς,
Κωκυτόν τ᾿ ἀθέμιστον ὑπ᾿ ὀφρύσι μειδήσαντα·
    ἠδὲ καὶ αἰνοτάτου βλέμμ᾿ ὑπέμεινε κυνός,
ἐν πυρὶ μὲν φωνὴν τεθοωμένου, ἐν πυρὶ δ᾿ ὄμμα
    σκληρόν, τριστοίχοις δεῖμα φέρον κεφαλαῖς.

---

17 No fragments of Lamynthius (4th century BCE or earlier)
are preserved, but cf. Epicr. fr. 4 (quoted at 13.605e).

18 Stephanis #1770.

19 Orpheus (named below), who descended to Hades to re-
claim his wife (normally called Eurydice).

20 One of the rivers of the Underworld, here personified. The
"horrid dog" is Cerberus.

Erotica (fr. 34 Wehrli = Antim. test. 10 Matthews), became
infatuated with the barbarian Lyde and wrote poems entitled *Lyde*, the former in elegiacs, the latter in lyric meters
(*PMG* 839).[17] I also left out Mimnermus' pipe-girl
Nanno[18] (cf. Hermesian. fr. 7.35–7, p. 99 Powell, below)
and Hermesianax of Colophon's Leontion; for he wrote
three books of elegiacs inspired by her when she was his
lover, in the third of which he offers a catalogue of love-
affairs, saying something along the following lines (fr. 7,
pp. 98–100 Powell):

> (A woman) such as Argiope of Thrace, whom the
>   beloved son
>   of Oeagrus,[19] wielding a lyre, brought up
> from Hades. He sailed to an unhappy spot in which
>   persuasion has no power,
>   where Charon hauls the souls of those who have
>   passed
> into a skiff we all share, and cries out far and wide
>   over the marshy water
>   whose stream flows through the dense reeds.
> But Orpheus had the courage to travel alone and to
>   play his lyre
>   beside its waves, and he persuaded gods of every
>   sort,
> including lawless Cocytus,[20] who squinted at him and
>   smiled.
>   He stood up as well to the gaze of the horrid dog,
> whose voice was keen with fire, and whose eyes were
>   harsh
>   with fire, and which produced terror with its
>   three-fold heads.

ATHENAEUS

ἔνθεν ἀοιδιάων μεγάλους ἀνέπεισεν ἄνακτας
  Ἀργιόπην μαλακοῦ πνεῦμα λαβεῖν βιότου.
οὐ μὴν οὐδ' υἱὸς Μήνης ἀγέραστον ἔθηκε |

d Μουσαῖος Χαρίτων ἤρανος Ἀντιόπην,
ἥ τε πολὺν μύστησιν Ἐλευσῖνος παρὰ πέζαν
  εὐασμὸν κρυφίων ἐξεφόρει λογίων,
Ῥάριον ὀργειῶνα νόμῳ διαπομπεύουσα
  Δημήτρᾳ· γνωστὴ δ' ἐστὶ καὶ εἰν Ἀΐδῃ.
φημὶ δὲ καὶ Βοιωτὸν ἀποπρολιπόντα μέλαθρον
  Ἡσίοδον πάσης ἤρανον ἱστορίης
Ἀσκραίων ἐσικέσθαι ἐρῶνθ' Ἑλικωνίδα κώμην·
  ἔνθεν ὅ γ' Ἠοίην μνώμενος Ἀσκραϊκὴν |

e πόλλ' ἔπαθεν, πάσας δὲ λόγων ἀνεγράψατο
    βίβλους
  ὑμνῶν, ἐκ πρώτης παιδὸς ἀνερχόμενος.
αὐτὸς δ' οὗτος ἀοιδός, ὃν ἐκ Διὸς αἶσα φυλάσσει
  ἥδιστον πάντων δαίμονα μουσοπόλων,
λεπτὴν ἧς Ἰθάκην ἐνετείνατο θεῖος Ὅμηρος
  ᾠδῇσιν πινυτῆς εἵνεκα Πηνελόπης, |

f ἣν διὰ πολλὰ παθὼν ὀλίγην ἐσενάσσατο νῆσον,
  πολλὸν ἀπ' εὐρείης λειπόμενος πατρίδος·
ἔκλεε δ' Ἰκαρίου τε γένος καὶ δῆμον Ἀμύκλου
  καὶ Σπάρτην, ἰδίων ἁπτόμενος παθέων.

---

[21] Hesiod himself has nothing good to say about the place (*Op.* 640).   [22] An inventive allusion to the fact that the individual items in Hesiod's *Catalogue of Women* all begin with the words *ê hoiê* ("or a woman such as"; cf. 13.590b n.).

[23] Icarius was Penelope's father (*Od.* 11.446), and Paus. 3.1.3–4 identifies him as a descendant of Amyclas of Sparta.

18

With his songs he convinced the great lords that
   Argiope
  should be granted the breath of soft life and
    escape from there.
Nor indeed did Mene's son Musaeus, guardian of the
   Graces,
  deprive Antiope of her fair share of honor,
she who upon Eleusis' plain expounded to initiates
  the long Bacchic cry of secret oracles,
duly escorting the Rarian priest
  for Demeter. She is known in Hades as well.
I also claim that Boeotian Hesiod, the guardian of
   tales
  of all sorts, abandoned his home
and came to the lovely Heliconian village of Ascra.[21]
  From there he courted Ascraean Eoie and
suffered much; and he wrote out all his books of
   poetic
  verses, setting off from his girl's name first.[22]
This very poet whom a decree from Zeus preserves
  as the most pleasant deity among all the Muses'
    servants,
the godlike Homer, described her meager Ithaca
  in his songs for thoughtful Penelope.
On her account he suffered much, and he settled on
   her tiny island,
  leaving far behind his broad fatherland,
and spread the fame of Icarius' family[23] and of the
   people of Amyclas
  and of Sparta, pursuing the theme of their private
   troubles.

Μίμνερμος δέ, τὸν ἡδὺν ὃς εὕρετο πολλὸν
  ἀνατλὰς ‖

598

ἦχον καὶ μαλακοῦ πνεῦμα τὸ πενταμέτρου,
καίετο μὲν Ναννοῦς, πολιῷ δ᾽ ἐπὶ πολλάκι λωτῷ
  κημωθεὶς κώμους εἶχε σὺν Ἐξαμύῃ,
ἤχθεε δ᾽ Ἑρμόβιον τὸν ἀεὶ βαρὺν ἠδὲ Φερεκλῆν
  ἐχθρόν, μισήσας οἷ᾽ ἀνέπεμψεν ἔπη.
Λυδῆς δ᾽ Ἀντίμαχος Λυδηίδος ἐκ μὲν ἔρωτος
  πληγεὶς Πακτωλοῦ ῥεῦμ᾽ ἐπέβη ποταμοῦ· |

b

† δαρδανη † δὲ θανοῦσαν ὑπὸ ξηρὴν θέτο γαῖαν
  κλαίων, † αιζαον † δ᾽ ἦλθεν ἀποπρολιπὼν
ἄκρην ἐς Κολοφῶνα, γόων δ᾽ ἐνεπλήσατο
    βίβλους
  ἱράς, ἐκ παντὸς παυσάμενος καμάτου.
Λέσβιος Ἀλκαῖος δὲ πόσους ἀνεδέξατο κώμους
  Σαπφοῦς φορμίζων ἱμερόεντα πόθον,
γιγνώσκεις· ὁ δ᾽ ἀοιδὸς ἀηδόνος ἠράσαθ᾽,
    ὕμνων |

c

Τήϊον ἀλγύνων ἄνδρα πολυφραδίῃ.
καὶ γὰρ τὴν ὁ μελιχρὸς ἐφημίλλητ᾽ Ἀνακρέων
  στελλομένην πολλαῖς ἄμμιγα Λεσβιάσιν·

---

[24] This passage = Antim. test. 11 Matthews; cf. 13.597a.

[25] Anacreon (cf. 13.599c–d, 600d–e), treated here as Alcaeus'
rival for Sappho's (i.e. "the nightingale's") love.

[26] For the chronological problem, see 13.599c–d.

But Mimnermus, who after enduring much
      discovered the sweet
  sound and breath of the sensuous pentameter,
burned for Nanno, and often with an ancient lotus-
      pipe strapped
  to his lips he wandered the streets drunk, along
      with Examue,
and quarreled with the eternally unpleasant
      Hermobius and with his enemy
  Pherecles, resenting the sort of remarks he
      produced.
Whereas Antimachus,[24] stung by love for Lydian
  Lyde, walked along the stream of the Pactolus
      River,
and [corrupt] placed her, after she was dead, beneath
      the dry earth,
  wailing all the while. And leaving behind
      [corrupt], he went
to steep Colophon, and he filled his sacred books
  with cries of lament, and gave up all his grief.
You know how many drunken wanderings Lesbian
      Alcaeus
  undertook, celebrating with his lyre his lovely
      desire
for Sappho. The bard loved the nightingale, and he
      caused grief
  for the man from Teos[25] by the eloquence of his
      hymns.
For Anacreon, sweet as honey, also competed for
      her[26]
  who was beautifully attired among Lesbos' many
      women.

φοίτα δ' ἄλλοτε μὲν λείπων Σάμον, ἄλλοτε δ'
    αὐτὴν
οἰνηρῇ δειρῇ κεκλιμένην πατρίδα
Λέσβον ἐς εὔοινον· τὸ δὲ Μύσιον εἴσιδε Λεκτὸν
πολλάκις Αἰολικοῦ κύματος ἀντιπέρας.
Ἀτθὶς δ' οἷα μέλισσα πολυπρήωνα Κολωνὸν
λείπουσ' ἐν τραγικαῖς ᾖδε χοροστασίαις |

d   Βάκχον καὶ τὸν ἔρωτα Θεωρίδος < . . . >
    < . . . > Ζεὺς ἔπορεν Σοφοκλεῖ.
φημὶ δὲ κἀκεῖνον τὸν ἀεὶ πεφυλαγμένον ἄνδρα
καὶ πάντων μῖσος κτώμενον ἐκ † συνοχῶν †
πάσας ἀμφὶ γυναῖκας, ὑπὸ σκολιοῖο τυπέντα
τόξου νυκτερινὰς οὐκ ἀποθέσθ' ὀδύνας·
ἀλλὰ Μακηδονίης πάσας κατενίσατο λαύρας
    † αιγειων †, μέθεπεν δ' Ἀρχελέω ταμίην, |

e   εἰσόκε <δὴ> δαίμων Εὐριπίδη εὗρ' ὄλεθρον
Ἀρριβίου στυγνῶν ἀντιάσαντι κυνῶν.
ἄνδρα δὲ τὸν Κυθέρηθεν, ὃν ἐθρέψαντο τιθῆναι
Βάκχου καὶ λωτοῦ πιστότατον ταμίην
Μοῦσαι παιδευθέντα Φιλόξενον, οἷα τιναχθεὶς
Ὀρτυγίῃ ταύτης ἦλθε διὰ πτόλεως

---

[27] Sophocles; this passage = S. test. 78. For his supposed lover Theoris, see 13.592a–b with n.

[28] Euripides, who at the end of his life moved to the court of Archelaus of Macedon, and who was supposedly torn apart by hunting dogs normally said to have belonged to his host rather than to the otherwise unknown Arrhibius (E. test. 122–5c). This passage = E. test. 106a.

[29] Sc. that belonging to Eros.   [30] The nymphs.

22

Sometimes he left Samos, at other times his own
     fatherland
  nestled against a grapevine-covered ridge, and
     went
to wine-filled Lesbos; and often he gazed upon
     Mysian
  Lectus on the other side of the Aeolian wave.
(You also know) how the Attic bee[27] left Colonus with
     its many
  little hills, and sang of Bacchus and of his love
for Theoris in choral performances of tragedy . . .
  . . . Zeus furnished to Sophocles.
I refer as well to that man[28] who remained eternally
     on guard
  and had secured universal dislike as a result of
     [corrupt]
regarding all women, but who, once wounded by a
     crooked
  bow,[29] did not set aside his nocturnal pangs.
Instead, he traveled through all the alleyways of
     Macedon
  [corrupt] and tagged behind Archelaus' steward,
until in fact a deity contrived destruction for
     Euripides,
  when he encountered Arrhibius' horrid dogs.
As for the man from Cythera, whom Bacchus'
     nurses[30]
  and the Muses raised—that is, Philoxenus, who
     was trained to be
the most trustworthy steward of the lotus-pipe—you
     know
  how shaken up he was when he passed through
     this city

23

γιγνώσκεις, ἀίουσα μέγαν πόθον ὃν Γαλατείη
αὐτοῖς μηλείοις θήκαθ᾽ ὑπὸ προγόνοις.
οἶσθα δὲ καὶ τὸν ἀοιδόν, ὃν Εὐρυπύλου
πολιῆται |

Κῷοι χάλκειον στῆσαν ὑπὸ πλατάνῳ
Βιττίδα μολπάζοντα θοήν, περὶ πάντα Φιλίταν
ῥήματα καὶ πᾶσαν τρυόμενον λαλιήν.
οὐδὲ μὲν οὐδ᾽ ὁπόσοι σκληρὸν βίον ἐστήσαντο
ἀνθρώπων, σκοτίην μαιόμενοι σοφίην,
οὓς αὐτὴ περὶ πυκνὰ λόγοις ἐσφίγξατο μῆτις,
καὶ δεινὴ μύθων κῆδος ἔχουσ᾽ ἀρετή,
οὐδ᾽ οἳ δ᾽ αἰνὸν ἔρωτος ἀπεστρέψαντο κυδοιμὸν ‖
μαινομένου, δεινὸν δ᾽ ἦλθον ὑφ᾽ ἡνίοχον.
οἵη μὲν Σάμιον μανίη κατέδησε Θεανοῦς
Πυθαγόρην, ἑλίκων κομψὰ γεωμετρίης
εὑρόμενον, καὶ κύκλον ὅσον περιβάλλεται αἰθὴρ
βαιῇ ἐνὶ σφαίρῃ πάντ᾽ ἀποπλασσάμενον.
οἵῳ δ᾽ ἐχλίηνεν, ὃν ἔξοχον ἔχρη Ἀπόλλων
ἀνθρώπων εἶναι Σωκράτη ἐν σοφίῃ, |

f

599

---

31 "This city" is presumably Colophon (Hermesianax's native
town). But it is unclear whether "Ortygia" is supposed to refer to
the island in the Great Harbor at Syracuse (and thus to Dionysius'
court there; thus Powell) or to Ephesus (where Hermesianax is
said to have died; thus Bergk).

32 Cf. 1.6e–7a with n.; 13.564e. Normally Galateia is a sea-
nymph, and the lambs would be expected to belong to her hapless
lover the Cyclops (cf. Antiph. fr. 131, quoted at 9.402e).

33 This passage = Philit. test. 2 Spanoudakis.

34 I.e. the philosophers.

for Ortygia,[31] for you have heard of his enormous
      longing, which Galateia[32]
   treated as less important than her most recently
   born lambs.
You are also familiar with the singer whom
      Eurypylus' fellow-citizens on
  Cos set up in bronze beneath a plane tree,
singing of swift Bittis—that is, Philitas,[33] who wore
      himself out
   on words of all kinds and on every sort of chatter.
Nor did any of those people who made their own
      lives
   difficult by pursuing obscure wisdom,[34]
whose very intelligence bound them tight in
      arguments,
   as did the fearsome skill that occupied itself with
   words—
not even they evaded the awful roil of insane
   love, but they were instead mastered by a dire
   charioteer.
A mad longing of this sort for Theano[35] overcame
   Pythagoras, who discovered the subtleties of
   geometric
cycles, and who created in a tiny sphere a model
   of everything about which the upper air is
   wrapped.
Whereas with what fiery heat did angry Cypris[36]
      warm
   Socrates—the man Apollo in an oracle declared

[35] Described by D.L. 8.42–3 as Pythagoras' wife.
[36] Aphrodite.

b   Κύπρις μηνίουσα πυρὸς μένει· ἐκ δὲ βαθείης
    ψυχῆς κουφοτέρας ἐξεπόνησ᾽ ἀνίας,
  οἰκί᾽ ἐς Ἀσπασίης πωλεύμενος· οὐδέ τι τέκμαρ
    εὗρε, λόγων πολλὰς εὑρόμενος διόδους.
  ἄνδρα ⟨δὲ⟩ Κυρηναῖον ἔσω πόθος ἔσπασεν
    Ἰσθμοῦ
  δεινός, ὅτ᾽ Ἀπιδανῆς Λαΐδος ἠράσατο
  ὀξὺς Ἀρίστιππος, πάσας δ᾽ ἠνήνατο λέσχας
    φεύγων, † ουδαμενον εξεφορησεβιωι †. |

c   ἐν τούτοις ὁ Ἑρμησιάναξ σφάλλεται συγχρονεῖν οἰόμενος Σαπφὼ καὶ Ἀνακρέοντα, τὸν μὲν κατὰ Κῦρον
καὶ Πολυκράτην γενόμενον, τὴν δὲ κατ᾽ Ἀλυάττην τὸν
Κροίσου πατέρα. Χαμαιλέων δ᾽ ἐν τῷ Περὶ Σαπφοῦς
καὶ λέγειν τινάς φησιν εἰς αὐτὴν πεποιῆσθαι ὑπὸ
Ἀνακρέοντος τάδε·

  σφαίρῃ δηὖτέ με πορφυρῇ
  βάλλων χρυσοκόμης Ἔρως
  νήνι ποικιλοσαμβάλῳ
  συμπαίζειν προκαλεῖται·
  ἡ δ᾽, ἐστὶν γὰρ ἀπ᾽ εὐκτίτου
  Λέσβου, τὴν μὲν ἐμὴν κόμην,

---

37 Cf. Pl. *Ap.* 21a, citing Delphic Oracle H3 Fontenrose (discussed also at 5.218e–f). For Socrates and Aspasia, cf. 5.219b–e
with n.   38 Cf. Herodicus *SH* 495 (preserved at 5.219c–e).

39 Aristippus of Cyrene, founder of the Cyrenaic school of philosophy (12.510a n.). This passage = fr. 63 Mannebach = *SSR* IV
A 94.

beyond all other humans in his wisdom![37] His
    profound soul
  only yielded him less stable sorrows
when he visited Aspasia's house.[38] Nor did he
    discover any cure
  for them, although he invented numerous
    pathways of argument.
And a fearful longing drew a man of Cyrene below
    the
  Isthmus, when insightful Aristippus[39] fell in love
with Laïs of Apidna; in his effort to escape, he
    refused
  all conversation, [corrupt].

Hermesianax is in error in this passage,[40] since he believes
that Sappho (fr. 250) and Anacreon are contemporaries,
whereas in fact Anacreon lived in the time of Cyrus and
Polycrates, but Sappho lived in the time of Croesus' father
Alyattes.[41] Chamaeleon in his *On Sappho* (fr. 26 Wehrli)
says that some authorities claim that Anacreon (*PMG* 358)
refers to her in the following passage:

When golden-haired Eros
strikes me with a purple ball,
he's challenging me to have fun with
that girl who's wearing the fancy sandals.
But since she's from Lesbos full of
lovely cities, she's unhappy

[40] I.e. in verses 51–2, quoted at 13.598c.
[41] Alyattes of Lydia ruled *c*.610–560 BCE, while Cyrus of Persia built his empire beginning about 550, and Polycrates of Samos seized power *c*.535.

λευκὴ γάρ, καταμέμφεται, |
d πρὸς δ' ἄλλην τινὰ χάσκει.

καὶ τὴν Σαπφὼ δὲ πρὸς αὐτὸν ταῦτά φησιν εἰπεῖν·

κεῖνον, ὦ χρυσόθρονε Μοῦσ', ἔνισπες
ὕμνον, ἐκ τᾶς καλλιγύναικος ἐσθλᾶς
Τήιος χώρας ὃν ἄειδε τερπνῶς
πρέσβυς ἀγαυός.

ὅτι δὲ οὔκ ἐστι Σαπφοῦς τοῦτο τὸ ᾆσμα παντί που
δῆλον· ἐγὼ δὲ ἡγοῦμαι παίζειν τὸν Ἑρμησιάνακτα
περὶ τούτου τοῦ ἔρωτος. καὶ γὰρ Δίφιλος ὁ κωμῳδιοποιὸς πεποίηκεν ἐν Σαπφοῖ δράματι Σαπφοῦς ἐραστὰς Ἀρχίλοχον καὶ Ἱππώνακτα.

Ταῦθ' ὑμῖν, | ὦ ἑταῖροι, οὐκ ἀμερίμνως δοκῶ τὸν
e ἐρωτικὸν τοῦτον πεποιῆσθαι κατάλογον, οὐκ ὢν οὕτως
ἐρωτομανὴς ὡς διαβάλλων μ' εἴρηκεν ὁ Κύνουλκος,
ἀλλ' ἐρωτικὸς μὲν εἶναι ὁμολογῶ, ἐρωτομανὴς δὲ οὔ.

τίς δ' ἔστ' ἀνάγκη δυστυχεῖν ἐν πλείοσιν,
ἐξὸν σιωπᾶν κἀν σκότῳ κρύπτειν τάδε;,

Αἰσχύλος ἔφη ὁ Ἀλεξανδρεὺς ἐν Ἀμφιτρύωνι. οὗτος
δέ ἐστιν Αἰσχύλος ὁ καὶ τὰ Μεσσηνιακὰ ἔπη συνθείς,

---

42 Cf. 13.598c n.

43 Archilochus probably belongs about a generation earlier
than Sappho, and Hipponax a generation or two after her. But
Diphilus was presumably not much concerned with chronological
niceties of this sort in any case.

28

with my hair, because it's gray,
and her attention's fixed on a different girl.

Sappho for her part, he says, offered the following response to Anacreon (adesp. *PMG* 953):

Muse seated on a gold throne—that hymn
you recited was the one the noble old man
from the fine land of Teos,[42] rich in beautiful women,
used to sing so nicely.

That this song is not by Sappho is obvious to everyone, I suppose, and in my judgment Hermesianax is joking when he refers to their love-affair. The comic poet Diphilus in his play *Sappho* (fr. 71), moreover, represents Archilochus and Hipponax as Sappho's lovers.[43]

I consider this a quite meticulous catalogue of love-affairs that I have produced for you, my friends, and although I am not as crazy about love (*erôtomanês*)[44] as Cynulcus claimed in his attack on me,[45] I confess that I am intrigued by it, if not crazy about it (*erôtomanês*).

But why should you confess your bad luck in public,
when you can keep these matters quiet and conceal
them in shadow?,

as Aeschylus of Alexandria said in *Amphitryon* (*TrGF* 179 F 1). This is the same Aeschylus who composed the epic poem *The History of Messenia* (*SH* 13); he was a well-

---

[44] For a catalogue of similar formations (to which the emphatic use of the adjective here suggests it is connected somehow), see 11.464d–e (citing Chrysippus).

[45] At 13.566e–7c, 568d–e.

f   ἀνὴρ εὐπαίδευτος. ὑπολαμβάνων οὖν | μέγαν εἶναι
δαίμονα καὶ δυνατώτατον τὸν Ἔρωτα, προσέτι τε καὶ
τὴν Ἀφροδίτην τὴν χρυσῆν, τὰ Εὐριπίδου ἐπὶ νοῦν
λαμβάνων λέγω·

> τὴν Ἀφροδίτην οὐχ ὁρᾷς ὅση θεός;
> ἣν οὐδ᾽ ἂν εἴποις οὐδὲ μετρήσειας ἂν
> ὅση πέφυκε κἀφ᾽ ὅσον διέρχεται.
> αὕτη τρέφει σὲ κἀμὲ καὶ πάντας βροτούς.
> τεκμήριον δέ, μὴ λόγῳ μόνον μάθῃς· ||

600
> ἔργῳ δὲ δείξω τὸ σθένος τὸ τῆς θεοῦ·[9]
> ἐρᾷ μὲν ὄμβρου γαῖ᾽, ὅταν ξηρὸν πέδον
> ἄκαρπον αὐχμῷ νοτίδος ἐνδεῶς ἔχῃ,
> ἐρᾷ δ᾽ ὁ σεμνὸς οὐρανὸς πληρούμενος
> ὄμβρου πεσεῖν εἰς γαῖαν Ἀφροδίτης ὕπο·
> ὅταν δὲ συμμιχθῆτον ἐς ταὐτὸν δύο,
> φύουσιν ἡμῖν πάντα καὶ τρέφουσ᾽ ἅμα
> δι᾽ ὧν βρότειον ζῇ τε καὶ θάλλει γένος.

καὶ ὁ σεμνότατος δ᾽ Αἰσχύλος ἐν ταῖς Δαναΐσιν αὐτὴν
παράγει τὴν Ἀφροδίτην λέγουσαν· |

b
> ἐρᾷ μὲν ἁγνὸς οὐρανὸς τρῶσαι χθόνα,
> ἔρως δὲ γαῖαν λαμβάνει γάμου τυχεῖν·
> ὄμβρος δ᾽ ἀπ᾽ εὐνάεντος οὐρανοῦ πεσὼν

[9] This verse appears to be an early (non-Euripidean) addition
to the text.

30

educated individual (*FGrH* 488 T 1). Since I believe, therefore, that Eros is an important and extremely powerful divinity, and that golden Aphrodite[46] is as well, I call to mind the passage from Euripides (fr. 898)[47] and say:

> Do you not see how powerful a goddess Aphrodite is?
> It would be impossible to describe or measure
> how great she is, or how wide her power extends.
> She is the one who sustains you, and me, and all
>   mortals.
> There is proof of this, and no need to rely on
>   argument alone;
> I will show you in practical terms how strong the
>   goddess is.
> The earth loves the rain, whenever the dry fields
> are parched, and fruitless, and in need of moisture;
> so too the sacred sky, when full of rain,
> loves to fall on the earth, under Aphrodite's direction.
> And when the two mix together into one,
> they produce and nourish for us everything
> that keeps the mortal race alive and flourishing.

The august Aeschylus in his *Danaids* (fr. 44) even brings Aphrodite herself onstage saying:

> The holy sky loves to penetrate the land,
> and a desire for marriage overwhelms the earth.
> The rain that falls from heaven kisses the earth,

---

[46] An echo of a common Homeric phrase (e.g. *Il.* 3.64; *Od.* 4.14).

[47] What follows appears to be from the same collection of material as 13.561a–c.

ἔκυσε γαῖαν· ἡ δὲ τίκτεται βροτοῖς
μήλων τε βοσκὰς καὶ βίον Δημήτριον
δένδρων τ᾽ ὀπώραν· ἐκ νοτίζοντος γάμου
τελεῖθ᾽ ὅσ᾽ ἔστι· τῶν δ᾽ ἐγὼ παραίτιος.

ἐν Ἱππολύτῳ Εὐριπιδείῳ πάλιν ἡ Ἀφροδίτη φησίν· |

c   ὅσοι τε Πόντου τερμόνων τ᾽ Ἀτλαντικῶν
ναίουσιν εἴσω, φῶς ὁρῶντες ἡλίου,
τοὺς μὲν σέβοντας τἀμὰ πρεσβεύω κράτη,
σφάλλω δ᾽ ὅσοι φρονοῦσιν εἰς ἡμᾶς μέγα.

νεανίσκῳ γὰρ τὴν πᾶσαν ἀρετὴν ἔχοντι τοῦτο μόνον
τὸ ἁμάρτημα προσόν, ὅτι οὐκ ἐτίμα τὴν Ἀφροδίτην,
αἴτιον ἐγένετο τοῦ ὀλέθρου· καὶ οὔτε ἡ Ἄρτεμις ἡ
περισσῶς ἀγαπήσασα οὔτε τῶν ἄλλων θεῶν τις ἢ
δαιμόνων ἐβοήθησεν αὐτῷ. κατὰ τὸν αὐτὸν οὖν ποι-
ητήν· |

d   ὅστις ⟨δ᾽⟩ Ἔρωτα μὴ μόνον κρίνει θεόν,[10]
ἢ σκαιός ἐστιν ἢ καλῶν ἄπειρος ὢν
οὐκ οἶδε τὸν μέγιστον ἀνθρώποις θεόν.

ὃν ὁ σοφὸς ὑμνῶν αἰεί ποτε Ἀνακρέων πᾶσίν ἐστιν

[10] Stobaeus has Ἔρωτα δ᾽ ὅστις μὴ θεὸν κρίνει μέγαν
(probably correct) and adds a second verse, καὶ τῶν ἀπάντων
δαιμόνων ὑπέρτατον.

with which heaven shares a bed, and the earth
    produces pasturage
for mortals' flocks, as well as the sustenance Demeter
    provides,
and fruit on the trees. From a moistening marriage
    comes
everything that is; and I am the joint cause of it all.

Again, in the Euripidean *Hippolytus* (3–6) Aphrodite says:

And all those who dwell between the Black Sea and
    Atlas' boundaries, and who see the light of the sun—
I give preference to those who respect my power,
but bring down any who confront me with a proud
    attitude.

For although this was an otherwise outstanding young
man,[48] who made only this one mistake, the fact that he
failed to honor Aphrodite was the cause of his destruction;
neither Artemis, who cared deeply for him, nor any other
god or divinity helped him. To quote the same poet (E. fr.
269), therefore:[49]

Anyone who does not consider Eros the most
    important god
is either stupid, or he lacks experience of what is
    good
and fails to realize who the most significant god for
    mortals is.

The wise Anacreon constantly sings of Eros and is thus on

[48] Referring to Hippolytus, who dies at the end of Euripides'
play.   [49] Identified by Stobaeus as coming from *Auge*.

διὰ στόματος. λέγει οὖν περὶ αὐτοῦ καὶ ὁ κράτιστος
Κριτίας τάδε·

τὸν δὲ γυναικείων μελέων πλέξαντά ποτ' ὠδὰς
ἡδὺν Ἀνακρείοντα Τέως εἰς Ἑλλάδ' ἀνῆγεν,
συμποσίων ἐρέθισμα, γυναικῶν ἠπερόπευμα, |
e   αὐλῶν ἀντίπαλον, φιλοβάρβιτον, ἡδύν, ἄλυπον.
οὔ ποτέ σου φιλότης γηράσεται οὐδὲ θανεῖται,
ἔστ' ἂν ὕδωρ οἴνῳ συμμειγνύμενον κυλίκεσσιν
παῖς διαπομπεύῃ προπόσεις ἐπὶ δεξιὰ νωμῶν
παννυχίδας θ' ἱερὰς θήλεις χοροὶ ἀμφιέπωσιν,
πλάστιγξ θ' ἡ χαλκοῦ θυγάτηρ ἐπ' ἄκραισι
        καθίζῃ
κοττάβου ὑψηλαῖς κορυφαῖς Βρομίου
        ψακάδεσσιν. |

f Ἀρχύτας δ' ὁ ἁρμονικός, ὥς φησι Χαμαιλέων,
Ἀλκμᾶνα γεγονέναι τῶν ἐρωτικῶν μελῶν ἡγεμόνα καὶ
ἐκδοῦναι πρῶτον μέλος ἀκόλαστον, ὄντα καὶ περὶ τὰς
γυναῖκας καὶ τὴν τοιαύτην μοῦσαν εἰς τὰς διατριβάς.
διὸ καὶ λέγειν ἔν τινι τῶν μελῶν·

Ἔρως με δηὖτε Κύπριδος Ϝέκατι
γλυκὺς κατείβων καρδίαν ἰαίνει.

λέγει δὲ καὶ ὡς τῆς Μεγαλοστράτης οὐ μετρίως ἐρα-

---

50 Cf. 13.598c with n.
51 A reference to the symposium game cottabus, for which cf.
15.665d–8f.

everyone's lips. The excellent Critias (88 B 1 D–K) accordingly says the following in regard to him:

> Teos brought to Greece delightful Anacreon,[50]
> who once wove together songs whose lyrics
>   concerned women;
> he stirred up drinking parties, cheated on ladies,
> opposed the pipes, loved the lyre, was pleasant, and
>   inflicted no pain.
> Affection for you will never age or die,
> for as long as a slave brings around water mixed with
>   wine
> for the cups, distributing the toasts from left to right,
> and female choruses participate in sacred all-night
>   festivals,
> and the disk, the daughter of bronze, sits upon the
>   highest
> upper point of the cottabus-stand, awaiting Bromius'
>   drops.[51]

According to Chamaeleon (fr. 25 Wehrli), the music-theorist Archytas[52] (claims that) Alcman invented erotic lyrics and was the first person to publish a depraved song, since he liked to spend his time around women and that kind of music. This is why he says in one of his songs (*PMG* 59(a)):

> When sweet Eros, at Cypris'[53]
> bidding, floods my heart and warms it.

Chamaeleon also claims that Alcman was madly in love

---

[52] Probably not the Pythagorean Archytas of Tarentum but the largely obscure Archytas of Mytilene (D.L. 8.82).

[53] Aphrodite's.

σθείς, ποιητρίας μὲν οὔσης, δυναμένης δὲ καὶ διὰ τὴν
601 ὁμιλίαν τοὺς ἐραστὰς προσελκύσασθαι. ‖ λέγει δ᾽
οὕτως περὶ αὐτῆς·

> τοῦτο Ϝαδειᾶν ἔδειξε Μωσᾶν
> δῶρον μάκαιρα παρσένων
> ἁ ξανθὰ Μεγαλοστράτα.

καὶ Στησίχορος δ᾽ οὐ μετρίως ἐρωτικὸς γενόμενος
συνέστησε καὶ τοῦτον τὸν τρόπον τῶν ἀσμάτων· ἃ δὴ
καὶ τὸ παλαιὸν ἐκαλεῖτο παίδεια καὶ παιδικά. οὕτω δ᾽
ἐναγώνιος ἦν ἡ περὶ τὰ ἐρωτικὰ πραγματεία, καὶ
οὐδεὶς ἡγεῖτο φορτικοὺς τοὺς ἐρωτικούς, ὥστε καὶ
Αἰσχύλος μέγας ὢν ποιητὴς καὶ Σοφοκλῆς ἦγον εἰς
b τὰ θέατρα διὰ τῶν τραγῳδιῶν τοὺς ἔρωτας, ὁ μὲν | τὸν
Ἀχιλλέως πρὸς Πάτροκλον, ὁ δ᾽ ἐν τῇ Νιόβῃ τὸν τῶν
παίδων, διὸ καὶ Παιδεράστριάν τινες καλοῦσι τὴν
τραγῳδίαν· καὶ ἐδέχοντο τὰ τοιαῦτα ἄσματα οἱ θεα-
ταί. καὶ ὁ Ῥηγῖνος δὲ Ἴβυκος βοᾷ καὶ κέκραγεν·

> ἦρι μὲν αἵ τε Κυδώνιαι
> μηλίδες ἀρδόμεναι ῥοᾶν
> ἐκ ποταμῶν, ἵνα Παρθένων
> κῆπος ἀκήρατος, αἵ τ᾽ οἰνανθίδες
> αὐξόμεναι σκιεροῖσιν ὑφ᾽ ἔρνεσιν
> οἰναρέοις θαλέθοισιν· ἐμοὶ δ᾽ ἔρος

---

54 The subject abruptly shifts here to pederastic (rather than
heterosexual) love.   55 Cf. A. frr. 135 (from *Myrmidons*;
quoted at 13.602e); 136; Pl. *Smp.* 180a (= A. fr. 134a).

with Megalostrate, who was a poetess and whose conversation allowed her to attract lovers. He says the following about her (Alcm. *PMG* 59(b)):

This is the gift of the sweet Muses that
a happy young woman, blonde
Megalostrate, showed me.

Stesichorus as well was profoundly erotic and composed songs of this sort, which were in fact referred to in ancient times as *paideia* and *paidika*.[54] Because people were so involved in love-affairs and because no one considered lovers despicable, Aeschylus—who was an important poet—and Sophocles introduced love-affairs to their audiences in their tragedies, the former by referring to Achilleus' love for Patroclus,[55] the latter by discussing the love of boys in his *Niobe*,[56] as a consequence of which some people refer to the play as the *Paiderastria*.[57] Audiences in fact welcomed songs of this sort. Ibycus of Rhegium (*PMG* 286) as well shouts and cries aloud:

In spring appear the Cydonian
apples,[58] watered by the rivers'
floods, in the untouched
garden of the Virgins,[59] while the grape-blossoms
swell and flourish beneath the shadows
grape-vines cast. But there is no season when

---

[56] Cf. S. fr. 448, in which (according to Plutarch) one of Niobe's dying sons called out for his lover.

[57] A feminine form of the normal masculine "pederast."

[58] I.e. quinces.

[59] I.e. the nymphs.

37

οὐδεμίαν κατάκοιτος ὥραν.
† τε † ὑπὸ στεροπᾶς φλέγων
Θρηίκιος βορέας
    ἀίσσων | παρὰ Κύπριδος ἀζαλέ-
      αις μανίαισιν ἐρεμνὸς ἀθαμβὴς
ἐγκρατέως παιδόθεν[11] † φυλάσσει †
ἡμετέρας φρένας.

καὶ Πίνδαρος δ' οὐ μετρίως ὢν ἐρωτικός φησιν·

εἴη καὶ ἐρᾶν καὶ ἔρωτι
χαρίζεσθαι κατὰ καιρόν·
μὴ πρεσβυτέραν ἀριθμοῦ
δίωκε, θυμέ, πρᾶξιν.

διόπερ καὶ ὁ Τίμων ἐν τοῖς Σίλλοις ἔφη·

ὥρη ἐρᾶν, ὥρη δὲ γαμεῖν, ὥρη δὲ πεπαῦσθαι,

καὶ μὴ ἀναμένειν ἔστ' ἂν ἐκεῖνό τις φθέγξηται κατὰ
τὸν αὐτὸν τοῦτον φιλόσοφον· |

ἡνίκ' ἐχρῆν δύνειν, νῦν ἄρχεται ἡδύνεσθαι.

μνησθεὶς δὲ καὶ τοῦ Τενεδίου Θεοξένου ὁ Πίνδαρος, ὃς
ἦν αὐτοῦ ἐρώμενος, τί φησιν;

---

[11] Better πεδόθεν (Naeke); but the verse is corrupt in any case.

my passion lays calm in bed.
† and † like the Thracian north wind,
burning from the lightning blast,
　　rushing from Cypris[60] with scorch-
　　　　ing madness, dark and fearless
powerfully ever since I was a boy † it guards †
my mind.

So too Pindar (fr. 127),[61] who was exceptionally erotic, says:

May I have the chance to love and to yield
to love at the appropriate moment!
Do not, my heart, pursue behavior
that is older than your years!

This is why Timo said in his *Silloi* (*SH* 791.2):[62]

There's a time for love, a time for marriage—and a
　　time for cutting it out,

and not to wait until someone quotes the well-known line from the same philosopher (*SH* 791.1):

When he should have been heading down, now he
　　starts living high.

And what does Pindar (fr. 123)[63] say when he refers to Theoxenus of Tenedos, who was his boyfriend?

---

[60] Aphrodite.

[61] The first two verses are quoted also at 13.561b.

[62] Quoted also (along with verse 1, which follows here) at 7.281e, where see n.

[63] Verses 2–6 are quoted also at 13.564d–e.

χρῆν μὲν κατὰ καιρὸν ἐρώ-
   των δρέπεσθαι, θυμέ, σὺν ἁλικίᾳ·
τὰς δὲ Θεοξένου ἀκτῖνας πρὸς ὄσσων
μαρμαριζοίσας δρακεὶς
ὃς μὴ πόθῳ κυμαίνεται, ἐξ ἀδάμαντος
ἢ σιδάρου κεχάλκευται μέλαιναν καρδίαν
ψυχρᾷ φλογί, πρὸς δ' Ἀφροδί-
   τας ἀτιμασθεὶς ἑλικογλεφάρου
ἢ περὶ χρήμασι μοχθίζει βιαίως
ἢ γυναικείῳ θράσει
ψυχρὰν † φορεῖται πᾶσαν | ὁδὸν θεραπεύων.
ἀλλ' ἐγὼ τᾶς ἕκατι κηρὸς ὣς δαχθεὶς ἕλᾳ
ἱρᾶν μελισσᾶν τάκομαι, εὖτ' ἂν ἴδω
παίδων νεόγυιον ἐς ἥβαν·
ἐν δ' ἄρα καὶ Τενέδῳ
Πειθώ τ' ἔναιεν καὶ Χάρις
υἱὸν Ἀγησίλα.

e

ὅλως δὲ τοὺς παιδικοὺς ἔρωτας τῶν ἐπὶ ταῖς θηλείαις
προκρίνουσι πολλοί· παρὰ γὰρ τὰς ἄλλας ταῖς εὐνο-
μουμέναις πόλεσιν ἐπὶ τῆς Ἑλλάδος σπουδασθῆναι
τόδε τὸ ἔθος. Κρῆτες γοῦν, ὡς ἔφην, καὶ οἱ ἐν Εὐβοίᾳ
Χαλκιδεῖς περὶ τὰ παιδικὰ δαιμονίως ἐπτόηνται. Ἐχε-
μένης γοῦν ἐν τοῖς Κρητικοῖς οὐ τὸν Δία φησὶν
ἁρπάσαι | τὸν Γανυμήδην ἀλλὰ Μίνωα. οἱ δὲ προ-
ειρημένοι Χαλκιδεῖς παρ' αὑτοῖς φασιν ἁρπασθῆναι

f

You should have picked love's flowers
    at the right time, my heart, when you were young.
But as for the sparkling rays from Theoxenus'
eyes, whoever looks on them
and is not roiled with longing has a black heart
forged with cold fire out of steel
or iron; and disregarded by
    Aphrodite of the glancing eyes,
he either toils furiously to earn money
or is no braver than a woman and
is carried along on every † cold road, like a servant.
But I on her[64] account, like wax produced by the
    sacred
bees when it is stung by the sun's rays, am melted
    whenever I gaze
upon the youthful beauty of boys with their fresh
    limbs.
It seems, then, that Persuasion
and Grace dwell on Tenedos,
in Hagesilas' son.

Many people wholeheartedly prefer love-affairs with boys to those with women; for the Greek cities that are best-governed in comparison with the others engage vigorously in this practice. The Cretans, for example, as I said (cf. 13.561e–f), and the inhabitants of Euboean Chalcis become extraordinarily excited about sex with boys. Echemenes in his *History of Crete* (*FGrH* 459 F 1), at any rate, claims that it was not Zeus who kidnapped Ganymede, but Minos. But the Chalcidians mentioned above claim that

---

[64] Aphrodite's.

τὸν Γανυμήδην ὑπὸ τοῦ Διὸς καὶ τὸν τόπον δεικνύντες
Ἁρπάγιον καλοῦσιν, ἐν ᾧ καὶ μυρρίναι διάφοροι πε-
φύκασιν. καὶ τὴν πρὸς Ἀθηναίους δ᾽ ἔχθραν διελύ-
σατο Μίνως, καίπερ ἐπὶ θανάτῳ παιδὸς συστᾶσαν,
Θησέως ἐρασθεὶς καὶ τὴν θυγατέρα τούτῳ γυναῖκα
ἔδωκε Φαίδραν, ὡς Ζῆνις ἢ Ζηνεύς φησιν ὁ Χῖος ἐν τῷ
602 περὶ τῆς πατρίδος συγγράμματι. ‖ Ἱερώνυμος δ᾽ ὁ
περιπατητικὸς περισπουδάστους φησὶν γενέσθαι τοὺς
τῶν παίδων ἔρωτας, ὅτι πολλάκις ἡ τῶν νέων ἀκμὴ
καὶ τὸ πρὸς ἀλλήλους ἑταιρικὸν συμφρονήσαν πολλὰς τυραννίδας καθεῖλεν· παιδικῶν γὰρ παρόντων
ἐραστὴς πᾶν ὁτιοῦν ἕλοιτ᾽ ἂν παθεῖν ἢ δειλοῦ δόξαν
ἀπενέγκασθαι παρὰ τοῖς παιδικοῖς. ἔργῳ γοῦν τοῦτο
ἔδειξεν ὁ συνταχθεὶς Θήβησιν ὑπὸ Ἐπαμινώνδου ἱε-
ρὸς λόχος καὶ ὁ κατὰ τῶν Πεισιστρατιδῶν θάνατος
ὑπὸ Ἁρμοδίου καὶ Ἀριστογείτονος γενόμενος, περὶ
b Σικελίαν δ᾽ ἐν Ἀκράγαντι ὁ Χαρίτωνος | καὶ Μελα-
νίππου ⟨ἔρως⟩.[12] Μελάνιππος δ᾽ ἦν τὰ παιδικά, ὡς
φησιν Ἡρακλείδης ὁ Ποντικὸς ἐν τῷ Περὶ Ἐρωτικῶν.
οὗτοι φανέντες ἐπιβουλεύοντες Φαλάριδι καὶ βασα-

[12] add. Schweighäuser

---

[65] Cognate with *harpazô* ("snatch, kidnap").   [66] Minos'
son Androgeos was killed in Athens, and Minos responded by requiring the city to furnish him with a tribute of young men and
women (to be given to the Minotaur), one of whom was eventually
Theseus. The normal story is not that Theseus was given Ariadne,
but that the two of them ran off together.

Ganymede was kidnapped in their territory by Zeus, and they point out the spot, which they refer to as Harpagion,[65] where exceptionally fine laurel trees grow. So too Minos abandoned his hostility toward the Athenians, even though it was caused by his son's death,[66] when he fell in love with Theseus, and he gave him his daughter Ariadne as his wife, according to Zenis (or Zeneus) of Chios in his treatise on his native land (*FGrH* 393 F 1).[67] Hieronymus the Peripatetic (fr. 34 Wehrli) claims that love-affairs with boys were treated with particular enthusiasm because the vigor of the young men and the friendly sympathy the pair felt for one another brought down a substantial number of tyrannies; for when his boyfriend is present, a lover would prefer to suffer absolutely anything rather than get a reputation for cowardice in the boy's eyes. The Sacred Band established in Thebes by Epaminondas,[68] for example, demonstrated this in practice, as did the assassination carried out by Harmodius and Aristogiton when Pisistratus' sons were in power,[69] as well as the love-affair of Chariton and Melanippus in Acragas in Sicily. According to Heracleides of Pontus in his *On Love-Affairs* (fr. 65 Wehrli = fr. 37 Schütrumpf), Melanippus was the boyfriend. They were caught plotting against Phalaris,[70] and when they were

[67] Additional fragments of very similar material are preserved at 13.602f–3a.

[68] The Sacred Band consisted of 150 pairs of male lovers. It was formed when Thebes was liberated in 379 BCE and thus, in fact, predates the period of Epaminondas' ascendancy.

[69] Cf. 13.596f n.

[70] Phalaris was tyrant of Acragas in Sicily *c*.570–*c*.549 BCE.

ATHENAEUS

νιζόμενοι ἀναγκαζόμενοί τε λέγειν τοὺς συνειδότας οὐ
μόνον οὐ κατεῖπον, ἀλλὰ καὶ τὸν Φάλαριν αὐτὸν εἰς
ἔλεον τῶν βασάνων ἤγαγον, ὡς ἀπολῦσαι αὐτοὺς
πολλὰ ἐπαινέσαντα. διὸ καὶ ὁ Ἀπόλλων ἡσθεὶς ἐπὶ
τούτοις ἀναβολὴν τοῦ θανάτου τῷ Φαλάριδι ἐχα-
ρίσατο, τοῦτο ἐμφήνας τοῖς πυνθανομένοις τῆς Πυ-
c θίας ὅπως αὐτῷ ἐπιθῶνται· ἔχρησεν | δὲ καὶ περὶ τῶν
ἀμφὶ τὸν Χαρίτωνα, προτάξας τοῦ ἑξαμέτρου τὸ πεν-
τάμετρον, καθάπερ ὕστερον καὶ Διονύσιος ὁ Ἀθηναῖος ἐποίησε ὁ ἐπικληθεὶς Χαλκοῦς ἐν τοῖς Ἐλεγείοις.
ἐστὶν δὲ ὁ χρησμὸς ὅδε·

εὐδαίμων Χαρίτων καὶ Μελάνιππος ἔφυ,
θείας ἁγητῆρες ἐφαμερίοις φιλότατος.

διαβόητα δ᾽ ἐστὶν καὶ τὰ ἐπὶ Κρατίνῳ τῷ Ἀθηναίῳ
γενόμενα· ὃς μειράκιον ⟨ὢν⟩[13] εὔμορφον, Ἐπιμενίδου
καθαίροντος τὴν Ἀττικὴν ἀνθρωπείῳ αἵματι διά τινα
d μύση παλαιά, ὡς ἱστορεῖ Νεάνθης ὁ Κυζικηνὸς | ἐν
δευτέρῳ Περὶ Τελετῶν, ἑκὼν αὐτὸν ἐπέδωκεν[14] ὑπὲρ
τῆς θρεψαμένης· ᾧ καὶ ἐπαπέθανεν ὁ ἐραστὴς Ἀρι-
στόδημος, λύσιν τ᾽ ἔλαβε τὸ δεινόν. διὰ τοὺς τοιού-

---

13 add. Dindorf
14 ἐπέδωκεν ὁ Κρατῖνος A: ὁ Κρατῖνος del. Kaibel

---

71 PAA 336985.
72 PAA 584305 (not the 5th-century comic poet); his lover
Aristodemus is PAA [168580].
73 According to [Arist.] Ath. 1.3 (cf. D.L. 1.110), Epimenides

tortured in an effort to force them to identify their fellow-conspirators, not only did they not give up the names but they made Phalaris himself feel pity for the pain they were suffering, to the extent that he praised them heartily and set them free. This is why Apollo, who was pleased at these events, rewarded Phalaris by delaying his death and explained this to people who asked the Pythia how to attack him. He also offered an oracle that concerned Chariton and his associates, putting the pentameter before the hexameter, just as Dionysius of Athens (nicknamed Chalcous)[71] did later on in his *Elegies*. The oracle runs as follows (Delphic Oracle Q85 Fontenrose):

> Chariton and Melanippus were happy men;
> they introduced mortals to an affection like that felt
> by gods.

The story of what happened to Cratinus of Athens[72] is also well-known. He was a good-looking boy, and when Epimenides[73] was purifying Attica with human blood on account of some ancient defilement, according to Neanthes of Cyzicus in Book II of *On Rites* (*FGrH* 84 F 16), he voluntarily gave himself up for the land that had raised him. His lover Aristodemus died after him, and the problem was resolved. On account of love-affairs of this type,[74]

---

of Crete (*FGrH* 457; D–K 3; *PAA* 396032) purified Attica after the murder of the would-be tyrant Cylon in the 630s BCE or so. The story is almost certainly legendary, as was suspected already in antiquity (cf. 13.602e–f).

[74] Returning to the topic momentarily abandoned above. Several documents have been roughly spliced together here; the discussion of Cratinus and Aristodemus resumes again briefly below.

τους οὖν ἔρωτας οἱ τύραννοι (πολέμιοι γὰρ αὐτοῖς
αὗται αἱ φιλίαι) τὸ παράπαν ἐκώλυον τοὺς παιδικοὺς
ἔρωτας, πανταχόθεν αὐτοὺς ἐκκόπτοντες. εἰσὶ δὲ οἳ
καὶ τὰς παλαίστρας ὥσπερ ἀντιτειχίσματα ταῖς ἰδί-
αις ἀκροπόλεσιν ἐνεπίμπρασάν τε καὶ κατέσκαψαν,
ὡς ἐποίησε Πολυκράτης ὁ Σαμίων τύραννος. παρὰ δὲ
e Σπαρτιάταις, ὡς Ἅγνων φησὶν ὁ Ἀκαδημαϊκός, | πρὸ
τῶν γάμων ταῖς παρθένοις ὡς παιδικοῖς νόμος ἐστὶν
ὁμιλεῖν. καὶ γὰρ ὁ νομοθέτης Σόλων ἔφη·

μηρῶν ἱμείρων καὶ γλυκεροῦ στόματος.

Αἰσχύλος τε καὶ Σοφοκλῆς ἀναφανδὸν ἔφασαν, ὁ μὲν
Μυρμιδόσιν·

σέβας δὲ μηρῶν ἁγνὸν οὐκ ἐπηδέσω,
ὦ δυσχάριστε τῶν πυκνῶν φιλημάτων,

ὁ δ' ἐν Κολχίσιν περὶ Γανυμήδους τὸν λόγον ποιού-
μενος·

μηροῖς ὑπαίθων τὴν Διὸς τυραννίδα.

οὐκ ἀγνοῶ δὲ ὅτι τὰ περὶ Κρατῖνον καὶ Ἀριστόδημον
f πεπλάσθαι | φησὶν Πολέμων ὁ περιηγητὴς ἐν ταῖς
Πρὸς τὸν Νεάνθην Ἀντιγραφαῖς. ὑμεῖς δέ, ὦ Κύνουλκε, τὰς διηγήσεις ταύτας, κἂν ψευδεῖς ὦσιν, ἀλη-
θεῖς εἶναι πιστεύετε, καὶ τὰ τοιαῦτα τῶν ποιημάτων ἃ

---

75 Polycrates reigned c.535–522 BCE.
76 I.e. anally.

46

therefore, tyrants—for these close personal relationships are contrary to their interests—by and large attempted to prevent pederastic love-affairs, working to eliminate them in any way possible. Some actually burned down or demolished the wrestling schools, as if they were counter-walls directed against their own citadels, as Polycrates, the tyrant of Samos,[75] did. In Sparta, according to Hagnon of the Academy, it is customary to have sex with girls before they marry in the same way one does with boys.[76] For the lawgiver Solon (fr. 25.2 West²) in fact said:[77]

> desiring thighs and a sweet mouth.

Both Aeschylus and Sophocles expressed this openly, the former in *Myrmidons* (A. fr. 135):[78]

> You showed no sacred respect for my thighs;
> how ungrateful you were for my frequent kisses!,

the latter in *Colchians* (S. fr. 345), where he is referring to Ganymede:

> setting Zeus' tyranny on fire with his thighs.

I am well aware, however, that the travel-writer Polemon in his *Treatise Responding to Neanthes* (fr. 53 Preller) claims that the story about Cratinus and Aristodemus is a fiction. Whereas your people,[79] Cynulcus, are confident that these narratives are true, even if they are false; and you enjoy occupying yourselves with poetry of this sort,

---

[77] This material appears to belong with the discussion at 13.601a–b rather than here, where it is patently out of place.

[78] Cf. 13.601a.

[79] The Cynics.

περὶ τοὺς παιδικούς ἐστιν ἔρωτας ἡδέως μελετᾶτε
< . . . > τοῦ παιδεραστεῖν παρὰ πρώτων Κρητῶν εἰς
τοὺς Ἕλληνας παρελθόντος, ὡς ἱστορεῖ Τίμαιος. ἄλλοι
δέ φασι τῶν τοιούτων ἐρώτων κατάρξασθαι Λάιον
603 ξενωθέντα παρὰ Πέλοπι καὶ ἐρασθέντα τοῦ ‖ υἱοῦ
αὐτοῦ Χρυσίππου, ὃν καὶ ἁρπάσαντα καὶ ἀναθέμενον
εἰς ἅρμα εἰς Θήβας φυγεῖν. Πράξιλλα δ᾽ ἡ Σικυωνία ὑπὸ
Διός φησιν ἁρπασθῆναι τὸν Χρύσιππον. καὶ Κελτοὶ
δὲ τῶν βαρβάρων καίτοι καλλίστας ἔχοντες γυναῖκας
παιδικοῖς μᾶλλον χαίρουσιν· ὡς πολλάκις ἐνίους ἐπὶ
ταῖς δοραῖς μετὰ δύο ἐρωμένων ἀναπαύεσθαι. Πέρσας
δὲ παρ᾽ Ἑλλήνων φησὶν Ἡρόδοτος μαθεῖν τὸ παισὶν
χρῆσθαι. φιλόπαις δ᾽ ἦν ἐκμανῶς καὶ Ἀλέξανδρος ὁ
βασιλεύς· Δικαίαρχος γοῦν ἐν τῷ Περὶ τῆς Ἐν Ἰλίῳ
b Θυσίας Βαγώου ‖ τοῦ εὐνούχου οὕτως αὐτόν φησιν
ἡττᾶσθαι ὡς ἐν ὄψει θεάτρου ὅλου καταφιλεῖν αὐτὸν
ἀνακλάσαντα, καὶ τῶν θεατῶν ἐπιφωνησάντων μετὰ
κρότου οὐκ ἀπειθήσας πάλιν ἀνακλάσας ἐφίλησεν.
Καρύστιος δ᾽ ἐν Ἱστορικοῖς Ὑπομνήμασι, Χάρωνι,
φησί, τῷ Χαλκιδεῖ παῖς καλὸς ἦν καὶ εἶχεν εὖ πρὸς
αὐτόν. ὡς δ᾽ Ἀλέξανδρος παρὰ Κρατερῷ αὐτὸν ἐπήνε-
σεν γενομένου πότου, ὁ Χάρων ἐκέλευσε τὸν παῖδα
καταφιλῆσαι τὸν Ἀλέξανδρον· καὶ ὅς, "μηδαμῶς,"
c εἶπεν, "οὐ γὰρ οὕτως ἐμὲ εὐφρανεῖ ‖ ὡς σὲ λυπήσει."
ὥσπερ γὰρ ἦν ἐρωτικὸς ὁ βασιλεὺς οὗτος, οὕτως καὶ

80 Cf. 13.601e–f.   81 The story provided the subject
matter for Euripides' *Chrysippus*; cf. Ael. *VH* 13.5.

which concerns pederastic love-affairs . . . since pederasty began with the Cretans and made its way to Greece from there, according to Timaeus (*FGrH* 566 F 144).[80] But other authorities claim that this type of love began with Laius, when he visited Pelops' house and fell in love with Pelops' son Chrysippus; he kidnapped the boy, put him in his chariot, and ran away to Thebes.[81] Praxilla of Sicyon (*PMG* 751), on the other hand, claims that Chrysippus was kidnapped by Zeus. So too the Celts, even though they have the most beautiful women of all the barbarians, prefer sex with boys; as a result, some of them routinely sleep on their animal-skins with two boyfriends. Herodotus (1.135) claims that the Persians learned about sex with boys from the Greeks. King Alexander was crazy about boys. Dicaearchus in his *On the Sacrifice at Ilium* (fr. 23 Wehrli = fr. 83 Mirhady), for example, says that he was so infatuated with the eunuch Bagoas[82] that he leaned back and kissed him in the sight of a theater full of people, and that when the spectators responded by clapping and cheering, he did what they wanted, and leaned back and kissed him again. Carystius says in his *Historical Commentaries* (fr. 5, *FHG* iv.357): Charon of Chalcis[83] had a good-looking slave-boy he was very fond of. When Alexander was at Craterus' house at a drinking party, he expressed admiration for the boy, and Charon ordered him to kiss Alexander. But Alexander said: "Absolutely not; the amount of pleasure he gives me will be less than the amount of pain he causes you." For even though this king was interested in

[82] Berve i #195; he originally belonged to Darius.

[83] Berve i #827. Craterus (below) is Berve i #446; he was one of Alexander's closest companions.

πρὸς τὸ καθῆκον ἐγκρατὴς καὶ πρὸς τὸ πρεπωδέ-
στατον· αἰχμαλώτους γοῦν λαβὼν τὰς Δαρείου θυγα-
τέρας καὶ τὴν γυναῖκα κάλλει διαπρεπεστάτην οὖσαν
οὐ μόνον ἀπέσχετο, ἀλλ᾽ οὐδὲ ἐκείνας μαθεῖν ἐποίησεν ὅτι εἰσὶν αἰχμάλωτοι, ἀλλ᾽ ὡς ἔτι Δαρείου ἐν τῇ
βασιλείᾳ ὄντος πάντα αὐταῖς χορηγεῖσθαι ἐκέλευσεν.
διόπερ καὶ Δαρεῖος τοῦτο μαθὼν ηὔξατο τῷ Ἡλίῳ τὰς
χεῖρας ἀνατείνας ἢ αὐτὸν βασιλεύειν ἢ Ἀλέξανδρον.

d Ῥαδαμάνθυος | δὲ τοῦ δικαίου Ἴβυκος ἐραστήν φησι
γενέσθαι Τάλων. Διότιμος δ᾽ ἐν τῇ Ἡρακλείᾳ Εὐρυ-
σθέα φησὶν Ἡρακλέους γενέσθαι παιδικά, διόπερ καὶ
τοὺς ἄθλους ὑπομεῖναι. Ἀγαμέμνονά τε Ἀργύννου
ἐρασθῆναι λόγος, ἰδόντα ἐπὶ τῷ Κηφισῷ νηχόμενον·
ἐν ᾧ καὶ τελευτήσαντα αὐτὸν (συνεχῶς γὰρ ἐν τῷ
ποταμῷ τούτῳ ἀπελούετο) θάψας εἵσατο καὶ ἱερὸν
αὐτόθι Ἀφροδίτης Ἀργυννίδος. Λικύμνιος δ᾽ ὁ Χῖος ἐν
Διθυράμβοις Ἀργύννου φησὶν ἐρώμενον Ὑμέναιον
e γενέσθαι. Ἀντιγόνου δὲ τοῦ βασιλέως ἐρώμενος | ἦν
Ἀριστοκλῆς ὁ κιθαρῳδός, περὶ οὗ Ἀντίγονος ὁ Καρύστιος ἐν τῷ Ζήνωνος Βίῳ γράφει οὕτως· Ἀντίγονος ὁ
βασιλεὺς ἐπεκώμαζε τῷ Ζήνωνι. καί ποτε καὶ μεθ᾽

---

84 I.e. to Ahura Mazda, the Persians' supreme god.

85 The story is attested nowhere else, and it is unclear whether
the Talus in question is the bronze guardian of Crete (A.R.
4.1638–88) or the nephew of Daedalus ([Apollod.] *Bib.* 3.15.8).

86 I.e. so as not to be embarrassed in front of the boy he loved;
cf. 13.602a. The normal story is that King Eurystheus was
Heracles' temporary master until he completed his labors.

love, he was equally in control of his feelings when it came
to what was appropriate and made the best appearance.
When he took Darius' daughters prisoner, for example,
along with his wife, who was extremely beautiful, he not
only kept his hands off of them but did not allow them to
learn that they were captives, and he instead ordered that
they be provided with everything they needed, as if Darius
was still on the throne. As a consequence, when Darius
learned about this, he stretched his hands up and prayed to
the Sun,[84] asking that either he be king or that Alexander
be. Ibycus (*PMG* 309) claims that Talus was the lover of
Rhadamanthys the Just.[85] And Diotimus in his *Epic of
Heracles* (*SH* 393) says that Eurystheus was Heracles' boyfriend, which is why Heracles endured his labors.[86] There
is a story that Agamemnon fell in love with Argynnus when
he saw him swimming in the Cephisus; after the boy died
in this river—because he was constantly taking baths in
it—Agamemnon buried him and founded a temple of
Aphrodite Argynnis there.[87] Licymnius of Chios in the
Dithyrambs (*PMG* 768), on the other hand, claims that
Hymenaeus was Argynnus' boyfriend. The citharode Aristocles[88] was the boyfriend of King Antigonus, and Antigonus of Carystus writes as follows about him in his *Life of
Zeno* (p. 117 Wilamowitz = fr. 35A Dorandi = Zeno fr. 23,
SVF i.10):[89] King Antigonus used to lead drunken proces-
sions to Zeno's house. On one occasion he left a party and

[87] For the story, cf. Phanocles fr. 5, p. 108 Powell; Propertius
3.7.21–4; St. Byz. A 402 Billerbeck.

[88] Stephanis #340. The Antigonus in question is Antigonus
Gonatas (reigned *c*.277–239 BCE).

[89] Cf. D.L. 7.13.

ἡμέραν ἐλθὼν ἔκ τινος πότου καὶ ἀναπηδήσας πρὸς
τὸν Ζήνωνα ἔπεισεν αὐτὸν συγκωμάσαι αὐτῷ πρὸς
Ἀριστοκλέα τὸν κιθαρῳδόν, οὗ σφόδρα ἦρα ὁ βασιλεύς. φιλομεῖραξ δὲ ἦν ὁ Σοφοκλῆς, ὡς Εὐριπίδης
φιλογύνης. Ἴων γοῦν ὁ ποιητὴς ἐν ταῖς ἐπιγραφομέ-
ναις Ἐπιδημίαις γράφει οὕτως· Σοφοκλεῖ τῷ ποιητῇ
f   ἐν Χίῳ συνήντησα, | ὅτε ἔπλει εἰς Λέσβον στρατηγός,
ἀνδρὶ παιδιώδει παρ᾽ οἶνον καὶ δεξιῷ. Ἑρμησίλεω δὲ
ξένου οἱ ἐόντος καὶ προξένου Ἀθηναίων ἑστιῶντος
αὐτόν, ἐπεὶ παρὰ τὸ πῦρ ἑστεὼς ὁ τὸν οἶνον ἐγχέων
παῖς < . . . > ἐὼν δῆλος ἦν εἶπέ τε· "βούλει με ἡδέως
πίνειν;" φάντος δ᾽ αὐτοῦ, "βραδέως τοίνυν καὶ πρόσ-
φερέ μοι καὶ ἀπόφερε τὴν κύλικα." ἔτι πολὺ μᾶλλον
ἐρυθριάσαντος τοῦ παιδὸς εἶπε πρὸς τὸν συγκατα-
κείμενον· "ὡς καλῶς Φρύνιχος ἐποίησεν εἶπας· ‖

604   λάμπει δ᾽ ἐπὶ πορφυρέαις παρῇσι φῶς ἔρωτος."

καὶ πρὸς τόδε ἠμείφθη ὁ Ἐρετριεὺς ἢ Ἐρυθραῖος
γραμμάτων ἐὼν διδάσκαλος· "σοφὸς μὲν δὴ σύ γε εἶ,
ὦ Σοφόκλεις, ἐν ποιήσει· ὅμως μέντοι γε οὐκ εὖ εἴρηκε
Φρύνιχος πορφυρέας εἰπὼν τὰς γνάθους τοῦ καλοῦ. εἰ
γὰρ ὁ ζωγράφος χρώματι πορφυρέῳ ἐναλείψειε τουδὶ
τοῦ παιδὸς τὰς γνάθους, οὐκ ἂν ἔτι καλὸς φαίνοιτο. οὐ
κάρτα δεῖ τὸ καλὸν τῷ μὴ καλῷ φαινομένῳ εἰκάζειν

90 Cf. 13.557e.
91 Quoted also at 13.564f.

got there after the sun was up; bounded in to see Zeno; and convinced him to join him on a drunken visit to the citharode Aristocles, with whom the king was deeply in love. Sophocles (test. 75) was partial to boys, in the same way that Euripides was partial to women.[90] The poet Ion (*TrGF* 19 T 4b), for example, writes as follows in his work entitled *Visits Abroad* (*FGrH* 392 F 6): I met the poet Sophocles on Chios, when he was sailing to Lesbos as a general; he was playful and witty when he was drinking. Hermesilaus, who was an old friend of his as well as the local representative of Athens' interests, gave a feast in his honor. When the slave-boy who was pouring the wine was standing by the fire, (Sophocles) was obviously . . . , and he said: "Do you want me to enjoy my drink?" When the boy said that he did, (Sophocles said:) "Then hand me the cup nice and slow, and take it back nice and slow too." When the boy blushed even more, Sophocles said to the man who was sharing his couch: "Phrynichus got it exactly right when he said in his poetry (*TrGF* 3 F 13):[91]

The light of love glows on his rosy cheeks."

The fellow from Eretria (or Erythrae),[92] who taught reading and writing, responded: "You're clever when it comes to poetry, Sophocles. But Phrynichus was still wrong to refer to a good-looking boy's cheeks as purple. Because if an artist covered this boy's jaws with purple paint, he wouldn't be handsome any longer—and you certainly shouldn't compare something that's beautiful with something that

---

[92] I.e. the man sharing Sophocles' couch, who was apparently well-educated enough by local standards that Hermesilaus had invited him to dinner with the visiting poetic luminary.

ἄν." γελάσας ἐπὶ τῷ Ἐρετριεῖ Σοφοκλῆς· "οὐδὲ τόδε
b σοι ἀρέσκει | ἄρα, ὦ ξένε, τὸ Σιμωνίδειον, κάρτα
δοκέον τοῖς Ἕλλησιν εὖ εἰρῆσθαι·

πορφυρέου ἀπὸ στόματος
ἱεῖσα φωνὰν παρθένος,

οὐδ' ὁ ποιητής, ἔφη, <ὁ>[15] λέγων χρυσοκόμαν Ἀπόλ-
λωνα· χρυσέας γὰρ εἰ ἐποίησεν ὁ ζωγράφος τὰς τοῦ
θεοῦ κόμας καὶ μὴ μελαίνας, χεῖρον ἂν ἦν τὸ ζω-
γράφημα. οὐδὲ ὁ φὰς "ῥοδοδάκτυλον·" εἰ γάρ τις εἰς
ῥόδεον χρῶμα βάψειε τοὺς δακτύλους, πορφυροβάφου
χεῖρας καὶ οὐ γυναικὸς καλῆς ποιήσειεν <ἄν>."[16] γελασάντων δὲ ὁ μὲν Ἐρετριεὺς ἐνωπήθη τῇ ἐπιραπίξει,
c ὁ δὲ πάλιν | τοῦ παιδὸς τῷ λόγῳ εἴχετο. εἴρετο γάρ μιν
ἀπὸ τῆς κύλικος κάρφος τῷ μικρῷ δακτύλῳ ἀφαι-
ρετέοντα, εἰ καθορᾷ τὸ κάρφος. φάντος δὲ καθορᾶν,
"ἄπο τοίνυν φύσησον αὐτό, ἵνα μὴ πλύνοιτο ὁ δάκτυ-
λός σευ." προσαγαγόντος δ' αὐτοῦ τὸ πρόσωπον πρὸς
τὴν κύλικα ἐγγυτέρω τὴν κύλικα τοῦ ἑαυτοῦ στόματος
ἦγεν, ἵνα δὴ ἡ κεφαλὴ τῇ κεφαλῇ ἀσσοτέρα γένηται.
ὡς δ' ἦν οἱ κάρτα πλησίον, περιλαβὼν τῇ χειρὶ
ἐφίλησεν. ἐπικροτησάντων δὲ πάντων σὺν γέλωτι καὶ
d βοῇ ὡς εὖ ὑπηγάγετο | τὸν παῖδα, "μελετῶ," εἶπεν,
"στρατηγεῖν, ὦ ἄνδρες· ἐπειδήπερ Περικλῆς ποιεῖν

15 add. Kaibel
16 add. Iacobs

doesn't seem to be!" Sophocles laughed at the Eretrian (and said): "Well then, stranger—you must disapprove of the following passage from Simonides (*PMG* 585) as well, although the Greeks generally consider it extremely well-expressed:

> a girl sending forth words
> from her rosy[93] mouth,

And you must also disapprove of the poet," he added, "who refers (Pi. *O.* 6.41) to Apollo as having golden hair; because if an artist made the god's hair golden rather than black, the painting would not be as good. So too with the poet who uses the word *rhododaktulos* ("rosy-fingered");[94] because if someone dipped (the goddess') fingers in rose-colored pigment, he would produce the hands of a purple-dyer, not of a beautiful woman." We laughed, and the Eretrian looked embarrassed by the scolding; but Sophocles began talking to the boy again. The boy was trying to get a bit of straw out of the cup with his little finger, and Sophocles asked if he saw the straw. When he said that he did, (Sophocles said): "Alright, then—blow it off, so your finger doesn't get wet!" But when the boy moved his face toward the cup, Sophocles brought the cup closer to his own mouth, so that his head would be closer to the boy's head. And when the boy was very close to him, Sophocles grabbed him and kissed him. Everyone applauded, and laughed and shouted that he had done a nice job of luring the boy toward himself, and he said: "I'm practicing my strategy, gentlemen; because Pericles claimed that I can

---

[93] Literally "purple."
[94] A common Homeric epithet of Dawn (e.g. *Od.* 2.1).

μέν ⟨με⟩[17] ἔφη, στρατηγεῖν δ᾽ οὐκ ἐπίστασθαι. ἆρ᾽
οὖν οὐ κατ᾽ ὀρθόν μοι πέπτωκεν τὸ στρατήγημα;"
τοιαῦτα πολλὰ δεξιῶς ἔλεγέν τε καὶ ἔπρησσεν ὅτε
πίνοι.[18] τὰ μέντοι πολιτικὰ οὔτε σοφὸς οὔτε ῥεκτήριος
ἦν, ἀλλ᾽ ὡς ἄν τις εἷς τῶν χρηστῶν Ἀθηναίων. καὶ
Ἱερώνυμος δ᾽ ὁ Ῥόδιος ἐν τοῖς Ἱστορικοῖς Ὑπομνή-
μασίν φησιν ὅτι Σοφοκλῆς εὐπρεπῆ παῖδα ἔξω τεί-
e χους ἀπήγαγε χρησόμενος αὐτῷ. ὁ μὲν οὖν | παῖς τὸ
ἴδιον ἱμάτιον ἐπὶ τῇ πόᾳ ὑπέστρωσεν, τὴν δὲ τοῦ
Σοφοκλέους χλανίδα περιεβάλοντο. μετ᾽ οὖν τὴν ὁμιλίαν ὁ παῖς ἁρπάσας τὸ τοῦ Σοφοκλέους χλανίδιον
ᾤχετο, καταλιπὼν τῷ Σοφοκλεῖ τὸ παιδικὸν ἱμάτιον.
οἷα δὲ εἰκὸς διαλαληθέντος τοῦ συμβεβηκότος Εὐριπίδης πυθόμενος καὶ ἐπιτωθάζων τὸ γεγονὸς καὶ
αὐτός ποτε ἔφη τούτῳ κεχρῆσθαι τῷ παιδί, ἀλλὰ
μηδὲν προσθεῖναι, τὸν δὲ Σοφοκλέα διὰ τὴν ἀκολασίαν καταφρονηθῆναι. καὶ ὁ Σοφοκλῆς ἀκούσας ἐποί-
f ησεν εἰς | αὐτὸν τὸ τοιοῦτον ἐπίγραμμα, χρησάμενος
τῷ περὶ τοῦ Ἡλίου καὶ Βορέου λόγῳ, καί τι πρὸς
μοιχείαν αὐτοῦ παραινιττόμενος·

[17] add. Kaibel: ἔφη ⟨με⟩ Musurus
[18] πίνοι ἢ πράσσοι A: ἢ πράσσοι del. Kaibel

write poetry, but I don't know how to be a general. So then—didn't my stratagem work out the way I wanted it to?" He spoke and behaved in many other similarly clever ways when he was drinking. As for politics, on the other hand, he was neither particularly wise nor particularly active, but behaved like a typical member of the Athenian upper class. So too Hieronymus of Rhodes in his *Historical Commentaries* (fr. 35 Wehrli) claims that Sophocles took a good-looking boy outside the city-walls to have sex with him. The boy accordingly put his own robe down on the grass beneath them, and they wrapped Sophocles' cloak around them. So after they were finished, the boy grabbed Sophocles' cloak and left, leaving Sophocles his own robe, which was the size a child would wear. As one might expect, what had happened was widely discussed; when Euripides heard about it, he made a nasty joke about the situation, saying that he had had sex with this boy himself once, but had not given him anything more than his usual fee, whereas Sophocles' lack of self-control had led to him being treated with contempt. When Sophocles heard this, he wrote an epigram along the following lines addressed to Euripides, using the story about the Sun and the North Wind,[95] but also alluding to Euripides' interest in seducing women ("Sophocles" *FGE* 1040–3):

[95] An allusion to Aes. *Fab*. 46 Perry: When the Sun and the North Wind argued about who was stronger, they agreed to see who could strip the clothes off a traveler. The North Wind tried to blow the man's clothes off but only succeeded in making him wrap them about himself more tightly, whereas the Sun, simply by shining on him, eventually made him strip himself and take a bath in a nearby river.

Ἥλιος ἦν, οὐ παῖς, Εὐριπίδη, ὅς με χλιαίνων
  γυμνὸν ἐποίησεν· σοὶ δὲ φιλοῦντι † ἑταίραν †
Βορρᾶς ὡμίλησε. σὺ δ᾽ οὐ σοφός, ὃς τὸν Ἔρωτα,
  ἀλλοτρίαν σπείρων, λωποδύτην ἀπάγεις.

Θεόπομπος δὲ ἐν τῷ Περὶ τῶν Συληθέντων Ἐκ ‖
605 Δελφῶν Χρημάτων Ἀσώπιχόν φησι τὸν Ἐπαμινώνδου ἐρώμενον τὸ Λευκτρικὸν τρόπαιον ἐντετυπωμένον
ἔχειν ἐπὶ τῆς ἀσπίδος καὶ θαυμαστῶς αὐτὸν κινδυ-
νεύειν, ἀνακεῖσθαί τε τὴν ἀσπίδα ταύτην ἐν Δελφοῖς
ἐν τῇ στοᾷ. ἐν δὲ τῷ αὐτῷ συγγράμματι Θεόπομπος
φιλογύναιον μέν φησι γεγονέναι Φάυλλον τὸν Φω-
κέων τύραννον, φιλόπαιδα δὲ Ὀνόμαρχον· καὶ ἐκ τῶν
τοῦ θεοῦ χαρίσασθαι τοῦτον εἰς Δελφοὺς παραγε-
νομένῳ < . . . > τῷ Πυθοδώρου τοῦ Σικυωνίου υἱῷ
b ἀποκερουμένῳ τὴν κόμην, | ὄντι καλῷ συγγενόμενον
τὰ Συβαριτῶν ἀναθήματα, στλεγγίδια χρυσᾶ τέσσα-
ρα. τῇ Δεινιάδου δὲ αὐλητρίδι Βρομιάδι Φάυλλος
καρχήσιον ἀργυροῦν Φωκαέων καὶ στέφανον χρυσοῦν κιττοῦ Πεπαρηθίων. αὕτη δέ, φησί, καὶ ἔμελλε
τὰ Πύθια αὐλεῖν, εἰ μὴ ὑπὸ τοῦ πλήθους ἐκωλύθη. τῷ
δὲ Λυκόλα τοῦ[19] Τριχονείου υἱῷ Φυσκίδᾳ ὄντι καλῷ

---

19 τῷ του A: τῷ del. Kaibel

---

96 Where the Thebans, with Epaminondas as general, defeated the Spartans in 371 BCE.

97 The brothers Phayllus and Onomarchus, along with the
chief commander Philemelus (below), were Phocian generals

It was the Sun, Euripides, and not a boy, that got me
    hot
    and stripped me naked. But the North Wind was
      with you
when you were kissing † a courtesan †. You're not so
    clever, if you arrest
    Eros for stealing clothes while you're sowing
      another man's field.

Theopompus in his *On the Goods Plundered from Delphi*
(*FGrH* 115 F 247) claims that Epaminondas' boyfriend
Asopichus had the victory-monument at Leuctra[96] en-
graved on his shield and took extraordinary risks and dedicated this shield in the stoa in Delphi. In this same treatise,
Theopompus (*FGrH* 115 F 248) says that the Phocian tyrant Phayllus[97] liked women, whereas Onomarchus liked
boys, and that from the god's property Onomarchus gave
. . . the son of Pythodorus of Sicyon, a good-looking boy
who was visiting Delphi in order to cut his hair,[98] the objects the Sybarites had dedicated, specifically four gold
strigils, after he had sex with him. But Phayllus gave the
pipe-girl Bromias,[99] who belonged to Deiniades, a silver
karchêsion dedicated by the Phocaeans and an ivy-garland
made of gold dedicated by the Peparethians. She was also
intending to play the pipe-music at the Pythian games,
he says, except that the crowd prevented this. And Onomarchus, he claims, gave Physcidas the son of Lycolas of
Trichonium, who was a good-looking boy, a laurel-garland

when the Phocians looted Delphi in 356 BCE; cf. 6.231c–d n.,
231d–e, 232e n.   [98] I.e. to mark that he had reached adult-
hood.   [99] Stephanis #535.

Ὀνόμαρχος ἔδωκεν, φησί, στέφανον ⟨χρυσοῦν⟩[20]
δάφνης, Ἐφεσίων ἀνάθημα. οὗτος ὁ παῖς πρὸς Φίλιππον ἀχθεὶς ὑπὸ τοῦ πατρὸς κἀκεῖ προαγωγευόμενος
c οὐδὲν λαβὼν | ἀπεστάλη. τῷ Ἐπιλύκου τοῦ Ἀμφιπο-
λίτου υἱῷ ὄντι καλῷ Δαμίππῳ ⟨ . . . ⟩ Πλεισθένους
ἀνάθημα Ὀνόμαρχος ἔδωκε. Φαρσαλίᾳ τῇ Θεσσαλίδι
ὀρχηστρίδι δάφνης στέφανον χρυσοῦν Φιλόμηλος
ἔδωκε, Λαμψακηνῶν ἀνάθημα. αὕτη ἡ Φαρσαλία ἐν
Μεταποντίῳ ὑπὸ τῶν ἐν τῇ ἀγορᾷ μάντεων, γενομένης
φωνῆς ἐκ τῆς δάφνης τῆς χαλκῆς, ἣν ἔστησαν Μετα-
ποντῖνοι κατὰ τὴν Ἀριστέα τοῦ Προκονησίου ἐπιδη-
μίαν, ὅτ᾽ ἔφησεν ἐξ Ὑπερβορέων παραγεγονέναι, ὡς
d τάχιστα ὤφθη εἰς τὴν ἀγορὰν ἐμβαλοῦσα, | ἐμμανῶν
γενομένων τῶν μάντεων διεσπάσθη ὑπ᾽ αὐτῶν. καὶ
τῶν ἀνθρώπων ὕστερον ἀναζητούντων τὴν αἰτίαν εὑ-
ρέθη διὰ τὸν τοῦ θεοῦ στέφανον ἀνῃρημένη. ὁρᾶτε οὖν
καὶ ὑμεῖς, ὦ φιλόσοφοι, οἱ παρὰ φύσιν τῇ Ἀφροδίτῃ
χρώμενοι καὶ ἀσεβοῦντες εἰς τὴν θεόν, μὴ τὸν αὐτὸν
διαφθαρῆτε τρόπον. τότε γὰρ καὶ οἱ παῖδές εἰσιν
καλοί, ὡς Γλυκέρα ἔφασκεν ἡ ἑταίρα, ὅσον ἐοίκασι
γυναιξὶ χρόνον, καθάπερ ἱστορεῖ Κλέαρχος. ἐμοὶ μὲν
γὰρ καὶ κατὰ φύσιν δοκεῖ πεποιηκέναι Κλεώνυμος ὁ
e Σπαρτιάτης, πρῶτος ἀνθρώπων | εἰς ὁμηρείαν λαβὼν
παρὰ Μεταποντίνων γυναῖκας καὶ παρθένους τὰς ἐν-

<hr>

[20] add. Meineke

[100] Stephanis #2462.

made of gold that had been dedicated by the Ephesians. This boy's father took him to Philip's court, where he was treated like a whore and then sent home with no reward. Onomarchus gave Damippus the son of Epilycus of Amphipolis, who was a good-looking boy, . . . that had been dedicated by Pleisthenes. Philomelus gave the Thessalian dancing-girl Pharsalia[100] a laurel-crown made of gold that had been dedicated by the Lampsacenes. As for this Pharsalia, there were seers in the marketplace in Metapontium, and when a voice came out of the bronze laurel tree the inhabitants of the city set up when Aristeas of Proconnesus (fr. 18 Bolton) visited, when he claimed to be on his way home from the land of the Hyperboreans—as soon as she was spotted entering the marketplace, the seers went crazy and tore her to pieces.[101] When people later on tried to discover the reason for this, they found that she had been killed because of her garland, which belonged to the god. You too should be careful, therefore, philosophers, if you engage in unnatural sex-acts and fail to show the goddess the respect she is due, or you may be destroyed in the same way. For as the courtesan Glycera[102] said, according to Clearchus (fr. 23 Wehrli), boys are attractive only as long as they resemble women. Cleonymus of Sparta[103] thus appears to me to have behaved normally when he became the first person to seize hostages, taking 200 of their most important and attractive women and girls from the inhabi-

---

[101] Plu. *Mor.* 397f–8a offers a different version of the story, in which Pharsalia (Stephanis #2462) was torn apart by young men who were fighting with one another to seize her garland.

[102] *PAA* 277490.　　　　[103] Pp. 246–7 Bradford (*c.*340–272 BCE). For the story, cf. D.S. 20.104.3 (303 BCE).

δοξοτάτας καὶ καλλίστας διακοσίας, ὡς ἱστορεῖ Δοῦρις ὁ Σάμιος ἐν τῇ τρίτῃ τῶν Περὶ Ἀγαθοκλέα Ἱστο-
ριῶν· κἀγὼ δὲ κατὰ τὴν Ἐπικράτους Ἀντιλαΐδα

τάρωτίκ᾽ ἐκμεμάθηκα ταῦτα παντελῶς
Σαπφοῦς, Μελήτου, Κλεομένους, Λαμυνθίου.

ὑμεῖς δέ, ὦ φιλόσοφοι, κἂν ἐρασθέντες ποτὲ γυναικῶν
ἐν ἐννοίᾳ λάβητε ὡς ἀδύνατόν ἐστι τὸ τυχεῖν, μάθετε
< . . . > παύονται οἱ ἔρωτες, ὥς φησι Κλέαρχος. τῇ τε
f γὰρ περὶ τὴν Πειρήνην χαλκῇ βοῒ βοῦς | ἐπανέβη·
καὶ γεγραμμένῃ κυνὶ καὶ περιστερᾷ καὶ χηνὶ τῇ μὲν
κύων, τῇ δὲ περιστερά, τῇ δὲ χὴν προσῆλθον καὶ
ἐπεπήδησαν· φανέντων δὲ πᾶσι τούτοις ἀδυνάτων
ἀπέστησαν, καθάπερ Κλείσοφος ὁ Σηλυμβριανός.
οὗτος γὰρ τοῦ ἐν Σάμῳ Παρίου ἀγάλματος ἐρασθεὶς
κατέκλεισεν αὐτὸν ἐν τῷ ναῷ, ὡς πλησιάσαι δυνη-
σόμενος· καὶ ὡς ἠδυνάτει διά τε τὴν ψυχρότητα καὶ τὸ
ἀντίτυπον τοῦ λίθου, τηνικαῦτα τῆς ἐπιθυμίας ἀπέστη
καὶ προβαλλόμενος τι[21] σαρκίον ἐπλησίασεν. τῆς
πράξεως ταύτης μνημονεύει καὶ Ἄλεξις ὁ ποιητὴς ἐν
τῷ ἐπιγραφομένῳ δράματι Γραφῇ λέγων ὧδε· ||

606   γεγένηται δ᾽, ὡς λέγουσιν, κἂν Σάμῳ
τοιοῦθ᾽ ἕτερον. λιθίνης ἐπεθύμησεν κόρης
ἄνθρωπος ἐγκατέκλεισέ θ᾽ αὑτὸν τῷ νεῷ.

καὶ Φιλήμων τοῦ αὐτοῦ μνημονεύων φησίν·

[21] τι Meineke: τὸ A

62

tants of Metapontium, according to Duris of Samos in
Book III of his *History involving Agathocles* (*FGrH* 76 F
18). I too, to quote Epicrates' *Antilaïs* (fr. 4),

> have systematically memorized this erotic poetry
>   produced
> by Sappho, Meletus, Cleomenes, and Lamynthius.[104]

But if you, my philosophers, ever fall in love with women
and realize that it is impossible to get what you want, understand . . . love fades, as Clearchus (fr. 26 Wehrli) says.
For a bull mounted the bronze cow in Pirene; and a male
dog, pigeon, and goose approached and mounted pictures
of, respectively, a female dog, pigeon, and goose. But when
it became apparent to them that it was impossible, they all
abandoned their efforts, just as Cleisophus of Selymbria
did. He fell in love with the statue made of Parian marble
on Samos, and he locked himself up in the temple in order
to have sex with it. But when he was unable to do so, because the stone was too cold and resistant, he immediately
abandoned his desire, put a small piece of meat in front of
himself, and had sex with that instead. The poet Alexis in
his play entitled *The Picture* (fr. 41) refers to the same set
of events, saying the following:

> People claim that something similar happened
> on Samos. A guy became infatuated with a girl
> made of stone and locked himself up in the temple.

Philemon (fr. 127) mentions the same person, saying:

[104] Meletus is presumably the tragic poet (*TrGF* 47; *PAA*
639320 = 639322; cf. Ar. *Ra.* 1302). For Cleomenes, cf. Chionid.
fr. 4 (quoted at 14.638d–e). For Lamynthius, cf. 13.597a with n.

ἀλλ' ἐν Σάμῳ μὲν τοῦ λιθίνου ζῴου ποτὲ
ἄνθρωπος ἠράσθη τις· εἶτ' εἰς τὸν νεὼν
κατέκλεισεν αὐτόν.

Κτησικλέους δ' ἐστὶν ἔργον τὸ ἄγαλμα, ὥς φησιν
Ἀδαῖος ὁ Μιτυληναῖος ἐν τῷ Περὶ Ἀγαλματοποιῶν.
Πολέμων δὲ ἢ ὁ ποιήσας τὸν ἐπιγραφόμενον Ἑλλα-
b δικόν, ἐν Δελφοῖς, φησίν, | ἐν τῷ Σπινατῶν θησαυρῷ
παῖδές εἰσιν λίθινοι δύο, ὧν τοῦ ἑτέρου Δελφοί φασι
τῶν θεωρῶν ἐπιθυμήσαντά τινα συγκατακλεισθῆναι
καὶ τῆς ὁμιλίας < . . . > καταλιπεῖν στέφανον. φωρα-
θέντος δ' αὐτοῦ τὸν θεὸν χρωμένοις τοῖς Δελφοῖς
συντάξαι ἀφεῖναι τὸν ἄνθρωπον· δεδωκέναι γὰρ αὐτὸν
μισθόν.

Καὶ ἄλογα δὲ ζῷα ἀνθρώπων ἠράσθη. Σεκούνδου
μέν τινος βασιλικοῦ οἰνοχόου ἀλεκτρυών· ἐκαλεῖτο δὲ
ὁ μὲν ἀλεκτρυὼν Κένταυρος, ὁ δὲ Σεκοῦνδος ἦν οἰκέτης Νικομήδους τοῦ Βιθυνῶν βασιλέως, ὡς ἱστορεῖ
c Νίκανδρος | ἐν ἕκτῳ Περιπετειῶν. ἐν Αἰγίῳ δὲ παιδὸς
ἠράσθη χήν, ὡς Κλέαρχος ἱστορεῖ ἐν πρώτῳ Ἐρω-
τικῶν· τὸν δὲ παῖδα τοῦτον Θεόφραστος ἐν τῷ Ἐρωτι-
κῷ Ἀμφίλοχον καλεῖσθαί φησι καὶ τὸ γένος Ὠλένιον
εἶναι, Ἑρμείας δ' ὁ τοῦ Ἑρμοδώρου, Σάμιος δὲ γένος,

---

105 This must be the individual to whom Polemon replied in
his *Response to Adaeus and Antigonus* (quoted at e.g. 5.210a;
11.462a; 15.690e). The sculptor Ctesicles is otherwise unknown.

106 Presumably the garland was made of gold, and the man had
not intended to leave it behind.

But on Samos, once upon a time, a guy fell in love
with a creature made of stone; then he locked
himself up in the temple.

The statue was made by Ctesicles, according to Adaeus of
Mitylene in his *On Sculptors*.[105] Polemon (fr. 28 Preller)—
or whoever the author of the work entitled *The Account of
Greece* is—says: There are two stone boys in the Treasury
of the Spinatae in Delphi, and the Delphians claim that
someone who came to see the place became infatuated
with one of them and locked himself up with it, and of having sex with it . . . left a garland behind. When he was
caught, the Delphians consulted the god, but he ordered
them to let the man go; because he had paid for his actions.[106]

Irrational animals have also fallen in love with human
beings. A rooster, for example, (fell in love with) a royal
wine-steward named Secundus. The rooster was named
Centaurus, and Secundus was a household-slave of Nicomedes, the king of Bithynia,[107] according to Nicander in
Book VI of the *Reversals of Fortune* (*FGrH* 700 F 2). In
Aegeum a goose fell in love with a boy, according to Clearchus in Book I of the *Erotica* (fr. 27 Wehrli); Theophrastus
in his *Erotic Essay* (fr. 567A Fortenbaugh) says that this
boy was named Amphilochus and that his family was from
Olene.[108] Hermeias the son of Hermodorus, whose family
was from Samos, on the other hand, (claims that the goose)

[107] Probably Nicomedes II (reigned 149–128/7 BCE). Cf. Ael.
NA 12.37.
[108] Cf. Ael. *NA* 5.29 (also citing Theophrastus); Plu. *Mor.* 972f
(who calls this a famous story).

ἐρασθῆναι Λακύδους τοῦ φιλοσόφου. ἐν δὲ Λευκαδίᾳ
φησὶν Κλέαρχος οὕτως ἐρασθῆναι ταὼν παρθένου ὡς
καὶ τὸν βίον ἐκλιπούσῃ συναποθανεῖν. δελφῖνα δ' ἐν
Ἰασῷ παιδὸς ἐρασθῆναι λόγος, ὡς ἱστορεῖ Δοῦρις ἐν
d τῇ ἐνάτῃ. ὁ δὲ λόγος ἐστὶν αὐτῷ περὶ | Ἀλεξάνδρου
καὶ λέγει οὕτως· μετεπέμψατο δὲ καὶ τὸν ἐκ τῆς Ἰασοῦ
παῖδα· περὶ γὰρ τὴν πόλιν ταύτην Διονύσιός τις ἦν
παῖς, ὃς μετὰ τῶν ἄλλων ἐκ παλαίστρας παραγινό-
μενος ἐπὶ τὴν θάλατταν ἐκολύμβα. δελφὶς δὲ πρὸς
αὐτὸν ἐκ τοῦ πελάγους ἀπῆντα καὶ ἀναλαμβάνων ἐπὶ
τὰ νῶτα ἔφερεν ἐπὶ πλεῖστον νηχόμενος καὶ πάλιν
ἀποκαθίστα εἰς τὴν γῆν. φιλανθρωπότατον δέ ἐστι
καὶ συνετώτατον τὸ ζῷον ὁ δελφὶς χάριν τε ἀποδιδόναι ἐπιστάμενον. Φύλαρχος γοῦν ἐν τῇ δωδεκάτῃ,
e Κοίρανος, φησίν, | ὁ Μιλήσιος ἰδὼν ἁλιέας τῷ δικτύῳ
λαβόντας δελφῖνα καὶ μέλλοντας κατακόπτειν ἀργύ-
ριον δοὺς καὶ παραιτησάμενος ἀφῆκεν εἰς τὸ πέλαγος.
καὶ μετὰ ταῦτα ναυαγίᾳ χρησάμενος περὶ Μύκονον
καὶ πάντων ἀπολομένων μόνος ὑπὸ δελφῖνος ἐσώθη ὁ
Κοίρανος. τελευτήσαντος δ' αὐτοῦ γηραιοῦ ἐν τῇ πα-
τρίδι καὶ τῆς ἐκφορᾶς παρὰ τὴν θάλατταν γιγνομένης
κατὰ τύχην,[22] ἐν τῷ λιμένι πλῆθος δελφίνων ἐφάνη ἐν
τῇ ἡμέρᾳ ἐκείνῃ μικρὸν ἀπωτέρω τῶν ἐκκομιζόντων

[22] κατὰ τύχην ἐν τῇ Μιλήτῳ A: ἐν τῇ Μιλήτῳ om. CE, del.
Meineke

fell in love with the philosopher Lacydes.[109] And in Leucadia, according to Clearchus (fr. 28 Wehrli), a peacock fell so deeply in love with a girl that when she passed away, it died at the same time. There is a story that a dolphin fell in love with a boy in Iasus, according to Duris in Book IX (*FGrH* 76 F 7).[110] His account involves Alexander, and goes as follows: (Alexander) also summoned the boy from Iasus. For there was a boy named Dionysius, who lived near this city, and who left the wrestling-school along with the other boys and was down by the sea swimming. A dolphin came up to him out of the sea; took him up on its back; swam around carrying him for a long time; and deposited him again on the shore. Dolphins are extremely friendly and intelligent creatures, and know how to return a favor. Phylarchus in Book XII (*FGrH* 81 F 26), for example, says:[111] When Coiranus of Miletus saw that some fishermen had caught a dolphin in their net and intended to butcher it, he gave them some money and, after they turned it over to him, released it back into the sea. Afterward, he was shipwrecked near Myconos, and although everyone else died, Coiranus alone was rescued by a dolphin. He died as an old man in his native country, and his funeral procession happened to proceed along the seashore; a school of dolphins appeared in the harbor that day, very close to the people accompanying Coiranus to his grave,

---

[109] Ael. *NA* 7.41 offers a more circumstantial version of the story. [110] Cf. Plu. *Mor.* 984e–f; Ael. *NA* 6.15 (a much more extensive and unhappy version of the same story); Plin. *Nat.* 9.25, 27; *Ep.* 9.33.

[111] Cf. Plu. *Mor.* 984f–5b (citing Archil. fr. 192 West²); Ael. *NA* 8.3 (both slightly more circumstantial versions of the story).

ATHENAEUS

f τὸν Κοίρανον, | ὡσεὶ συνεκφερόντων καὶ συγκηδευ-
όντων τὸν ἄνθρωπον. ὁ δὲ αὐτὸς ἱστορεῖ Φύλαρχος
διὰ τῆς εἰκοστῆς ὅσην ἐλέφας²³ φιλοστοργίαν ἔσχεν
εἰς παιδίον. γράφει δ᾽ οὕτως· τούτῳ δὲ τῷ ἐλέφαντι
συνετρέφετο θήλεια ἐλέφας, ἣν Νίκαιαν ἐκάλουν· ᾧ
τελευτῶσα ἡ τοῦ τρέφοντος Ἰνδοῦ γυνὴ παιδίον αὐτῆς
τριακοσταῖον παρακατέθετο. ἀποθανούσης δὲ τῆς ἀνθρώπου δεινή τις φιλοστοργία γέγονε τοῦ θηρίου
πρὸς τὸ παιδίον· οὔτε γὰρ ἀπ᾽ αὐτοῦ χωριζόμενον τὸ
βρέφος ὑπέμενεν, τὸ δὲ εἰ μὴ βλέποι τὸ παιδίον
ἤσχαλλεν. ὅτ᾽ οὖν ἡ τροφὸς ἐμπλήσειεν αὐτὸ τοῦ
γάλακτος, ἀνὰ μέσον τῶν ποδῶν τοῦ θηρίου ἐτίθει
607 αὐτὸ ἐν σκάφῃ. ‖ εἰ δὲ μὴ τοῦτο πεποιήκοι, τροφὴν
οὐκ ἐλάμβανεν ἡ ἐλέφας. καὶ μετὰ ταῦτα δι᾽ ὅλης τῆς
ἡμέρας τοὺς καλάμους λαμβάνων ἐκ τῶν παρατιθε-
μένων χορτασμάτων καθεύδοντος τοῦ βρέφους τὰς
μυίας ἀπεσόβει· ὅτε δὲ κλαίοι, τῇ προβοσκίδι τὴν
σκάφην ἐκίνει καὶ κατεκοίμιζεν αὐτό. τὸ δ᾽ αὐτὸ ἐποίει
καὶ ὁ ἄρρην ἐλέφας πολλάκις. ὑμεῖς δέ, ὦ φιλόσοφοι,
καὶ τῶν δελφίνων καὶ τῶν ἐλεφάντων ἐστὲ κατὰ τὴν
γνώμην ἀγριώτεροι ἔτι τε ἀνημερώτεροι, καίτοι Περ-
σαίου τοῦ Κιτιέως ἐν τοῖς Συμποτικοῖς Ὑπομνήμασιν |
b βοῶντος καὶ λέγοντος περὶ ἀφροδισίων ἁρμοστὸν
εἶναι ἐν τῷ οἴνῳ μνείαν ποιεῖσθαι· καὶ γὰρ πρὸς ταῦτα
ἡμᾶς ὅταν ὑποπίωμεν ἐπιρρεπεῖς εἶναι. καὶ ἐνταῦθα
τοὺς μὲν ἡμέρως τε καὶ μετρίως αὐτοῖς χρωμένους
ἐπαινεῖν δεῖ, τοὺς δὲ θηριωδῶς καὶ ἀπλήστως ψέγειν.

68

as if the dolphins as well were part of the procession and were participating in his burial. In Book XX the same Phylarchus (*FGrH* 81 F 36) describes how devoted an elephant was to a baby. He writes as follows:[112] A she-elephant known as Nicaea was kept along with this elephant, and when the wife of the Indian to whom the elephants belonged was dying, she entrusted her month-old baby to it. After the woman died, the beast became deeply devoted to the baby; it refused to be separated from the child, and if it could not see the baby, it became upset. So once the nurse had filled the child with milk, she would set it in a trough between the beast's feet; if she failed to do so, the elephant refused to eat. After that, all day long the elephant would take stalks from the fodder it was given and would shoo the flies away from the child as it slept. And whenever the child cried, the elephant rocked the trough with its trunk and tried to put it to sleep; and the male elephant often behaved the same way. But your minds, my philosophers, are more savage and untamed than those of dolphins or elephants, even though Persaeus of Citium in his *Drinking Party Commentaries*[113] (*FGrH* 584 F 4 = Persaeus fr. 451, *SVF* i.100) shouts and proclaims that it is appropriate to discuss sex while drinking wine; because when we have a bit to drink, we incline in that direction. This is also a fitting context in which to praise people who enjoy sex in a mild and moderate way, and to criticize those who behave like wild animals and cannot get enough of it. Whereas if

[112] Ael. *NA* 11.14 offers a slightly different version of the story.
[113] Cf. 4.162b–c.

23 ἐλέφας τὸ ζῷον A: τὸ ζῷον del. Olson

καὶ εἰ διαλεκτικοὶ συνελθόντες εἰς πότον περὶ συλλο-
γισμῶν διαλέγοιντο, ἀλλοτρίως ἂν αὐτοὺς ὑπολάβοι
τις ποιεῖν τοῦ παρόντος καιροῦ, <ὅτε>[24] καὶ ὁ καλὸς
κἀγαθὸς ἀνὴρ μεθυσθείη ἄν. οἱ δὲ βουλόμενοι σωφρο-
c νικοὶ εἶναι σφόδρα μέχρι τινὸς διατηροῦσιν | ἐν τοῖς
πότοις τὸ τοιοῦτον· εἶθ' ὅταν παρεισδυῇ τὸ οἰνάριον,
τὴν πᾶσαν ἀσχημοσύνην ἐπιδείκνυνται· ὃ καὶ πρώην
ἐγένετο ἐπὶ τῶν ἐξ Ἀρκαδίας θεωρῶν πρὸς Ἀντίγονον
παραγενομένων. ἐκεῖνοι γὰρ ἠρίστων σφόδρα σκυ-
θρωπῶς καὶ εὐσχημόνως, ὡς ᾤοντο, οὐχ ὅτι ἡμῶν τινα
προσβλέποντες, ἀλλ' οὐδὲ ἀλλήλους. ὡς δὲ ὁ πότος
προέβαινεν καὶ εἰσῆλθεν ἄλλα τε ἀκροάματα καὶ αἱ
Θετταλαὶ αὗται ὀρχηστρίδες, καθάπερ αὐταῖς ἔθος
ἐστίν, ἐν ταῖς διαζώστραις γυμναὶ ὠρχοῦντο, οὐκ ἔτι
d κατεῖχον αὐτοὺς | οἱ ἄνδρες, ἀλλὰ ἐκ τῶν κλινῶν
ἀνώρμων καὶ ἐβόων ὡς θαυμαστόν τι θέαμα θεώμενοι·
καὶ μακάριον τὸν βασιλέα ἀπεκάλουν, ὅτι ἔξεστιν
αὐτῷ τούτων ἀπολαύειν, καὶ ἕτερα τούτοις παραπλή-
σια πάνυ πολλὰ τῶν φορτικῶν ἐποίουν. τῶν φιλοσόφων δέ τις συμπίνων ἡμῖν εἰσελθούσης αὐλητρίδος
καὶ οὔσης εὐρυχωρίας παρ' αὐτῷ, βουλομένης τῆς
παιδίσκης παρακαθίσαι οὐκ ἐπέτρεψεν, ἀλλὰ σκληρὸν αὐτὸν εἰσῆγεν. εἶθ' ὕστερον πωλουμένης τῆς αὐλητρίδος, καθάπερ ἔθος ἐστὶν ἐν τοῖς πότοις γίνεσθαι,
e ἔν τε τῷ | ἀγοράζειν πάνυ νεανικὸς ἦν καὶ τῷ πωλοῦντι
ἄλλῳ τινὶ θᾶττον προσθέντι ἠμφισβήτει καὶ οὐκ ἔφη

[24] add. Kaibel

individuals trained in dialectic gather for a drinking party and spend their time discussing syllogisms, one might feel that they are not behaving as they should in the situation, given that an individual with good manners would get drunk. People interested in behaving in a profoundly sober fashion manage to keep this up for a while at a drinking party; but then, once a little wine is inside them, they put on an extremely ugly show. This happened just the other day, when the sacred delegates from Arcadia visited Antigonus.[114] They were eating lunch with big scowls on their faces, and were making a great show of their manners—or so they thought—and avoiding eye-contact with any of us, or even with one another. But as the party went on, and entertainers of various sorts came in, and the famous Thessalian dancing-girls were prancing around half-naked in their underwear, as they always do, these men could no longer control themselves, but started jumping up off of their couches and shouting that they were watching an amazing show; and they said that the king was very lucky, since he could enjoy himself like this, and they behaved in many other, similarly low-class ways. When a pipe-girl came in and wanted to sit beside one of the philosophers who was drinking with us, he refused to let her, even though there was plenty of room next to him, and acted like a tough guy. Then later on, when the pipe-girl was being auctioned off, as commonly happens at drinking parties, he acted like a wild young man as the bidding was going on, and when the auctioneer awarded her prematurely to someone else, he argued with him and claimed that the

---

[114] Antigonus Gonatas (reigned c.277–239 BCE).

αὐτὸν πεπρακέναι· καὶ τέλος εἰς πυγμὰς ἦλθεν ὁ
σκληρὸς ἐκεῖνος φιλόσοφος καὶ ἐν ἀρχῇ οὐδ' ἂν
παρακαθίσαι ἐπιτρέπων τῇ αὐλητρίδι. μήποτε αὐτός
ἐστιν Περσαῖος ὁ περὶ τῆς αὐλητρίδος διαπυκτεύσας.
φησὶν γὰρ Ἀντίγονος ὁ Καρύστιος ἐν τῷ Περὶ Ζήνωνος γράφων ὧδε· Ζήνων ὁ Κιτιεὺς Περσαίου παρὰ
πότον αὐλητρίδιον πριαμένου καὶ διοκνοῦντος εἰσ-
f αγαγεῖν πρὸς αὐτὸν | διὰ τὸ τὴν αὐτὴν οἰκεῖν οἰκίαν,
συναισθόμενος εἰσείλκυσε τὴν παιδίσκην καὶ συγ-
κατέκλεισε τῷ Περσαίῳ. οἶδα δὲ καὶ Πολύστρατον τὸν
Ἀθηναῖον, μαθητὴν δὲ Θεοφράστου, τὸν ἐπικαλούμενον Τυρρηνόν, ὅτι τῶν αὐλητρίδων τὰ ἱμάτια περι-
έδυεν. ἐσπουδάκεσαν δὲ καὶ οἱ βασιλεῖς περὶ τὰς
μουσουργούς, ὡς δῆλον ποιεῖ Παρμενίων ἐν τῇ Πρὸς
Ἀλέξανδρον Ἐπιστολῇ, ἣν ἐπέστειλεν αὐτῷ μετὰ τὸ
Δαμασκὸν ἑλεῖν καὶ τῆς ἀποσκευῆς τῆς Δαρείου
ἐγκρατὴς γενέσθαι. καταριθμησάμενος οὖν τὰ αἰχμ-
άλωτα γράφει καὶ ταῦτα· παλλακίδας εὗρον μουσουρ-
608 γοὺς τοῦ βασιλέως ‖ τριακοσίας εἴκοσι ἐννέα, ἄνδρας
στεφανοπλόκους ἓξ καὶ τεσσαράκοντα, ὀψοποιοὺς
διακοσίους ἑβδομήκοντα ἑπτά, χυτρεψοὺς εἴκοσι ἐννέα, γαλακτουργοὺς τρισκαίδεκα, ποτηματοποιοὺς
ἑπτακαίδεκα, οἰνοηθητὰς ἑβδομήκοντα, μυροποιοὺς
τεσσαράκοντα.

Καὶ ὑμῖν δέ, ὦ ἑταῖροι, λέγω ὅτι οὐδέν ἐστιν
ὀφθαλμῶν οὕτως εὐφραντικὸν ὡς γυναικὸς κάλλος. ὁ
γοῦν τοῦ τραγικοῦ Χαιρήμονος Οἰνεὺς περὶ παρθένων

sale was invalid. In the end our tough-guy philosopher found himself involved in a fistfight—even though he initially refused even to let the pipe-girl sit down next to him! Perhaps the man who traded punches over the pipe-girl was Persaeus himself. For Antigonus of Carystus says in his *On Zeno* (p. 117 Wilamowitz = fr. 34A Dorandi), writing as follows:[115] When Persaeus was the high bidder for a pipe-girl at a drinking party, but was reluctant to take her home because he lived in the same house as Zeno of Citium, Zeno realized what was going on, dragged the girl inside, and locked her up with Persaeus. I am also aware that Polystratus of Athens[116]—he was a student of Theophrastus and was nicknamed the Etruscan—used to put on the pipe-girls' clothing. Even kings were intrigued by women who played musical instruments, as Parmenion makes clear in his *Letter to Alexander*, which he sent to Alexander after capturing Damascus[117] and seizing control of Darius' household property. After listing the captured goods, he writes as follows: I found 329 royal concubines trained to play musical instruments; 46 men who weave garlands; 277 who produce fancy dishes; 29 who make soup; 13 who process milk; 17 who mix drinks; 70 who strain wine; and 40 who produce perfume.

I tell you, my friends: nothing makes a man's eyes happier than a beautiful woman! The tragic author Chaeremon's *Oineus* (*TrGF* 71 F 14), for example, describes some

[115] Cf. D.L. 7.13.

[116] *PAA* 780975. His nickname presumably reflects his devotion to extreme luxury; cf. 12.517d–18c.

[117] After the Battle of Issus in 330 BCE. Parmenion is Berve i #606.

τινῶν διηγούμενος ὧν ἐθεᾶτό φησιν ἐν τῷ ὁμωνύμῳ
δράματι· |

b   ἔκειτο δ' ἡ μὲν λευκὸν εἰς σεληνόφως
    φαίνουσα μαστὸν λελυμένης ἐπωμίδος,
    τῆς δ' αὖ χορεία λαγόνα τὴν ἀριστερὰν
    ἔλυσε· γυμνὴ δ' αἰθέρος θεάμασιν
    ζῶσαν γραφὴν ἔφαινε, χρῶμα δ' ὄμμασιν
    λευκὸν μελαίνης ἔργον ἀντηύγει σκιᾶς.
    ἄλλη δ' ἐγύμνου καλλίχειρας ὠλένας,
    ἄλλης προσαμπέχουσα θῆλυν αὐχένα.
    ἡ δὲ ῥαγέντων χλανιδίων ὑπὸ πτυχαῖς |
c   ἔφαινε μηρόν, κἀξεπεσφραγίζετο
    ὥρας γελώσης χωρὶς ἐλπίδων ἔρως.
    ὑπνωμέναι δ' ἔπιπτον ἐλενίων ἔπι,
    ἴων τε μελανόφυλλα συγκλῶσαι πτερὰ
    κρόκον θ', ὃς ἡλιῶδες εἰς ὑφάσματα
    πέπλων σκιᾶς εἴδωλον ἐξωμόργνυτο,
    ἕρσῃ δὲ θαλερὸς ἐκτραφεὶς ἀμάρακος
    λειμῶσι μαλακοὺς ἐξέτεινεν αὐχένας. |

d ἐπικατάφορος δὲ ὢν ὁ ποιητὴς οὗτος ἐπὶ τὰ ἄνθη καὶ
ἐν Ἀλφεσιβοίᾳ φησίν·

    καὶ σώματος μὲν † ὄψεις κατειργάζετο
    στίλβοντα λευκῷ † χρώματι διαπρεπῆ.
    αἰδὼς δ' ἐπερρύθμιζεν ἠπιώτατον

young women[118] he saw and says, in the play that bears his
name:

> One of them was lying there, putting her pale breast
> on display in the moonlight, since her dress had
>   slipped down,
> while the dancing had exposed the left hip
> of another. Exposed to open view,
> it made a living image visible, and its white tint
> balanced the effect of the shadowy darkness on my
>   eyes.
> A third exposed her forearms and lovely hands,
> wrapping them around the female neck of another
>   girl.
> This one allowed a glimpse of her thigh beneath the
>   folds
> of her shredded robes, and hopeless longing
> for her radiant beauty impressed itself upon me.
> They sprawled out asleep on calamint,
> and had woven black-flowered violet-petals together
> with crocus, which wiped a shade
> that resembled sunlight onto their woven robes.
> And dew-swollen marjoram that had grown
> in the marshes extended its tender stalks.

Because this poet was fascinated by flowers, he says in
Alphesiboea (*TrGF* 71 F 1):

> and of her body † sights it was being produced
> glistening with white † magnificently colored.
> But a sense of decency altered it, adding

118 Most likely maenads.

ἐρύθημα λαμπρῷ προστιθεῖσα χρώματι·
κόμαι δὲ κηρόχρωτος ὡς ἀγάλματος
αὐτοῖσι βοστρύχοισιν ἐκπεπλασμένου
ξουθοῖσιν ἀνέμοις ἐνετρύφων φορούμεναι.

ἐν δὲ τῇ Ἰοῖ ἔαρος τέκνα προσηγόρευε τὰ ἄνθη· |

e   ἀνθηροῦ τέκνα
ἔαρος πέριξ στρώσαντες.

ἐν δὲ Κενταύρῳ, ὅπερ δρᾶμα πολύμετρόν ἐστιν, λει-
μῶνος τέκνα·

     ἔνθ᾽ αἱ μὲν αὐτῶν εἰς ἀπείρονα στρατὸν
     ἀνθέων ἄλογχον ἐστράτευσαν, ἡδοναῖς
     θηρώμεν‹αι . . . ›οντα λειμώνων τέκνα.

ἐν δὲ Διονύσῳ·

     χορῶν ἐραστὴς κισσός, ἐνιαυτοῦ δὲ παῖς.

περὶ δὲ ῥόδων ἐν Ὀδυσσεῖ φησιν οὕτως·

     κόμαισιν ὡρῶν σώματ᾽ εὐανθῆ ῥόδα
     εἶχον, τιθήνημ᾽ ἔαρος ἐκπρεπέστατον. |

f   καὶ ἐν Θυέστῃ·

     ῥόδ᾽ ὀξυφεγγῆ κρίνεσιν ἀργεννοῖς ὁμοῦ.

ἐν δὲ Μινύαις·

     πολλὴν ὀπώραν Κύπριδος εἰσορᾶν παρῆν
     ἄκραισι περκάζουσαν οἰνάνθαις χρόνου.

a slight blush to the tint with which she shone.
Her hair, like that of a wax-colored statue
on which even the tresses are sculpted,
spilled about, blown by the trilling breezes.

And in his *Io* (*TrGF* 71 F 9) he refers to the flowers as "children of the spring":

strewing the children
of the flowery spring everywhere about.

Whereas in *The Centaur* (*TrGF* 71 F 10), which is a polymetrical play, (he calls them) "children of the meadow":

There some of them attacked the boundless,
unarmed army of flowers, joyfully
hunting . . . –ing children of the meadows.

And in *Dionysus* (*TrGF* 71 F 5):

Ivy, the lover of choruses and child of the year.

He says the following about roses in *Odysseus* (*TrGF* 71 F 13):

In their hair they wore roses, the fair-flowering
    embodiment
of the seasons, a gorgeous nursling of spring.

And in *Thyestes* (*TrGF* 71 F 8):

a brightly shining rose, along with white lilies.

And in *Minyans* (*TrGF* 71 F 12):

You could see a great deal of Cypris'[119] fruit
turning dark on the tendril-tips of time.

[119] Aphrodite's.

ἐπὶ κάλλει δὲ –

ἔτι γὰρ[25] γέρων ἀοιδὸς
κελαδεῖ[26] Μναμοσύναν,

κατὰ τὸν Εὐριπίδην – διαβόητοι γεγόνασι γυναῖκες
Θαργηλία ἡ Μιλησία, ἥτις καὶ τεσσαρεσκαίδεκα ||
609 ἀνδράσιν ἐγαμήθη, οὖσα καὶ τὸ εἶδος πάνυ καλὴ καὶ
σοφή, ὥς φησιν Ἱππίας ὁ σοφιστὴς ἐν τῷ ἐπιγραφομένῳ Συναγωγή. Δίνων δ' ἐν τῇ πέμπτῃ τῶν Περ-
σικῶν τῆς πρώτης συντάξεώς φησιν ὅτι ἡ Βαγαβάζου
γυνή, ἥτις ἦν ὁμοπάτριος Ξέρξου ἀδελφή, ὄνομα
Ἀνοῦτις, καλλίστη ἦν τῶν ἐν τῇ Ἀσίᾳ γυναικῶν καὶ
ἀκολαστοτάτη. Φύλαρχος δὲ ἐν τῇ ἐννεακαιδεκάτῃ
Τιμῶσάν φησι τὴν Ὀξυάρτου παλλακίδα πάσας γυναῖκας ὑπερβεβληκέναι κάλλει· ταύτην δ' ἀπεστάλκει
b δῶρον | ὁ τῶν Αἰγυπτίων βασιλεὺς Στατίρᾳ τῇ βασι-
λέως γυναικί. Θεόπομπος δὲ ἐν τῇ ἕκτῃ καὶ πεντη-
κοστῇ τῶν Ἱστοριῶν Ξενοπείθειαν τὴν Λυσανδρίδου
μητέρα πασῶν τῶν κατὰ Πελοπόννησον γυναικῶν
γεγονέναι καλλίονα· ἀπέκτειναν δὲ αὐτὴν Λακεδαιμόνιοι καὶ τὴν ἀδελφὴν αὐτῆς Χρύσην, ὅτε καὶ τὸν
Λυσανδρίδαν ἐχθρὸν ὄντα Ἀγησίλαος ὁ βασιλεὺς
καταστασιάσας φυγαδευθῆναι ἐποίησεν ὑπὸ Λακεδαιμονίων. καλλίστη δ' ἦν καὶ Παντίκα ἡ Κυπρία,
c περὶ ἧς φησι Φύλαρχος ἐν τῇ δεκάτῃ τῶν | Ἱστοριῶν

---

[25] L (the only manuscript that preserves the complete text of
the HF) has τοι.   [26] κελαδῶ Diggle

78

Women notorious for their beauty—

> for an aged singer can still
> celebrate Mnemosyne ("Memory"),

to quote Euripides (*HF* 678–9)—include Thargelia of Miletus, who was married to 14 different men and was extremely beautiful and wise, according to the sophist Hippias in his work entitled *The Collection* (*FGrH* 6 F 3). Dinon in the opening section of Book V of his *History of Persia* (*FGrH* 690 F 1) says that Bagabyzus' wife, who had the same father as Xerxes and was named Anoutis, was the most beautiful woman in Asia, as well as the most sexually ravenous. Phylarchus in Book XIX (*FGrH* 81 F 34) says that Oxyartis' concubine Timosa was more beautiful than any woman in the world; the king of Egypt sent her as a gift to the Persian king's wife, Statira.[120] Theopompus in Book LVI of his *History* (*FGrH* 115 F 240) (claims that) Xenopeitheia[121] the mother of Lysandridas was the most beautiful woman in the Peloponnese; the Spartans executed her and her sister Chryse when King Agesilaus outmaneuvered Lysandridas, who was his enemy, and convinced the Spartans to send him into exile. Pantica of Cyprus was also extremely beautiful; Phylarchus in Book X of his *History* (*FGrH* 81 F 21) claims that when she was

[120] The location of this anecdote in Phylarchus Book XIX would seem to place these events sometime in the mid-230s BCE.

[121] Poralla #570. Lysandridas is Poralla #503, and Chryse is Poralla #769. The Agesilaus referred to below is Agesilaus II (Poralla #9; reigned 400–360/59 BCE).

ὅτι παρ' Ὀλυμπιάδι οὖσαν τῇ Ἀλεξάνδρου μητρὶ ᾔτει
πρὸς γάμον Μόνιμος ὁ Πυθίωνος. καὶ ἐπεὶ ἦν ἀκό-
λαστος ἡ γυνή, ἔφη ἡ Ὀλυμπιάς· "ὦ πόνηρε, τοῖς
ὀφθαλμοῖς γαμεῖς καὶ οὐ τῷ νῷ." καὶ τὴν καταγα-
γοῦσαν δὲ Πεισίστρατον ἐπὶ τὴν τυραννίδα, ὡς Ἀθηνᾶς † πειραν † εἶδος ἔχουσαν, καλήν φησι γεγονέναι,
ἥτις καὶ τῇ θεῷ εἴκαστο τὴν μορφήν. στεφανόπωλις δ'
ἦν· καὶ αὐτὴν ἐξέδωκε πρὸς γάμου κοινωνίαν ὁ Πει-
σίστρατος Ἱππάρχῳ τῷ υἱῷ, ὡς Ἀντικλείδης²⁷ ἱστορεῖ
d ἐν ὀγδόῳ Νόστων· ἐξέδωκεν | δὲ καὶ Ἱππάρχῳ τῷ υἱεῖ
τὴν παραιβατήσασαν αὐτῷ γυναῖκα Φύην τὴν Σωκράτους θυγατέρα, καὶ Χάρμου τοῦ πολεμαρχήσαν-
τος θυγατέρα ἔλαβεν Ἱππίᾳ περικαλλεστάτην οὖσαν
τῷ μετ' αὐτὸν τυραννεύσαντι. συνέβη δέ, ὥς φησι, τὸν
Χάρμον ἐραστὴν τοῦ Ἱππίου γενέσθαι καὶ τὸν πρὸς
Ἀκαδημίᾳ Ἔρωτα ἱδρύσασθαι πρῶτον, ἐφ' οὗ ἐπι-
γέγραπται·

ποικιλομήχαν' Ἔρως, σοὶ τόνδ' ἱδρύσατο βωμὸν
   Χάρμος ἐπὶ σκιεροῖς τέρμασι γυμνασίου. |

e Ἡσίοδος δ' ἐν τρίτῳ Μελαμποδίας τὴν ἐν Εὐβοίᾳ
Χαλκίδα καλλιγύναικα εἶπεν· εὐπρεπεῖς γὰρ αὐτόθι
γίγνονται γυναῖκες, ὡς καὶ Θεόφραστος εἴρηκεν. καὶ
Νυμφόδωρος δ' ἐν τῷ τῆς Ἀσίας Περίπλῳ καλλίονάς

²⁷ Ἀντικλείδης Stiehle: Κλείδημος A

----

122 Monimus was the ruler of Pella; cf. D.S. 19.50.3.

visiting Alexander's mother Olympias, Monimus the son of Pythion asked to marry her.[122] Because Pantica had an uncontrollable sexual appetite, Olympias said: "You poor bastard—you're marrying with your eyes, not your brain!" He also says that the woman who restored Pisistratus to the tyranny was beautiful,[123] since her [corrupt] looked like Athena's; she was also built like the goddess. She was a garland-seller, and Pisistratus gave her to his son Hipparchus to marry, according to Anticleides[124] in Book VIII of the *Returns* (*FGrH* 140 F 6): He gave his son Hipparchus Phye the daughter of Socrates, who had been by his side, as his wife; and he got the daughter of the polemarch Charmus,[125] who was extremely beautiful, for Hippias, who succeeded him as tyrant. Charmus, he claims, happened to have been Hippias' lover and was responsible for the erection of the (statue of) Eros that stands in the Academy and bears the inscription (anon. *FGE* 1482–3):[126]

> Eros of many wiles—Charmus had this altar
>   constructed
>   for you at the shady edge of the park.

Hesiod in Book III of the *Melampodia* (fr. 277) referred to Euboean Chalcis as "having beautiful women"; for the women are good-looking there, according to Theophrastus (fr. 562 Fortenbaugh). So too Nymphodorus in his *Voyage along the Coast of Asia* (*FGrH* 572 F 7) claims that the

---

[123] For the story (set in the mid-550s BCE), see Hdt. 1.60.3–5. Phye is *PAA* 966190.

[124] For the error in the author's name (see the Greek apparatus), cf. 9.409f–10a.   [125] *PAA* 988430.

[126] For the story, cf. Paus. 1.30.1.

φησι γίνεσθαι γυναῖκας τῶν πανταχοῦ γυναικῶν ἐν
Τενέδῳ τῇ Τρωικῇ νήσῳ. οἶδα δὲ καὶ περὶ κάλλους
γυναικῶν ἀγῶνά ποτε διατεθέντα· περὶ οὗ ἱστορῶν
Νικίας ἐν τοῖς Ἀρκαδικοῖς διαθεῖναί φησιν αὐτὸν
Κύψελον, πόλιν κτίσαντα ἐν τῷ πεδίῳ περὶ τὸν Ἀλ-
f φειόν· | εἰς ἣν κατοικίσαντα Παρρασίων τινὰς τέμενος
καὶ βωμὸν ἀναστῆσαι Δήμητρι Ἐλευσινίᾳ, ἧς ἐν τῇ
ἑορτῇ καὶ τὸν τοῦ κάλλους ἀγῶνα ἐπιτελέσαι· καὶ
νικῆσαι πρῶτον αὐτοῦ τὴν γυναῖκα Ἡροδίκην. ἐπι-
τελεῖται δὲ καὶ μέχρι νῦν ὁ ἀγὼν οὗτος, καὶ αἱ ἀγωνι-
ζόμεναι γυναῖκες χρυσοφόροι ὀνομάζονται. Θεόφραστος δὲ ἀγῶνα κάλλους φησὶ γίνεσθαι παρὰ Ἠλείοις,
καὶ τὴν κρίσιν ἐπιτελεῖσθαι μετὰ σπουδῆς λαμβάνειν
τε τοὺς νικήσαντας ἆθλα ὅπλα· ἅπερ ἀνατίθεσθαί
610 φησιν Διονύσιος ὁ Λευκτρικὸς τῇ Ἀθηνᾷ, ‖ τὸν δὲ
νικήσαντα ταινιούμενον ὑπὸ τῶν φίλων καὶ πομπεύ-
οντα ἕως τοῦ ἱεροῦ παραγίνεσθαι. τὸν στέφανον δ᾽
αὐτοῖς δίδοσθαι μυρρίνης ἱστορεῖ Μυρσίλος ἐν Ἱστορικοῖς Παραδόξοις. ἐνιαχοῦ δέ φησιν ὁ αὐτὸς Θεόφραστος καὶ κρίσεις γυναικῶν περὶ σωφροσύνης
γίνεσθαι καὶ οἰκονομίας, ὥσπερ ἐν τοῖς βαρβάροις·
ἑτέρωθι δὲ κάλλους, ὡς δέον καὶ τοῦτο τιμᾶσθαι,
καθάπερ καὶ παρὰ Τενεδίοις καὶ Λεσβίοις. ταύτην δὲ
τύχης ἢ φύσεως εἶναι τιμήν, δέον προκεῖσθαι σωφρο-

---

127 The late 7th-century BCE Corinthian tyrant. According to
Paus. 8.29.5, the city he founded was called Basilis.

128 Not much of a surprise; but this is cult aetiology, not history. For beauty-contests, see also 13.565f–6a.

most beautiful women anywhere are found on the island of Tenedos near Troy. I am also aware that a beauty contest for women was established at one point; Nicias discusses it in his *History of Arcadia* (*FGrH* 318 F 1), claiming that Cypselus[127] himself organized it after he founded a city in the plain near the Alpheus River. He settled some Parrhasians in the city and established a sacred precinct and an altar dedicated to Eleusinian Demeter, at whose festival he held the beauty contest; the first winner was his own wife Herodice.[128] This contest is still held today, and the women who compete are referred to as *chrusophoroi* ("gold-bearers, wearers of gold"). Theophrastus (fr. 563 Fortenbaugh) claims that there is a beauty contest in Elis, and that the verdict is treated as a serious matter and the winners[129] receive military gear as a prize; Dionysius of Leuctra says that this gear is dedicated to Athena, and that the winner's friends tie a ribbon around his head and act as his escort for the duration of the festival. Myrsilus in the *Historical Oddities* (fr. 16, *FHG* iv.460) records that the garland they are given is made of laurel. The same Theophrastus (fr. 564 Fortenbaugh) reports that in some places contests were held for women in modesty and domestic skills, as happens among the barbarians; beauty contests are held elsewhere, for example on Tenedos[130] and Lesbos, since this quality too deserves recognition. But because this honor comes as a result of luck or genetics, modesty should be treated as more important; for this way[131] beauty will actually be

---

[129] The participle is masculine.

[130] See above (citing Nymphodorus).

[131] Sc. if a woman is modest as well as beautiful.

b σύνης· τὸ κάλλος γὰρ οὕτως | καλόν, εἰ δὲ μή, κίν-
δυνον ἔχον ἐπ' ἀκολασίαν.

Τοσαῦτα τοῦ Μυρτίλου ἑξῆς καταλέξαντος καὶ
πάντων αὐτὸν ἐπὶ τῇ μνήμῃ θαυμασάντων ὁ Κύνουλκος ἔφη·

πουλυμαθημοσύνης, τῆς οὐ κενεώτερον οὐδέν,

Ἵππων ἔφη ὁ ἄθεος. ἀλλὰ καὶ Ἡράκλειτος ὁ θεῖός
φησι· πουλυμαθίη νόον ἔχειν οὐ διδάσκει. καὶ ὁ Τίμων δὲ ἔφη·

ἐν δὲ πλατυσμὸς
πουλυμαθημοσύνης, τῆς οὐ κενεώτερον ἄλλο. |

c τί γὰρ ὄφελος τῶν τοσούτων ὀνομάτων, ὦ γραμ-
ματικέ, πάντων ἐπιτρῖψαι μᾶλλον ἢ σωφρονίσαι δυ-
ναμένων τοὺς ἀκούοντας; καὶ ἐὰν μέν τίς σου πύθηται
τίνες ἦσαν οἱ εἰς τὸν δούρειον ἵππον ἐγκατακλει-
σθέντες, ἑνὸς καὶ δευτέρου ἴσως ἐρεῖς ὄνομα· καὶ οὐδὲ
ταῦτ' ἐκ τῶν Στησιχόρου, σχολῇ γάρ, ἀλλ' ἐκ τῆς
Ἀγία τοῦ Ἀργείου Ἰλίου Πέρσιδος· οὗτος γὰρ παμ-
πόλλους τινὰς κατέλεξεν. ἀλλὰ μὴν οὐδὲ τῶν Ὀδυσ-
σέως ἑταίρων ἔχοις ἂν οὕτως εὐρύθμως καταλέξαι τὰς
d προσηγορίας | καὶ τίνες οἱ ὑπὸ τοῦ Κύκλωπος αὐτῶν
καταβρωθέντες ἢ ὑπὸ τῶν Λαιστρυγόνων καὶ εἰ ὄντως
κατεβρώθησαν· ὅστις οὖν οὐδὲ τοῦτ' οἶδας, καίτοι
συνεχῶς Φυλάρχου μνήμην ποιούμενος ὅτι ἐν ταῖς
Κείων πόλεσιν οὔτε ἑταίρας οὔτε αὐλητρίδας ἰδεῖν
ἔστι.

beautiful, whereas otherwise there is a risk of it leading to uncontrolled behavior.

After Myrtilus recited this enormous catalogue from one end to the other and everyone expressed astonishment at his memory, Cynulcus said:

> enormous learning, than which nothing is more
> vapid,

as Hippon the Atheist (38 B 3 D–K) put it.[132] But the divine Heraclitus (22 B 40 D–K) also says: Enormous learning doesn't teach good sense. Timo (*SH* 794) as well said:

> In it was the blathering of
> enormous learning, than which nothing else is more
> vapid.

Because what use are all these names, my grammarian, which have more power to annoy their audience than to improve it? If someone asks you who was shut up inside the Wooden Horse, you will be able to offer the names of one or perhaps two people—and they will not be drawn from Stesichorus' poems (*PMG* 199)—scarcely so!—but from the *Sack of Troy* by Agias of Argos (test. 3 Bernabé); for he recorded an enormous number of them. Nor would you be able to list so glibly the names of Odysseus' companions, and which of them were eaten by the Cyclops or the Laestrygonians, or whether they really *were* eaten. So you do not even know this—despite the fact that you constantly cite Phylarchus (*FGrH* 81 F 42) to the effect that courtesans and pipe-girls cannot be seen in the cities on Ceos!

---

[132] Cf. Timo *SH* 794.2 below.

Καὶ ὁ Μυρτίλος· τοῦτο δὲ ποῦ εἴρηκεν ὁ Φύλαρχος;
κατανέγνων γὰρ αὐτοῦ πᾶσαν τὴν Ἱστορίαν. εἰπόντος
δ'· ἐν τῇ τρίτῃ καὶ εἰκοστῇ, ὁ Μυρτίλος ἔφη· εἶτ' οὐκ
ἐγὼ δικαίως πάντας ὑμᾶς τοὺς φιλοσόφους μισῶ
e μισοφιλολόγους ὄντας; οὓς οὐ μόνον | Λυσίμαχος ὁ
βασιλεὺς ἐξεκήρυξε τῆς ἰδίας βασιλείας ἀπελαύνων,
ὡς ὁ Καρύστιός φησιν ἐν Ἱστορικοῖς Ὑπομνήμασιν,
ἀλλὰ καὶ Ἀθηναῖοι. Ἄλεξις γοῦν ἐν Ἵππει[28] φησίν·

> τοῦτ' ἔστιν Ἀκαδήμεια, τοῦτο Ξενοκράτης;
> πόλλ' ἀγαθὰ δοῖεν οἱ θεοὶ Δημητρίῳ
> καὶ τοῖς νομοθέταις, διότι τοὺς τὰς τῶν λόγων,
> ὥς φασι, δυνάμεις παραδιδόντας τοῖς νέοις
> ἐς κόρακας ἔρρειν φασὶν ἐκ τῆς Ἀττικῆς.

καὶ Σοφοκλῆς δέ τις ψηφίσματι ἐξήλασε πάντας |
f φιλοσόφους τῆς Ἀττικῆς, καθ' οὗ λόγον ἔγραψε Φίλων ὁ Ἀριστοτέλους γνώριμος, ἀπολογίαν ὑπὲρ τοῦ
Σοφοκλέους Δημοχάρους πεποιηκότος τοῦ Δημοσθέ-
νους ἀνεψιοῦ. καὶ Ῥωμαῖοι δ' οἱ πάντα ἄριστοι ἐξέβα-
λον τοὺς σοφιστὰς τῆς Ῥώμης ὡς διαφθείροντας τοὺς
νέους· ἔπειτ' οὐκ οἶδ' ὅπως κατεδέξαντο. ἐμφανίζει δ'

---

28 Ἵππει Schweighäuser: Ἵππῳ A

---

133 *PAA* 732995; head of the Academy 339–314 BCE. The
Demetrius referred to in the next line is Demetrius Poliorcetes.
134 *PAA* 829235. The decree (for which, cf. D.L. 5.38; Poll.
9.42) dates to 307 BCE and was repealed in 306 as a result of the
suit brought by Philo, referred to below.

Myrtilus (responded): Where does Phylarchus say this? For I read his entire *History*. When (Cynulcus) replied: In Book XXIII, Myrtilus said: Am I not right to despise all you philosophers who are hostile to philology? It was not just King Lysimachus who issued a proclamation banishing you from the territory he controlled, as Carystius asserts in the *Historical Commentaries* (fr. 9, *FHG* iv.358), but the Athenians as well. Alexis in *The Knight* (fr. 99), at any rate, says:

> Is this the Academy? Is this Xenocrates?[133]
> May the gods confer many blessings on Demetrius
> and our legislators, since they're telling these people
> who are able to bestow verbal power on our young
>   men—
> or so they say—to get the hell out of Attica!

A certain Sophocles[134] also proposed a decree that expelled all philosophers from Attica; Aristotle's student Philo[135] wrote a speech attacking him (cf. Baiter–Sauppe ii.343), while Demosthenes' cousin Demochares composed a defense speech supporting Sophocles (I, Baiter–Sauppe ii.341–2).[136] So too the Romans, who do everything right, expelled the sophists from their city on the ground that they were corrupting the young men[137]—but then later, for reasons I fail to understand, they let them back in. The comic poet Anaxippus in *The Man Who Was*

---

[135] *PAA* 953760.

[136] Cf. 5.187d; 11.508f. Demochares (*PAA* 321970) was actually Demosthenes' nephew.

[137] Cf. 12.547a (perhaps another fragment of the same source-document being quoted here).

ὑμῶν καὶ τὸ ἀνόητον Ἀνάξιππος ὁ κωμῳδιοποιὸς ἐν
Κεραυνουμένῳ λέγων οὕτως·

οἴμοι, φιλοσοφεῖς. ἀλλὰ τούς γε φιλοσόφους ‖
611   ἐν τοῖς λόγοις φρονοῦντας εὑρίσκω μόνον,
ἐν τοῖσι δ' ἔργοις ὄντας ἀνοήτους ὁρῶ.

εἰκότως οὖν πολλαὶ τῶν πόλεων καὶ μάλιστα ἡ Λακεδαιμονίων, ὡς Χαμαιλέων φησὶν ἐν τῷ Περὶ Σιμωνίδου, οὐ προσίενται οὔτε ⟨φιλοσοφίαν οὔτε⟩[29] ῥητο-
ρικὴν διὰ τὰς ἐν τοῖς λόγοις ὑμῶν φιλοτιμίας καὶ
ἔριδας καὶ τοὺς ἀκαίρους ἐλέγχους. δι' οὓς Σωκράτης
μὲν ἀπέθανεν ὁ πρὸς τοὺς εἰς τὰ δικαστήρια ἀπο-
κληρουμένους διαλεγόμενος περὶ τοῦ δικαίου κλεπτι-
στάτους ὄντας· ἀπέθανεν δὲ διὰ ταῦτα καὶ Θεόδωρος ὁ
b   ἄθεος | καὶ Διαγόρας[30] ἐφυγαδεύθη.[31] Διότιμος δ' ὁ
γράψας τὰ κατ' Ἐπικούρου βιβλία ὑπὸ Ζήνωνος τοῦ
Ἐπικουρείου ἐξαιτηθεὶς ἀνῃρέθη, ὥς φησι Δημήτριος
ὁ Μάγνης ἐν τοῖς Ὁμωνύμοις. συνελόντι δὲ εἰπεῖν
κατὰ τὸν Σολέα Κλέαρχον οὐ καρτερικὸν βίον ἀσκεῖ-
τε, κυνικὸν δὲ τῷ ὄντι ζῆτε· καίτοι τοῦ ζῴου τούτου ἐν
τέτταρσι τὴν φύσιν περιττὴν ἔχοντος, ὧνπερ ὑμεῖς τὰ
χείρω μερισάμενοι τηρεῖτε. αἰσθήσει τε γὰρ τῇ πρὸς
ὄσφρανσιν καὶ πρὸς τὸ οἰκεῖον καὶ ἀλλότριον θαυ-
c   μαστὸν | καὶ τῷ συνανθρωπίζον οἰκουρὸν εἶναι καὶ

    29 add. Musurus   30 Διαγόρας ⟨ἐξεκηρύχθη καὶ Πρω-
ταγόρας⟩ Wilamowitz   31 ἐφυγαδεύθη· ὅτε καὶ πλέων
ναυαγίῳ ἐχρήσατο ACE: ὅτε καὶ κτλ. del. Olson

Struck by Lightning (fr. 4) brings out your folly when he says the following:

> Oh no—you're a philosopher! As far as I can tell,
> the philosophers only make sense when they talk,
> whereas their behavior looks crazy to me.

It is therefore understandable that many cities, and Sparta in particular, according to Chamaeleon in his *On Simonides* (fr. 35 Wehrli), refuse to allow philosophy or rhetoric to be taught, on account of how you wrangle and quarrel in your discussions, and because of the untimely nature of your arguments. You are the reason Socrates died—he discussed justice with the men who had been chosen by lot to serve as jurors, and who were the biggest thieves imaginable! This is also why Theodorus the Atheist (*SSR* IV H 11) died,[138] and why Diagoras was driven into exile.[139] And Diotimus, who wrote the books that attack Epicurus,[140] was tracked down and murdered by the Epicurean Zeno, according to Demetrius of Magnesia in his *Men Who Share a Name* (fr. 7 Mejer). To sum up, you do not live a hard (*karterikos*) life, to quote Clearchus of Soli (fr. 16 Wehrli), but a veritable hound's (*kunikos*) life. That creature, in fact, has four pronounced natural characteristics, which you have split up, retaining the worst ones. For a dog is remarkable for its sense of smell and its ability to tell what belongs to it from what does not; and it has an exceptional ability to live with people as a domestic animal and

---

[138] Cf. D.L. 2.101 (citing Amphicrates' *On Famous Men*).

[139] Apparently a garbled reference to the decree against Diagoras of Melos (cf. Ar. *Av.* 1073 with Dunbar ad loc.).

[140] For Diotimus' attack on Epicurus, cf. D.L. 10.3.

φυλακτικὸν τοῦ τῶν εὖ δρώντων βίου πάντων περιτ-
τότατον· ὧν οὐδέτερον πρόσεστιν ὑμῖν τοῖς τὸν κυνικὸν βίον μιμουμένοις. οὔτε γὰρ συνανθρωπίζετε οὔτε
διαγινώσκετε οὐδένα τῶν ὁμιλούντων, αἰσθήσει τε
πολλῷ ὑστεροῦντες ἀργῶς ᵃκαὶ ἀφυλάκτως ζῆτε. λοι-
δόρου δὲ καὶ παμφάγου τοῦ ζῴου πεφυκότος, ἔτι δὲ
ταλαιπώρου καὶ γυμνοῦ τὸν βίον, ἄμφω ταῦτα μελετᾶτε, κακολόγοι καὶ βοροὶ πρός τε τούτοις ἄνοικοι καὶ
d   ἀνέστιοι βιοῦντες. ἐξ ὧν | ἁπάντων ἀλλότριοι μὲν
ἀρετῆς, μάταιοι δὲ ⟨ἐστὲ⟩[32] εἰς τὸ τοῦ βίου χρήσιμον·
οὐδὲν γάρ ἐστι τῶν καλουμένων φιλοσόφων ἀφιλο-
σοφώτερον. τίς γὰρ ἤλπισεν ⟨ἂν⟩[33] Αἰσχίνην τὸν
Σωκρατικὸν τοιοῦτον γεγενῆσθαι τοὺς τρόπους ὁποῖόν
φησι Λυσίας ὁ ῥήτωρ ἐν τοῖς τῶν συμβολαίων λόγοις; ὃν ἐκ τῶν φερομένων ὡς αὑτοῦ διαλόγων θαυ-
μάζομεν ὡς ἐπιεικῆ καὶ μέτριον, πλὴν εἰ μὴ ὡς
ἀληθῶς τοῦ σοφοῦ Σωκράτους ἐστὶν συγγράμματα,
ἐχαρίσθη δὲ αὐτῷ ὑπὸ Ξανθίππης τῆς Σωκράτους
e   γυναικὸς μετὰ τὸν ἐκείνου | θάνατον, ὡς οἱ ἀμφὶ τὸν
Ἰδομενέα φασίν. ἀλλ᾽ ὅ γε Λυσίας ἐν τῷ ἐπιγραφομένῳ λόγῳ οὑτωσί, πρὸς Αἰσχίνην τὸν Σωκρατικὸν
Χρέως – ἀπομνημονεύσω δ᾽ ἐγώ, εἰ καὶ πολλά ἐστι τὰ
λεχθέντα, διὰ τὸν βρένθον ὑμῶν τὸν πολύν, ὦ φιλόσοφοι – ἄρχεται δ᾽ οὕτως ὁ ῥήτωρ· οὐκ ἄν ποτ᾽ ᾠήθην,
ἄνδρες δικασταί, Αἰσχίνην τολμῆσαι οὕτως αἰσχρὰν

32 add. Kaibel
33 add. Kaibel

to protect the property of the rich. But although you try to imitate the way dogs live, you lack either quality; for you are bad company and fail to understand the people you associate with, and because your powers of perception are vastly inferior, you live idly and carelessly. But the creature also has an abusive mouth and is willing to eat anything, and in addition it leads an impoverished existence, stripped of all possessions—and you devote yourselves to both qualities, since you are foul-mouthed gluttons, and on top of that you live without a hearth or a home![141] As a consequence of all this, you are divorced from any sort of virtuous behavior and are worthless when it comes to discovering how to lead a useful existence; for nothing is less philosophical than the so-called philosophers! Who would have expected Aeschines Socraticus[142] to behave the way the orator Lysias describes in his speeches about the contracts (fr. 1 Carey, quoted below)? On the basis of the dialogues attributed to him, I respect him as a decent, moderate individual—unless the texts were actually composed by the wise Socrates and given to Aeschines by Socrates' wife Xanthippe[143] after his death, as Idomeneus[144] (*FGrH* 338 F 17c) claims. But the orator Lysias in his speech with the following title: *A Response to Aeschines Socraticus in the Matter of a Debt* (fr. 1 Carey)—I intend to quote it, even if his remarks are quite extended, because of your excessive swaggering, my philosophers—begins as follows: I would never have expected, gentlemen of the jury, that Aeschines would have dared to become involved in such an

---

[141] An echo of *Il.* 9.63. [142] *PAA* 115140.
[143] *PAA* 730275. [144] Literally "those around Idomeneus, Idomeneus' followers."

δίκην δικάσασθαι, νομίζω δ᾽ οὐκ ἂν ῥᾳδίως αὐτὸν
ἑτέραν ταύτης συκοφαντωδεστέραν ἐξευρεῖν. οὗτος
f γάρ, ὦ ἄνδρες δικασταί, ὀφείλων ἀργύριον | ἐπὶ τρισὶ
δραχμαῖς Σωσινόμῳ τῷ τραπεζίτῃ καὶ Ἀριστογείτονι
προσελθὼν πρὸς ἐμὲ ἐδεῖτο μὴ περιδεῖν αὐτὸν διὰ
τοὺς τόκους ἐκ τῶν ὄντων ἐκπεσόντα. "κατασκευάζο-
μαι δ᾽," ἔφη, "τέχνην μυρεψικήν· ἀφορμῆς δὲ δέομαι,
καὶ οἴσω δέ σοι ἐννέ᾽ ὀβολοὺς τῆς μνᾶς τόκους."
612 καλόν γε τὸ τέλος ‖ τῆς εὐδαιμονίας τῷ φιλοσόφῳ ἡ
μυρεψικὴ τέχνη ἀκόλουθός τε τῇ Σωκράτους φιλοσοφίᾳ, ἀνδρὸς τοῦ καὶ τὴν τοιαύτην χρῆσιν τῶν
μύρων ἀποδοκιμάσαντος, Σόλωνος δὲ τοῦ νομοθέτου
οὐδ᾽ ἐπιτρέποντος ἀνδρὶ τοιαύτης προΐστασθαι
τέχνης· διὸ καὶ Φερεκράτης ἐν Ἴπνῳ ἢ Παννυχίδι
φησίν·

κᾆτα μυροπωλεῖν τί μαθόντ᾽ ἄνδρ᾽ ἐχρῆν
       καθήμενον
ὑψηλῶς ὑπὸ σκιαδείῳ, κατεσκευασμένον
συνέδριον τοῖς μειρακίοις ἐλλαλεῖν δι᾽ ἡμέρας;

εἶθ᾽ ἑξῆς φησιν·

b   αὐτίκ᾽ οὐδεὶς οὔτε μαγείραιναν | εἶδε πώποτε
       οὔτε μὴν οὐδ᾽ ἰχθυοπώλαιναν.

---

145 Sosinomus is *PAA* 862820. Aristogiton is *PAA* 168110.
146 I.e. per 100, making the annual rate 36%—which explains
why Aeschines was allegedly so eager to make other arrange-
ments.
147 Nine obols = 1½ drachmas; a *mina* = 100 drachmas; and

embarrassing case, and I believe it would be difficult for him to find another that so blatantly abuses our legal system. For this man, gentlemen of the jury, owed Sosinomus the banker and Aristogiton[145] money, on which he was paying three drachmas[146] per month; and he came to me and asked me not to stand by and watch him lose all his property because of the interest. "I'm setting up a business to make perfume," he said; "I need start-up money, and I can offer you nine obols per *mina*[147] as interest."[148] What perfect happiness for the philosopher a business producing perfume is! And how exactly in line with the philosophy of Socrates—who disapproved of using perfume this way (X. *Smp.* 2.3–4)![149] Nor did the law-giver Solon (fr. 73b Ruschenbusch)[150] allow a man to run a business of this sort, which is why Pherecrates says in *The Kitchen* or *The All-Night Festival* (fr. 70, encompassing both quotations):

> And then—what could a man be thinking, to sit haughtily
> under a sun-shade, selling perfume, providing
> a spot for the young men to hang around and talk nonsense all day?

Then immediately after this he says:

> For example, no one's ever seen a female cook,
> and certainly not a female fishseller.[151]

the interest is to be paid monthly, making the rate about 18 percent per year (normal for commercial loans in classical Athens and only half of what Aeschines was paying previously).
[148] The quotation from Lysias breaks off abruptly here and resumes at 13.612b.
[149] Quoted at 15.686d–f.   [150] Cf. 15.687a.
[151] Sc. because those are allegedly properly male occupations.

ἑκάστῳ γὰρ γένει ἁρμόζοντα δεῖ εἶναι καὶ τὰ τῆς
τέχνης. ἑξῆς δὲ τούτοις ὁ ῥήτωρ τάδε λέγει· πεισθεὶς
δ᾽ ὑπ᾽ αὐτοῦ τοιαῦτα λέγοντος καὶ ἅμα οἰόμενος τοῦ-
τον³⁴ Σωκράτους γεγονότα μαθητὴν καὶ περὶ δικαιο-
σύνης καὶ ἀρετῆς πολλοὺς καὶ σεμνοὺς λέγοντα
λόγους οὐκ ἄν ποτε ἐπιχειρῆσαι οὐδὲ τολμῆσαι ἅπερ
οἱ πονηρότατοι καὶ ἀδικώτατοι ἄνθρωποι ἐπιχειροῦσι
πράττειν. καὶ μετὰ ταῦτα πάλιν καταδρομὴν αὐτοῦ
c   ποιησάμενος, ὡς δανεισάμενος οὔτε | τόκους οὔτε
τἀρχαῖον ἀπεδίδου καὶ ὅτι ὑπερήμερος ἐγένετο γνώμῃ
δικαστηρίου ἐρήμην καταδικασθεὶς καὶ ὡς ἠνεχυ-
ράσθη οἰκέτης αὐτοῦ στιγματίας, καὶ πολλὰ ἄλλα
κατειπὼν αὐτοῦ ἐπιλέγει ταῦτα· ἀλλὰ γάρ, ὦ ἄνδρες
δικασταί, οὐκ εἰς ἐμὲ μόνον τοιοῦτός ἐστιν, ἀλλὰ καὶ
εἰς τοὺς ἄλλους ἅπαντας τοὺς αὐτῷ κεχρημένους. οὐχ
οἱ μὲν κάπηλοι οἱ ἐγγὺς οἰκοῦντες, παρ᾽ ὧν προδόσεις
λαμβάνων οὐκ ἀποδίδωσι, δικάζονται αὐτῷ συγκλεί-
σαντες τὰ καπηλεῖα, οἱ δὲ γείτονες οὕτως ὑπ᾽ αὐτοῦ |
d   δεινὰ πάσχουσιν ὥστ᾽ ἐκλιπόντες τὰς αὑτῶν οἰκίας
ἑτέρας πόρρω μισθοῦνται; ὅσους δ᾽ ἐράνους συνεί-
λεκται, τὰς μὲν ὑπολοίπους φορὰς οὐ κατατίθησιν,
⟨ . . . ⟩ ἀλλὰ περὶ τοῦτον τὸν κάπηλον ὡς περὶ στήλην
διαφθείρονται. τοσοῦτοι δὲ ἐπὶ τὴν οἰκίαν ἅμα τῇ
ἡμέρᾳ ἀπαιτήσοντες τὰ ὀφειλόμενα ἔρχονται ὥστε
οἴεσθαι τοὺς παριόντας ἐπ᾽ ἐκφορὰν αὐτοὺς ἥκειν
τούτου τεθνεῶτος. οὕτω δ᾽ οἱ ἐν τῷ Πειραιεῖ διάκεινται

³⁴ τοῦτον Αἰσχίνην Α: Αἰσχίνην del. Kaibel

For the character of any business ought to fit one sex or the other. And immediately after this the orator says the following (Lys. fr. 1 Carey, continued): I was convinced by him, because he made remarks along these lines, and also because I thought that, since he was one of Socrates' students and made many elevated speeches about justice and virtue, he would never attempt or dare to behave as the most miserable, utterly dishonest people try to do. After this he attacks him again, alleging that after (Aeschines) borrowed the money, he paid back neither the interest nor the principal; that he missed his due-date and lost the ensuing court-case by default; and that a tattooed domestic slave who belonged to him was made surety for the loan. And after denouncing him for many additional misbehaviors, he concludes as follows (Lys. fr. 1 Carey, continued): But the fact is, gentlemen of the jury, it is not just me he treats this way, but everyone who comes in contact with him. Don't the shopkeepers in his neighborhood, from whom he gets goods on credit and then fails to pay for them, lock up their stores and bring him into court? And doesn't he make the people who live near him so miserable that they abandon their own houses and rent others far away? Whenever he gathers contributions for a group dinner, he doesn't return the money that's left over . . . but when they come in contact with this huckster, it's like hitting a turning post,[152] and they're ruined. So many people come to his house at dawn to ask for the money they're owed, that passers-by think he's dead and they've come for his funeral! And the people in the Piraeus[153] have adopted

---

[152] Sc. in a chariot race.   [153] I.e. the bankers, much of whose money was used for bottomry loans.

ὥστε πολὺ ἀσφαλέστερον εἶναι δοκεῖν εἰς τὸν Ἀδρίαν
e πλεῖν ἢ | τούτῳ συμβάλλειν· πολὺ γὰρ μᾶλλον ἃ ἂν
δανείσηται αὐτοῦ νομίζει εἶναι ἢ ἃ ὁ πατὴρ αὐτῷ
κατέλιπεν. ἀλλὰ γὰρ οὐ τὴν οὐσίαν κέκτηται Ἑρμαίου
τοῦ μυροπώλου, τὴν γυναῖκα διαφθείρας ἑβδομήκοντα ἔτη γεγονυῖαν; ἧς ἐρᾶν προσποιησάμενος οὕτω
διέθηκεν ὥστε τὸν μὲν ἄνδρα αὐτῆς καὶ τοὺς υἱοὺς
πτωχοὺς ἐποίησεν, αὐτὸν δὲ ἀντὶ καπήλου μυροπώλην
ἀπέδειξεν· οὕτως ἐρωτικῶς τὸ κόριον μετεχειρίζετο
τῆς ἡλικίας αὐτῆς ἀπολαύων, ἧς ῥᾷον τοὺς ὀδόντας
f ἀριθμῆσαι[35] | ἢ τῆς χειρὸς τοὺς δακτύλους. καί μοι
ἀνάβητε τούτων μάρτυρες. ὁ μὲν οὖν βίος τοῦ σοφι-
στοῦ τοιοῦτος. ὁ μὲν οὖν Λυσίας, ὦ Κύνουλκε, οὕτως·
ἐγὼ δέ, κατὰ τὸν Ἀρίσταρχον τὸν τραγικὸν ποιητήν,

τάδ᾽ οὐχ ὑπάρχων, ἀλλὰ τιμωρούμενος,

καταπαύσω τὸν πρὸς σὲ καὶ τοὺς ἄλλους κύνας ἐνταῦθα λόγον.

[35] ἀριθμῆσαι ὅσου ἐλάττους ἦσαν ACE: ὅσου ἐλάττους
ἦσαν del. Casaubon

the attitude that it looks much safer to sail to the Adriatic than to get involved with him; because he regards any money he's been loaned as much more his own than what his father left him. And hasn't he got hold of the property of Hermaeus the perfume-maker[154] by seducing his wife— even though she's 70 years old? He pretended to be in love with her, and arranged matters in such a way that he's reduced her husband and sons to poverty, and has turned himself into a perfume-vendor rather than a simple shopkeeper. That's the sort of erotic handling he subjected this "young woman" to, taking advantage of her age—although it would be easier to count her teeth than the fingers on your hand. Let the witnesses to these matters come up onto the speaker's stand, please! That, then, is how the sophist lives! Thus Lysias, Cynulcus. I, on the other hand, to quote the tragic poet Aristarchus (*TrGF* 14 F 4),

> not initiating these deeds, but exacting vengeance for
> them,

will conclude my speech addressed to you and the other dogs[155] at this point.

[154] *PAA* 401965.
[155] I.e. the other Cynic philosophers.

613 Τὸν Διόνυσον, ἑταῖρε Τιμόκρατες, μαινόμενον οἱ πολλοὶ λέγουσιν ἀπὸ τοῦ τοὺς πλείονας ἀκράτου σπῶντας
θορυβώδεις γίνεσθαι·

οἶνός σε τρώει μελιηδής, ὅς τε καὶ ἄλλους
βλάπτει, ὃς ἄν μιν χανδὸν ἕλῃ μηδ᾽ αἴσιμα
πίνῃ.
οἶνος καὶ κένταυρον, ἀγακλυτὸν Εὐρυτίωνα,
ὦλεσ᾽[1] ἐνὶ μεγάρῳ μεγαθύμου Πειριθόοιο
ἐς Λαπίθας ἐλθόνθ᾽. ὁ δ᾽ ἐπεὶ φρένας ἄασεν
οἴνῳ, |
b   μαινόμενος κάκ᾽ ἔρεξε δόμοις ἐνὶ[2] Πειριθόοιο.

κατιόντος γοῦν τοῦ οἴνου ἐς τὸ σῶμα, ὥς φησιν
Ἡρόδοτος, ἐπαναπλέει κακὰ ἔπεα καὶ μαινόμενα.
Κλέαρχός τε ὁ κωμῳδιοποιὸς ἐν Κορινθίοις φησίν·

εἰ τοῖς μεθυσκομένοις ἑκάστης ἡμέρας
ἀλγεῖν συνέβαινε τὴν κεφαλὴν πρὸ τοῦ πιεῖν
τὸν ἄκρατον, ἡμῶν οὐδὲ εἷς ἔπινεν ἄν.

[1] The traditional text of Homer has ἄασ᾽.
[2] The traditional text of Homer has δόμον κατὰ.

BOOK XIV

Many authorities, my friend Timocrates, refer to Dionysus as insane as a consequence of the fact that most people grow boisterous when they gulp down strong wine (*Od.* 21.293–8):

> The honey-sweet wine is injuring you; it hurts anyone
> who consumes it greedily and drinks more than he
>   should.
> Wine ruined the centaur, the famous Eurytion,
> for example, in the house of great-hearted Perithous,
> when he visited the Lapiths. When the wine
>   unbalanced his mind, he
> went crazy and behaved badly in Perithous' house.

The fact is, according to Herodotus (1.212.2), that when wine descends into our body, foul, insane words emerge in its wake. The comic poet Clearchus says in *Corinthians* (fr. 3):

> If people who get loaded every day
> suffered their hangovers before they drank
> their strong wine, none of us would indulge!

νῦν δὲ πρότερόν γε τοῦ πόνου τὴν ἡδονὴν
προλαμβάνοντες ὑστεροῦμεν τἀγαθοῦ. |

c Ξενοφῶντος δὲ τὸν Ἀγησίλαον· μέθης μὲν ἀπέχεσθαι
ὁμοίως ᾤετο χρῆναι καὶ μανίας, σίτων δὲ ὑπερκαίρων[3]
ὁμοίως καὶ ἀργίας. ἀλλ᾽ οὐχ ἡμεῖς γε οὔτε τῶν πλεῖον
πινόντων ὄντες ⟨οὔτε⟩[4] τῶν ἐξοίνων γινομένων πλη-
θούσης ἀγορᾶς ἐπὶ τὰ μουσικὰ ταῦτα ἐρχόμεθα συμπόσια. καὶ γὰρ ὁ φιλεπιτιμητὴς Οὐλπιανὸς πάλιν
τινὸς ἐπείληπτο εἰπόντος, ἔξοινος οὔκ εἰμι, λέγων, ὁ δ᾽
ἔξοινος ποῦ; καὶ ὅς, παρ᾽ Ἀλέξιδι ἐν Εἰσοικιζομένῳ·

ἔξοινος ἐποίει ταῦτά γε,

ἔφη.

Ἐπεὶ δὲ ἑκάστης ἡμέρας μετὰ τοὺς παρ᾽ ἡμῶν
d καινοὺς αἰεὶ λεγομένους | λόγους καὶ ἀκροάματα
ἑκάστοτε διάφορα ἐπεισάγει ὁ λαμπρὸς ἡμῶν ἑστι-
άτωρ Λαρήνσιος ἔτι τε καὶ γελωτοποιούς, φέρε λέγω-
μέν τι καὶ ἡμεῖς περὶ τούτων. καίτοι γε οἶδα καὶ
Ἀνάχαρσιν τὸν Σκύθην ἐν συμποσίῳ γελωτοποιῶν
εἰσαχθέντων ἀγέλαστον διαμείναντα, πιθήκου δ᾽ ἐπει-
σαχθέντος γελάσαντα φάναι, ὡς οὗτος μὲν φύσει
γελοῖός ἐστιν, ὁ δ᾽ ἄνθρωπος ἐπιτηδεύσει. καὶ Εὐριπίδης δὲ ἐν τῇ Δεσμώτιδι Μελανίππῃ ἔφη·

---

[3] The manuscripts of Xenophon have ὑπὲρ καιρόν.
[4] add. Casaubon

But as it is, we enjoy the pleasure before
the pain, so we miss out on what's good.

(Contrast) Xenophon's Agesilaus (*Ages.* 5.1); he thought it
important to avoid not just getting drunk and acting crazy,
but also eating more food than is appropriate and laziness.
But we, who are not among those who drink more than
they should or who become intoxicated (*exoinos*) when the
marketplace is crowded,[1] attend these intellectual gatherings. When someone said, I am not *exoinos*, Ulpian—who
liked criticizing others—went on the attack again and
asked: Where is the word *exoinos* attested? The other man
replied: In Alexis' *The Man Who Was Moving In* (fr. 64):

This is what he was doing when he was *exoinos*.

Since our distinguished host Larensius brought in musical entertainment of various sorts, as well as comedians, every day at the end of the ever-new conversations in
which we engaged, let me say something about them.[2] I am
certainly aware that when Anacharsis the Scythian (A11A
Kindstrand) was at a party and some comedians were introduced, he failed to laugh, whereas when a monkey was
brought in, he laughed and said: "This creature is naturally
funny—but a human being has to work at it!" So too Euripides said in his *Melanippe the Prisoner* (fr. 492):

[1] I.e. "during normal working hours, in the middle of the day."
[2] In this opening section of Book 14, the words of the external
narrator Athenaeus and of Ulpian blend imperceptibly into one
another; cf. 14.615e, where the speech that follows here is expressly assigned to Ulpian.

ἀνδρῶν δὲ πολλοὶ τοῦ γέλωτος οὕνεκα
ἀσκοῦσι χάριτας κερτόμους· ἐγὼ δέ πως
μισῶ γελοίους, οἵτινες τήτῃ σοφῶν ‖
614   ἀχάλιν᾽ ἔχουσι στόματα, κὰς ἀνδρῶν μὲν οὐ
τελοῦσιν ἀριθμόν, ἐν γέλωτι δ᾽ εὐπρεπεῖς.[5]

οἰκοῦσιν[6] οἴκους καὶ τὰ ναυστολούμενα
ἔσω δόμων σῴζουσι.

Παρμενίσκος δὲ ὁ Μεταποντῖνος, ὥς φησιν Σῆμος ἐν
πέμπτῃ Δηλιάδος, καὶ γένει καὶ πλούτῳ πρωτεύων εἰς
Τροφωνίου καταβὰς καὶ ἀνελθὼν οὐκ ἔτι γελᾶν ἐδύ-
νατο. καὶ χρηστηριαζομένῳ περὶ τούτου ἡ Πυθία ἔφη·

εἴρῃ μ᾽ ἀμφὶ γέλωτος, ἀμείλιχε, μειλιχίοιο. |
b   δώσει σοι μήτηρ οἴκοι· τὴν ἔξοχα τῖε.

ἐλπίζων δ᾽ ἂν ἐπανέλθῃ εἰς τὴν πατρίδα γελάσειν, ὡς
οὐδὲν ἦν πλέον, οἰόμενος ἐξηπατῆσθαι ἔρχεταί ποτε
κατὰ τύχην εἰς Δῆλον· καὶ πάντα τὰ κατὰ τὴν νῆσον
θαυμάζων ἦλθεν καὶ εἰς τὸ Λητῷον, νομίζων τῆς
Ἀπόλλωνος μητρὸς ἄγαλμα τι θεωρήσειν ἀξιόλογον.
ἰδὼν δ᾽ αὐτὸ ξύλον ὂν ἄμορφον παραδόξως ἐγέλασεν·
καὶ τὸν τοῦ θεοῦ χρησμὸν συμβάλλων καὶ τῆς ἀρρω-

[5] The verse and a half that follows is preserved in a papyrus
(probably from *Melanippe the Captive*), but is not connected
there to the first five verses Athenaeus quotes. Whether
Athenaeus (or his source) has scrambled the text, or whether a
lacuna ought to be marked instead, is unclear.

[6] The papyrus has νέμουσι δ᾽.

Many men generate witty insults
to make others laugh. But I, for some reason,
hate jokers who have nothing clever to say and
so let their mouths run wild; they do not count
as men, although they look good when it comes to
  getting laughs.

They are in charge of houses and keep whatever
goods we trade for inside our residences (E. fr.
  494.9–10).[3]

According to Semus in Book V of the *History of Delos*
(*FGrH* 396 F 10), Parmeniscus of Metapontum, who was
both from a distinguished family and very rich, descended
into Trophonius' shrine, and after he emerged from it, he
was no longer able to laugh. When he consulted the oracle
about his situation, the Pythia said (Delphic Oracle Q185
Fontenrose):

You ask me, harsh one, about mild laughter.
Mother will give it to you at home; show her
  tremendous honor.

Parmeniscus expected that once he was back in his own
country, he would be able to laugh. But when nothing
changed, he decided that he had been tricked; and then he
happened to go to Delos at some point. In the course of ad-
miring everything on the island, he visited the sanctuary of
Leto, expecting to view an impressive statue of Apollo's
mother. But when he saw that it was made of wood and
ugly, he laughed spontaneously; after he recognized the

---

[3] Also from *Melanippe the Prisoner*; but the subject of the
verbs is now women (i.e. wives) rather than men.

ATHENAEUS

στίας ἀπαλλαγεὶς μεγαλωστὶ τὴν θεὸν ἐτίμησεν.
c Ἀναξανδρίδης | δ' ἐν Γεροντομανίᾳ καὶ εὑρετὰς τῶν
γελοίων φησὶ γενέσθαι Ῥαδάμανθυν καὶ Παλαμήδην,
λέγων οὕτως·

καίτοι πολλοί γε πονοῦμεν.
τὸν ἀσύμβολον εὗρε γέλοια λέγειν Ῥαδάμανθυς
καὶ Παλαμήδης.

γελωτοποιῶν δὲ μέμνηται Ξενοφῶν ἐν τῷ Συμποσίῳ
Φιλίππου μέν, περὶ οὗ καὶ οὑτωσὶ λέγει· Φίλιππος δ' ὁ
γελωτοποιὸς κρούσας τὴν θύραν εἶπε τῷ ὑπακούσαντι
εἰσαγγεῖλαι ὅστις τε εἴη καὶ διότι κατάγεσθαι βούλ-
εται· συνεσκευασμένος δὲ ἔφη παρεῖναι πάντα τἀπι-
d τήδεια ὥστε | δειπνεῖν τἀλλότρια. καὶ τὸν παῖδα δ'
ἔφη πάνυ πιέζεσθαι διά τε τὸ φέρειν μηδὲν καὶ διὰ τὸ
ἀνάριστον εἶναι. Ἱππόλοχος δ' ὁ Μακεδὼν ἐν τῇ πρὸς
Λυγκέα Ἐπιστολῇ γελωτοποιῶν μέμνηται Μανδρογέ-
νους καὶ Στράτωνος τοῦ Ἀττικοῦ. πλῆθος δ' ἦν Ἀθήνησι τῆς σοφίας ταύτης· ἐν γοῦν τῷ Διομέων Ἡρα-
κλείῳ συνελέγοντο ἑξήκοντα ὄντες τὸν ἀριθμὸν καὶ ἐν
τῇ πόλει διωνομάζοντο ὡς "οἱ ἑξήκοντα τοῦτ' εἶπον"
καὶ "ἀπὸ τῶν ἑξήκοντα ἔρχομαι." ἐν δὲ τούτοις ἦσαν
e Καλλιμέδων τε ὁ Κάραβος καὶ | Δεινίας, ἔτι τε Μνα-

---

4 Apollo was referring not to Parmeniscus' mother but to his
own.   5 Rhadamanthys (a son of Zeus and Europa) was
known for his wisdom, while Palamedes was a proverbially clever
member of the expedition against Troy (cf. 1.11d, 17e).
6 I.e. a parasite; cf. 6.234c–48c, esp. 235e–40c.

104

meaning of Apollo's oracle[4] and was cured of his malady, he showed the goddess enormous honor. Anaxandrides in *The Madness of Old Men* (fr. 10) claims that Rhadamanthys and Palamedes[5] invented the idea of jokes, putting it as follows:

> Many of us certainly work hard.
> Rhadamanthys and Palamedes came up with the idea
>   of the person who doesn't contribute to the
>   dinner-expenses[6] telling jokes.

Xenophon in his *Symposium* (1.11) mentions comedians, including Philip,[7] about whom he says the following: The comedian Philip knocked on the door and told the person who answered it to announce who he was and that he wanted to be admitted to the party; he claimed to have arrived with everything he needed in order to eat someone else's food. He added that his slave was in some distress, because he wasn't carrying anything and hadn't had lunch.[8] Hippolochus of Macedon in his *Letter to Lynceus*[9] mentions the comedians Mandrogenes and Straton of Athens. A large number of people in Athens had this talent. 60 of them used to gather, at any rate, in Heracles' sanctuary in Diomeia, and this is how people referred to them in the city, for example "The 60 said this" or "I'm on my way from the 60." Callimedon the Crayfish and Deinias[10] belonged

---

[7] Stephanis #2498; *PAA* 929295. The same passage of Xenophon is cited at 1.20b.   [8] Cf. Ar. *Ra.* 1–3, 25–30.

[9] The passage in question is quoted at 4.130c. Mandrogenes is Stephanis #1600; *PAA* 632020. Straton is Stephanis #2314; *PAA* 839370.

[10] Callimedon (cf. 3.100c n.) is Stephanis #1343; *PAA* 558185. Deinias is Stephanis #587; *PAA* 302175.

σιγείτων καὶ Μέναιχμος, ὥς φησι Τηλεφάνης ἐν τῷ
Περὶ τοῦ Ἄστεος. τοσαύτη δ' αὐτῶν δόξα τῆς ῥᾳθυ-
μίας ἐγένετο ὡς καὶ Φίλιππον ἀκούσαντα τὸν Μακε-
δόνα πέμψαι αὐτοῖς τάλαντον, ἵν' ἐκγραφόμενοι τὰ
γελοῖα πέμπωσιν αὐτῷ. ὅτι δὲ ἦν περὶ τὰ γελοῖα
ἐσπουδακὼς ὁ βασιλεὺς οὗτος μαρτυρεῖ Δημοσθένης
ὁ ῥήτωρ ἐν τοῖς Φιλιππικοῖς. φιλόγελως δὲ ἦν καὶ
Δημήτριος ὁ Πολιορκητής, ὥς φησι Φύλαρχος ἐν τῇ
ἕκτῃ τῶν Ἱστοριῶν, ὅς γε καὶ τὴν Λυσιμάχου αὐλὴν |
f κωμικῆς σκηνῆς οὐδὲν διαφέρειν ἔλεγεν· ἐξιέναι γὰρ
ἀπ' αὐτῆς πάντας δισυλλάβους, τόν τε Βίθυν χλευ-
άζων καὶ τὸν Πάριν, μεγίστους ὄντας παρὰ τῷ Λυσιμάχῳ, καί τινας ἑτέρους τῶν φίλων· παρὰ δ' αὐτοῦ
Πευκέστας καὶ Μενελάους, ἔτι δὲ Ὀξυθέμιδας. ταῦτα
δ' ἀκούων ὁ Λυσίμαχος, "ἐγὼ τοίνυν," ἔφη, "πόρνην ἐκ
τραγικῆς σκηνῆς οὐχ ἑώρακα ἐξιοῦσαν," τὴν αὐλη-
615 τρίδα Λάμιαν λέγων. ‖ ἀπαγγελθέντος δὲ καὶ τούτου
πάλιν ὑπολαβὼν ὁ Δημήτριος ἔφη· "ἀλλ' ἡ παρ' ἐμοὶ
πόρνη σωφρονέστερον τῆς παρ' ἐκείνῳ Πηνελόπης
ζῇ." ὅτι δὲ καὶ Σύλλας ὁ Ῥωμαίων στρατηγὸς φιλόγελως ἦν προείρηται. Λεύκιος δὲ Ἀνίκιος, καὶ αὐτὸς
Ῥωμαίων στρατηγήσας, Ἰλλυριοὺς καταπολεμήσας
καὶ αἰχμάλωτον ἀγαγὼν Γένθιον τὸν τῶν Ἰλλυριῶν
βασιλέα σὺν τοῖς τέκνοις, ἀγῶνας ἐπιτελῶν τοὺς ἐπι-

---

11 Mnasigiton is Stephanis #1714; *PAA* 654660. Menaechmus
is Stephanis #1640; *PAA* 640910.

12 Cf. 6.261b (citing Phylarchus Book X).

13 Peucestas is Berve i #634; Billows #90. Menelaus is perhaps

to this group, as did Mnasigiton and Menaechmus,[11] according to Telephanes in his *On the City* (*FHG* iv.507). They had such a reputation for being amusing, that when Philip of Macedon heard about them, he sent them a talent of silver to get them to write down their jokes and send them to him. The orator Demosthenes in his *Philippics* (2.19) attests to the fact that this king was very interested in jokes. According to Phylarchus in Book VI of his *History* (*FGrH* 81 F 12), Demetrius Poliorcetes also liked to laugh.[12] Demetrius used to say that Lysimachus' court was no different from a comic stage, since everyone who played a part there was only two syllables long (which was his way of making fun of Lysimachus' favorites Bithys and Paris, and of some of his other friends), whereas he had people with names like Peucestas and Menelaus, and even Oxythemis.[13] When Lysimachus heard this, he said: "I've certainly never seen a whore come out on the tragic stage," referring to the pipe-girl Lamia.[14] This remark made its way back to Demetrius, and he responded by saying: "Well, my whore leads a more respectable life than Penelope would with him."[15] That the Roman general Sulla liked to laugh was noted earlier (6.261c). When Lucius Anicius, another Roman general, defeated the Illyrians and brought the Illyrian king Genthius back as a prisoner,[16] along with his children, he held victory games in

Berve i #505, who was primarily associated with Ptolemy but was Demetrius' captive at one point. Oxythemis is Billows #86.

[14] Stephanis #1527; *PAA* 601325. For her close association with Demetrius, e.g. 3.101e; 4.128a–b; 6.253a–b; 13.577c.

[15] The same anecdote is preserved at Plu. *Demetr.* 25.6.

[16] In 168 BCE.

107

νικίους ἐν τῇ Ῥώμῃ παντὸς γέλωτος ἄξια πράγματα
ἐποίησεν, ὡς Πολύβιος ἱστορεῖ ἐν τῇ τριακοστῇ. |
b μεταπεμψάμενος γὰρ τοὺς ἐκ τῆς Ἑλλάδος ἐπιφανε-
στάτους τεχνίτας καὶ σκηνὴν κατασκευάσας μεγί-
στην ἐν τῷ κίρκῳ πρώτους εἰσῆγεν αὐλητὰς ἅμα
πάντας. οὗτοι δ᾽ ἦσαν Θεόδωρος ὁ Βοιώτιος, Θεόπομπος, Ἕρμιππος, Λυσίμαχος,[7] οἵτινες ἐπιφανέστατοι
ἦσαν. τούτους οὖν στήσας ἐπὶ τὸ προσκήνιον μετὰ
τοῦ χοροῦ αὐλεῖν ἐκέλευσεν ἅμα πάντας. τῶν δὲ δια-
πορευομένων τὰς κρούσεις μετὰ τῆς ἁρμοζούσης
κινήσεως προσπέμψας οὐκ ἔφη καλῶς αὐτοὺς αὐλεῖν,
c ἀλλ᾽ ἀγωνίζεσθαι | μᾶλλον ἐκέλευσεν. τῶν δὲ διαπο-
ρούντων ὑπέδειξέν τις τῶν ῥαβδούχων, ἐπιστρέψαν-
τας ἐπαγαγεῖν ἐπ᾽ αὐτοὺς καὶ ποιεῖν ὡσανεὶ μάχην.
ταχὺ δὲ συννοήσαντες οἱ αὐληταὶ καὶ λαβόντες ⟨ . . . ⟩
οἰκείαν ταῖς ἑαυτῶν ἀσελγείαις μεγάλην ἐποίησαν
σύγχυσιν. συνεπιστρέψαντες δὲ τοὺς μέσους χοροὺς
πρὸς τοὺς ἄκρους οἱ μὲν αὐληταὶ φυσῶντες ἀδιανόητα
καὶ διαφέροντες τοὺς αὐλοὺς ἐπῆγον ἀνὰ μέρος ἐπ᾽
ἀλλήλους, ἅμα δὲ τούτοις ἐπικτυποῦντες οἱ χοροὶ καὶ
d συνεπισείοντες τὴν σκευὴν | ἐπεφέροντο τοῖς ἐναν-
τίοις καὶ πάλιν ἀνεχώρουν ἐκ μεταβολῆς. ὡς δὲ καὶ
περιζωσάμενός τις τῶν χορευτῶν ἐκ τοῦ καιροῦ στρα-

7 Ἕρμιππος ὁ Λυσίμαχος A (Ἕρμιππος tantum CE): ὁ del.
Kaibel: Ἕρμιππος ὁ Λυσιμαχεύς Schweighäuser

17 Stephanis #1159, 1180, 898, and 1582, respectively.

Rome and arranged matters to provoke a great deal of laughter, according to Polybius in Book XXX (22). Because he sent for the most distinguished Greek musicians; erected an enormous stage in the Circus; and began by bringing all the pipe-players on together. The individuals in question were Theodorus of Boeotia, Theopompus, Hermippus, and Lysimachus,[17] who were extremely distinguished. He put them up on the stage, then, and ordered them all to play their pipes in accompaniment to their choruses simultaneously. They started to perform their music, along with the movement that went with it;[18] but he sent them a message, telling them that they were playing poorly, and ordered them to compete with one another more aggressively. When they expressed puzzlement, one of the officials made gestures indicating that they were to wheel around and advance on one another, producing something resembling a battle. The pipe-players quickly caught his meaning and taking their own . . . produced immense confusion with their own lewd behavior. The pipe-players pivoted the central sections of their choruses around to face the wings, and attacked their competitors, one after another, producing incomprehensible sounds and playing their pipes discordantly.[19] Meanwhile the choruses, stamping their feet and shaking their costumes in time with the pipe-players, advanced on their opponents, and then turned around and withdrew again. And when one of the dancers wrapped his robes tight around himself, spun around at exactly the right moment, and

[18] I.e. "while the dancers moved in time to it."

[19] Individual pipers played two pipes simultaneously; here they make no effort to coordinate the tones.

φεὶς ἦρε τὰς χεῖρας ἀπὸ πυγμῆς πρὸς τὸν ἐπιφε-
ρόμενον αὐλητήν, τότ᾽ ἤδη κρότος ἐξαίσιος ἐγένετο
καὶ κραυγὴ τῶν θεωμένων. ἔτι δὲ τούτων ἐκ παρα-
τάξεως ἀγωνιζομένων ὀρχησταὶ δύο εἰσήγοντο μετὰ
συμφωνίας εἰς τὴν ὀρχήστραν, καὶ πύκται τέσσαρες
ἀνέβησαν ἐπὶ τὴν σκηνὴν μετὰ σαλπιγκτῶν καὶ βυ-
κανιστῶν. ὁμοῦ δὲ τούτων πάντων ἀγωνιζομένων
e ἄλεκτον ἦν τὸ συμβαῖνον. | περὶ δὲ τῶν τραγῳδῶν,
φησὶν ὁ Πολύβιος, ὅ τι ἂν ἐπιβάλωμαι λέγειν, δόξω
τισὶν διαχλευάζειν.

Ταῦτα τοῦ Οὐλπιανοῦ διεξελθόντος καὶ πάντων
ἀνακαγχασάντων ἐπὶ ταῖς Ἀνικίκοις[8] ταύταις θέαις
ἐγένοντό τινες λόγοι καὶ περὶ τῶν καλουμένων πλά-
νων, καὶ ἐζητεῖτο εἰ μνήμη τις καὶ περὶ τούτων ἐγένετο
παρὰ τοῖς παλαιοτέροις· περὶ γὰρ θαυματοποιῶν ἤδη
προειρήκαμεν. καὶ ὁ Μάγνος ἔφη· Διονύσιος μὲν ὁ
Σινωπεὺς ὁ τῆς κωμῳδίας[9] ποιητὴς ἐν τῷ ἐπιγραφομένῳ Ὁμώνυμοι μνημονεύει Κηφισοδώρου τοῦ πλά-
νου διὰ τούτων·

Κηφισόδωρόν φασιν ἐπικαλούμενον
f πλάνον τιν᾽ ἐν Ἀθήναις | γενέσθαι, τὴν σχολὴν
εἰς τοῦτο τὸ μέρος τοῦ βίου καταχρώμενον.
† τοῦτον ἐντυχόντα † πρὸς τὸ σιμὸν ἀνατρέχειν,
† ἢ συγκαθεῖναι τηπι † τῇ βακτηρίᾳ.

8 Ἀνικίκοις Olson: Ἀνικίοις A
9 τῆς ⟨μέσης⟩ κωμῳδίας Gulick

110

raised his fists as if intending to punch the pipe-player who was moving toward him, at that point the audience applauded and cheered wildly. While this group was still competing in a battle line, two dancers, accompanied by a group of musicians, invaded the dancing area, and four boxers got up onstage, along with trumpeters and horn-players. The situation as all these groups wrestled with one another was beyond description; and as for what I could add about the tragic actors, says Polybius, some people will think that I am joking.

After Ulpian completed these remarks and everyone burst out laughing at this show Anicius put on,[20] there was discussion of the individuals known as *planoi*,[21] and the question came up as to whether the older authorities ever referred to them; for I have discussed magicians earlier (1.19e, 20a). Magnes said: The comic poet Dionysius of Sinope in his play entitled *Men Who Shared a Name* (fr. 4) refers to the *planos* Cephisodorus[22] in the following passage:

> People say there's a *planos* named
> Cephisodorus in Athens, who dedicates
> his free time to this aspect of life.
> † this man coming upon † to race up to the top,
> † or to let down together [corrupt] † with his stick.

[20] But also, punningly, "this incomparable show."
[21] Literally "wanderers," i.e. show-men of various sorts who made their way from one town to the next; cf. 1.19d, 20a.
[22] Stephanis #1395; *PAA* 568055; also mentioned (along with Pantaleon) at 1.20a.

μνημονεύει δ᾽ αὐτοῦ καὶ Νικόστρατος ἐν Σύρῳ·

Κηφισόδωρον οὐ κακῶς μὰ τὸν Δία
τὸν πλάνον φασὶ στενωπὸν εἰς μέσον στῆσαί
τινας
ἀγκαλίδας ἔχοντας, ὥστε μὴ παρελθεῖν
μηδένα. ‖

616 Πανταλέοντος δὲ μνημονεύει Θεόγνητος ἐν Φιλο-
δεσπότῳ·

ὁ Πανταλέων μὲν αὐτὸς αὐτοὺς τοὺς ξένους
τούς τ᾽ ἀγνοοῦντας αὐτὸν ἐπλάνα, καὶ σχεδὸν
ἀπεκραιπάλα τὰ πλεῖστα τοῦ γελάσαι χάριν,
ἰδίαν τιν᾽ αὑτῷ θέμενος ἀδολεσχίαν.

καὶ Χρύσιππος δ᾽ ὁ φιλόσοφος ἐν πέμπτῳ Περὶ τοῦ
Καλοῦ Καὶ τῆς Ἡδονῆς περὶ τοῦ Πανταλέοντος τάδε
b γράφει· ὁ δὲ πλάνος Πανταλέων τελευτᾶν | μέλλων
ἑκάτερον τῶν υἱῶν κατ᾽ ἰδίαν ἐξηπάτησε, φήσας μόνῳ
αὐτῷ λέγειν ὅπου κατορύχοι τὸ χρυσίον· ὥστε μάτην
ὕστερον κοινῇ σκάπτοντας αἰσθέσθαι ἐξηπατημέ-
νους.

Οὐκ ἠπόρει δ᾽ ἡμῶν τὸ συμπόσιον οὐδὲ τῶν φιλο-
σκωπτούντων. περὶ δὲ τοιούτου τινὸς πάλιν ὁ Χρύσιππος ἐν τῷ αὐτῷ γράφει· φιλοσκώπτης τις μέλλων ὑπὸ
τοῦ δημίου σφάττεσθαι ἔτι ἕν τι ἔφη θέλειν ὥσπερ τὸ
κύκνειον ᾄσας ἀποθανεῖν. ἐπιτρέψαντος δ᾽ ἐκείνου

Nicostratus in *The Syrian* (fr. 25) also mentions him:

> They say the *planos* Cephisodorus, by Zeus,
> is quite right to put people holding bundles of stuff
> in the middle of an alley, so no one can get through.

Theognetus in *The Man Who Loved His Master* (fr. 2)
mentions Pantaleon:[23]

> Pantaleon himself used to fool (*eplana*) the foreigners
> in particular, as well as anyone who didn't know him;
>   and he turned
> almost everything into a wild party to get a laugh,
> having a private conversation with himself.

So too the philosopher Chrysippus in Book V of *On the
Good and Pleasure* (xxviii fr. 7, *SVF* iii.199) writes the following about Pantaleon: When the *planos* Pantaleon was
about to die, he tricked both his sons individually, by
claiming to be telling each of them, but not his brother,
where his money was buried. The result was that later on
they both tried to dig it up and found nothing, and they
came to the joint conclusion that they had been taken in.

Nor did our party lack people who like to make fun of
others. Chrysippus writes again in the same work (xxviii fr.
8, *SVF* iii.199) about someone of this sort: When a man
who loved to mock others was about to be put to death by
the public executioner, he said that he wanted to offer his
final swan-song,[24] as it were, and then die. When the executioner granted him permission, he made fun of him.

[23] Stephanis #1996; *PAA* 764430.
[24] For the tradition of the swan-song, cf. 9.393d.

113

ἔσκωψεν. ὑπὸ δὴ τῶν τοιούτων πολλάκις ὁ Μυρτίλος |
c σκωφθέντα καὶ ἀγανακτήσαντα εἶπεν καλῶς Λυσίμαχον τὸν βασιλέα πεποιηκέναι. Τελέσφορον γὰρ ἕνα
τῶν ὑπάρχων αὐτοῦ, ἐπειδὴ ἔσκωψέ ποτε ἐν συμποσίῳ
τὴν Ἀρσινόην (γυνὴ δ' ἦν τοῦ Λυσιμάχου) ὡς ἐμετι-
κὴν οὖσαν, εἰπών·

   "κακῶν κατάρχεις τήνδ' ἐμοῦσαν[10] εἰσάγων,"

ὁ Λυσίμαχος ἀκούσας ἐμβληθῆναι αὐτὸν ἐκέλευσεν
εἰς γαλεάγραν καὶ δίκην θηρίου περιφερόμενον καὶ
τρεφόμενον, κολαζόμενον οὕτως ἐποίησεν ἀποθανεῖν.
σὺ δέ, ὦ Οὐλπιανέ, εἰ τὴν γαλεάγραν ζητεῖς, ἔχεις
d παρ' | Ὑπερείδῃ τῷ ῥήτορι· ὅπου δέ, σὺ ζήτει. καὶ
Ταχὼς δ' ὁ Αἰγυπτίων βασιλεὺς Ἀγησίλαον σκώψας
τὸν Λακεδαιμονίων βασιλέα, ὅτ' ἦλθεν αὐτῷ συμ-
μαχήσων (ἦν γὰρ βραχὺς τὸ σῶμα), ἰδιώτης ἐγένετο,
ἀποστάντος ἐκείνου τῆς συμμαχίας. τὸ δὲ σκῶμμα
τοῦτ' ἦν·

   ὤδινεν ὄρος, Ζεὺς δ' ἐφοβεῖτο, τὸ δ' ἔτεκεν μῦν.

[10] Euripides wrote τήνδε μοῦσαν.

---

25 One of Alexander's successors (d. 281 BCE). Arsinoe II (below) was his second wife, whom he married in 300/299.

26 Sc. in order that, with her stomach now empty, she could
continue to eat and drink.

27 A witty adaptation of E. fr. 183.1, with *tênd' emousan* ("this
vomiting woman") replacing the original *tênde Mousan* ("this
Muse").

Myrtilus remarked that King Lysimachus[25] had behaved appropriately when he was repeatedly mocked by people like this and became annoyed. For at one point when Telesphorus, who was one of his chief officials, made fun of Arsinoe—this was Lysimachus' wife—at a party, for forcing herself to throw up,[26] by saying:

"You are causing trouble by bringing in this vomiting woman,"[27]

Lysimachus heard the remark, and he ordered the man to be thrown in a cage (*galeagra*) and carried around and fed like a wild animal; after punishing him this way, he had him put to death.[28] As for you, Ulpian, if you have a question about the word *galeagra*, you can find it in the orator Hyperides (fr. 34 Jensen); as for precisely where— you can look for it yourself![29] So too when the Egyptian king Tachos mocked Agesilaus, the king of Sparta,[30] when Agesilaus visited him in the hope of forming an alliance, because Agesilaus was not very tall, he was reduced to a private citizen when Agesilaus abandoned the alliance. The mocking remark was as follows:

A mountain cried in pain, and Zeus was terrified; but what it bore was a mouse.

[28] Two fragments of a very similar story are preserved at Plu. *Mor.* 606b, 634e; cf. Sen. *de Ira* 3.17.3–4 (a far more detailed and much uglier account).

[29] Ulpian never responds to the implied challenge.

[30] Agesilaus II (Poralla #9). For his visit to Egypt in 361 BCE, cf. 9.384a (also citing Theopompus); Plu. *Ages.* 36–8, esp. 36.5 (quoting a prose version of this verse, for which cf. also Hor. *AP* 139 *parturiunt montes, nascetur ridiculus mus*).

ὅπερ ἀκούσας ὁ Ἀγησίλαος καὶ ὀργισθεὶς ἔφη, "φα-
νήσομαί σοί ποτε καὶ λέων·" ὕστερον γὰρ ἀφισταμέ-
νων τῶν Αἰγυπτίων, ὥς φησι Θεόπομπος καὶ Λυκέας ὁ
e Ναυκρατίτης ἐν τοῖς | Αἰγυπτιακοῖς, οὐδὲν αὐτῷ συμ-
πράξας ἐποίησεν ἐκπεσόντα τῆς ἀρχῆς φυγεῖν εἰς
Πέρσας.

Πολλῶν οὖν πολλάκις ὄντων τῶν ἀκροαμάτων καὶ
τῶν αὐτῶν οὐκ αἰεί, ἐπειδὴ πολλοὶ περὶ αὐτῶν ἐγί-
νοντο λόγοι, τὰ ὀνόματα τῶν εἰπόντων παραλιπὼν τῶν
πραγμάτων μνησθήσομαι. περὶ μὲν γὰρ αὐλῶν ὁ μέν
τις ἔφη τὸν Μελανιππίδην καλῶς ἐν τῷ Μαρσύᾳ
διασύροντα τὴν αὐλητικὴν εἰρηκέναι περὶ τῆς Ἀθη-
νᾶς·

ἁ μὲν Ἀθάνα
τὦργαν᾽ ἔρριψέν θ᾽ ἱερᾶς ἀπὸ χειρὸς
εἶπέ τ᾽· "ἔρρετ᾽ αἴσχεα, σώματι λύμα·
† ἐμὲ δ᾽ ἐγὼ † κακότατι δίδωμι."

f πρὸς ὃν ἀντιλέγων | ἄλλος ἔφη· ἀλλ᾽ ὅ γε Σελινούν-
τιος Τελέστης τῷ Μελανιππίδῃ ἀντικορυσσόμενος ἐν
Ἀργοῖ ἔφη· ὁ δὲ λόγος ἐστὶ περὶ τῆς Ἀθηνᾶς·

† ὃν † σοφὸν σοφὰν λαβοῦσαν οὐκ ἐπέλπομαι
      νόῳ
δρυμοῖς ὀρείοις ὄργανον

When Agesilaus heard this, he became angry and said: "Someday I'll look like a lion to you!"; for later on, when the Egyptians revolted, according to Theopompus (*FGrH* 115 F 108) and Lyceas of Naucratis in his *History of Egypt* (*FGrH* 613 F 2), he refused to cooperate with Tachos, and deposed him and drove him into exile in Persia.

There was frequently musical entertainment of various sorts, and always something different; since we discussed these matters on numerous occasions, I will omit the names of the speakers and will simply offer an account of the topics we took up. On the subject of pipes, one man said that Melanippides in his *Marsyas* (*PMG* 758) was quite right to disparage the music played on them, when he said about Athena:

> Athena
> cast the instrument from her sacred hand
> and said: "To hell with you, ugly device that damages
> my body;[31]
> † but me I † give to baseness."

Someone else responded to him and said: But Telestes of Selinus took up arms against Melanippides in *The Argo* (*PMG* 805a) and said—the story involves Athena—:

> † whom † I do not expect in my mind that after the
> wise, bright Athena
> in the mountain thickets picked up

[31] Sc. because they distorted her features when she blew into them; cf. Plu. *Mor.* 456b; [Apollod.] *Bib.* 1.4.2. The satyr Marsyas picked up the pipes Athena discarded (below).

δίαν Ἀθάναν δυσόφθαλμον αἶσχος ἐκφοβη-
    θεῖσαν αὖθις χερῶν ἐκβαλεῖν
νυμφαγενεῖ χειροκτύπῳ φηρὶ Μαρσύᾳ κλέος· ‖
617   τί γάρ νιν εὐηράτοιο κάλλεος ὀξὺς ἔρως ἔτειρεν,
    ᾇ παρθενίαν ἄγαμον καὶ ἄπαιδ᾽ ἀπένειμε
        Κλωθώ;,

ὡς οὐκ ἂν εὐλαβηθείσης τὴν αἰσχρότητα τοῦ εἴδους
διὰ τὴν παρθενίαν. ἑξῆς τέ φησι·

ἀλλὰ μάταν ἀχόρευτος ἅδε ματαιολόγων
φάμα προσέπταθ᾽ Ἑλλάδα μουσοπόλων
σοφᾶς ἐπίφθονον βροτοῖς τέχνας ὄνειδος.

μετὰ ταῦτα δὲ ἐγκωμιάζων τὴν αὐλητικὴν λέγει·

ἂν συνεριθοτάταν Βρομίῳ παρέδωκε σεμνᾶς
δαίμονος ἀερόεν πνεῦμ᾽ αἰολοπτέρυγον
b   σὺν ἀγλαᾶν ὠκύτατι ǀ χειρῶν.

κομψῶς δὲ κἀν τῷ Ἀσκληπιῷ ὁ Τελέστης ἐδήλωσε τὴν
τῶν αὐλῶν χρείαν ἐν τούτοις·

ἢ Φρύγα καλλιπνόων αὐλῶν ἱερῶν βασιλῆα,
Λυδὸν ὃς ἅρμοσε πρῶτος
Δωρίδος ἀντίπαλον Μούσας † νομοαίολον
    ὀρφναι †
πνεύματος εὔπτερον αὔραν ἀμφιπλέκων
καλάμοις.

---

32 One of the Fates.

the wise instrument, she was terrified of ugliness that
  displeases
    the eye and cast it from her hand again
to be a source of glory for the wild, hand-clapping
    beast Marysas, born of a nymph.
For what piercing desire for lovely beauty distressed
    her,
to whom Clotho[32] allotted unmarried, childless
    virginity?,

as if Athena would not have been concerned about looking
ugly, because of her commitment to virginity! And immediately after this he says (*PMG* 805b):

But this story, hostile to the dance, spread pointlessly
through Greece, perpetuated by nonsense-spouting
    poets,
a grudging complaint in mortal ears about a wise art.

After this he praises the art of pipe-playing and says (*PMG*
805c):

which the quick-flitting, airy breath of the august
    deity, joined to the speed of her splendid hands,
handed over to Bromius to be his chief assistant.

Telestes in his *Asclepius* (*PMG* 806) offered an elegant
description of how the pipes are played, in the following
passage:

or the Phrygian king of the fair-blowing, sacred pipes,
who was the first to join a Lydian
[corrupt] to match a Doric muse,
twining the swift-flying breeze of his breath about its
    reeds.

119

Πρατίνας δὲ ὁ Φλιάσιος αὐλητῶν καὶ χορευτῶν
μισθοφόρων κατεχόντων τὰς ὀρχήστρας ἀγανακτεῖν
τινας ἐπὶ τῷ τοὺς αὐλητὰς μὴ συναυλεῖν τοῖς χοροῖς,
καθάπερ ἦν πάτριον, ἀλλὰ τοὺς χοροὺς συνᾴδειν τοῖς
c αὐληταῖς. | ὃν οὖν εἶχεν κατὰ τῶν ταῦτα ποιούντων
θυμὸν ὁ Πρατίνας ἐμφανίζει διὰ τοῦδε τοῦ ὑπορ-
χήματος·

τίς ὁ θόρυβος ὅδε; τί τάδε τὰ χορεύματα;
τίς ὕβρις ἔμολεν ἐπὶ Διονυσιάδα πολυπάταγα
θυμέλαν;
d ἐμὸς ἐμὸς ὁ Βρόμιος, ἐμὲ δεῖ κελαδεῖν, | ἐμὲ δεῖ
παταγεῖν
ἀν᾽ ὄρεα σύμενον μετὰ Ναϊάδων
οἷά τε κύκνον ἄγοντα ποικιλόπτερον μέλος.
τὰν ἀοιδὰν κατέστασε Πιερὶς βασίλειαν· ὁ δ᾽
αὐλὸς
ὕστερον χορευέτω· καὶ γάρ ἐσθ᾽ ὑπηρέτας.
e κώμῳ μόνον θυραμάχοις τε πυγμαχίαισι | νέων
θέλοι παροίνων
ἔμμεναι στρατηλάτας.
παῖε τὸν φρυνεοῦ ποικίλαν πνοὰν ἔχοντα,
φλέγε τὸν ὀλεσισιαλοκάλαμον
λαλοβαρύοπα παραμελορυθμοβάταν
ὑπαὶ τρυπάνῳ δέμας πεπλασμένον.

---

33 Sc. in theaters.   34 Pieria is the region just north of
Mt. Olympus, where the Muses were born (Hes. *Th.* 53–4 with
West ad loc.), and Pieris presumably refers to one of them, or to

120

Pratinas of Phlius (claims) that when hired pipe-players
and dancers took over the dancing-areas,[33] some people
became annoyed at the fact that the pipe-players did not
play music to accompany the choruses, as was traditional,
but the choruses instead sang to accompany the pipes.
Pratinas (*PMG* 708) brings out the anger he felt against
those who behaved this way in the following hyporcheme:

> What uproar is this? What dances are these?
> What outrageous behavior has come to Dionysus'
>   tumultuous altar?
> Bromius is mine, mine! It is I who must shout, I who
>   must create a clatter
> as I rush over the mountains with the naiads,
> producing a song that flits this way and that, like a
>   swan.
> Pieris[34] gave the throne to song; let the pipe
> take second position when it dances, since it is a
>   servant!
> Let it aspire to serve as general only for drunken
>   wanderings and for the fist-fights in which
>   intoxicated
> young men engage in front of others' doors.
> Punch the man with the spotted breath of a toad![35]
> Set fire to the chatteringly-deep-voiced,
> out-of-time-with-the-music-marching, spit-wasting-
>   made-of-reed (pipe),
> whose form was moulded by an auger!

their mother Mnemosyne ("Memory"), or to the art they represent.   [35] I.e. whose cheeks bulge out like a toad's when he
plays the pipes?

121

f   ἢν ἰδού· ἅδε | σοι δεξιᾶς καὶ ποδὸς διαρριφά·
Θρίαμβε Διθύραμβε κισσόχαιτ᾽ ἄναξ,
<ἄκου᾽> ἄκουε τὰν ἐμὰν Δώριον χορείαν.

περὶ δὲ τῆς αὐλῶν πρὸς λύραν κοινωνίας, ἐπεὶ πολλάκις καὶ αὐτὴ ἡμᾶς ἡ συναυλία ἔθελγεν, Ἔφιππος ἐν
Ἐμπολῇ φησιν· ||

618   κοινωνεῖ γὰρ, ὦ μειράκιον, ἡ
ἐν τοῖσιν αὐλοῖς μουσικὴ κἂν τῇ λύρᾳ
τοῖς ἡμετέροισι παιγνίοις· ὅταν γὰρ εὖ
συναρμόσῃ τις τοῖς συνοῦσι τὸν τρόπον,
τόθ᾽ ἡ μεγίστη τέρψις ἐξευρίσκεται.

τὴν δὲ συναυλίαν τί ποτ᾽ ἐστὶν ἐμφανίζει Σῆμος ὁ
Δήλιος ἐν πέμπτῃ Δηλιάδος γράφων οὕτως· ἀγνο-
ουμένης δὲ παρὰ πολλοῖς τῆς συναυλίας, λεκτέον. ἦν
τις ἀγὼν συμφωνίας ἀμοιβαῖος αὐλοῦ καὶ ῥυθμοῦ,
b χωρὶς τοῦ[11] προσμελῳδοῦντος. | ἀστείως δὲ αὐτὴν
Ἀντιφάνης φανερὰν ποιεῖ ἐν τῷ Αὐλητῇ λέγων·

ποίαν, φράσον γάρ, † ηδε † τὴν συναυλίαν
ταύτην ἐπίσταται γάρ † ἀλλ᾽ ηὔλουν ἔτι
μαθόντες < . . . > ὥστε τοὺς αὐλοὺς σύ τε
αὐτή τε λήψεσθ᾽, εἶθ᾽ ἃ μὲν σὺ τυγχάνεις
αὐλῶν πέραινε. δέξεται δὲ τἆλλά σοι

---

[11] χωρὶς λόγου τοῦ A: λόγου del. Kaibel

---

36 Two cult-titles of Dionysus.

Look at this! Here is a tossing of my right hand and
　　my foot for you!
Thriambos, Dithyrambos,[36] ivy-crowned lord—
listen, listen to my Doric dance-song!

As for the coordination of pipes with the lyre—for this
combination of instruments frequently charmed us—
Ephippus says in *Merchandise* (fr. 7):

　　　　　For music produced
　on the pipes and the lyre, my boy, is an integral part
　of the entertainment we provide. Since whenever
　　　someone
　carefully matches his behavior to the people he's
　　　with,
　that's when we find the most pleasure.

Semus of Delos in Book V of the *History of Delos* (*FGrH*
396 F 11) brings out what a *sunaulia* is when he writes as
follows: Since many people do not know what a *sunaulia*
is, the matter requires discussion. This was a musical competition that alternated between pipe-music (*aulos*) and
dancing, with no one singing along. Antiphanes in his *The
Pipe-Player* (fr. 49) offers a witty description of it, saying:[37]

　Because tell me—what sort of [corrupt] *sunaulia* is
　this he/she knows about for † but they were still
　　　playing pipes
　after they learned . . . so that you and her will take
　the pipes, and then what you happen
　to be playing—finish it! She'll take the rest for you

---

[37] The fragment is seriously corrupt but appears to describe a
joint performance by two pipers.

† ἡδύ τι κοινόν ἐστιν † οὗ χωρὶς πάλιν
συννεύματ᾿ οὐ προβλήμαθ᾿ οἷς σημαίνεται
ἕκαστα.

Λίβυν δὲ τὸν αὐλὸν προσαγορεύουσιν οἱ ποιηταί,
c φησὶ Δοῦρις ἐν δευτέρᾳ τῶν Περὶ Ἀγαθοκλέα, | ἐπειδὴ
Σειρίτης δοκεῖ πρῶτος εὑρεῖν τὴν αὐλητικήν, Λίβυς
ὢν τῶν Νομάδων, ὃς καὶ κατηύλησεν τὰ μητρῷα
πρῶτος. αὐλήσεων δ᾿ εἰσὶν ὀνομασίαι, ὥς φησι Τρύφων ἐν δευτέρῳ Ὀνομασιῶν, αἵδε· κῶμος, βουκο-
λισμός, γίγγρας, τετράκωμος, ἐπίφαλλος, χορεῖος,
καλλίνικος, πολεμικόν, ἡδύκωμος, σικιννοτύρβη,
θυροκοπικόν (τὸ δ᾿ αὐτὸ καὶ κρουσίθυρον), κνισμός,
μόθων. ταῦτα δὲ πάντα μετ᾿ ὀρχήσεως ηὐλεῖτο. καὶ
ᾠδῆς δὲ ὀνομασίας καταλέγει ὁ Τρύφων τάσδε· ἱμαῖος
d ἡ ἐπιμύλιος | καλουμένη, ἣν παρὰ τοὺς ἀλέτους ᾖδον,
ἴσως ἀπὸ τῆς ἱμαλίδος. ἱμαλὶς δ᾿ ἐστὶν παρὰ Δωρι-
εῦσιν ὁ νόστος καὶ τὰ ἐπίμετρα τῶν ἀλεύρων. ἡ δὲ τῶν

---

38 I.e. the Mother of the Gods, often referred to as Cybele.

39 "a drunken revel, wandering the streets drunk (sc. with a
pipe-player)."   40 I.e. *boukoliasmos*, "singing pastoral
poetry"; cf. 14.619a–b.   41 Eastern pipes of some sort; cf.
4.174f–5b (also citing Tryphon).

42 "quadruple-*kômos*" (cf. above).   43 "associated with
phallic dances."

44 "associated with a chorus, with dancing."

45 "gloriously victorious"; cf. Olson on Ar. *Ach.* 1227.

46 "war-[song]."   47 "pleasant-*kômos*" (see above).

48 < *sikinnis* (a dance associated with satyr play; cf. 1.20e;
14.629d) + *turbê* ("revelry, wild dance").

† something pleasant is in common † where separate
   again
nods rather than questions used to signal
everything.

The poets refer to pipes as Libyan, according to Duris in
Book II of his *On Agathocles* (*FGrH* 76 F 16), because
Sirites, a Libyan nomad, appears to have invented the art
of pipe-playing; he was the first person to accompany the
rites of the Mother[38] with pipe-music. The following terms
are connected with playing the pipes, according to Tryphon in Book II of *Terminology* (fr. 109 Velsen): *kômos*,[39]
boukolismos,[40] *gingras*,[41] *tetrakômos*,[42] *epiphallos*,[43] *cho-
reios*,[44] *kallinikos*,[45] *polemikon*,[46] *hêdukômos*,[47] *sikinno-
turbê*,[48] *thurokopikon*[49] (*krousithuron* has the same
sense), *knismos*,[50] *mothôn*.[51] These were all played on the
pipes to accompany dancing. Tryphon (fr. 113 Velsen)[52]
also lists the following terms for songs: the *himaios*, also
known as an *epimulios* ("mill-stone-[song]"), which they
sang while milling grain; perhaps derived from *himalis*.
Himalis is a Doric word that means "homecoming" and
"extra measures of flour."[53] The song sung by women work-

---

[49] "door-pounding-[song]," i.e. what is sung or played when
the *kômos* (above) reaches its destination.

[50] Literally "itching, tickling," although the word sometimes
has erotic connotations.

[51] A lewd dance of some sort; cf. Ar. *Eq.* 697.

[52] Presumably another excerpt from *On Terminology* (cf.
4.174e; 14.618b–c, 634d–e).

[53] Cf. 4.109a; 10.416c (*Himalis* as a Sicilian epithet of Demeter, the goddess of grain).

ἱστουργῶν ᾠδὴ αἴλινος, ὡς Ἐπίχαρμος ἐν Ἀταλάνταις ἱστορεῖ, ἡ δὲ τῶν ταλασιουργῶν ἴουλος. Σῆμος δ᾽
ὁ Δήλιος ἐν τῷ Περὶ Παιάνων φησί· τὰ δράγματα τῶν
κριθῶν αὐτὰ καθ᾽ αὑτὰ προσηγόρευον ἀμάλας· συν-
αθροισθέντα δὲ καὶ ἐκ πολλῶν μίαν γενόμενα δέσμην
οὔλους καὶ ἰούλους· καὶ τὴν Δήμητρα ὁτὲ μὲν Χλόην,
e ὁτὲ δὲ Ἰουλώ. ἀπὸ | τῶν οὖν τῆς Δήμητρος εὑρημάτων
τούς τε καρποὺς καὶ τοὺς ὕμνους τοὺς εἰς τὴν θεὸν
οὔλους καλοῦσι καὶ ἰούλους. Δημήτρουλοι καὶ καλ-
λίουλοι. καὶ

πλεῖστον οὖλον ἵει, ἴουλον ἵει.

ἄλλοι δέ φασιν ἐριουργῶν εἶναι τὴν ᾠδήν. αἱ δὲ τῶν
τιτθευουσῶν ᾠδαὶ καταβαυκαλήσεις ὀνομάζονται. ἦν
δὲ καὶ ἐπὶ ταῖς Ἐώραις τις ἐπ᾽ Ἠριγόνῃ, ἣν καὶ ἀλῆτιν
λέγουσιν, ᾠδή. Ἀριστοτέλης γοῦν ἐν τῇ Κολοφωνίων
Πολιτείᾳ φησίν· ἀπέθανεν δὲ καὶ αὐτὸς ὁ Θεόδωρος
f ὕστερον βιαίῳ θανάτῳ. λέγεται δὲ γενέσθαι | τρυφῶν
τις, ὡς ἐκ τῆς ποιήσεως δῆλόν ἐστιν· ἔτι γὰρ καὶ νῦν
619 αἱ γυναῖκες ᾄδουσιν αὐτοῦ μέλη ‖ περὶ τὰς Ἐώρας. ἡ
δὲ τῶν θεριστῶν ᾠδὴ Λιτυέρσης καλεῖται. καὶ τῶν
μισθωτῶν δέ τις ἦν ᾠδὴ τῶν ἐς τοὺς ἀγροὺς φοι-

---

54 The *ailinos* is generally assumed to be a song of lamentation
(cf. 14.619c; Bond on E. *HF* 348 [quoted at 14.619c]) and under-
stood to mean "Woe for Linus!" (cf. Hes. fr. 305); but cf. *linon*
("thread"), with which the word would seem to be connected
here.   55 Literally "Demeter-*ouloi* and beauty-*ouloi*." See
below (presumably from a different source).

126

ing at a loom is an *ailinos*,[54] according to Epicharmus in *Atalantas* (fr. 14), while the one sung by women spinning wool is an *ioulos*. Semus of Delos says in his *On Paeans* (*FGrH* 396 F 23): They referred to the individual handfuls of cut barley as *amalai*; but when these were gathered together and a number of them were made into a single bundle, (they called them) *ouloi* or *iouloi*; they also referred to Demeter sometimes as Chloê ("Green"), at other times as Ioulô. As a consequence of Demeter's innovations, therefore, they refer to both the crops and the hymns directed to the goddess as *ouloi* or *iouloi*. (There are) *Dêmêtrouloi* and *kalliouloi*.[55] Also (carm. pop. *PMG* 849):

Produce a full *oulos*! Produce an *ioulos*!

But other authorities claim that the song is sung by wool-workers. The songs sung by wet-nurses are known as *katabaukalêseis* ("lullabies"). There was also a song sung at the Eôrai festival in honor of Erigone, which they call an *alêtis*.[56] Aristotle, for example, says in his *Constitution of the Colophonians* (fr. 520.1): Theodorus (*SH* 753) himself died a violent death later on. He is said to have been addicted to luxury, as his poetry makes apparent; because even today the women sing his songs at the Eôrai festival.[57] The song sung by harvesters is called the Lityersês.[58] There was also a song sung by hired laborers as they made

[56] Erigone hanged herself after the death of her father, Icarius, who introduced wine into Attica. The festival is more often referred to as the Aiôra (literally "Swing/Noose-[Festival]").

[57] Cf. 3.122b = *SH* 754; Poll. 4.55.

[58] Cf. Gow on Theoc. 10.41.

τώντων, ὡς Τηλεκλείδης φησὶν ἐν Ἀμφικτύοσιν· καὶ
βαλανέων ἄλλαι, ὡς Κράτης ἐν Τόλμαις, καὶ τῶν
πτισσουσῶν ἄλλη τις, ὡς Ἀριστοφάνης ἐν Θεσμοφο-
ριαζούσαις καὶ Νικοχάρης ἐν Ἡρακλεῖ Χορηγῷ. ἦν
δὲ καὶ τοῖς ἡγουμένοις τῶν βοσκημάτων ὁ βουκο-
λιασμὸς καλούμενος. Δίομος δ᾽ ἦν βουκόλος Σικε-
λιώτης ὁ πρῶτος εὑρὼν τὸ εἶδος· μνημονεύει δ᾽ αὐτοῦ |
b Ἐπίχαρμος ἐν Ἀλκυόνι καὶ ἐν Ὀδυσσεῖ Ναυαγῷ. ἡ δ᾽
ἐπὶ τοῖς θανάτοις καὶ λύπαις ᾠδὴ ὀλοφυρμὸς καλεῖται. αἱ δὲ ἴουλοι καλούμεναι ᾠδαὶ Δήμητρι καὶ Φερ-
σεφόνῃ πρέπουσι. ἡ δὲ εἰς Ἀπόλλωνα ᾠδὴ φιληλιάς,
ὡς Τελέσιλλα παρίστησιν· οὔπιγγοι δὲ αἱ εἰς Ἄρ-
τεμιν. ἤδοντο δὲ Ἀθήνησι καὶ οἱ Χαρώνδου νόμοι παρ᾽
οἶνον, ὡς Ἑρμιππός φησιν ἐν ἕκτῳ Περὶ Νομοθετῶν.
Ἀριστοφάνης δ᾽ ἐν Ἀττικαῖς φησιν Λέξεσιν· ἱμαῖος
ᾠδὴ μυλωθρῶν· ἐν δὲ γάμοις ὑμέναιος· ἐν δὲ πένθεσιν
c ἰάλεμος. λίνος | δὲ καὶ αἴλινος οὐ μόνον ἐν πένθεσιν,
ἀλλὰ καὶ

ἐπ᾽ εὐτυχεῖ

μολπᾷ

κατὰ τὸν Εὐριπίδην. Κλέαρχος δ᾽ ἐν πρώτῳ Ἐρωτικῶν
νόμιον καλεῖσθαί τινά φησιν ᾠδὴν ἀπ᾽ Ἠριφανίδος,
γράφων οὕτως· Ἠριφανὶς ἡ μελοποιὸς Μενάλκου

---

[59] I.e. the lost play by that title, not the preserved one of 411
BCE.   [60] Cf. 14.618c n.

[61] I.e. Persephone, Demeter's daughter. For these songs, see
14.618d–e (presumably from a different source).

their way into the fields, according to Teleclides in *Amphictyonies* (fr. 8); there were others sung by bathmen, according to Crates in *Daring Deeds* (fr. 42), and one sung by women winnowing grain, according to Aristophanes in *Women Celebrating the Thesmophoria*[59] (fr. 352) and Nicochares in *Heracles the Choregos* (fr. 9). People driving herds out to pasture also had the so-called *boukoliasmos*.[60] The Sicilian cowherd Diomus invented the genre; Epicharmus mentions him in *The Halcyon* (fr. 4) and in *Odysseus Shipwrecked* (fr. 104). The song sung in response to death or grief is referred to as an *olophurmos*. The songs known as *iouloi* are appropriate for Demeter and Phersephonê.[61] The song that honors Apollo is a *philêlias*, as Telesilla (*PMG* 718) establishes, while those that honor Artemis are *oupingoi*. Charondas' laws[62] were sung at drinking parties in Athens, according to Hermippus in Book VI of *On Law-Givers* (fr. 88 Wehrli). Aristophanes says in *Attic Vocabulary* (Ar. Byz. fr. 340 Slater): A *himaios* is a song sung by millers; a *humenaios* is sung at wedding celebrations; and an *ialemos* is sung as a dirge. The *linos* and the *ailinos* are sung not only as dirges, but also

> at the happy
dance,

to quote Euripides (*HF* 348–9). Clearchus in Book I of the *Erotica* (fr. 32 Wehrli) reports that a certain pastoral song got its name from Eriphanis. He writes as follows: The lyric poetess Eriphanis fell in love with Menalces when he

---

[62] Or "melodies." Charondas was the lawgiver of Catana in Sicily; presumably his laws were set in verse and had a general moralizing character.

κυνηγετοῦντος ἐρασθεῖσα ἐθήρευεν μεταθέουσα ταῖς
ἐπιθυμίαις· φοιτῶσα γὰρ καὶ πλανωμένη πάντας τοὺς
ὀρείους ἐπεξῄει δρυμούς, ὡς μῦθον εἶναι τοὺς λεγο-
μένους Ἰοῦς δρόμους· ὥστε μὴ μόνον τῶν ἀνθρώπων
τοὺς ἀστοργίᾳ διαφέροντας, ἀλλὰ καὶ τῶν θηρῶν τοὺς

d ἀνημερωτάτους | συνδακρῦσαι τῷ πάθει, λαβόντας
αἴσθησιν ἐρωτικῆς ἐλπίδος. ὅθεν ἐποίησέ τε καὶ ποιή-
σασα περιήει κατὰ τὴν ἐρημίαν, ὥς φασιν, ἀναβοῶσα
καὶ ᾄδουσα τὸ καλούμενον νόμιον, ἐν ᾧ ἐστιν·

μακραὶ δρύες, ὦ Μέναλκα.

Ἀριστόξενος δὲ ἐν τετάρτῳ Περὶ Μουσικῆς, ᾖδον,
φησίν, αἱ ἀρχαῖαι γυναῖκες Καλύκην τινὰ ᾠδήν. Στησιχόρου δ᾽ ἦν ποίημα, ἐν ᾧ Καλύκη τις ὄνομα ἐρῶσα
Εὐάθλου νεανίσκου εὔχεται τῇ Ἀφροδίτῃ γαμηθῆναι
αὐτῷ· ἐπεὶ δὲ ὑπερεῖδεν ὁ νεανίσκος, κατεκρήμνισεν
ἑαυτήν. ἐγένετο δὲ τὸ πάθος περὶ Λευκάδα. σωφρο-

e νικὸν | δὲ πάνυ κατεσκεύασεν ὁ ποιητὴς τὸ τῆς παρ-
θένου ἦθος, οὐκ ἐκ παντὸς τρόπου θελούσης συγγενέ-
σθαι τῷ νεανίσκῳ, ἀλλ᾽ εὐχομένης εἰ δύναιτο γυνὴ
τοῦ Εὐάθλου γενέσθαι κουριδία ἢ εἰ τοῦτο μὴ δυνα-
τόν, ἀπαλλαγῆναι τοῦ βίου. ἐν δὲ τοῖς Κατὰ Βραχὺ
Ὑπομνήμασιν ὁ Ἀριστόξενος, Ἴφικλος, φησίν, Ἁρ-
παλύκην ἐρασθεῖσαν ὑπερεῖδεν. ἡ δὲ ἀπέθανεν καὶ

was out hunting, and she began to hunt herself, as a way of pursuing her desires; for she visited all the mountain thickets in her travels and her wanderings, making Io's so-called courses[63] an empty story by comparison. As a consequence, not only did people known for their cold temperament weep at her suffering, but even the most savage beasts did, when they recognized her erotic longing. This is what inspired her poetry, and after she composed it, they say, she wandered through the wilderness, shouting and singing her so-called pastoral song, which includes the words (carm. pop. *PMG* 850):

The oaks are tall, Menalcas!

Aristoxenus says in Book IV of *On Music* (fr. 89 Wehrli): Ancient women sang a song called the *Calycê*. This was a poem by Stesichorus (*PMG* 277), in which a girl named Calycê, who is in love with a young man named Euathlus, prays to Aphrodite, asking to marry him; when the young man showed no interest in her, she hung herself. This unfortunate incident took place in Leucas. The poet characterized the girl as extremely chaste, in that she does not want to sleep with the young man on any terms, but asks in her prayer that she be allowed to become Euathlus' bride or, if that proves impossible, that she be allowed to die. In his *Abbreviated Commentaries*, Aristoxenus (fr. 129 Wehrli) says: Iphiclus showed no interest in Harpalycê after she fell in love with him. She died, and a singing-

---

63 Sc. as she wandered from Argos to Egypt, after having been raped by Zeus and transformed into a cow by Hera; cf. [A.] *PV* 561–886, esp. 707–35, 788–815. Gulick suggests that "courses" (*dromous*) is a painfully weak pun on "thickets" (*drumous*).

γίνεται ἐπ᾽ αὐτῇ παρθένοις ἀγὼν ᾠδῆς, ἥτις Ἀρπα-
λύκη, φησί, καλεῖται. Νύμφις δ᾽ ἐν πρώτῳ Περὶ Ἡρα-
κλείας περὶ Μαριανδυνῶν διηγούμενός φησιν· ὁμοίως
δὲ καὶ τῶν ᾠδῶν ἐνίας κατανοήσειεν ἄν τις, ἃς ἐκεῖνοι
f κατά τινα ἐπιχωριαζομένην | παρ᾽ αὐτοῖς ‹ . . . ›
ᾄδοντες ἀνακαλοῦνταί τινα τῶν ἀρχαίων, προσαγορεύοντες Βῶρμον. τοῦτον δὲ λέγουσιν υἱὸν γενέσθαι
620 ἀνδρὸς ἐπιφανοῦς καὶ πλουσίου, τῷ δὲ κάλλει καὶ ‖ τῇ
κατὰ τὴν ἀκμὴν ὥρᾳ πολὺ τῶν ἄλλων διενεγκεῖν· ὃν
ἐφεστῶτα ἔργοις ἰδίοις καὶ βουλόμενον τοῖς θερί-
ζουσιν δοῦναι πιεῖν βαδίζοντα ἐφ᾽ ὕδωρ ἀφανισθῆναι.
ζητεῖν οὖν αὐτὸν τοὺς ἀπὸ τῆς χώρας μετά τινος
μεμελωδημένου θρήνου καὶ ἀνακλήσεως,[12] ᾧ καὶ νῦν
ἔτι πάντες χρώμενοι διατελοῦσι. τοιοῦτος δ᾽ ἐστὶ καὶ ὁ
παρ᾽ Αἰγυπτίοις καλούμενος Μάνερως.

Οὐκ ἀπελείποντο δὲ ἡμῶν τῶν συμποσίων οὐδὲ
b ῥαψῳδοί· | ἔχαιρε γὰρ τοῖς Ὁμήρου ὁ Λαρήνσιος ὡς
ἄλλος οὐδὲ εἷς, ὡς λῆρον ἀποφαίνειν Κάσανδρον τὸν
Μακεδονίας βασιλεύσαντα, περὶ οὗ φησι Καρύστιος
ἐν Ἱστορικοῖς Ὑπομνήμασιν ὅτι οὕτως ἦν φιλόμηρος
ὡς διὰ στόματος ἔχειν τῶν ἐπῶν τὰ πολλά· καὶ Ἰλιὰς
ἦν αὐτῷ καὶ Ὀδυσσεία ἰδίως γεγραμμέναι. ὅτι δ᾽
ἐκαλοῦντο οἱ ῥαψῳδοὶ καὶ Ὁμηρισταὶ Ἀριστοκλῆς
εἴρηκεν ἐν τῷ Περὶ Χορῶν. τοὺς δὲ νῦν Ὁμηριστὰς
ὀνομαζομένους πρῶτος εἰς τὰ θέατρα παρήγαγε

---

[12] καὶ ἀνακλήσεως del. Kaibel

contest for girls is held in her honor; he reports that it is known as the Harpalycê. Nymphis says in Book I of *On Heracleia* (*FGrH* 432 F 5b), in the course of his discussion of the Mariandynoi: One might similarly note some of the songs they sing at one of their local . . . invoking a boy from the distant past, whom they address as Bormus. They claim that he was the son of an important, wealthy man, and was much better looking than any of his contemporaries, and was at the height of his youthful beauty. He was overseeing the work in some fields that belonged to him, and he wanted to give the harvesters a drink, so he went to fetch water—and disappeared.[64] The local people accordingly began to look for him, singing a dirge that had been set to music and calling out his name, and even today they all continue to do this. What the Egyptians call the Manerôs is similar.[65]

Our parties also featured rhapsodes. For Larensius was more fond of Homer's poetry than anyone you can imagine—fond enough to render insignificant Cassander, the king of Macedon,[66] who Carystius in his *Historical Commentaries* (fr. 8, *FHG* iv.358) claims liked Homer so much that he routinely recited long passages from the poems. Cassander also owned an *Iliad* and an *Odyssey* that had been privately copied for him. Aristocles in his *On Choruses* (fr. 10, *FHG* iv.331) reports that rhapsodes were also referred to as *Homeristai*. The first person to introduce the individuals known today as *Homeristai* into the theaters

[64] Hsch. β 1394 says specifically that Bormus was abducted by nymphs.   [65] Cf. Poll. 4.55 (= Arist. fr. 520.2).

[66] Cassander (Berve i #414) formally claimed the title of king of Macedon *c*.305 BCE; he died in 297.

c Δημήτριος ὁ Φαληρεύς. Χαμαιλέων | δὲ ἐν τῷ Περὶ
Στησιχόρου καὶ μελῳδηθῆναί φησιν οὐ μόνον τὰ
Ὁμήρου, ἀλλὰ καὶ τὰ Ἡσιόδου καὶ Ἀρχιλόχου, ἔτι δὲ
Μιμνέρμου καὶ Φωκυλίδου. Κλέαρχος δ' ἐν τῷ προ-
τέρῳ Περὶ Γρίφων, τὰ Ἀρχιλόχου, φησίν, Σιμωνίδης[13]
ὁ Ζακύνθιος ἐν τοῖς θεάτροις ἐπὶ δίφρου καθήμενος
ἐραψῴδει. Λυσανίας δ' ἐν τῷ πρώτῳ Περὶ Ἰαμβοποιῶν
Μνασίωνα τὸν ῥαψῳδὸν λέγει ἐν ταῖς δείξεσι τῶν
Σιμωνίδου τινὰς ἰάμβων ὑποκρίνεσθαι. τοὺς δ' Ἐμ-
d πεδοκλέους Καθαρμοὺς ἐραψῴδησεν | Ὀλυμπίασι
Κλεομένης ὁ ῥαψῳδός, ὥς φησιν Δικαίαρχος ἐν τῷ
Ὀλυμπικῷ. Ἰάσων δ' ἐν τρίτῳ Περὶ τῶν Ἀλεξάνδρου
Ἱερῶν ἐν Ἀλεξανδρείᾳ φησὶν ἐν τῷ μεγάλῳ θεάτρῳ
ὑποκρίνασθαι Ἡγησίαν τὸν κωμῳδὸν τὰ Ἡσιόδου,
Ἑρμόφαντον δὲ τὰ Ὁμήρου.

Καὶ οἱ καλούμενοι δὲ ἱλαρῳδοί, οὓς νῦν τινες
σιμῳδοὺς καλοῦσιν, ὡς Ἀριστοκλῆς φησιν ἐν πρώτῳ
Περὶ Χορῶν, τῷ τὸν Μάγνητα Σῖμον διαπρέψαι μᾶλλον τῶν διὰ τοῦ ἱλαρῳδεῖν ποιητῶν, συνεχῶς ἡμῖν
e ἐπεφαίνοντο. καταλέγει | δ' ὁ Ἀριστοκλῆς καὶ τούσδε
ἐν τῷ Περὶ Μουσικῆς γράφων ὧδε· μαγῳδός· οὗτος δ'

---

[13] Σιμωνίδης CE: ὁ Σιμωνίδης A

---

[67] Demetrius (*PAA* 312150) controlled Athens from 317–307
BCE and was a great patron of the literary arts.
[68] Stephanis #2281.   [69] Stephanis #1721.
[70] Confused here (as routinely elsewhere) with Semonides of
Amorgos.

was Demetrius of Phaleron (fr. 33 Wehrli = fr. 55A Forten-
baugh–Schütrumpf).[67] According to Chamaeleon in his
On Stesichorus (fr. 28 Wehrli), it was not just Homer's
poems that were recited, but also those of Hesiod and
Archilochus, and of Mimnermus and Phocylides as well.
Clearchus says in Book I of *On Riddles* (fr. 92 Wehrli):
Simonides of Zacynthus[68] used to recite Archilochus' poems in the theaters while seated on a stool. Lysanias in
Book I of *On Iambic Poets* reports that the rhapsode
Mnasion[69] gave public performances in which he acted out
some of Simonides'[70] iambs. The rhapsode Cleomenes[71]
recited Empedocles' *Purifications* (31 A 12 D–K) at Olympia, according to Dicaearchus in his *History of Olympia*
(fr. 87 Wehrli = fr. 85 Mirhady). Iason in Book III of *On
Alexander's Offerings*[72] (*FGrH* 632 F 1) claims that the
comic actor Hegesias[73] performed Hesiod's poems in the
large theater in Alexandria, and that Hermophantus[74] performed Homer's.

The so-called hilarodes—some people today refer to
them as *simôidoi*, according to Aristocles in Book I of *On
Choruses* (fr. 7, *FHG* iv.331, including the excerpt from
On Music below), because Simus of Magnesia[75] was the
best-known hilarodic poet—likewise appeared constantly
at our parties. Aristocles also includes them in the catalogue in his *On Music*, writing as follows: *Magôidos*: this

[71] Stephanis #1445. Cf. D.L. 8.63 (citing Favorinus).

[72] Or perhaps *On the Offerings Made in Alexander's Honor*.

[73] O'Connor #209; Stephanis #1055.

[74] Stephanis #908 (floruit 240s BCE).

[75] Discussed also at Strabo 14.648, but otherwise unknown.

135

ἐστὶν ὁ αὐτὸς τῷ λυσιῳδῷ. Ἀριστόξενος δέ φησι τὸν
μὲν ἀνδρεῖα καὶ γυναικεῖα πρόσωπα ὑποκρινόμενον
μαγῳδὸν καλεῖσθαι, τὸν δὲ γυναικεῖα ἀνδρείοις λυσι-
ῳδόν· τὰ αὐτὰ δὲ μέλη ᾄδουσιν, καὶ τἆλλα πάντα δ'
ἐστὶν ὅμοια. ὁ δὲ Ἰωνικολόγος τὰ Σωτάδου καὶ τῶν
πρὸ τούτου Ἰωνικὰ καλούμενα ποιήματα Ἀλεξάνδρου
τε τοῦ Αἰτωλοῦ καὶ Πύρητος τοῦ Μιλησίου καὶ
f Ἀλέξου καὶ ἄλλων τοιούτων | ποιητῶν προφέρεται·
καλεῖται δ' οὗτος καὶ κιναιδολόγος. ἤκμασεν δ' ἐν τῷ
εἴδει τούτῳ Σωτάδης ὁ Μαρωνείτης, ὥς φησι Καρύστιος ὁ Περγαμηνὸς ἐν τῷ περὶ αὐτοῦ[14] συγγράμματι
καὶ ὁ τοῦ Σωτάδου υἱὸς Ἀπολλώνιος. ἔγραψεν δὲ καὶ
οὗτος περὶ τῶν τοῦ πατρὸς ποιημάτων σύγγραμμα, ἐξ
οὗ ἔστι κατιδεῖν τὴν ἄκαιρον παρρησίαν τοῦ Σωτάδου, κακῶς μὲν εἰπόντος Λυσίμαχον τὸν βασιλέα ἐν
Ἀλεξανδρείᾳ, Πτολεμαῖον δὲ τὸν Φιλάδελφον παρὰ
Λυσιμάχῳ, καὶ ἄλλους τῶν βασιλέων ἐν ἄλλαις τῶν
πόλεων. διόπερ τῆς δεούσης ἔτυχε τιμωρίας· ἐκ-
621 πλεύσαντα γὰρ ‖ αὐτὸν τῆς Ἀλεξανδρείας, ὥς φησιν
Ἡγήσανδρος ἐν τοῖς Ὑπομνήμασιν, καὶ δοκοῦντα
διαπεφευγέναι τὸν κίνδυνον (εἰρήκει γὰρ εἰς τὸν βασιλέα Πτολεμαῖον πολλὰ δεινά, ἀτὰρ καὶ τόδε, ὅτε τὴν
ἀδελφὴν Ἀρσινόην ἐγεγαμήκει·

_____

[14] αὐτοῦ Σωτάδου A: del. Σωτάδου Wilamowitz

_____

[76] At 5.211b–c, however, the *lusiôidos* is a woman who wears
male clothing.
[77] Suda σ 871 offers a slightly different version of the list: "Al-

136

individual is the same as a *lusiôidos*. But Aristoxenus (fr. 111 Wehrli) claims that a man who plays male and female parts is referred to as a *magôidos*, whereas a man who plays female parts dressed in male clothing is a *lusiôidos*;[76] but they perform the same songs, and everything else about them is identical. An *Ionikologos* performs the so-called Ionian poems of Sotades and his predecessors, meaning Alexander Aetolus (fr. 21, p. 129 Powell = fr. 18 Magnelli), Pyretus of Miletus (*SH* 714), Alexas (*SH* 41), and other poets of the same sort;[77] this type of performer is also known as a *kinaidologos*.[78] Sotades of Maroneia excelled in this genre, according to Carystius of Pergamum in his treatise on him (fr. 19, *FHG* iv.359), and according to Sotades' son Apollonius as well. The latter also wrote a treatise on his father's poems, which allows one to catch a glimpse of Sotades' tendency to open his mouth at the wrong moment, as when he criticized King Lysimachus in Alexandria, Ptolemy Philadelphus in Lysimachus' court,[79] and other kings in other cities. He accordingly got the punishment he deserved; after he sailed out of Alexandria, according to Hegesander in his *Commentaries* (fr. 12, *FHG* iv.415–16), and seemed to have escaped the danger— for he had made numerous nasty remarks regarding King Ptolemy, including the following, after Ptolemy had married his sister Arsinoe (fr. 1, p. 238 Powell):

exander of Aetolus, Pyrhus of Miletus (*SH* 714), Theodorus (*SH* 756), Timocharidas, and Xenarchus."

[78] "obscenity-speaker" *vel sim.* For Ionian depravity, cf. 12.524f–6e.

[79] Ptolemy Philadelphus is Ptolemy II (reigned 285/3–246 BCE); he married Arsinoe II in around 270. Lysimachus (another of Alexander's successors, and Arsinoe's first husband) died in 281.

εἰς οὐχ ὁσίην τρυμαλιὴν τὸ κέντρον ὠθεῖς),

Πάτροκλος οὖν ὁ τοῦ Πτολεμαίου στρατηγὸς ἐν Καύ-
b νῳ τῇ νήσῳ λαβὼν αὐτὸν | καὶ εἰς μολυβῆν κεραμίδα
ἐμβαλὼν καὶ ἀναγαγὼν εἰς τὸ πέλαγος κατεπόντωσε.
τοιαύτη δ᾽ ἐστὶν αὐτοῦ ἡ ποίησις· Θεοδώρου τοῦ αὐλη-
τοῦ Φιλῖνος ἦν πατήρ, εἰς ὃν ταῦτ᾽ ἔγραψεν·

ὁ δ᾽ ἀποστεγάσας τὸ τρῆμα τῆς ὄπισθε λαύρης
διὰ δενδροφόρου φάραγγος ἐξέωσε βροντὴν
ἠλέματον, ὁκοίην ἀροτὴρ γέρων χαλᾷ βοῦς.

σεμνότερος δὲ τῶν τοιούτων ἐστὶ ποιητῶν ὁ ἱλαρῳδὸς |
c καλούμενος· οὐδὲ γὰρ σχινίζεται, χρῆται δ᾽ ἐσθῆτι
λευκῇ ἀνδρείᾳ καὶ στεφανοῦται χρυσοῦν στέφανον,
καὶ τὸ μὲν παλαιὸν ὑποδήμασιν ἐχρῆτο, ὥς φησιν ὁ
Ἀριστοκλῆς, νῦν δὲ κρηπῖσιν, ψάλλει δ᾽ αὐτῷ ἄρρην ἢ
θήλεια, ὡς καὶ τῷ αὐλῳδῷ. δίδοται δὲ ὁ στέφανος τῷ
ἱλαρῳδῷ καὶ τῷ αὐλῳδῷ, οὐ τῷ ψάλτῃ οὐδὲ τῷ αὐλητῇ. ὁ δὲ μαγῳδὸς καλούμενος τύμπανα ἔχει καὶ
κύμβαλα καὶ πάντα τὰ περὶ αὐτὸν ἐνδύματα γυναικεῖα, σχινίζεται δὲ καὶ πάντα ποιεῖ τὰ ἔξω κόσμου,
ὑποκρινόμενος ποτὲ μὲν γυναῖκας μοιχοὺς[15] καὶ
μαστροπούς, ποτὲ δὲ ἄνδρα μεθύοντα καὶ ἐπὶ κῶμον
παραγινόμενον πρὸς τὴν ἐρωμένην. φησὶ δὲ ὁ

[15] γυναῖκας καὶ μοιχοὺς CE: γυναῖκα καὶ μοιχοὺς A: καὶ
del. Kaibel

You're thrusting your poker into an unholy slot—

Ptolemy's general Patroclus captured him on the island of Caunus, stuck his feet in a jar full of lead, took him out to sea, and drowned him. This is the type of poetry he produced: Philinus was the father of the pipe-player Theodorus,[80] and Sotades wrote the following about him (fr. 2, p. 238 Powell):

> He opened up the hole of his back alley
> and expelled an idle blast through his bushy
> crack, the type an old plow-ox lets loose.

The so-called *hilarôidoi* are more respectable than poets of this sort; for they do not *schinizomai*,[81] and they wear white, male clothing and have a gold garland on their head, and in the old days they wore sandals, according to Aristocles (fr. 8, *FHG* iv.331), although nowadays they wear high boots; a man or a woman plays the harp to accompany them, as also in the case of *aulôidoi*.[82] *Hilarôidoi* and *aulôidoi* are allowed to wear garlands, whereas harp-players and pipe-players are not. The so-called *magôidoi* have drums and cymbals, and wear only female clothing; they *schinizomai* and behave in all the ways no one should, sometimes pretending to be women who are having affairs or arranging liaisons for others, at other times playing a man who is drunk or who appears at his girlfriend's house with a group of troublemakers. Aristoxenus (fr. 110

---

[80] Stephanis #1173.   [81] Obscure, but used again below to describe the behavior of the cross-dressing *magôidoi*.

[82] I.e. individuals who sing to flute music and for whom the flute player may once again be either a man or a woman.

ATHENAEUS

d Ἀριστόξενος | τὴν μὲν ἱλαρῳδίαν σεμνὴν οὖσαν παρὰ
τὴν τραγῳδίαν εἶναι, τὴν δὲ μαγῳδίαν παρὰ τὴν
κωμῳδίαν. πολλάκις δὲ οἱ μαγῳδοὶ καὶ κωμικὰς ὑπο-
θέσεις λαβόντες ὑπεκρίθησαν κατὰ τὴν ἰδίαν ἀγωγὴν
καὶ διάθεσιν. ἔσχεν δὲ τοὔνομα ἡ μαγῳδία ἀπὸ τοῦ
οἱονεὶ μαγικὰ προφέρεσθαι καὶ φαρμάκων ἐμφανίζειν
δυνάμεις.

Παρὰ δὲ Λακεδαιμονίοις κωμικῆς παιδιᾶς ἦν τις
τρόπος παλαιός, ὥς φησι Σωσίβιος, οὐκ ἄγαν σπου-
δαῖος, ἅτε δὴ κἀν τούτοις τὸ λιτὸν τῆς Σπάρτης
μεταδιωκούσης. ἐμιμεῖτο γάρ τις ἐν εὐτελεῖ τῇ λέξει
κλέπτοντάς τινας ὀπώραν ἢ ξενικὸν ἰατρὸν τοιαυτὶ
e λέγοντα, ὡς | Ἄλεξις ἐν Μανδραγοριζομένῃ διὰ τού-
των παρίστησιν·

            ἐὰν ἐπιχώριος
    ἰατρὸς εἴπῃ, "τρύβλιον τούτῳ δότε
    πτισάνης ἕωθεν," καταφρονοῦμεν εὐθέως·
    ἂν δὲ "πτισάνας" καὶ "τρούβλιον," θαυμάζομεν.
    καὶ πάλιν ἐὰν μὲν "τευτλίον," παρείδομεν·
    ἐὰν δὲ "σεῦτλον," ἀσμένως ἠκούσαμεν,
    ὡς οὐ τὸ σεῦτλον ταὐτὸν ὂν τῷ τευτλίῳ.

ἐκαλοῦντο δ' οἱ μετιόντες τὴν τοιαύτην παιδιὰν παρὰ
τοῖς Λάκωσι δικηλισταί,[16] ὡς ἄν τις σκευοποιοὺς εἴπῃ

[16] δεικηλισταί CE

140

Wehrli) claims that because *hilarôidia* is respectable, it is connected with tragedy, whereas *magôidia* is connected with comedy. *Magôidoi* frequently took over comic plots and acted them out in their own fashion and style. *Magôidia* got its name from the fact that they pronounced *magika* ("magic spells"), as it were, and displayed unnatural powers.[83]

The Spartans had an old style of comic entertainment, according to Sosibius (*FGrH* 595 F *7 = com. dor. test. 2), which was not particularly elevated, since Sparta pursued simplicity even in matters of this sort. For someone would use unrefined language to imitate people stealing fruit, or a foreign doctor making remarks like those Alexis presents in the following passage from *The Woman Who Ate Mandrake* (fr. 146):

> If a local
> doctor says "Give him a bowl (*trublion*)
> of wheat-gruel (*ptisanê*) first thing in the morning,"
>   we immediately ignore him;
> but if he says *"ptisana"* and *"troublion,"*[84] we're
>   impressed.
> So too if he says *"teutlion"* ("beet"), we pay no
>   attention;
> but if it's *"seutlon,"* we're happy to listen—
> as if a *seutlon* weren't the same thing as a *teutlion*!

They used to call the people who practiced this form of entertainment in Sparta *dikêlistai*, which is to say "trick-

---

[83] The actual etymology of the first element in the word is obscure.   [84] Doric forms of the same word, as again below with *seutlon* for *teutlion*.

f   καὶ μιμητάς. τοῦ δὲ εἴδους τῶν δικηλιστῶν | πολλαὶ
κατὰ τόπους εἰσὶ προσηγορίαι. Σικυώνιοι μὲν γὰρ
φαλλοφόρους αὐτοὺς καλοῦσιν, ἄλλοι δ᾽ αὐτοκαβδά-
λους, οἱ δὲ φλύακας, ὡς Ἰταλοί, σοφιστὰς δὲ οἱ
πολλοί· Θηβαῖοι δὲ καὶ τὰ πολλὰ ἰδίως ὀνομάζειν
εἰωθότες ἐθελοντάς. ὅτι δὲ καινουργοῦσιν κατὰ τὰς
φωνὰς οἱ Θηβαῖοι Στράττις ἐπιδείκνυσιν ἐν Φοινίσσαις διὰ τούτων·

    ξυνίετ᾽ οὐδέν, πᾶσα Θηβαίων πόλις· ‖
622   οὐδέν ποτ᾽ ἀλλ᾽. οἳ πρῶτα μὲν τὴν σηπίαν
    ὀπιτθοτίλαν, ὡς λέγουσ᾽, ὀνομάζετε,
    τὸν ἀλεκτρύονα δ᾽ † ὀρτάλιχον, τὸν ἰατρὸν δὲ †
    σάκταν, βέφυραν τὴν γέφυραν, τῦκα δὲ
    τὰ σῦκα, κωτιλάδας δὲ τὰς χελιδόνας,
    τὴν ἔνθεσιν δ᾽ ἄκολον, τὸ γελᾶν δὲ κριδδέμεν,
    νεασπάτων δ᾽, ἤν τι νεοκάττυτον ᾖ.

Σῆμος δ᾽ ὁ Δήλιος ἐν τῷ Περὶ Παιάνων, οἱ αὐτο-
b   κάβδαλοι, | φησί, καλούμενοι ἐστεφανωμένοι κιττῷ
σχέδην ἐπέραινον ῥήσεις· ὕστερον δὲ ἴαμβοι ὠνο-
μάσθησαν αὐτοί τε καὶ τὰ ποιήματα αὐτῶν. οἱ δὲ

---

85 Or "fabricators."   86 Literally "backward-diarrhea-
squirter," referring to the creature's ink.

87 The word as it is preserved in the manuscript normally
means "young bird, chick" and is put in a Boeotian's mouth also at
Ar. *Ach.* 871.

88 *beta* for common *gamma* is a not-uncommon variant in
Aeolic dialects such as Boeotian.

sters"[85] or "mimes." There are many terms for this type of *dikêlistai* in different places: the Sicyonians call them *phallophoroi* ("phallus-bearers"); others call them *autokabdaloi* ("improvisers"); some call them *phluakes*, as the Italians do; and many refer to them as "sophists." But the Thebans, who are generally accustomed to using their own names for things, call them "volunteers." That the Thebans tend to invent new words is pointed out by Strattis in *Phoenician Women* (fr. 49), in the following passage:

> City of Thebes, none of you understand anything
>   whatsoever—
> and that's the end of it! People claim, first of all, that
> you call a cuttlefish (*sêpia*) an *opitthotila*;[86]
> a rooster (*alektruôn*) an † *ortalichos*;[87] a doctor
>   (*iatros*) †
> a *sakta*; a bridge (*gephura*) a *bephura*;[88] figs (*suka*)
> *tuka*; swallows (*chelidones*) *kôtilades*;[89]
> a mouthful of food (*enthesis*) an *akolos*; and laughing
>   (*gelan*) *kriddemen*.
> And if a shoe's been re-soled (*neokattutos*), it's
>   *neaspatôtos*.[90]

Semus of Delos says in his *On Paeans* (*FGrH* 396 F 24): The so-called *autokabdaloi* wore ivy-wreaths and recited their speeches slowly; later on they and their poems were referred to as *iamboi*. The so-called *ithyphalloi*,[91] he re-

---

[89] Cognate with the verb *kôtillein* ("to speak sweetly"; cf. Anacr. *PMG* 453).

[90] Hsch. σ 1437 glosses *spatos* (the second element in the compound) as meaning "hide, piece of leather."

[91] Literally "men with erect phalluses."

143

ἰθύφαλλοι, φησί, καλούμενοι προσωπεῖα μεθυόντων
ἔχουσιν καὶ ἐστεφάνωνται, χειρῖδας ἀνθινὰς ἔχοντες·
χιτῶσι δὲ χρῶνται μεσολεύκοις καὶ περιέζωνται Ταραντῖνον καλυπτὸν αὐτοὺς μέχρι τῶν σφυρῶν. σιγῇ
δὲ διὰ τοῦ πυλῶνος εἰσελθόντες, ὅταν κατὰ μέσην τὴν
ὀρχήστραν γένωνται, ἐπιστρέφουσιν εἰς τὸ θέατρον
λέγοντες· |

c   ἀνάγετ᾽, εὐρυχωρίαν
    τῷ θεῷ ποιεῖτε·
    θέλει γὰρ ὁ θεὸς ὀρθὸς ἐσφυδωμένος
    διὰ μέσου βαδίζειν.

οἱ δὲ φαλλοφόροι, φησίν, προσωπεῖον μὲν οὐ λαμ-
βάνουσιν, προπόλιον δ᾽ ἐξ ἑρπύλλου περιτιθέμενοι
καὶ παιδέρωτος ἐπάνω τούτου ἐπιτίθενται στέφανον[17]
δασὺν ἴων καὶ κιττοῦ. καυνάκας τε περιβεβλημένοι
παρέρχονται οἱ μὲν ἐκ παρόδου, οἱ δὲ κατὰ μέσας τὰς
θύρας, βαίνοντες ἐν ῥυθμῷ καὶ λέγοντες·

    σοί, Βάκχε, τάνδε Μοῦσαν ἀγλαΐζομεν,
    ἁπλοῦν ῥυθμὸν χέοντες αἰόλῳ μέλει, |
d   καινὰν ἀπαρθένευτον, οὔ τι ταῖς πάρος
    κεχρημέναν ᾠδαῖσιν, ἀλλ᾽ ἀκήρατον
    κατάρχομεν τὸν ὕμνον.

εἶτα προστρέχοντες ἐτώθαζον οὕς[18] προέλοιντο, στά-

---

[17] στέφανόν τε ACE: τε del. Meineke
[18] οὓς ἂν ACE: ἂν del. Kaibel

144

ports, have masks that look like drunks, put garlands on
their heads, and wear long, embroidered sleeves; they
dress in off-white tunics and wrap a Tarentine robe that ex-
tends down to their ankles around themselves. They enter
through the gateway in silence, and once they are in the
middle of the dancing-area, they turn to the audience and
say (carm. pop. *PMG* 851a):

> Get back! Clear
> the way for the god!
> For the god wants to pass through your midst
> erect and swollen!

Whereas the *phallophoroi*,[92] he says, do not wear masks,
and instead put a *prospolion* made of tufted thyme and
paiderôs around their heads, and place a thick garland of
violets and ivy on top of that. And they wrap themselves in
heavy blankets and come in, some of them via a side-
entrance, others through the central doors, marching in
step and saying (carm. pop. *PMG* 851b):

> Bacchus—we offer this composition in your honor,
> pouring forth an elaborate song set to a simple
> rhythm.
> Our composition is new and virginal, and was never
> used
> in odes performed in the past; the hymn
> we offer is undefiled.

Then they ran up to the people they selected and made fun

[92] Literally "phallus-bearers"; cf. 10.445b; 14.621f.

145

δην δὲ ἔπραττον· ὁ δὲ φαλλοφόρος ἰθὺ βαδίζων κατα-
πασθεὶς αἰθάλῳ.

Ἐπεὶ δ' ἐνταῦθα τοῦ λόγου ἐσμέν, οὐκ ἄξιον ἡγοῦμαι παραλιπεῖν τὰ περὶ Ἀμοιβέως τοῦ καθ' ἡμᾶς
κιθαρῳδοῦ,

ἀνδρὸς τεχνίτου κατὰ νόμους τοὺς μουσικούς.

οὗτός ποτε βράδιον ἥκων ἐπὶ τὸ συμπόσιον ἡμῶν ὡς
e ἔμαθεν παρά τινος | τῶν οἰκετῶν ἀποδειπνήσαντας,
ἐβουλεύετο τί χρὴ ποιεῖν, ἕως παρελθὼν ὁ Σόφων
αὐτῷ μάγειρος (γεγωνότερον δ' ἐφθέγγετο ὡς πάντας
ἀκούειν) τὰ ἐξ Αὔγης εἶπεν Εὐβούλου·

τί, ὦ πόνηρ', ἕστηκας ἐν πύλαις ἔτι,
ἀλλ' οὐ βαδίζεις; τοῖσδε γενναίως πάλαι
διεσπάρακται θερμὰ χηνίσκων μέλη,
διερράχισται σεμνὰ δελφάκων κρέα,
κατηλόηται γαστρὸς ἐν μέσῳ κύκλος,
κατησίμωται πάντα τἀκροκώλια, |
f νενωγάλισται σεμνὸς ἀλλᾶντος τόμος,
παρεντέτρωκται τευθὶς ἐξωπτημένη,
παρεγκέκαπται † στερανι † ἐννέ' ἢ δέκα.
ὥστ' εἴ τι βούλει τῶν λελειμμένων φαγεῖν,
ἔπειγ' ἔπειγε, μή ποθ' ὡς λύκος χανὼν

---

93 Stephanis #160.
94 An adespota iambic trimeter line, accepted neither by Radt
among the tragic adespota nor by Kassel–Austin among the comic
adespota.

146

of them; they did this while standing in one spot. But the man who carried the phallus kept moving forward, sprinkled with soot.

Since I have reached this point in my account, I consider it inappropriate to omit the anecdotes I have to offer about the contemporary citharode Amoebeus,[93]

a man skilled in music's rules.[94]

He came a bit late to our party once, and one of the servants informed him that we were done with dinner. He was trying to decide what to do, until the cook Sophon[95] came over and quoted the lines from Eubulus' *Auge* (fr. 14) to him—he spoke loud enough for all of us to hear:

Why are you still standing here in the doorway, you
    poor bastard,
instead of going in? They've long ago neatly
ripped apart the warm limbs of little geese,
carved up the sacred flesh of pigs,
finished off the central circle of a stomach-sausage,
consumed all the pigs' trotters,
nibbled on a sacred slice of sausage,
eaten a roasted squid as well,
and gulped down nine or ten [corrupt] on top of that.
So if you want to eat some of the leftovers,
hurry, hurry! Otherwise you'll be like a wolf with
    empty jaws,[96]

93 Comic cooks by the same name (cognate with the adjective *sophos*, "wise") are mentioned at Anaxipp. fr. 1.1 (preserved at 9.403e) and Bato fr. 4.4 (preserved at 14.662c).

96 Proverbial; cf. 9.380b with n.

καὶ τῶνδ᾽ ἁμαρτὼν ὕστερον † συχνω δραχμης †.

(A.) πάντ᾽ ἐστὶν ἡμῖν,

κατὰ τὸν ἥδιστον Ἀντιφάνην, ὃς ἐν τῷ Φιλοθηβαίῳ
φησίν·

> ἥ τε γὰρ συνώνυμος
> τῆς ἔνδον οὔσης ἔγχελυς Βοιωτία ‖

623
> τμηθεῖσα[19] κοίλοις ἐν βυθοῖσι κακκάβης
> χλιαίνετ᾽, αἴρεθ᾽, ἕψεται, παφλάζεται,
> προσκάεθ᾽· ὥστε μηδ᾽ ἂν εἰ χαλκοῦς ἔχων
> μυκτῆρας εἰσέλθοι τις, ἐξελθεῖν πάλιν
> εἰκῇ· τοσαύτην ἐξακοντίζει πνοήν.
> (B.) λέγεις μάγειρον ζῶντα. (A.) πλησίον δέ γε
> ταύτης ἄσιτος ἡμέραν καὶ νύχθ᾽ ὅλην
> κεστρεύς, λοπισθείς < . . . > πασθείς, στραφείς,
> χρωσθείς, ὁμοῦ τι πρὸς τέλος δρόμου περῶν, |

b
> σίζει κεκραγώς, παῖς δ᾽ ἐφέστηκε ῥανῶν
> ὄξει, Λίβυς τε καυλὸς ἐξηρασμένος
> ἀκτῖσι θείαις σιλφίου παραστατεῖ.
> (B.) εἶτ᾽ οὐκ ἐπῳδούς φασιν ἰσχύειν τινές·
> ἐγὼ γὰρ ἤδη τρεῖς ὁρῶ μασωμένους,
> σοῦ ταῦτα συστρέφοντος. (A.) ἥ τε σύννομον

---

[19] μιχθεῖσα 4.169c

---

[97] A more complete version of the first four verses (with a variant in verse 3) is preserved at 4.169c–d.

[98] It is unclear whether the woman's name is supposed to be

and you'll miss this too and later [corrupt].

(A.) We've got everything!,

to quote the delightful Antiphanes, who says in his *The Man Who Loved Thebes* (fr. 216):[97]

> For the Boeotian eel,
> whose name's the same as the woman's inside,[98]
> has been cut up and is within the hollow depths of a
>   casserole-dish,
> where it's growing hot, swelling up, stewing,
>   spluttering,
> even burning; so that even if a man had bronze
> nostrils, once he got inside, he wouldn't get out again,
> I suspect. That's the sort of smell it's generating.
> (B.) You're talking about a real, live cook! (A.) And
>   next to
> the eel is a gray mullet that never eats at any point,
>   day
> or night;[99] it's been scaled . . . sprinkled, flipped,
> and browned, is nearing the end of the race,
> sizzling and shrieking. A slave stands beside it,
>   sprinkling
> it with vinegar, while a dried Libyan stalk
> is at hand with divine beams of silphium.
> (B.) And some people claim sorcerers don't have any
>   power!
> Because I already see three people chewing—

Boeotia (thus Meineke) or Eel (thus Kock), but she must in any case be a courtesan.

[99] For "fasting mullets," cf. 7.307c–8b.

τῆς κυφονώτου σῶμ' ἔχουσα σηπίας,
ξιφηφόροισι χερσὶν ἐξωπλισμένη
τευθίς, μεταλλάξασα λευκαυγῆ φύσιν
σαρκὸς πυρωτοῖς ἀνθράκων ῥιπίσμασιν, |

c ξανθαῖσιν αὔραις σῶμα πᾶν ἀγάλλεται,
δείπνου προφήτην λιμὸν ἐκκαλουμένη.
<   . . .   > ὥστε γ' εἴσιθι·
μὴ μέλλε, χώρει. δεῖ γὰρ ἠριστηκότας
πάσχειν, ἐάν τι καὶ παθεῖν ἡμᾶς δέῃ.

καὶ ὃς πάνυ ἐμμελέστατα ἀπαντήσας αὐτῷ ἀντεφώ-
νησε τὰ ἐκ τοῦ Κλεάρχου Κιθαρῳδοῦ τάδε·

γόγγρων τε λευκῶν πᾶσι τοῖς κολλώδεσι
βρόχθιζε. τούτοις γὰρ τρέφεται τὸ πνεῦμα καὶ
τὸ φωνάριον ἡμῶν † περίσαργον † γίνεται. |

d κρότου δ' ἐπὶ τούτοις γενομένου καὶ πάντων ὁμοθυ-
μαδὸν αὐτὸν καλεσάντων εἰσελθὼν καὶ πιὼν ἀναλα-
βών τε τὴν κιθάραν εἰς τοσοῦτον ἡμᾶς ᾖσεν ὡς
πάντας θαυμάζειν τήν τε κιθάρισιν μετὰ τῆς τέχνης
ταχίστην οὖσαν καὶ τῆς φωνῆς τὴν ἐμμέλειαν· ἐμοὶ
μὲν γὰρ οὐδὲν ἐλάττων εἶναι νομίζεται τοῦ παλαιοῦ
Ἀμοιβέως, ὅν φησιν Ἀριστέας ἐν τῷ Περὶ Κιθαρῳδῶν
ἐν Ἀθήναις κατοικοῦντα καὶ πλησίον τοῦ θεάτρου
οἰκοῦντα, εἰ ἐξέλθοι ᾀσόμενος, τάλαντον Ἀττικὸν τῆς
ἡμέρας λαμβάνειν.

while you're still spinning these remarks! (A.) And
    she whose
body is akin to that of the hunch-backed cuttlefish
and is equipped with sword-bearing hands,
the squid, altering the shining character
of her flesh under the fiery blasts of the coals,
exults in the browning scent throughout her body,
summoning hunger, the harbinger of dinner.
. . . So go inside!
Don't wait! Move! If something bad's going to happen
to us, let's make sure it happens after lunch!

Amoebeus responded in harmony with this, and quoted
back to him the following lines from Clearchus' *Citharode*
(fr. 2):

Treat your throat with all the gummy parts of white
eels; because they help us breathe and
our voice becomes [corrupt].

These remarks were met with applause, and we unani-
mously invited him in. After he entered the room and had
a drink, he picked up his lyre and delighted us so much
that we were all astonished at his playing, which was rapid
and technically accomplished, and at how well-trained his
voice was; for in my opinion he was as good as the ancient Amoebeus,[100] who according to Aristeas in his *On
Citharodes* was a resident of Athens and lived near the
Theater; whenever he went onstage to sing, he was paid an
Attic talent[101] per day.

---

[100] Stephanis #159; *PAA* 124327. He belongs to the middle of
the 3rd century BCE.

[101] = 6,000 drachmas, a preposterous sum.

e   Περὶ δὲ | μουσικῆς τῶν μὲν τάδε λεγόντων, ἄλλων
δ' ἄλλα γ' ὁσημέραι, πάντων δ' ἐπαινούντων τὴν
παιδείαν ταύτην, Μασούριος ὁ πάντα ἄριστος καὶ
σοφὸς (καὶ γὰρ νόμων ἐξηγητὴς οὐδενὸς δεύτερος καὶ
περὶ μουσικὴν ἐνδιατρίβων αἰεί· ἅπτεται γὰρ καὶ τῶν
ὀργάνων) ἔφη· ὁ μὲν κωμῳδιοποιὸς Εὔπολις, ἄνδρες
φίλοι, φησί·

   καὶ μουσικὴ πρᾶγμ' ἐστὶ βαθύ τι † καὶ
      καμπύλον,

αἰεί τε καινὸν ἐξευρίσκει τι τοῖς ἐπινοεῖν δυναμένοις.
διόπερ καὶ Ἀναξίλας ἐν Ὑακίνθῳ φησίν· |

f   ἡ μουσικὴ δ' ὥσπερ Λιβύη, πρὸς τῶν θεῶν,
   ἀεί τι καινὸν κατ' ἐνιαυτὸν θηρίον
   τίκτει.

                                           μέγας

γάρ, ὦ μακάριοι, κατὰ τὸν Θεοφίλου Κιθαρῳδόν,

   θησαυρός ἐστι καὶ βέβαιος μουσικὴ
   ἅπασι τοῖς μαθοῦσι παιδευθεῖσί τε.

καὶ γὰρ τὰ ἤθη παιδεύει καὶ τοὺς θυμοειδεῖς καὶ τὰς
γνώμας διαφόρους καταπραΰνει. Κλεινίας γοῦν ὁ
624 Πυθαγόρειος, ὡς Χαμαιλέων ὁ Ποντικὸς ἱστορεῖ, ‖ καὶ
τῷ βίῳ καὶ τοῖς ἤθεσιν διαφέρων, εἴ ποτε συνέβαινεν

───────────────

102 Cf. the even more extravagant praise of Masurius at 1.1c
(composed by the Epitomator, but presumably drawing on Athenaeus himself in the full version of Book 1).

Music was discussed every day, with some guests offering the comments quoted above, while others made remarks of different sorts, although everyone spoke highly of this type of training. The universally excellent and wise Masurius—he is in fact second to no one as a legal exegete, and has always devoted himself to music; for he plays various instruments[102]—said: The comic poet Eupolis (fr. 366), my friends, remarks:

> Music's a profound business—† and a complicated
> one,

which always presents those capable of appreciating it with something new. This is why Anaxilas says in *Hyacinthus* (fr. 27):

> Music's like Libya, by the gods—
> it's always producing a new monster
> every year!

Because, my fortunate friends, to quote Theophilus' *Citharode* (fr. 5):

> Music's
> a vast, secure storeroom
> for anyone who studied it and got an education.

For the fact is that it shapes our character and calms individuals who are hot-tempered or argumentative. Cleinias the Pythagorean, for example, according to Chamaeleon of Pontus (fr. 4 Wehrli),[103] lived and behaved in an exem-

---

[103] Material very similar to this (but not attributed to Chamaeleon) is preserved at Ael. *VH* 14.23.

χαλεπαίνειν αὐτὸν δι' ὀργήν, ἀναλαμβάνων τὴν λύραν ἐκιθάριζεν. πρὸς δὲ τοὺς ἐπιζητοῦντας τὴν αἰτίαν
ἔλεγεν, "πραΰνομαι." καὶ ὁ Ὁμηρικὸς δὲ Ἀχιλλεὺς τῇ
κιθάρᾳ κατεπραΰνετο, ἣν αὐτῷ ἐκ τῶν Ἠετίωνος
λαφύρων μόνην Ὅμηρος χαρίζεται, καταστέλλειν τὸ
πυρῶδες αὐτοῦ δυναμένην· μόνος γοῦν ἐν Ἰλιάδι ταύτῃ χρῆται τῇ μουσικῇ. ὅτι δὲ καὶ νόσους ἰᾶται μουσικὴ Θεόφραστος ἱστόρησεν ἐν τῷ Περὶ Ἐνθουσι-
b   ασμοῦ, ἰσχιδιακοὺς[20] | φάσκων ἀνόσους διατελεῖν, εἰ
καταυλήσοι τις τοῦ τόπου τῇ Φρυγιστὶ ἁρμονίᾳ. ταύτην δὲ τὴν ἁρμονίαν Φρύγες πρῶτοι εὗρον καὶ μετ-
εχειρίσαντο· διὸ καὶ τοὺς παρὰ τοῖς Ἕλλησιν αὐλητὰς Φρυγίους καὶ δουλοπρεπεῖς τὰς προσηγορίας
ἔχειν. οἷός ἐστιν ὁ παρὰ Ἀλκμᾶνι Σάμβας καὶ Ἄδων
καὶ Τῆλος, παρὰ δὲ Ἱππώνακτι Κίων καὶ Κώδαλος καὶ
Βάβυς, ἐφ' ᾧ καὶ ἡ παροιμία ἐπὶ τῶν αἰεὶ πρὸς τὸ
χεῖρον αὐλούντων·

κάκιον Βάβυς[21] αὐλεῖ.

ὁ δ' Ἀριστόξενος τὴν εὕρεσιν αὐτῆς Ὑάγνιδι τῷ
c   Φρυγὶ ἀνατίθησιν. | Ἡρακλείδης δ' ὁ Ποντικὸς ἐν
τρίτῳ Περὶ Μουσικῆς οὐδ' ἁρμονίαν φησὶ δεῖν καλεῖ-

---

20 ἰσχιδιακοὺς Olson: ἰσχιακοὺς ACE
21 καὶ κίων ἢ Βάβυς ACE: κάκιον Casaubon, ἢ del. Kaibel

---

104 But cf. Il. 3.54 (of Paris); 18.570 (on the Shield of Achilleus).   105 Sambas is Stephanis #2209, Adon is Stephanis
#53, Telus is Stephanis #2409, Cion (or Cicon) is Stephanis #1404,

plary fashion, and if he ever happened to get angry or upset, he picked up his lyre and started playing it. When
asked why, he would say: "I'm calming myself down." The
Homeric Achilleus similarly used his lyre to get control
of his temper (cf. *Il.* 9.186–8); this was the only object
Homer awarded him from the plunder of Eetion, and it
had the power to control the fiery aspect of his personality.
He is the only character in the *Iliad*, at any rate, who plays
this sort of music.[104] Theophrastus in his *On Inspiration*
(fr. 726B Fortenbaugh) reported that music cures diseases,
claiming that individuals who suffer from sciatica have
their symptoms relieved if someone plays the lyre over
the affected spot using the Phrygian scale. The Phrygians
invented and developed this scale, which is why the pipe-
players in Greece are Phrygians or have names appropriate for slaves. Examples include Alcman's (*PMG* 109)
Sambas, Adon, and Telus, and Hipponax' (fr. 153 Degani)
Cion, Codalus, and Babys,[105] to whom the proverb (Zenob.
4.81) about people whose pipe-playing constantly deterio-
rates refers:

Babys' pipe-playing is getting worse.

Aristoxenus (fr. 78 Wehrli) attributes the invention of the
scale to Hyagnis of Phrygia.[106] But Heracleides of Pontus in Book III of *On Music* (fr. 163 Wehrli = fr. 114
Schütrumpf) claims that it should not be referred to as

Codalus is Stephanis #1523, and Babys is Stephanis #506. Nothing
further is known about any of them.

[106] Plu. *Mor.* 1132f calls Hyagnis the father of the satyr Marsyas; cf. Antip. Thess. *AP* 9.266 = *GPh* 681–6.

σθαι τὴν Φρύγιον, καθάπερ οὐδὲ τὴν Λύδιον· ἁρμονίας γὰρ εἶναι τρεῖς, τρία γὰρ καὶ γενέσθαι Ἑλλήνων
γένη, Δωριεῖς, Αἰολεῖς, Ἴωνας. οὐ μικρᾶς οὖν οὔσης
διαφορᾶς ἐν τοῖς τούτων ἤθεσιν, Λακεδαιμόνιοι μὲν
μάλιστα τῶν ἄλλων Δωριέων τὰ πάτρια διαφυλάτ-
τουσιν, Θεσσαλοὶ δὲ (οὗτοι γάρ εἰσιν ⟨οἱ⟩²² τὴν
ἀρχὴν τοῦ γένους Αἰολεῦσιν μεταδόντες) παραπλήσιον ἀεὶ ποιοῦνται τοῦ βίου τὴν ἀγωγήν, Ἰώνων δὲ τὸ
d   πολὺ | πλῆθος ἠλλοίωται διὰ τὸ συμπεριφέρεσθαι
τοῖς ἀεὶ δυναστεύουσιν αὐτοῖς τῶν βαρβάρων. τὴν
οὖν ἀγωγὴν τῆς μελῳδίας ἣν οἱ Δωριεῖς ἐποιοῦντο
Δώριον ἐκάλουν ἁρμονίαν, ἐκάλουν δὲ καὶ Αἰολίδα
ἁρμονίαν ἣν Αἰολεῖς ᾖδον, Ἰαστὶ δὲ τὴν τρίτην ἔφασκον ἣν ἤκουον ᾀδόντων τῶν Ἰώνων. ἡ μὲν οὖν
Δώριος ἁρμονία τὸ ἀνδρῶδες ἐμφαίνει καὶ τὸ μεγαλοπρεπὲς καὶ οὐ διακεχυμένον οὐδ᾽ ἱλαρόν, ἀλλὰ
σκυθρωπὸν καὶ σφοδρόν, οὔτε δὲ ποικίλον οὔτε πολύ-
τροπον. τὸ δὲ τῶν Αἰολέων ἦθος ἔχει τὸ γαῦρον καὶ |
e   ὀγκῶδες, ἔτι δὲ ὑπόχαυνον, ὁμολογεῖ δὲ ταῦτα ταῖς
ἱπποτροφίαις αὐτῶν καὶ ξενοδοχίαις· οὐ πανοῦργον
δέ, ἀλλὰ ἐξηρμένον καὶ τεθαρρηκός, διὸ καὶ οἰκεῖόν
ἐστ᾽ αὐτοῖς ἡ φιλοποσία καὶ τὰ ἐρωτικὰ καὶ πᾶσα ἡ
περὶ τὴν δίαιταν ἄνεσις. διόπερ ἔχουσι τὸ τῆς ὑπο-
δωρίου καλουμένης ἁρμονίας ἦθος· αὕτη γάρ ἐστι,
φησὶν ὁ Ἡρακλείδης, ἣν ἐκάλουν Αἰολίδα, ὡς καὶ

²² add. Kaibel

Phrygian any more than as Lydian; for there are three
scales, inasmuch as there are three types of Greeks: Dorians, Aeolians, and Ionians. There are substantial differ-
ences in the character of these groups: the Spartans cling
more closely to their ancestral customs than the other
Dorians do; the Thessalians—because the origin of the
Aeolian group can be traced back to them—continue to
live much as they always have; but the vast majority of
Ionians have changed their life-style, as a consequence of
their interaction with whichever barbarians have power
over them at the moment. People accordingly came to refer to the melodic tradition the Dorians practiced as the
Doric scale; referred to the scale in which the Aeolians
sang as the Aeolic scale; and called the third scale, in which
they heard the Ionians singing, Ionic. The Doric scale,
then, expresses masculinity and ostentation, and is not
frivolous or light-hearted but fierce and serious, and is
neither elaborate nor complex. The Aeolic character is
haughty and bombastic, as well as a bit conceited, and
these characteristics fit their interest in horse-breeding
and their emphasis on hospitality; they are not treacherous
but dignified and confident, which is why they enjoy drinking, sex, and everything else associated with a relaxed life-
style. Their character thus fits the so-called hypodoric[107]
scale; for according to Heracleides, this is how people referred to the Aeolic scale, as for example Lasus of Her-

---

[107] I.e. "sub-Doric."

Λᾶσος ὁ Ἑρμιονεὺς ἐν τῷ Εἰς τὴν ‹Ἐν›[23] Ἑρμιόνι
Δήμητρα Ὕμνῳ λέγων οὕτως·

> Δάματρα μέλπω Κόραν τε Κλυμένοι' ἄλοχον
> f   μελιβόαν | ὕμνον ἀναγνέων,
> Αἰολίδ' ἂμ βαρύβρομον ἁρμονίαν.

ταῦτα δ' ᾄδουσιν πάντες ὑποδώρια[24] τὰ μέλη. ἐπεὶ οὖν
τὸ μέλος ἐστὶν ὑποδώριον,[25] εἰκότως Αἰολίδα φησὶν
εἶναι τὴν ἁρμονίαν ὁ Λᾶσος. καὶ Πρατίνας δέ πού
φησι·

> μήτε σύντονον δίωκε
> μήτε τὰν ἀνειμέναν
> Μοῦσαν, ἀλλὰ τὰν μέσαν
> νεῶν ἄρουραν Αἰόλιζε τῷ μέλει.

ἐν δὲ τοῖς ἑξῆς σαφέστερόν φησιν·

>   πρέπει τοι
> πᾶσιν ἀοιδολαβράκταις
> Αἰολὶς ἁρμονία. ‖

625 πρότερον μὲν οὖν, ὡς ἔφην, Αἰολίδα αὐτὴν ἐκάλουν,
ὕστερον δ' ὑποδώριον, ὥσπερ ἔνιοί φασιν, ἐν τοῖς
αὐλοῖς τετάχθαι νομίσαντες αὐτὴν ὑπὸ τὴν Δώριον
ἁρμονίαν. ἐμοὶ δὲ δοκεῖ ὁρῶντας αὐτοὺς τὸν ὄγκον καὶ

---

[23] add. Schweighäuser
[24] ὑποδώρια τὰ μέλη A: τὰ μέλη del. Kaibel
[25] ὑποδώριον τὰ μέλη A: τὰ μέλη del. Casaubon

mione in his *Hymn to the Demeter in Hermione* (*PMG* 702),[108] where he says the following:

> I sing of Damater and Cora, the wife of Clymenus,[109]
> lifting up a honey-toned hymn
> in a deep-sounding Aeolic scale.

Everyone sings this passage in the hypodoric scale; since the song is hypodoric, it is unsurprising that Lasus refers to the scale as Aeolic. Pratinas as well (*PMG* 712a) says somewhere:

> Do not pursue an intense
> Muse or the one who is
> relaxed; but as you plow, Aeolize
> the center of the field in your song.

And in the section immediately after this he puts it more clearly (*PMG* 712b):

> The Aeolic scale,
> I assure you, is appropriate for anyone
> who is greedy for songs.

Previously, then, as I said, they referred to this as the Aeolic scale, but later as hypodoric, according to some authorities because they believed that it was pitched lower than (*hupo*) the Doric scale on the pipes. But in my opin-

---

[108] The first verse is quoted also at 10.455d, where Athenaeus (again citing Heracleides of Pontus) claims that the entire poem was asigmatic.

[109] Literally "the Famous One" (i.e. Hades).

τὸ προσποίημα τῆς καλοκἀγαθίας ἐν τοῖς τῆς ἁρμονίας ἤθεσιν Δώριον μὲν αὐτὴν οὐ νομίζειν, προσεμ-
φερῆ δέ πως ἐκείνῃ. διόπερ ὑποδώριον ἐκάλεσαν, ὡς
τὸ προσεμφερὲς τῷ λευκῷ ὑπόλευκον καὶ τὸ μὴ γλυκὺ
μὲν ἐγγὺς δὲ τούτου λέγομεν ὑπόγλυκυ· οὕτως καὶ
b   ὑποδώριον τὸ μὴ πάνυ | Δώριον. ἑξῆς ἐπισκεψώμεθα
τὸ τῶν Μιλησίων ἦθος, ὃ διαφαίνουσιν οἱ Ἴωνες, ἐπὶ
ταῖς τῶν σωμάτων εὐεξίαις βρενθυόμενοι καὶ θυμοῦ
πλήρεις, δυσκατάλλακτοι, φιλόνεικοι, οὐδὲν φιλάν-
θρωπον οὐδ᾽ ἱλαρὸν ἐνδιδόντες, ἀστοργίαν ⟨δὲ⟩[26] καὶ
σκληρότητα ἐν τοῖς ἤθεσιν ἐμφανίζοντες. διόπερ οὐδὲ
τὸ τῆς Ἰαστὶ γένος[27] οὔτ᾽ ἀνθηρὸν οὔτε ἱλαρόν ἐστιν,
ἀλλὰ αὐστηρὸν καὶ σκληρόν, ὄγκον δ᾽ ἔχον οὐκ ἀγεν-
νῆ· διὸ καὶ τῇ τραγῳδίᾳ προσφιλὴς ἡ ἁρμονία. τὰ δὲ
τῶν νῦν Ἰώνων ἤθη τρυφερώτερα καὶ πολὺ παραλ-
c   λάττον τὸ | τῆς ἁρμονίας ἦθος. φασὶ δὲ Πύθερμον τὸν
Τήιον ἐν τῷ γένει τῆς ἁρμονίας τούτῳ ποιῆσαι σκολιὰ
μέλη, καὶ διὰ τὸ εἶναι τὸν ποιητὴν Ἰωνικὸν Ἰαστὶ
κληθῆναι τὴν ἁρμονίαν. οὗτός ἐστι Πύθερμος οὗ μνημονεύει Ἀνάνιος ἢ Ἱππῶναξ ἐν τοῖς Ἰάμβοις· ⟨ . . .
καὶ⟩[28] ἐν ἄλλῳ οὕτως·

χρυσὸν λέγει Πύθερμος ὡς οὐδὲν τἆλλα.

λέγει δ᾽ οὕτως ὁ Πύθερμος·

26 add. Kaibel
27 γένος ἁρμονίας ACE: ἁρμονίας del. Olson
28 add. Kaibel

160

ion they saw the haughtiness and false nobility characteristic of the scale, and regarded it not as Doric but as somehow similar to Doric. They accordingly referred to it as hypodoric, in the same way that we refer to the color that resembles white (*leukon*) as *hupoleukon*, and to something that is not sweet (*gluku*) but almost is as *hupogluku*. So too that which is not precisely Doric is hypodoric. Let us next consider the character of the Milesians, which the Ionians illustrate by acting proud of their fine physiques; being high-spirited, difficult to bring to terms, and quarrelsome; displaying neither kindness nor good humor; and exhibiting cold, harsh behavior instead. This is why the Ionic type is neither exuberant nor cheerful, but harsh and austere, and features a rather noble dignity; as a consequence, the scale is particularly well-suited to tragedy. The behavior of today's Ionians, however, is more effeminate, and the character of their scale is considerably different. People say that Pythermus of Teos composed lyric skolia in this sort of scale, and that because the poet was an Ionian, the scale came to be referred to as Ionic. This is the Pythermus mentioned by Ananius (fr. 2 West²) or Hipponax in his *Iambs* (fr. spurium 218 Degani): . . . ¹¹⁰ Also in another passage, as follows:

> Pythermus talks about gold as if nothing else
> mattered.

Pythermus says the following (*PMG* 910):

---

110 The quotation has fallen out of the text.

οὐδὲν ἦν ἄρα τἆλλα πλὴν ⟨ὁ⟩ χρυσός.

οὐκοῦν καὶ κατὰ τοῦτον τὸν λόγον πιθανόν ἐστι τὸν
d Πύθερμον ἐκεῖθεν ὄντα ποιήσασθαι τὴν | ἀγωγὴν τῶν
μελῶν ἁρμόττουσαν τοῖς ἤθεσι τῶν Ἰώνων· διόπερ
ὑπολαμβάνω οὐχ ἁρμονίαν εἶναι τὴν Ἰαστί, τρόπον
δέ τινα θαυμαστὸν σχήματος ἁρμονίας. καταφρονη-
τέον οὖν τῶν τὰς μὲν κατ᾽ εἶδος διαφορὰς οὐ δυναμέ-
νων θεωρεῖν, ἐπακολουθούντων δὲ τῇ τῶν φθόγγων
ὀξύτητι καὶ βαρύτητι καὶ τιθεμένων ὑπερμιξολύδιον
ἁρμονίαν καὶ πάλιν ὑπὲρ ταύτης ἄλλην. οὐχ ὁρῶ γὰρ
οὐδὲ τὴν ὑπερφρύγιον ἴδιον ἔχουσαν ἦθος· καίτοι
e τινές φασιν ἄλλην ἐξευρηκέναι | καινὴν ἁρμονίαν
ὑποφρύγιον. δεῖ δὲ τὴν ἁρμονίαν εἶδος ἔχειν ἤθους ἢ
πάθους, καθάπερ ἡ Λοκριστί· ταύτῃ γὰρ ἔνιοι τῶν
γενομένων κατὰ Σιμωνίδην καὶ Πίνδαρον ἐχρήσαντό
ποτε, καὶ πάλιν κατεφρονήθη. τρεῖς οὖν αὗται, καθάπερ ἐξ ἀρχῆς εἴπομεν εἶναι ἁρμονίας, ὅσα καὶ τὰ
ἔθνη. τὴν δὲ Φρυγιστὶ καὶ τὴν Λυδιστὶ παρὰ τῶν
βαρβάρων οὔσας γνωσθῆναι τοῖς Ἕλλησιν ἀπὸ τῶν
σὺν Πέλοπι κατελθόντων εἰς τὴν Πελοπόννησον Φρυ-
γῶν καὶ Λυδῶν· Λυδοὶ μὲν γὰρ αὐτῷ συνηκολούθησαν |
f διὰ τὸ τὴν Σίπυλον εἶναι τῆς Λυδίας, Φρύγες δὲ οὐχ
ὅτι ὁμοτέρμονες τοῖς Λυδοῖς εἰσιν, ἀλλ᾽ ὅτι καὶ αὐτῶν
ἦρχεν ὁ Τάνταλος. ἴδοις δ᾽ ἂν καὶ τῆς Πελοποννήσου

---

[111] Both poets belong to the end of the 6th and the first half of
the 5th centuries BCE.

It appears that nothing actually matters except gold.

On the basis of this remark, then, it is believable that because Pythermus was from there, he produced a style of lyric poetry that fit the Ionian character. I accordingly suspect that the scale in question was not Ionic but an unusual scale of some other type. We should accordingly ignore individuals who are unable to see any difference among the types, and who rely instead on how high or low the sounds are pitched, and who postulate the existence of a hypermixolydian scale, and of yet another higher than it. For I do not see that the hyperphrygian has a distinctive character; and indeed, some authorities claim to have discovered yet another new scale, the hypophrygian. But a scale must have a particular character or effect, as the Locrian scale does; for some contemporaries of Simonides and Pindar[111] employed this at one point, and then afterward it fell out of favor again. There are thus these three scales, as I noted at the beginning (14.624c), and they match the number of types of Greeks. As for the Phrygian and Lydian scales, which originated with the barbarians, the Greeks learned about them from the Phrygians and Lydians who moved down into the Peloponnese along with Pelops;[112] for Lydians accompanied him, on account of the fact that Sipylus[113] was a Lydian city, while the Phrygians did so not because they shared a border with the Lydians, but because Tantalus was their king. You can see large mounds everywhere in the Peloponnese, but especially in Lacedaemon,

[112] Sc. when he married Hippodameia and became king of Elis.   [113] The city of Pelops' father, Tantalus, and thus originally of Pelops himself.

παντα χοῦ, μάλιστα δὲ ἐν Λακεδαίμονι χώματα μεγά-
λα, ἃ καλοῦσι τάφους τῶν μετὰ Πέλοπος Φρυγῶν.
μαθεῖν οὖν τὰς ἁρμονίας ταύτας τοὺς Ἕλληνας παρὰ
τούτων, διὸ καὶ Τελέστης ὁ Σελινούντιός φησιν· ‖

626   πρῶτοι παρὰ κρατῆρας Ἑλλάνων ἐν αὐλοῖς
     συνοπαδοὶ Πέλοπος Ματρὸς ὀρείας
     Φρύγιον ἄεισαν νόμον·
     τοὶ δ᾽ ὀξύφωνοις πηκτίδων ψαλμοῖς κρέκον
     Λύδιον ὕμνον.

Οὐ παραληπτέον δὲ τὴν μουσικήν, φησὶν Πολύβιος ὁ Μεγαλοπολίτης, ὡς Ἔφορος ἱστορεῖ, ἐπὶ
ἀπάτῃ καὶ γοητείᾳ παρεισῆχθαι τοῖς ἀνθρώποις, οὐδὲ
b τοὺς παλαιοὺς | Κρητῶν καὶ Λακεδαιμονίων αὐλὸν καὶ
ῥυθμὸν εἰς τὸν πόλεμον ἀντὶ σάλπιγγος εἰκῇ νομιστέον εἰσαγαγεῖν, οὐδὲ τοὺς πρώτους Ἀρκάδων εἰς
τὴν ὅλην πολιτείαν τὴν μουσικὴν παραλαβεῖν, ὥστε
μὴ μόνον παισὶν ἀλλὰ καὶ νεανίσκοις[29] γενομένοις
ἕως τριάκοντα ἐτῶν κατ᾽ ἀνάγκην σύντροφον ποιεῖν
αὐτήν, τἆλλα τοῖς βίοις ὄντας αὐστηροτάτους. παρὰ
γοῦν μόνοις Ἀρκάσιν οἱ παῖδες ἐκ νηπίων ᾄδειν
ἐθίζονται κατὰ νόμον τοὺς ὕμνους καὶ παιᾶνας, οἷς
ἕκαστοι κατὰ τὰ πάτρια τοὺς ἐπιχωρίους ἥρωας καὶ
θεοὺς ὑμνοῦσι. μετὰ δὲ ταῦτα τοὺς Τιμοθέου καὶ
Φιλοξένου νόμους μανθάνοντες χορεύουσι κατ᾽ ἐνι-

---

[29] ἐν παισὶν ἀλλὰ καὶ ἐν νεανίσκοις A; but the traditional
text of Polybius omits the prepositions.

which people identify as tombs of the Phrygians who accompanied Pelops. The Greeks, then, learned these scales from them, which is why Telestes of Selinus (*PMG* 810) says:

> The first to sing a Phrygian tune in honor of the
> Mountain Mother
> beside the Greeks' mixing-bowls as the flutes played
> were Pelops' companions;
> they struck up a Lydian hymn with the high-pitched
> vibrations of harps.

Polybius of Megalopolis (4.20.5–21.9) says that we should reject Ephorus' (*FGrH* 70 F 8) claim that music was introduced to human beings to trick and deceive them. Nor should we believe that the ancient inhabitants of Crete and Lacedaemon introduced rhythmic movements coordinated with pipes into war in place of trumpets without any reason, or that the earliest Arcadians lacked a motivation for incorporating music into every aspect of their society, forcing not just their boys but their young men up to the age of 30 to immerse themselves in it, despite the fact that they otherwise led extraordinarily austere lives. It is only Arcadian boys, at any rate, who are required by law to become accustomed from the time they are toddlers to singing their hymns and paeans, which they universally use to offer praise to the local heroes and gods in their traditional fashion. After these they learn the tunes of Timotheus and Philoxenus, and they dance every year in their

ATHENAEUS

c   αὐτὸν τοῖς Διονυσιακοῖς αὐληταῖς | ἐν τοῖς θεάτροις,
οἱ μὲν οὖν παῖδες τοὺς παιδικοὺς ἀγῶνας, οἱ δὲ νεα-
νίσκοι τοὺς τῶν ἀνδρῶν. καὶ παρ᾽ ὅλον δὲ τὸν βίον ἐν
ταῖς συνουσίαις ταῖς κοιναῖς οὐχ ‹οὕτω ποιοῦνται τὰς
ἀγωγὰς›³⁰ διὰ τῶν ἐπεισάκτων ἀκροαμάτων ὡς δι᾽
αὐτῶν, ἀνὰ μέρος ᾄδειν ἀλλήλοις προστάττοντες. καὶ
τῶν μὲν ἄλλων μαθημάτων ἀρνηθῆναί τι μὴ εἰδέναι
οὐδενὶ αὐτῶν αἰσχρόν ἐστιν, τὸ δὲ ᾄδειν ἀποτρί-
βεσθαι αἰσχρὸν παρ᾽ αὐτοῖς νομίζεται. καὶ μὴν ἐμβα-
τήρια μετ᾽ αὐλοῦ καὶ τάξεως ἀσκοῦντες, ἔτι δὲ
ὀρχήσεις ἐκπονοῦντες μετὰ κοινῆς ἐπιστροφῆς καὶ
d   δαπάνης κατ᾽ | ἐνιαυτὸν ἐν τοῖς θεάτροις ἐπιδείκνυν-
ται. ταῦτ᾽ οὖν αὐτοὺς εἴθισαν οἱ παλαιοὶ οὐ τρυφῆς
καὶ περιουσίας χάριν, ἀλλὰ θεωροῦντες τὴν ἑκάστου
κατὰ τὸν βίον σκληρότητα καὶ τὴν τῶν ἠθῶν αὐστη-
ρίαν, ἥτις αὐτοῖς παρέπεται διὰ τὴν τοῦ περιέχοντος
ψυχρότητα καὶ στυγνότητα τὴν κατὰ ‹τὸ›³¹ πλεῖστον
ἐν τοῖς τόποις ὑπάρχουσαν, οἷς καὶ συνεξομοιοῦσθαι
πεφύκαμεν πάντες ἄνθρωποι· διὸ καὶ κατὰ τὰς ἐθνικὰς
διαστάσεις πλεῖστον ἀλλήλων διαφέρομεν ἤθεσι καὶ
μορφαῖς καὶ χρώμασιν. πρὸς δὲ τούτοις συνόδους
e   κοινὰς καὶ θυσίας ἀνδράσι καὶ | γυναιξὶ κατείθισαν,
ἔτι δὲ χοροὺς παρθένων ὁμοῦ καὶ παίδων, σπεύδοντες
τὸ τῆς φύσεως ἀτέραμνον διὰ τῆς τῶν ἐθισμῶν κατα-
σκευῆς ἐξημεροῦν καὶ πραΰνειν. ὧν Κυναιθεῖς ὀλιγω-

³⁰ add. Kaibel e Polybio
³¹ add. Kaibel e Polybio

theaters along with the Dionysiac pipe-players;[114] the boys
dance in their own contests, while the young men dance in
the men's contests. And at no point in their lives do they or-
ganize matters at their public festivals using entertainers
imported from elsewhere, but they rely instead on their
own abilities, requiring one another to take turns singing.
None of them is embarrassed to confess ignorance of any
other subject; but they do consider a lack of musical training something to be ashamed of. They practice marching-
songs drawn up in lines and accompanied by pipes, and
they also work hard on their dancing and put on shows in
their theaters every year with public support and funding.
The ancients accustomed themselves to practices of this
sort, then, not out of an interest in luxury and excess, but
because they knew that individual lives were difficult, and
recognized the harshness of their manners, which dogged
them on account of the frigidity of their environment and
the general gloominess that prevailed in their territory,
to both of which human beings have a universal natural
tendency to assimilate themselves; this is why we differ
widely from one another along ethnic lines in our behavior,
physical build, and skin-color. In addition, they made it
their custom to have public gatherings and sacrifices for
men and women, as well as dances for both girls and boys,
since they were eager to use the practices they devised to
tame and calm their natural rigidity. The inhabitants of
Cynaetha ultimately came to feel contempt for such prac-

114 I.e. those who play to accompany events at Dionysiac festivals, such as the dithyrambic dance-competitions referred to
here.

ρήσαντες εἰς τέλος, καίτοι σκληρότατον παρὰ πολὺ
τῆς Ἀρκαδίας ὁμοῦ τῷ τόπῳ καὶ τὸν ἀέρα ἔχοντες,
πρὸς μὲν αὐτὰς τὰς ἐν ἀλλήλοις παρατριβὰς καὶ
φιλοτιμίας ὁρμήσαντες τέλος ἀπεθηριώθησαν οὕτως
ὡς μέγιστα ἀσεβήματα παρὰ μόνοις αὐτοῖς γίνεσθαι.
f καθ᾽ οὓς δὲ καιροὺς τὴν μεγάλην σφαγὴν | ἐποι-
ήσαντο, εἰς ἅς ποτε πόλεις Ἀρκαδικὰς κατὰ τὴν
δίοδον εἰσῆλθον, οἱ μὲν ἄλλοι παραχρῆμα πάντες
αὐτοὺς ἐξεκήρυξαν, Μαντινεῖς δὲ καὶ μετὰ τὴν ἀπαλ-
λαγὴν αὐτῶν καθαρμὸν τῆς πόλεως ἐποιήσαντο
σφάγια περιαγαγόντες κύκλῳ τῆς χώρας ἁπάσης.

Ἀγίας δ᾽ ὁ μουσικὸς ἔφη τὸν στύρακα τὸν ἐν ταῖς
ὀρχήστραις θυμιώμενον τοῖς Διονυσίοις Φρύγιον ποιεῖν ὀδμὴν τοῖς αἰσθανομένοις.

Τὸ δ᾽ ἀρχαῖον ἡ μουσικὴ ἐπ᾽ ἀνδρείαν προτροπὴ
627 ἦν. ‖ Ἀλκαῖος γοῦν ὁ ποιητής, εἴ τις καὶ ἄλλος
μουσικώτατος γενόμενος, πρότερα τῶν κατὰ ποιητικὴν τὰ κατὰ τὴν ἀνδρείαν τίθεται, μᾶλλον τοῦ δέον-
τος πολεμικὸς γενόμενος. διὸ καὶ ἐπὶ τοῖς τοιούτοις
σεμνυνόμενός φησιν·

μαρμαίρει δὲ μέγας δόμος
    χάλκῳ, παῖσα δ᾽ Ἄρη κεκόσμηται στέγα
λάμπραισιν κυνίαισι, κὰτ
    τᾶν λεύκοι κατέπερθεν ἵππιοι λόφοι
νεύοισιν, κεφάλαισιν ἄν-
b   δρων ἀγάλματα· | χάλκιαι δὲ πασσάλοις

tices, even though they occupy far and away the most rugged part of Arcadia, as far as both topography and climate are concerned; they plunged into open conflict and rivalry with one another, and in the end were so brutalized that the most appalling acts of impiety occurred exclusively in their country. At the time they were carrying out their enormous massacre,[115] whenever they entered other Arcadian cities in the course of their travels, everyone immediately issued a public proclamation expelling them, and after they left, the Mantineans purified their city by carrying sacrificial victims around the perimeter of the entire area.

Agias (fr. 4, *FHG* iv.293), who wrote on music, said that the storax-gum burned in the dancing-areas at Dionysiac festivals produced a Phrygian scent for anyone who caught a whiff of it.

In the old days, music encouraged bravery. The poet Alcaeus, for example, who was as devoted to music as anyone ever has been, ranks brave deeds ahead of poetic accomplishments, but was more devoted to war than necessary. This is why he expresses pride in matters of this sort and says (fr. 140):

> The huge house shines
>   with bronze; the entire place has been decorated
>   by Ares
> with gleaming helmets, and white
>   crests of horse-hair nod from
> their tops, ornaments for
>   men's heads. Brilliant bronze

---

[115] The events in question probably took place sometime in the 230s BCE.

κρύπτοισιν περικείμεναι
  λάμπραι κνάμιδες, ἕρκος ἰσχύρω βέλεος·
θόρρακές τε νέω λίνω,
  κόιλαί τε κὰτ ἄσπιδες βεβλήμεναι·
πὰρ δὲ Χαλκίδικαι σπάθαι,
  πὰρ δὲ ζώματα πόλλα καὶ κυπάσσιδες.
τῶν οὐκ ἔστι λάθεσθ' ἐπεὶ
  δὴ πρώτιστ' ὑπὰ τῶργον ἔσταμεν τόδε.

καίτοι μᾶλλον ἴσως ἥρμοττε τὴν οἰκίαν πλήρη εἶναι
μουσικῶν ὀργάνων. ἀλλ' οἱ παλαιοὶ τὴν ἀνδρείαν
c ὑπελάμβανον | εἶναι μεγίστην τῶν πολιτικῶν ἀρετῶν,
καὶ ταύτῃ τὰ πολλὰ προσνέμειν < . . . > οὐ τοῖς
ἄλλοις. Ἀρχίλοχος γοῦν ἀγαθὸς ὢν ποιητὴς πρῶτον
ἐκαυχήσατο τῷ δύνασθαι μετέχειν τῶν πολιτικῶν
ἀγώνων, δεύτερον δὲ ἐμνήσθη τῶν περὶ τὴν ποιητικὴν
ὑπαρχόντων αὐτῷ, λέγων·

εἰμὶ δ' ἐγὼ θεράπων μὲν Ἐνναλίοιο ἄνακτος
  καὶ Μουσέων ἐρατὸν δῶρον ἐπιστάμενος.

ὁμοίως δὲ καὶ Αἰσχύλος τηλικαύτην δόξαν ἔχων διὰ
τὴν ποιητικὴν οὐδὲν ἧττον ἐπὶ τοῦ τάφου ἐπιγραφῆναι |
d ἠξίωσεν μᾶλλον τὴν ἀνδρείαν, ποιήσας·

greaves, a defense against
    powerful missiles, conceal the pegs they hang
      upon.
Likewise breastplates of fresh linen,
    and hollow shields thrown on the floor;
and Chalcidian swords are there,
    and numerous loin-cloths and short tunics.
We cannot forget these objects, now
    that we have undertaken this project.

It might actually have been more appropriate for his house to be full of musical instruments. But the ancients regarded courage as the most important public virtue, and to assign to this the majority . . . rather than to others. Although Archilochus, for example, was a good poet, he boasted first about his ability to participate in political struggles and mentioned his poetic accomplishments second, saying (fr. 1 West²):

I am a servant of Lord Enyalius,[116]
    and I understand the lovely gift of the Muses.

So too, even though Aeschylus had a substantial reputation for his poetry, he nonetheless preferred to have a reference to his bravery inscribed on his tomb, and he wrote (test. 162 = *FGE* 478–9):[117]

[116] Sometimes identified with Ares, sometimes a separate figure.

[117] Two additional lines of the epitaph, which identify the tomb as Aeschylus' and place it in Gela in Syracuse, are preserved in the anonymous *Life of Aeschylus* (test. 1.42–3) and at Plu. *Mor.* 604e–f.

ἀλκὴν δ᾽ εὐδόκιμον Μαραθώνιον ἄλσος ἂν εἴποι
καὶ βαθυχαιτήεις Μῆδος ἐπιστάμενος.

διόπερ καὶ οἱ ἀνδρειότατοι Λακεδαιμόνιοι μετ᾽ αὐλῶν
στρατεύονται, Κρῆτες δὲ μετὰ λύρας, μετὰ δὲ συρίγ-
γων καὶ αὐλῶν Λυδοί, ὡς Ἡρόδοτος ἱστορεῖ. πολλοὶ
δὲ καὶ τῶν βαρβάρων τὰς ἐπικηρυκείας ποιοῦνται μετ᾽
αὐλῶν καὶ κιθάρας, καταπραΰνοντες τῶν ἐναντίων τὰς
e ψυχάς. Θεόπομπος δ᾽ ἐν | τεσσαρακοστῇ ἕκτῃ τῶν
Ἱστοριῶν, Γέται, φησί, κιθάρας ἔχοντες καὶ κιθαρί-
ζοντες τὰς ἐπικηρυκείας ποιοῦνται. ὅθεν ἔοικεν καὶ
Ὅμηρος διατηρῶν τὴν ἀρχαίαν τῶν Ἑλλήνων κατά-
στασιν λέγειν·

φόρμιγγός θ᾽, ἣν δαιτὶ θεοὶ ποίησαν ἑταίρην,[32]

ὡς καὶ τοῖς εὐωχουμένοις χρησίμης οὔσης τῆς
τέχνης. ἦν δ᾽ ὡς ἔοικε τοῦτο νενομισμένον, πρῶτον
μὲν ὅπως ἕκαστος τῶν εἰς μέθην καὶ πλήρωσιν ὡρμη-
μένων ἰατρὸν λαμβάνῃ τῆς ὕβρεως καὶ τῆς ἀκοσμίας
τὴν μουσικήν, εἶθ᾽ ὅτι τὴν αὐθάδειαν πραΰνει· περιαι-
f ρουμένη | γὰρ τὴν στυγνότητα ποιεῖ πρᾳότητα καὶ
χαρὰν ἐλευθέριον, ὅθεν καὶ Ὅμηρος εἰσήγαγε τοὺς

[32] A combination of *Od.* 8.99 φόρμιγγός θ᾽, ἣ δαιτὶ
συνήορός ἐστι θαλείῃ and 17.270–1 φόρμιγξ / ἠπύει, ἣν ἄρα
δαιτὶ θεοὶ ποίησαν ἑταίρην.

[118] A reference to the famous battle of 490 BCE, when the
Athenians defeated a large Persian expeditionary force. Aeschy-

The grove at Marathon could describe the might that
    won me a fine reputation,
        as could the long-haired Mede who came to know
            it.[118]

This[119] is why the Spartans, who are extremely courageous,
go into battle accompanied by pipes, the Cretans accompanied by the lyre, and the Lydians accompanied by pan-
pipes and pipes, according to Herodotus (1.17.1). Many
barbarian peoples also arrange for their embassies to be
accompanied by pipes and lyres, as a way of calming their
enemies' tempers. Theopompus says in Book XLVI of his
History (*FGrH* 115 F 216): When the Getae enter into
diplomatic negotiations, they have lyres in their hands and
play them. Homer thus apparently preserves the ancient
situation in Greece when he says:

and the lyre, which the gods made to accompany
    feasts,[120]

since this skill is useful for people attending a banquet.
This was apparently the custom first in order that anyone
who wanted to get drunk and stuff himself would have music as a physician to treat his reckless, disorderly behavior,
and next because it tempers surliness; for when it strips off
one's gloom, it produces gentleness and the happiness that
befits a free person, which is why Homer brought the gods

lus' brother Cynegirus died in the battle, trying to capture a Persian ship (A. test. 16–48).

119 The fact that music can be used to encourage bravery
(14.626f). For what follows, cf. 12.517a–b.

120 A garbled combination of *Od*. 8.99 and 17.270–1; see critical n.

θεοὺς χρωμένους ἐν τοῖς πρώτοις τῆς Ἰλιάδος τῇ
μουσικῇ. μετὰ γὰρ τὴν περὶ τὸν Ἀχιλλέα φιλοτιμίαν
διετέλουν[33] ἀκροώμενοι

> φόρμιγγος περικαλλέος, ἣν ἔχ᾽ Ἀπόλλων,
> Μουσάων,[34] αἳ ἄειδον ἀμειβόμεναι ὀπὶ καλῇ·

παύσασθαι γὰρ ἔδει τὰ νείκη καὶ τὴν στάσιν, καθάπερ ἐλέγομεν. ἐοίκασιν οὖν οἱ πολλοὶ τὴν ἐπιστήμην
ἀποδιδόναι ταῖς συνουσίαις ἐπανορθώσεως χάριν καὶ
ὠφελείας. ἀλλὰ μὴν οἱ ἀρχαῖοι καὶ περιέλαβον ἔθεσι
628 καὶ νόμοις τοὺς τῶν θεῶν ὕμνους ‖ ᾄδειν ἅπαντας ἐν
ταῖς ἑστιάσεσιν, ὅπως καὶ διὰ τούτων τηρῆται τὸ
καλὸν καὶ σωφρονικὸν ἡμῶν· ἐναρμονίων γὰρ ὄντων
τῶν ᾀσμάτων προσγινόμενος ὁ τῶν θεῶν λόγος ἀπο-
σεμνύνει τὸν ἑκάστων τρόπον. Φιλόχορος δέ φησιν ὡς
οἱ παλαιοὶ[35] οὐκ αἰεὶ διθυραμβοῦσιν, ἀλλ᾽ ὅταν σπέν-
b δωσι, τὸν μὲν Διόνυσον ἐν οἴνῳ | καὶ μέθῃ, τὸν δ᾽
Ἀπόλλωνα μεθ᾽ ἡσυχίας καὶ τάξεως μέλποντες. Ἀρχίλοχος γοῦν φησιν·

> ὡς Διωνύσου ἄνακτος καλὸν ἐξάρξαι μέλος
> οἶδα διθύραμβον οἴνῳ συγκεραυνωθεὶς φρένας.

καὶ Ἐπίχαρμος δ᾽ ἐν Φιλοκτήτῃ ἔφη·

> οὐκ ἔστι διθύραμβος, ὅκχ᾽ ὕδωρ πίῃς.

---

[33] μετὰ δὲ τὴν . . . διετέλουν γὰρ A: corr. Kaibel
[34] The traditional text of Homer has Μουσάων θ᾽.
[35] παλαιοὶ σπένδοντες A: παλαιοὶ ἔσπενδον CE: σπένδοντες del. Wilamowitz

on at the beginning of the *Iliad* enjoying music. For after their argument about Achilleus, they spend their time listening (1.603–4)

> to a beautiful lyre, which Apollo was holding,
> that belonged to the Muses, who sang responsively
>   with their lovely voices;

since their quarrels and division needed to be brought to an end, as I was saying. Most people thus appear to incorporate this knowledge into social occasions to correct and improve them. The ancients, in fact, enshrined in their customs and rules that everyone who attended their feasts was to sing the hymns that honor the gods, the idea being that these would preserve our sense of what is good and decent; for when songs are sung in harmony, the remarks about the gods that accompany them lend dignity to everyone's behavior. Philochorus (*FGrH* 328 F 172) claims that the ancients did not perform dithyrambs on all occasions but only when pouring libations, and that they sang about Dionysus when they were drinking wine and getting drunk, but about Apollo in calm, orderly situations. Archilochus (fr. 120 West[2]), at any rate, says:

> Since I know how to initiate the dithyramb, the
>   beautiful song devoted to
> King Dionysus, when my mind has been lightning-
>   blasted with wine.

So too Epicharmus said in *Philoctetes* (fr. 131):

> It's not a dithyramb, when you drink water!

ATHENAEUS

ὅτι μὲν οὖν οὐχ ἡδονῆς χάριν ἐπιπολαίου καὶ δημο-
τικῆς ἡ μουσικὴ προῆλθεν κατ᾽ ἀρχὰς εἰς τὰς ἑστιάσεις, ὥσπερ ἔνιοι νομίζουσιν, φανερὸν ἐκ τῶν εἰρημένων. Λακεδαιμόνιοι δ᾽ ὅτι μὲν ἐμάνθανον τὴν
μουσικὴν οὐδὲ λέγουσιν· ὅτι δὲ κρίνειν δύνανται
καλῶς τὴν τέχνην ὁμολογεῖται παρ᾽ αὐτῶν, καί φασιν
τρὶς ἤδη σεσωκέναι διαφθειρομένην αὐτήν. καὶ πρὸς
c γυμνασίαν δὲ καὶ ὀξύτητα | διανοίας συμβάλλεται ἡ
μουσική· διὸ καὶ τῶν Ἑλλήνων ἕκαστοι καὶ τῶν βαρβάρων οἱ γινωσκόμενοι τυγχάνουσιν χρώμενοι. οὐ
κακῶς δ᾽ ἔλεγον οἱ περὶ Δάμωνα τὸν Ἀθηναῖον ὅτι καὶ
τὰς ᾠδὰς καὶ τὰς ὀρχήσεις ἀνάγκη γίνεσθαι κινου-
μένης πως τῆς ψυχῆς· καὶ αἱ μὲν ἐλευθέριοι καὶ καλαὶ
ποιοῦσι τοιαύτας, αἱ δ᾽ ἐναντίαι τὰς ἐναντίας. ὅθεν καὶ
τὸ Κλεοσθένους τοῦ Σικυωνίων τυράννου χαρίεν καὶ
σημεῖον διανοίας πεπαιδευμένης· ἰδὼν γάρ, ὥς φασι,
d φορτικῶς ὀρχησάμενον ἕνα τῶν τῆς θυγατρὸς | μνη-
στήρων (Ἱπποκλείδης δ᾽ ἦν ὁ Ἀθηναῖος) ἀπωρχῆσθαι
τὸν γάμον αὐτὸν ἔφησεν, νομίζων ὡς ἔοικεν καὶ τὴν
ψυχὴν τἀνδρὸς εἶναι τοιαύτην. καὶ γὰρ ἐν ὀρχήσει καὶ
πορείᾳ καλὸν μὲν εὐσχημοσύνη καὶ κόσμος, αἰσχρὸν
δὲ ἀταξία καὶ τὸ φορτικόν. διὰ τοῦτο γὰρ καὶ ἐξ
ἀρχῆς συνέταττον οἱ ποιηταὶ τοῖς ἐλευθέροις τὰς
ὀρχήσεις καὶ ἐχρῶντο τοῖς σχήμασι σημείοις μόνον

---

121 Casaubon took this to be a reference to the careers of
Terpander, Timotheus, and Phrynis.

176

That music was not originally introduced into feasts for the sake of superficial pleasure catering to conventional tastes, as some authorities believe, is apparent from what has been said. The Spartans do not claim to have invested any time in learning about music; but they generally maintain that they are good judges of the art, and they allege that they have rescued it three times when it was in decline.[121] Music also contributes to the training and sharpening of the intellect; this is why all the Greek and barbarian peoples known to us use it. Damon of Athens[122] (37 B 6 D–K) was accordingly quite right to say that songs and dances can only be produced when the soul is somehow set in motion; free, beautiful souls produce songs and dances that resemble them in that respect, and *vice versa*. Hence the witty remark of Cleosthenes, the tyrant of Sicyon, which shows that he had an educated intellect; for they say that when he saw one of his daughters' suitors—specifically Hippocleides of Athens—doing a vulgar dance, he commented that the man had danced away his marriage,[123] since he thought that his soul most likely matched his actions. For grace and dignity in how a person dances and carries himself are in fact attractive, whereas clumsiness and low-class behavior are embarrassing. This is why the poets from the very beginning designed their dances for free people and used the movements only to illustrate the

[122] Or perhaps "The followers/students of Damon of Athens." Damon (mid-5th century BCE) is *PAA* 301540.

[123] The story comes from Hdt. 6.129, where the tyrant's name is given as Cleisthenes (tyrant of Sicyon *c*.600–570 BCE). According to Herodotus, the rejected suitor had the last word: "Hippocleides could not care less." Hippocleides is *PAA* 538230.

τῶν ᾀδομένων, τηροῦντες αἰεὶ τὸ εὐγενὲς καὶ ἀνδρῶδες
ἐπ᾽ αὐτῶν, ὅθεν καὶ ὑπορχήματα τὰ τοιαῦτα προσηγό-
e ρευον. εἰ δέ τις ἀμέτρως | διαθείη τὴν σχηματοποιίαν
καὶ ταῖς ᾠδαῖς ἐπιτυγχάνων μηδὲν λέγοι κατὰ τὴν
ὄρχησιν, οὗτος δ᾽ ἦν ἀδόκιμος. διὸ καὶ Ἀριστοφάνης
ἢ Πλάτων ἐν ταῖς Σκευαῖς, ὡς Χαμαιλέων φησίν,
εἴρηκεν οὕτως·

> ὥστ᾽ εἴ τις ὀρχοῖτ᾽ εὖ, θέαμ᾽ ἦν· νῦν δὲ δρῶσιν
> οὐδέν,
> ἀλλ᾽ ὥσπερ ἀπόπληκτοι στάδην ἑστῶτες
> ὠρύονται.

ἦν γὰρ τὸ τῆς ὀρχήσεως γένος τῆς ἐν τοῖς χοροῖς
εὔσχημον τότε καὶ μεγαλοπρεπὲς καὶ ὡσανεὶ τὰς ἐν
τοῖς ὅπλοις κινήσεις ἀπομιμούμενον. ὅθεν καὶ Σω-
f κράτης ἐν τοῖς ποιήμασιν τοὺς κάλλιστα | χορεύοντας
ἀρίστους φησὶν εἶναι τὰ πολέμια λέγων οὕτως·

> οἳ δὲ χοροῖς κάλλιστα θεοὺς τιμῶσιν, ἄριστοι
> ἐν πολέμῳ.

σχεδὸν γὰρ ὥσπερ ἐξοπλισία τις ἦν ἡ χορεία καὶ
ἐπίδειξις οὐ μόνον τῆς λοιπῆς εὐταξίας, ἀλλὰ καὶ τῆς
τῶν σωμάτων ἐπιμελείας. ‖

---

124 Apparently taken here to mean "(compositions) in which
the dancing (orchêsis) takes a subordinate (hupo) part"; cf.
14.631c.

words that were sung, making a consistent effort to preserve the nobility and manliness associated with them, as a
consequence of which they referred to compositions of
this sort as *huporchêmata*.[124] But if someone's choreogra-
phy was excessive, or if, when it came to the songs, his lyrics were unconnected to the dance-steps, he got a bad reputation. This is why Aristophanes or Plato (fr. 138) in his
Equipment,[125] according to Chamaeleon (fr. 42 Wehrli),
says the following:

> So that if someone was a good dancer, it was worth
>   watching. But nowadays they're worthless,
> and they just stand in one spot and howl, as if they
>   were having a seizure.

For the type of dancing in which the choruses engaged in
those days was graceful and impressive, and imitated, as it
were, the movements of men wearing armor. This is why
Socrates (fr. 3 West[2]) in his poetry claims that the best
dancers are also the best warriors, putting it as follows:[126]

> Those who show the gods the finest honors in
>   choruses are the best
> in war.

For choral dance represented something approaching military drill, and was a way of demonstrating not just good
discipline generally but specifically the care they took of
their bodies.

[125] The play is elsewhere consistently attributed to Plato
Comicus rather than to Aristophanes.

[126] It is unclear whether these are both hexameters or part of
an elegiac couplet.

629 Ἀμφίων δ᾽ ὁ Θεσπιεὺς ἐν δευτέρῳ Περὶ τοῦ ἐν
Ἑλικῶνι Μουσείου ἄγεσθαί φησιν ἐν Ἑλικῶνι παίδων
ὀρχήσεις μετὰ σπουδῆς, παρατιθέμενος ἀρχαῖον ἐπί-
γραμμα τόδε·

> ἀμφότερ᾽, ὠρχεύμην τε καὶ ἐν Μώσαις ἐδίδασκον
> ἄνδρας· ὁ δ᾽ αὐλητὰς ἦν Ἄνακος Φιαλεύς.
> εἰμὶ δὲ Βακχιάδας Σικυώνιος. ἦ ῥα θεοῖσι
> ταῖς Σικυῶνι καλὸν τοῦτ᾽ ἀπέκειτο γέρας.

οὐ κακῶς δὲ καὶ Καφισίας ὁ αὐλητής, ἐπιβαλλομένου |
b τινὸς τῶν μαθητῶν αὐλεῖν μέγα καὶ τοῦτο μελετῶντος,
πατάξας εἶπεν οὐκ ἐν τῷ μεγάλῳ τὸ εὖ κείμενον εἶναι,
ἀλλὰ ἐν τῷ εὖ τὸ μέγα. ἐστὶ δὲ καὶ τὰ τῶν ἀρχαίων
δημιουργῶν ἀγάλματα τῆς παλαιᾶς ὀρχήσεως
λείψανα. διὸ καὶ συνέστη τὰ κατὰ τὴν χειρονομίαν
ἐπιμελεστέρως διὰ ταύτην τὴν αἰτίαν· ἐζήτουν γὰρ
κἂν ταύτῃ κινήσεις καλὰς καὶ ἐλευθερίους, ἐν τῷ εὖ τὸ
μέγα περιλαμβάνοντες, καὶ τὰ σχήματα μετέφερον
ἐντεῦθεν εἰς τοὺς χοροὺς, ἐκ δὲ τῶν χορῶν εἰς τὰς
c παλαίστρας. καὶ γὰρ ἐν τῇ μουσικῇ κἂν τῇ | τῶν
σωμάτων ἐπιμελείᾳ περιεποιοῦντο τὴν ἀνδρείαν καὶ
πρὸς τὰς ἐν τοῖς ὅπλοις κινήσεις ἐγυμνάζοντο μετὰ
τῆς ᾠδῆς· ὅθεν ἐκινήθησαν αἱ καλούμεναι πυρρίχαι

---

127 Stephanis #172. Bacchiades (who appears to have erected
a statue of himself in the Muses' sanctuary on Helicon, although
he dedicated it to the Muses of his native city, whom he regarded
as responsible for his success) is Stephanis #510.

Amphion of Thespiae in Book II of *On the Sanctuary of the Muses on Mount Helicon* (*FGrH* 387 F 1) says that boys danced on Helicon and that the celebrations were taken seriously. He cites the following ancient epigram (anon. *FGE* 1844–7):

> I did both—I danced and I trained a men's chorus in
>   the sanctuary
>   of the Muses; Anacus of Phigaleia[127] played the
>   pipes.
> I am Bacchiades of Sicyon. I assuredly set money
>   aside
>   for this fine offering to the goddesses in Sicyon.

The pipe-player Caphisias[128] was entirely justified, when one of his students was trying to play the pipes loudly and was concerned about nothing else, to hit him and say that quality is not defined by volume, but that volume is instead defined by quality. The statues produced by early artists also preserve traces of the ancient style of dance. As a consequence, everything connected with gesture was done more carefully for this reason; for in this area as well they aspired to attractive movements appropriate to free people, and they attempted to incorporate volume in quality, and transferred the postures from there to their dances, and from their dances to their wrestling schools. For the fact is that they acquired courage through their music, as well as through the care they took of their bodies, and they practiced the movements they made when wearing armor to musical accompaniment. This is the origin of the so-

---

[128] Stephanis #1387. A very similar anecdote is recorded at D.L. 7.21, where Zeno is said to have repeated it.

καὶ πᾶς ὁ τοιοῦτος τρόπος τῆς ὀρχήσεως· πολλαὶ γὰρ
αἱ ὀνομασίαι[36] αὐτῶν, ὡς παρὰ Κρησὶν ὀρσίτης καὶ
ἐπικρήδιος. τὴν δ' ἀπόκινον καλουμένην ὄρχησιν, ἧς
μνημονεύει Κρατῖνος ἐν Νεμέσει καὶ Κηφισόδωρος ἐν
Ἀμαζόσιν Ἀριστοφάνης τ' ἐν Κενταύρῳ καὶ ἄλλοι
πλείονες, ὕστερον μακτρισμὸν ὠνόμασαν· ἦν καὶ πολ-
d λαὶ γυναῖκες ὠρχοῦντο, ἃς καὶ | μακτιστρίας ὀνομα-
ζομένας οἶδα. τὰ δὲ στασιμώτερα καὶ πυκνότερα καὶ
τὴν ὄρχησιν ἁπλουστέραν ἔχοντα καλεῖται δάκτυλοι,
ἰαμβική, Μολοσσική, ἐμμέλεια, κόρδαξ, σίκιννις,
Περσική, Φρύγιος, νιβατισμός, Θράκιος, κολαβρι-
σμός, Τελεσιάς· Μακεδονικὴ δ' ἐστὶν αὕτη ὄρχησις, ᾗ
χρησάμενοι οἱ περὶ Πτολεμαῖον Ἀλέξανδρον τὸν Φιλίππου ἀδελφὸν ἀνεῖλον, ὡς ἱστορεῖ Μαρσύας ἐν
τρίτῳ Μακεδονικῶν. μανιώδεις δ' εἰσὶν ὀρχήσεις κερ-
e νοφόρος καὶ | μογγὰς καὶ θερμαυστρίς. ἦν δὲ καὶ
παρὰ τοῖς ἰδιώταις ἡ καλουμένη ἄνθεμα. ταύτην δὲ
ὠρχοῦντο μετὰ λέξεως τοιαύτης μιμούμενοι καὶ λέ-
γοντες·

---

[36] αιπολλαι παραιονομασίαι A: corr. Kaibel

[129] A dance that imitated movements associated with hoplite
combat; cf. 14.630d–1b; Pl. *Lg.* 815a.

[130] Included in a list of humorous dances at 14.629f.

[131] A tragic dance; cf. 1.20e; 14.630d–e.

[132] A comic dance; cf. 1.20e; 14.630e.

[133] A dance associated with satyr play; see 1.20e; 14.618c n.,
630b.

called *purrhichai*[129] and of all other dances of this type; for there are many names for them, for example *orsitês* and *epikrêdios* on Crete. As for the so-called *apokinos* dance, which is mentioned by Cratinus in *Nemesis* (fr. 127), Cephisodorus in *Amazons* (fr. 2), Aristophanes in *The Centaur* (fr. 287), and numerous other authors, it was later referred to as a *maktrismos*;[130] many women used to dance it, and I know that they were referred to as *maktristriai*. Dances that are more static and contained, on the other hand, and that involve simpler steps, are known as *daktuloi* ("fingers"), *iambikê* ("iambic"), Molossian, *emmeleia*,[131] *kordax*,[132] *sikinnis*,[133] Persian, Phrygian, *nibatismos*, Thracian, *kolabrismos*, and *Telesias*;[134] the latter is a Macedonian dance, which Ptolemy's men[135] did when they killed Philip's brother Alexander,[136] according to Marsyas in Book III of the *History of Macedon* (*FGrH* 135 F 11). Dances that resemble the movements of lunatics are the *kernophoros* ("*kernos*-bearer"[137]), *mongas*, and *thermaustris* ("tongs"). There was also a dance known as the *anthema*, which was performed by private citizens.[138] They used to match their gestures to lyrics along the following lines when they performed it, saying (carm. pop. *PMG* 852):

[134] Cf. 14.630a.

[135] Or perhaps simply "Ptolemy."

[136] Alexander II of Macedon (reigned 370/69–367 BCE), who was murdered and replaced by Ptolemy of Alorus. The Philip in question is Philip II, Alexander the Great's father.

[137] For the *kernos* (a small pot used to carry offerings), cf. 11.476e–f.

[138] I.e. rather than by performers in public festivals.

πoῦ μοι τὰ ῥόδα, πoῦ μοι τὰ ἴα,
   πoῦ μοι τὰ καλὰ σέλινα;
ταδὶ τὰ ῥόδα, ταδὶ τὰ ἴα,
   ταδὶ τὰ καλὰ σέλινα.

παρὰ δὲ Συρακοσίοις καὶ Χιτωνέας Ἀρτέμιδος ὄρ-
χησίς τίς ἐστιν ἴδιος καὶ αὔλησις. ἦν δέ τις καὶ
Ἰωνικὴ ὄρχησις παροίνιος, καὶ τὴν ἀγγελικὴν δὲ
πάροινον ἠκρίβουν ὄρχησιν. καλεῖται δέ τις καὶ ἄλλη
ὄρχησις κόσμου ἐκπύρωσις, ἧς μνημονεύει Μένιππος
f ὁ κυνικὸς ἐν τῷ Συμποσίῳ. καὶ γελοῖαι | δ᾽ εἰσὶν
ὀρχήσεις ἴγδις καὶ μακτρισμὸς ἀπόκινός τε καὶ σο-
βάς, ἔτι δὲ μορφασμὸς καὶ γλαὺξ καὶ λέων ἀλφίτων
τε ἔκχυσις καὶ χρεῶν ἀποκοπὴ καὶ στοιχεῖα καὶ πυρρίχη. μετ᾽ αὐλῶν δ᾽ ὠρχοῦντο τὴν τοῦ κελευστοῦ καὶ
τὴν καλουμένην πινακίδα. σχήματα δέ ἐστιν ὀρχήσεως ξιφισμός, καλαθίσκος, καλλαβίδες, σκώψ, σκώ-
πευμα. ἦν δὲ ὁ σκὼψ τῶν ἀποσκοπούντων τι σχῆμα
ἄκραν τὴν χεῖρα ὑπὲρ τοῦ μετώπου κεκυρτωκότων.
μνημονεύει Αἰσχύλος ἐν Θεωροῖς·

καὶ μὴν παλαιῶν τῶνδέ σοι σκωπευμάτων. ||

630 καλλαβίδων δ᾽ Εὔπολις ἐν Κόλαξιν·

---

139 At 14.629c *maktrismos* and *apokinos* are said to be different names for the same dance.
140 Doubtless wildly celebratory.
141 Patently out of place in this list; cf. 14.629c n., 630d–1b.

Where are my roses? Where are my violets?
    Where is my lovely celery?
Here are my roses! Here are my violets!
    Here is my lovely celery!

The Syracusans have a unique style of dancing and pipe-playing performed in honor of Artemis Chitônea. There was also a dance called the Ionian that imitated a drunk's movements; in addition, they perfected a drunk-dance known as the *angelikê* ("messenger-[dance]"). Another dance is referred to as the *kosmou ekpurôsis* ("cosmic conflagration"); Menippus the Cynic mentions it in his *Symposium* (fr. IV, p. 246 Riese). There are humorous dances as well: the *igdis* ("mortar"), *maktrismos*, *apokinos*,[139] and *sobas*, as well as the *morphasmos*, little owl, lion, barley-groat-dumping, debt-cancellation,[140] letters, and *purrhichê*.[141] They performed the bosun's dance and the so-called *pinakis* to pipe-music. Dance-steps include: the sword-play, basket, *kallabides*, scops owl,[142] and *skôpeuma*. The scops owl was a step in which the dancers cupped their hand, placed it over their brow, and looked off into the distance. Aeschylus mentions it in *Sacred Ambassadors* (fr. 79):

And look at these ancient *skôpeumata* you've got![143]

Eupolis (mentions) *kallabides* in *Flatterers* (fr. 176.2–3):[144]

142 Cf. 9.391a–c with n.; Poll. 4.103.
143 But the definition given above seems unlikely to be the sense intended here.
144 Quoted at greater length at 14.646f.

καλλαβίδας δὲ βαίνει,
σησαμίδας δὲ χέζει.

θερμαυστρίς, ἑκατερίδες, σκοπός, χεὶρ καταπρηνής,
χεὶρ σιμή, διποδισμός, ξύλου παράληψις, ἐπαγκωνι-
σμός, καλαθίσκος, στρόβιλος. καὶ Τελεσιὰς δ' ἐστὶν
ὄρχησις καλουμένη· στρατιωτικὴ δ' ἐστὶν αὕτη ἀπό
τινος ἀνδρὸς Τελεσίου λαβοῦσα τοὔνομα, μεθ' ὅπλων
τὸ πρῶτον αὐτὴν ἐκείνου ὀρχησαμένου, ὥς φησιν
Ἱππαγόρας ἐν τῷ πρώτῳ Περὶ τῆς Καρχηδονίων Πο-
λιτείας. |

b   Καλεῖται δ' ἡ μὲν σατυρικὴ ὄρχησις, ὥς φησιν
Ἀριστοκλῆς ἐν πρώτῳ Περὶ Χορῶν, σίκιννις καὶ οἱ
σάτυροι σικιννισταί· τινὲς δέ φασιν Σίκιννόν τινα
βάρβαρον εὑρετὴν αὐτῆς γενέσθαι, ἄλλοι δὲ Κρῆτα
λέγουσι τὸ γένος εἶναι τὸν Σίκιννον. ὀρχησταὶ δ' οἱ
Κρῆτες, ὥς φησιν Ἀριστόξενος. Σκάμων δ' ἐν πρώτῳ
Περὶ Εὑρημάτων σίκιννιν αὐτὴν εἰρῆσθαι ἀπὸ τοῦ
σείεσθαι, καὶ πρῶτον ὀρχήσασθαι τὴν σίκιννιν Θέρ-
σιππον. προτέρα δ' εὕρηται ἡ περὶ τοὺς πόδας κίνησις
c τῆς διὰ τῶν χειρῶν | οἱ γὰρ παλαιοὶ τοὺς πόδας
μᾶλλον ἐγυμνάζοντο ἐν τοῖς ἀγῶσι καὶ τοῖς κυνη-
γεσίοις. οἱ δὲ Κρῆτες κυνηγετικοί, διὸ καὶ ποδώκεις.
εἰσὶ δέ τινες οἵ φασι τὴν σίκιννιν ποιητικῶς ὀνο-

---

145 Cf. Apolloph. fr. 1 (quoted at 11.467f).
146 Stephanis #2387 (where the reference is to this passage);
otherwise unknown. For the dance itself, cf. 14.629d.
147 Cf. 1.20e (citing Aristonicus).

who does *kallabides*-dances when he walks,
and shits sesame cakes.

The *thermaustris* ("tongs"), *hekaterides* ("alternate
[hands]"), look-out, down-turned hand, cupped hand,
two-footer, club-grabbing, *epankônismos* ("nudging"),
basket,[145] and top. The so-called *Telesias* is another dance;
it is performed by soldiers and got its name from a man
named Telesias,[146] who was wearing hoplite armor when
he danced it for the first time, according to Hippagoras
in Book I of *On the Carthaginian Constitution* (*FGrH* 743
F 1).

According to Aristocles in Book I of *On Choruses* (fr. 9,
FHG iv.331), the dance used in satyr plays is a *sikinnis*, and
the satyrs are *sikinnistai*; some authorities claim that a
barbarian named Sicinnus invented (this dance),[147] while
others say that Sicinnus' family was from Crete. The Cretans are dancers, according to Aristoxenus (fr. 107 Wehrli).
Scamon in Book I of *On Inventions* (*FGrH* 476 F 2) says
that it gets the name *sikinnis* from the verb *seiesthai* ("to
shake oneself"),[148] and that the first person to dance it
was Thersippus.[149] Movements involving the feet were invented before those that involve the hands; for the ancients gave their feet more exercise in their contests and
when they hunted. The Cretans like to hunt, which is why
they are fast on their feet.[150] But some authorities[151] claim

---

[148] A preposterous etymology.

[149] Stephanis #1196; otherwise unknown.

[150] Presumably another observation taken from Aristoxenus
(cited above).   [151] Sc. in contrast to Scamon (cited above);
several source-documents appear to have been crudely spliced together in this section.

μάσθαι ἀπὸ τῆς κινήσεως, ἣν καὶ οἱ σάτυροι ὀρχοῦνται ταχυτάτην οὖσαν· οὐ γὰρ ἔχει πάθος[37] αὕτη ἡ
ὄρχησις, διὸ οὐδὲ βραδύνει. συνέστηκεν δὲ καὶ σατυρικὴ πᾶσα ποίησις τὸ παλαιὸν ἐκ χορῶν, ὡς καὶ ἡ
τότε τραγῳδία· διόπερ οὐδὲ ὑποκριτὰς εἶχον. τρεῖς δ᾽
d εἰσὶ τῆς σκηνικῆς | ποιήσεως ὀρχήσεις, τραγική,
κωμική, σατυρική. ὁμοίως δὲ καὶ τῆς λυρικῆς ποιήσεως τρεῖς, πυρρίχη, γυμνοπαιδική, ὑπορχηματική.
καὶ ἐστὶν ὁμοία ἡ μὲν πυρρίχη τῇ σατυρικῇ· ἀμφότεραι γὰρ διὰ τάχους. πολεμικὴ δὲ δοκεῖ εἶναι ἡ πυρ-
ρίχη· ἔνοπλοι γὰρ αὐτὴν παῖδες ὀρχοῦνται. τάχους δὲ
δεῖ τῷ πολέμῳ εἰς τὸ διώκειν καὶ εἰς τὸ ἡττωμένους

φεύγειν μηδὲ μένειν, μηδ᾽ αἰδεῖσθαι κακοὺς[38]
    εἶναι.

e ἡ δὲ γυμνοπαιδικὴ παρεμφερής ἐστι | τῇ τραγικῇ
ὀρχήσει, ἥτις ἐμμέλεια καλεῖται· ἐν ἑκατέρᾳ δὲ ὁρᾶται
τὸ βαρὺ καὶ σεμνόν. ἡ δ᾽ ὑπορχηματικὴ τῇ κωμικῇ
οἰκειοῦται, ἥτις καλεῖται κόρδαξ· παιγνιώδεις δ᾽ εἰσὶν
ἀμφότεραι. Ἀριστόξενος δέ φησι τὴν πυρρίχην ἀπὸ
Πυρρίχου Λάκωνος τὸ γένος τὴν προσηγορίαν
λαβεῖν· Λακωνικὸν δ᾽ εἶναι μέχρι καὶ νῦν ὄνομα τὸν
Πύρριχον. ἐμφανίζει δ᾽ ἡ ὄρχησις πολεμικὴ οὖσα ὡς

---

[37] ἦθος Meineke   [38] Unmetrical (κακὸς Herodotus)

152 Another fanciful etymology; "poetically" apparently means
"via an anagrammatic rearrangement of the letters."

that the word *sikinnis* is derived poetically from *kinêsis* ("movement"),[152] because the satyrs move with great rapidity when they dance; for this dance involves no suffering, and it is therefore not done slowly. In ancient times, all satyric poetry consisted of choruses, like the tragedy of that period; as a consequence, neither included actors. Three dance-styles are associated with dramatic poetry: tragic, comic, and satyric. Likewise three dance-styles are associated with lyric poetry: *purrhichê*, *gumnopaidikê*,[153] and *huporchêmatikê*.[154] The *purrhichê* resembles satyric dancing, inasmuch as both are done rapidly. The *purrhichê* appears to be associated with warfare, since boys perform it dressed in hoplite equipment. Speed is needed in war to pursue the enemy, and when defeated

> to try to escape and not remain, and not be ashamed
> of being cowards.[155]

The *gumnopaidikê* is similar to the tragic dance known as an *emmeleia*; for seriousness and gravity are apparent in both. The *huporchêmatikê* is related to the comic dance known as a *kordax*; both are playful. Aristoxenus (fr. 103 Wehrli) claims that the *purrhichê* got its name from a Spartan named Pyrrhichus;[156] the name Pyrrhichus is still used in Sparta even today. The fact that this style of dance

---

[153] Literally "naked-boy (dance)"; cf. 14.631b–c.

[154] Cf. 14.631c.

[155] Adopted from Delphic Oracle Q101.3 Fontenrose (quoted at Hdt. 1.55.2).

[156] Poralla #653 (but almost certainly a mythical rather than a historical character).

Λακεδαιμονίων τὸ εὕρημα· πολεμικοὶ δ' εἰσὶν οἱ
f Λάκωνες, ὧν καὶ οἱ υἱοὶ τὰ ἐμβατήρια | μέλη ἀναλαμ-
βάνουσιν, ἅπερ καὶ ἐνόπλια καλεῖται. καὶ αὐτοὶ δ' οἱ
Λάκωνες ἐν τοῖς πολέμοις τὰ Τυρταίου ποιήματα
ἀπομνημονεύοντες ἔρρυθμον κίνησιν ποιοῦνται. Φιλόχορος δέ φησιν κρατήσαντας Λακεδαιμονίους Μεσ-
σηνίων διὰ τὴν Τυρταίου στρατηγίαν ἐν ταῖς στρα-
τείαις ἔθος ποιήσασθαι, ἂν δειπνοποιήσωνται καὶ
παιωνίσωσιν, ᾄδειν καθ' ἕνα <τὰ>[39] Τυρταίου· κρίνειν
δὲ τὸν πολέμαρχον καὶ ἆθλον διδόναι τῷ νικῶντι
631 κρέας. ‖ ἡ δὲ πυρρίχη παρὰ μὲν τοῖς ἄλλοις Ἕλλησιν
οὐκ ἔτι παραμένει· ἐκλιπούσης δὲ αὐτῆς συμβέβηκε
καὶ τοὺς πολέμους καταλυθῆναι. παρὰ μόνοις δὲ
Λακεδαιμονίοις διαμένει προγύμνασμα οὖσα τοῦ
πολέμου· ἐκμανθάνουσί τε πάντες ἐν τῇ Σπάρτῃ ἀπὸ
πέντε ἐτῶν πυρριχίζειν. ἡ δὲ καθ' ἡμᾶς πυρρίχη
Διονυσιακή τις εἶναι δοκεῖ, ἐπιεικεστέρα οὖσα τῆς
ἀρχαίας· ἔχουσι γὰρ οἱ ὀρχούμενοι θύρσους ἀντὶ
δοράτων, προΐενται δὲ ἐπ' ἀλλήλους νάρθηκας[40] καὶ
λαμπάδας φέρουσιν ὀρχοῦνταί τε τὰ περὶ τὸν Διό-
b νυσον καὶ | τοὺς Ἰνδούς,[41] ἔτι τε τὰ περὶ τὸν Πενθέα.
τακτέον δὲ ἐπὶ τῆς πυρρίχης τὰ κάλλιστα μέλη καὶ

39 add. Kaibel
40 καὶ νάρθηκας ACE: καὶ del. Olson
41 τὰ περὶ τοὺς Ἰνδοὺς A: τὰ περὶ del. Kaibel

157 Literally "armed," i.e. "martial (songs)."
158 Sc. as they march toward the enemy.

has a warlike character supports the notion that the Spartans invented it; the Spartans dedicate themselves to war, and their sons memorize their marching-songs, known as *enoplia*.[157] So too the Spartans themselves recite Tyrtaeus' poems during their wars and move in time with them.[158] Philochorus (*FGrH* 328 F 216) says that after the Spartans defeated the Messenians because of Tyrtaeus' generalship,[159] they made it a custom during their campaigns that, after they have dinner and sing a paean, they take turns singing Tyrtaeus' poems; the polemarch judges among them[160] and awards the winner a piece of meat as a prize. The other Greeks no longer dance the *purrhichê*; after it fell out of use, their wars coincidentally came to an end as well. Only the Spartans continue to perform the *purrhichê*, which serves as a form of military training, and everyone in Sparta learns to dance it, beginning at age five. The *purrhichê* performed in our time appears to have a Dionysiac character and is more presentable than the ancient one; for the dancers hold thyrsuses rather than spears, throw fennel-stalks at one another and carry torches, and perform dances that represent the story of Dionysus and the Indians,[161] as well as the story of Pentheus.[162] The most attractive melodies and rapid rhythms

---

[159] During the Second Messenian War. Tyrtaeus (Poralla #709) belongs to the mid-7th century BCE. Substantial portions of his poetry are preserved, but none of them in Athenaeus.

[160] Sc. as to who has sung the best.   [161] I.e. the story of Dionysus' conquest of the East; cf. 5.200c–d with n.

[162] The young king of Thebes who was first driven mad by Dionysus and then torn apart by the maenads (including his own mother and aunts), as in Euripides' *Bacchae*.

τοὺς ὀρθίους ῥυθμούς. ἔοικεν δὲ ἡ γυμνοπαιδικὴ τῇ
καλουμένῃ ἀναπάλῃ παρὰ τοῖς παλαιοῖς· γυμνοὶ γὰρ
ὀρχοῦνται οἱ παῖδες πάντες, ἐρρύθμους φοράς τινας
ἀποτελοῦντες καὶ σχήματά τινα τῶν χειρῶν κατὰ τὸ
ἀνάπαλον, ὥστ' ἐμφαίνειν θεωρήματά τινα τῆς παλαίστρας καὶ τοῦ παγκρατίου, κινοῦντες ἐρρύθμως τοὺς
πόδας. τρόποι δ' αὐτῆς οἵ τε Ὠσχοφορικοὶ καὶ οἱ
βακχικοί, ὥστε καὶ τὴν ὄρχησιν ταύτην[42] εἰς τὸν
c   Διόνυσον ἀναφέρεσθαι. | Ἀριστόξενος δέ φησιν ὡς οἱ
παλαιοὶ γυμναζόμενοι πρῶτον ἐν τῇ γυμνοπαιδικῇ εἰς
τὴν πυρρίχην ἐχώρουν πρὸ τοῦ εἰσιέναι εἰς τὸ θέατρον. καλεῖται δ' ἡ πυρρίχη καὶ χειρονομία. ἡ δ'
ὑπορχηματική ἐστιν ἐν ᾗ ᾄδων ὁ χορὸς ὀρχεῖται.
φησὶ γοῦν ὁ Βακχυλίδης·

οὐχ ἕδρας ἔργον οὐδ' ἀμβολᾶς.

καὶ Πίνδαρος δέ φησιν·

Λάκαινα μὲν παρθένων ἀγέλα.

ὀρχοῦνται δὲ ταύτην παρὰ τῷ Πινδάρῳ οἱ Λάκωνες,
καὶ ἔστιν ὄρχησις[43] ἀνδρῶν καὶ γυναικῶν. βέλτιστοι
d   δέ εἰσι τῶν τρόπων οἵτινες καὶ ὀρχοῦνται. | εἰσὶ δὲ
οἵδε· προσοδιακοί,[44] ἀποστολικοί (οὗτοι δὲ καὶ παρ-

---

[42] τὴν ὄρχησιν ταύτην A: τὴν ὄρχησιν del. Kaibel
[43] ὑπορχηματικὴ ὄρχησις A: ὑπορχηματικὴ del. Kaibel
[44] προσοδιακοί Dindorf: προσῳδιακοί ACE

---

[163] An adjective derived from Ôschophoria (literally "Grape-

should be used for the *purrhichê*. The *gumnopaidikê* resembles what the ancients referred to as an *anapalê*; because all the boys (*paides*) dance in the nude (*gumnoi*), producing rhythmic movements and hand-gestures in an *anapalon* style reminiscent of what one might see in a wrestling-school or at a pancration competition, moving their feet to the beat. *Ôschophorikoi*[163] and Bacchic dances are varieties of this type, which is accordingly associated with Dionysus. Aristoxenus (fr. 108 Wehrli) claims that the ancients first practiced (*gumnazomenoi*) the *gumnopaidikê* and then moved on to the *purrhichê* before entering the theater. The *purrhichê* is also known as a *cheironomia*.[164] The *huporchêmatikê* is a style in which the chorus dances while singing. Bacchylides (fr. 15.1), for example, says:

There's no time for sitting around or delay.

Pindar (fr. 112) as well says:

A Spartan herd of girls.[165]

The Spartans do this dance in Pindar, and both men and women perform it. The best styles[166] are those that involve dancing. They are the following: *prosodiakoi* ("processional [songs]"), *apostolikoi* ("departure [songs]")—these

vine-tendril-bearing"; cf. 11.495f), the name of an Athenian festival celebrated in honor of Dionysus.   [164] Literally "gesticulation"; cf. 14.629b–c.   [165] The quotation seems out of place here and might be better at 14.632f–3a.   [166] Sc. of poetry. Kaibel marked a lacuna before this sentence, but more likely the problem is to be traced to Athenaeus' clumsy combination of a number of separate source-documents.

θένιοι καλοῦνται), καὶ οἱ τούτοις ὅμοιοι. τῶν γὰρ
ὕμνων οἱ μὲν ὠρχοῦντο, οἱ δὲ οὐκ ὠρχοῦντο < ... > ἢ
τοὺς εἰς Ἀφροδίτην καὶ Διόνυσον, καὶ τὸν παιᾶνα δὲ
ὁτὲ μέν, ὁτὲ δὲ οὔ. εἰσὶ δὲ καὶ παρὰ τοῖς βαρβάροις
ὥσπερ καὶ παρὰ τοῖς Ἕλλησι σπουδαῖαι καὶ φαῦλαι
ὀρχήσεις. ὁ μὲν κόρδαξ παρ' Ἕλλησι φορτικός, ἡ δὲ
ἐμμέλεια σπουδαία, καθάπερ καὶ ἡ παρὰ Ἀρκάσι
κίδαρις, παρὰ Σικυωνίοις τε ὁ ἀλητήρ. οὕτως δὲ καὶ ἐν
Ἰθάκῃ καλεῖται ἀλητήρ, ὡς ἱστορεῖ Ἀριστόξενος ἐν |
e πρώτῳ Συγκρίσεων. καὶ περὶ μὲν ὀρχήσεως τοσαῦτά
μοι ἐπὶ τοῦ παρόντος λέλεκται.

Τὸ δὲ παλαιὸν ἐτηρεῖτο περὶ τὴν μουσικὴν τὸ
καλὸν καὶ πάντ' εἶχε κατὰ τὴν τέχνην τὸν οἰκεῖον
αὐτοῖς κόσμον· διόπερ ἦσαν ἴδιοι καθ' ἑκάστην ἁρμονίαν αὐλοὶ καὶ ἑκάστοις αὐλητῶν ὑπῆρχον αὐλοὶ
ἑκάστῃ ἁρμονίᾳ πρόσφοροι ἐν τοῖς ἀγῶσι. Πρόνομος
δ' ὁ Θηβαῖος πρῶτος ηὔλησεν ἀπὸ τῶν αὐτῶν
<πάσας>[45] τὰς ἁρμονίας. νῦν δὲ εἰκῇ καὶ ἀλόγως
ἅπτονται τῆς μουσικῆς. καὶ πάλαι μὲν τὸ παρὰ τοῖς
f ὄχλοις εὐδοκιμεῖν σημεῖον | ἦν κακοτεχνίας· ὅθεν καὶ
Ἀσωπόδωρος ὁ Φλιάσιος κροταλιζομένου ποτέ τινος
τῶν αὐλητῶν διατρίβων αὐτὸς ἔτι ἐν τῷ ὑποσκηνίῳ,
"τί τοῦτ';" εἶπεν· "δῆλον ὅτι μέγα κακὸν γέγονεν," ὡς
οὐκ ἂν ἄλλως ἐν τοῖς πολλοῖς εὐδοκιμήσαντος. οἶδα
δέ τινας τοῦθ' ἱστορήσαντας ὡς Ἀντιγενείδου εἰπόν-

45 add. Meineke

are also referred to as *parthenioi* ("[songs] of unmarried girls")—and the like. For some hymns are accompanied by dancing, while others are not . . . or those in honor of Aphrodite or Dionysus, while the paean sometimes is and sometimes is not. The barbarians have both serious and vulgar dances, just like the Greeks. Among the Greeks, the *kordax* is low-class, whereas the *emmeleia* is serious, like the Arcadian *kidaris* and the Sicyonian *alêtêr*. The term *alêtêr* is also used on Ithaca, according to Aristoxenus in Book I of *Comparisons* (fr. 109 Wehrli). That is all I have to say about dancing for the moment.

Efforts were made in ancient times to keep music beautiful, and all its technical elements served to maintain its proper organization; this is why every scale had a specific set of pipes, and every pipe-player owned pipes suited to each scale used in the competitions. Pronomus of Thebes[167] was the first person to play all the scales using a single set of pipes. Nowadays, on the other hand, people approach music in a random, careless manner. In the past, moreover, being a popular favorite was regarded as evidence of bad technique; as a consequence, when a pipe-player got applause once while Asopodorus of Phlius[168] (*SH* 224) was still killing time backstage, he said: "What was that? Apparently something terrible happened!", as if that were the only way the crowd could have given the other man a favorable reception. But I am aware that some authorities report that it was Antigeneidas[169] who said this.

---

[167] Stephanis #2149; *PAA* 789605. This comment interrupts the flow of the argument, which resumes in the next sentence.

[168] Stephanis #468; cf. 14.639a n.

[169] Stephanis #196.

τος. καίτοι οἱ καθ᾽ ἡμᾶς γε τέλος ποιοῦνται τῆς τέχνης
632 τὴν παρὰ τοῖς θεάτροις ‖ εὐημερίαν. διόπερ Ἀριστόξενος ἐν τοῖς Συμμίκτοις Συμποτικοῖς, ὅμοιον,
φησί, ποιοῦμεν Ποσειδωνιάταις τοῖς ἐν τῷ Τυρσηνικῷ
κόλπῳ κατοικοῦσιν. οἷς συνέβη τὰ μὲν ἐξ ἀρχῆς
Ἕλλησιν οὖσιν ἐκβεβαρβαρῶσθαι Τυρρηνοῖς ἢ Ῥωμαίοις[46] γεγονόσι, καὶ τήν τε φωνὴν μεταβεβληκέναι
τά τε λοιπὰ τῶν ἐπιτηδευμάτων, ἄγειν δὲ μίαν τινὰ
αὐτοὺς τῶν ἑορτῶν τῶν Ἑλληνικῶν ἔτι καὶ νῦν, ἐν ᾗ
συνιόντες ἀναμιμνήσκονται τῶν ἀρχαίων ἐκείνων ὀνο-
b μάτων τε καὶ νομίμων καὶ ἀπολοφυράμενοι | πρὸς
ἀλλήλους καὶ ἀποδακρύσαντες ἀπέρχονται. οὕτω δὴ
οὖν, φησί, καὶ ἡμεῖς, ἐπειδὴ καὶ τὰ θέατρα ἐκβεβαρ-
βάρωται καὶ εἰς μεγάλην διαφθορὰν προελήλυθεν ἡ
πάνδημος αὕτη μουσική, καθ᾽ αὑτοὺς γενόμενοι ὀλί-
γοι ἀναμιμνησκόμεθα οἵα ἦν ἡ μουσική. ταῦτα μὲν ὁ
Ἀριστόξενος· κἀμοὶ δὲ διὰ τοῦτο φαίνεται φιλοσο-
φητέον εἶναι περὶ μουσικῆς. καὶ γὰρ Πυθαγόρας ὁ
Σάμιος τηλικαύτην δόξαν ἔχων ἐπὶ φιλοσοφίᾳ κατα-
φανής ἐστιν ἐκ πολλῶν οὐ παρέργως ἁψάμενος |
c μουσικῆς· ὅς γε καὶ τὴν τοῦ παντὸς οὐσίαν διὰ μουσικῆς ἀποφαίνει συγκειμένην. τὸ δ᾽ ὅλον ἔοικεν ἡ πα-
λαιὰ τῶν Ἑλλήνων σοφία τῇ μουσικῇ μάλιστ᾽ εἶναι
δεδομένη. καὶ διὰ τοῦτο τῶν μὲν θεῶν Ἀπόλλωνα, τῶν
δὲ ἡμιθέων Ὀρφέα μουσικώτατον καὶ σοφώτατον
ἔκρινον, καὶ πάντας τοὺς χρωμένους τῇ τέχνῃ ταύτῃ

[46] ἢ Ῥωμαίοις del. Wilamowitz

The fact is that our contemporaries regard a successful public performance as the ultimate aim of their craft. This is why Aristoxenus says in his *Sympotic Miscellany* (fr. 124 Wehrli): We act like the inhabitants of the Posidonia located on the Tyrrhenian Gulf. What happened to them is that they were originally Greeks but have turned into barbarians and become Etruscans or Romans, and their language has changed,[170] along with all their other practices. They continue today to celebrate only one Greek festival, in which they get together and imitate their ancient way of speaking and behaving; after they wail about them with one another and cry their hearts out, they go back home. We are actually in the same situation, he says; for our theaters have been barbarized, and popular music itself has been utterly degraded, and only a few of us recall privately what music was once like. Thus Aristoxenus; but it seems to me as well on this account that music deserves to be a subject of philosophical inquiry. There is in fact considerable evidence that Pythagoras of Samos, who has such a great reputation in philosophy, took a more than passing interest in music; indeed, he insists that music holds the fabric of the entire universe together. And by and large ancient Greek wisdom (*sophia*) appears to have been closely connected with music. This is why they regarded Apollo and Orpheus as the most musical and the wisest (*sophôtatos*) of the gods and demigods, respectively, and why they referred to everyone who practiced this art as a

[170] Latin was sometimes thought to be merely a dialect of Greek; see Stevens, *CJ* 102 (2006/7) 115–44.

197

σοφιστὰς ἀπεκάλουν, ὥσπερ καὶ Αἰσχύλος ἐποίησε·

εἴτ᾽ οὖν σοφιστὴς † καλὰ † παραπαίων χέλυν.

d ὅτι δὲ πρὸς τὴν μουσικὴν οἰκειότατα διέκειντο | οἱ
ἀρχαῖοι δῆλον καὶ ἐξ Ὁμήρου· ὃς διὰ τὸ μεμελο-
ποιηκέναι πᾶσαν ἑαυτοῦ τὴν ποίησιν ἀφροντιστὶ πολ-
λούς⁴⁷ ἀκεφάλους ποιεῖ στίχους καὶ λαγαρούς, ἔτι δὲ
μειούρους. Ξενοφάνης δὲ καὶ Σόλων καὶ Θέογνις καὶ
Φωκυλίδης, ἔτι δὲ Περίανδρος ὁ Κορίνθιος ἐλεγειο-
ποιὸς καὶ τῶν λοιπῶν οἱ μὴ προσάγοντες πρὸς τὰ
ποιήματα μελῳδίαν ἐκπονοῦσι τοὺς στίχους τοῖς
ἀριθμοῖς καὶ τῇ τάξει τῶν μέτρων καὶ σκοποῦσιν
ὅπως αὐτῶν μηθεὶς <μήτε>⁴⁸ ἀκέφαλος ἔσται μήτε
e λαγαρὸς μήτε μείουρος. ἀκέφαλοι | δέ εἰσιν οἱ ἐπὶ τῆς
ἀρχῆς τὴν χωλότητα ἔχοντες·

ἐπεὶ δὴ νῆάς τε καὶ Ἑλλήσποντον ἵκοντο.
ἐπίτονος τετάνυστο βοὸς ἶφι κταμένοιο.⁴⁹

λαγαροὶ δὲ οἱ ἐν μέσῳ, οἷον·

αἶψα δ᾽ ἄρ᾽ Αἰνείαν φίλον υἱὸν⁵⁰ Ἀγχίσαο.

⁴⁷ τοὺς πολλοὺς ACE: τοὺς del. Meineke
⁴⁸ add. Meineke   ⁴⁹ cf. Od. 12.423 ἐπίτονος βέβλητο,
βοὸς ῥινοῖο τετευχώς; Il. 3.375 ἥ οἱ ῥῆξεν ἱμάντα βοὸς ἶφι
κταμένοιο.   ⁵⁰ φίλον υἱὸν Meineke: υἱὸν φίλον A

171 Literally "mouse-tailed."
172 I.e. that begin with what ought properly to be a short syllable, where a dactylic hexameter requires a long.

sophistês ("wise man, intellectual"), as Aeschylus (fr. 314) wrote:

> So then, a *sophistês* † beautiful † striking a false note on a tortoise-shell lyre.

That the ancients were intimately familiar with music is also apparent from Homer, who in the course of composing all his poetry carelessly produces numerous headless and hollow, as well as tapering[171] lines. Xenophanes, Solon, Theognis, and Phocylides, as well as the elegiac poet Periander of Corinth and the others who do not set their poems to music, carefully construct their lines as regards the number and arrangement of the metrical units, and see to it that none of them will be headless, hollow, or tapering. Headless lines are those that limp at the beginning:[172]

> when in fact they came to the ships and the Hellespont. (*Il.* 23.2)
> a strap made of a slaughtered bull's hide was stretched over it.[173]

Hollow lines are those (that limp) in the middle, for example:

> straightaway, then, Aeneas the beloved son of Anchises.[174]

---

[173] A conflation of *Od*. 12.423 (which begins with the metrical anomaly referred to here) and *Il*. 3.375 (which does not).

[174] An adespota dactylic hexameter not found in the traditional text of Homer. The verse (as emended by Meineke) has a short in the second syllable of *huion*, where a dactylic hexameter requires a long.

τῶν αὖθ᾽ ἡγείσθην Ἀσκληπιοῦ δύο παῖδε.

μείουροι δ᾽ εἰσὶν οἱ ἐπὶ τῆς ἐκβολῆς, οἷον· |

f Τρῶες δ᾽ ἐρρίγησαν, ὅπως ἴδον αἰόλον ὄφιν.
καλὴ Κασσιέπεια θεοῖς δέμας ἐοικυῖα.⁵¹
τοῦ φέρον ἐμπλήσας ἀσκὸν μέγαν, ἐν δὲ καὶ ἥια.

διετήρησαν δὲ μάλιστα τῶν Ἑλλήνων Λακεδαιμόνιοι
τὴν μουσικήν, πλείστῃ αὐτῇ χρώμενοι, καὶ συχνοὶ
παρ᾽ αὐτοῖς ἐγένοντο μελῶν ποιηταί. τηροῦσιν δὲ καὶ
633 νῦν τὰς ἀρχαίας ᾠδὰς ἐπιμελῶς ‖ πολυμαθεῖς τε εἰς
ταύτας εἰσὶ καὶ ἀκριβεῖς. ὅθεν καὶ Πρατίνας φησί·

Λάκων ὁ τέττιξ εὔτυκος ἐς χορόν.

διὸ καὶ οἱ ποιηταὶ διετέλουν προσαγορεύοντες οὕτως
τὰς ᾠδάς·

⟨ . . . ⟩ γλυκυτάτων πρύτανιν ὕμνων,

καί·

⟨ . . . ⟩ μέλεα μελιπτέρωτα Μουσᾶν.⁵²

⁵¹ cf. Il. 8.305 καλὴ Καστιάνειρα δέμας εἰκυῖα θεῇσιν.
⁵² διὸ καὶ . . . Μουσᾶν del. Wilamowitz

175 For the verse to scan as a dactylic hexameter, the *iota* in
Asklêpiou must be treated as long rather than as short (as expected).   176 For the verse to scan as a dactylic hexameter,
the first syllable in *ophin* must be treated as long rather than as
short (as expected); West prints *opphin*.

177 An adespota dactylic hexameter not found in the tradi-

The two sons of Asclepius, again, were their
    leaders.[175] (*Il.* 2.731)

Tapering lines are those (that limp) at the end, for example:

The Trojans shuddered when they saw the glistening
    serpent.[176] (*Il.* 12.208)
Lovely Cassiepeia, like to the gods in appearance.[177]
I filled a large goatskin sack with this and brought it;
    provisions were inside.[178] (*Od.* 9.212)

The Spartans were the Greeks who preserved their music
most faithfully, inasmuch as they were deeply immersed in
it, and they produced large numbers of lyric poets. Even
today they carefully preserve their ancient songs and have
a great deal of precise information about them. Pratinas
(*PMG* 709) accordingly says:

The Spartan cicada is well-suited to a chorus.[179]

This is why the poets constantly referred to their songs as
follows (adesp. *PMG* 954a):

leader of sweetest hymns,

and (adesp. *PMG* 954b):

honey-winged songs of the Muses.

---

tional text of Homer (cf. *Il.* 8.305). For the verse to scan as a dactylic hexameter, the first syllable in *eoikuia* must be treated as long rather than as short (as expected).

[178] The final word in the line as Athenaeus gives it has three syllables, which will not do at the end of a dactylic hexameter; the problem can be resolved by converting the *iota* to a subscript.

[179] For "Spartan cicadas," cf. 15.680d.

ἀπὸ γὰρ τῆς τοῦ βίου σωφροσύνης καὶ αὐστηρίας μετέβαινον ἀσμένως ἐπὶ τὴν μουσικήν, ἐχούσης τὸ κηλητικὸν τῆς ἐπιστήμης. εἰκότως οὖν ἐγίνετο χαίρειν τοὺς ἀκροωμένους.

Ἐκάλουν δὲ καὶ χορηγούς, ὥς φησιν ὁ Βυζάντιος
b Δημήτριος ἐν τετάρτῳ Περὶ | Ποιημάτων, οὐχ ὥσπερ νῦν τοὺς μισθουμένους τοὺς χορούς, ἀλλὰ τοὺς καθηγουμένους τοῦ χοροῦ, καθάπερ αὐτὸ τοὔνομα σημαίνει.

Καὶ τὸ χρηστομουσεῖν καὶ μὴ παραβαίνειν τοὺς ἀρχαίους τῆς μουσικῆς νόμους.

Συνέβαινε δὲ τὸ μὲν παλαιὸν φιλομουσεῖν τοὺς Ἕλληνας· μετὰ δὲ ταῦτα γενομένης ἀταξίας καταγηρασάντων σχεδὸν ἁπάντων τῶν ἀρχαίων νομίμων ἥ τε προαίρεσις αὕτη κατελύθη καὶ τρόποι μουσικῆς φαῦλοι κατεδείχθησαν, οἷς ἕκαστος τῶν χρωμένων
c ἀντὶ μὲν πρᾳότητος | περιεποιεῖτο μαλακίαν, ἀντὶ δὲ σωφροσύνης ἀκολασίαν καὶ ἄνεσιν. ἔσται δ' ἴσως τοῦτο ⟨ἔτι⟩[53] μᾶλλον καὶ ἐπὶ πλέον προαχθήσεται, ἐὰν μή τις ἀγάγῃ πάλιν εἰς τοὐμφανὲς τὴν πάτριον μουσικήν· τὸ παλαιὸν γὰρ καὶ τῶν ἡρώων τὰς πράξεις καὶ τῶν θεῶν τοὺς ὕμνους δι' ᾠδῆς ἐποιοῦντο. Ὅμηρος γοῦν φησιν ἐπ' Ἀχιλλέως·

[53] add. Kaibel

[180] These last few remarks represent another fragment of the brief "history of music" that forms the framework for this section

For they were happy to make the transition from the sober austerity in which they lived to music, since the science has a charming effect. It was accordingly unsurprising that those who listened to it became happy.[180]

They used the term *chorêgos*,[181] according to Demetrius of Byzantium in Book IV of *On Poems* (*FHG* ii.624), not to refer to the individuals who hired and paid the chorus, as people do today, but to those who danced at the head of one (e.g. Alcm. *PMG* 1.44), as the name itself suggests.

(They) also (used the verb) *chrêstomousein*[182] to mean "not to violate the ancient principles of music."

In ancient times, the fact was that the Greeks enjoyed music. But afterward, when the situation became chaotic and almost all the old customs grew antiquated, this tendency was abandoned and low-class musical styles emerged; everyone who composed in them opted for effeminacy rather than gentleness, and for loose licentiousness rather than self-control. This state of affairs will perhaps continue to develop and grow even more pronounced, unless the traditional style of music is brought back to general attention. For in ancient times they produced songs that described the heroes' deeds or were hymns of praise honoring the gods. Homer (*Il.* 9.189) says of Achilleus, for example:

of the *Learned Banqueters*, and into which a wide variety of other material has been inserted here and there.

181 Literally "chorus-leader."

182 Literally "to be devoted to good music" *vel sim.*; the word is not attested elsewhere.

< . . . > ἄειδε δ' ἄρα κλέα ἀνδρῶν ἡρώων.[54]

καὶ τὸν Φήμιον δέ φησιν ὅτι

πολλὰ < . . . > βροτῶν θελκτήρια οἶδεν,[55]
ἔργ' ἀνδρῶν τε θεῶν τε, τά τε κλείουσιν ἀοιδοί. |

d τὸ δὲ ἔθος τοῦτο καὶ παρὰ τοῖς βαρβάροις ἐσῴζετο,
ὥς φησι Δίνων ἐν τοῖς Περσικοῖς. τὴν γοῦν Κύρου τοῦ
πρώτου ἀνδρείαν καὶ τὸν μέλλοντα πόλεμον ἔσεσθαι
πρὸς Ἀστυάγην προείδοντο οἱ ᾠδοί. ὅτε γάρ, φησίν,
ᾐτήσατο τὴν εἰς Πέρσας ἀποδημίαν ὁ Κῦρος (ἐγε-
γόνει δ' αὐτοῦ πρότερον ἐπὶ τῶν ῥαβδοφόρων, εἶθ'
ὕστερον ἐπὶ τῶν ὁπλοφόρων) < . . . > καὶ ἀπῆλθεν.
εὐωχουμένου οὖν τοῦ Ἀστυάγους μετὰ τῶν φίλων τότε
Ἀγγάρης ὄνομα (οὗτος δ' ἦν τῶν ᾠδῶν ὁ ἐνδοξότατος)
e ᾖδεν εἰσκληθεὶς τά τε ἄλλα τῶν εἰθισμένων καὶ | τὸ
ἔσχατον εἶπεν ὡς ἀφεῖται εἰς τὸ ἕλος θηρίον μέγα,
θρασύτερον ὑὸς ἀγρίου· ὃ ἂν κυριεύσῃ τῶν καθ' αὑτὸ
τόπων, πολλοῖς μετ' ὀλίγον ῥᾳδίως μαχεῖται. ἐρομένου δὲ τοῦ Ἀστυάγους "ποῖον θηρίον;", ἔφη Κῦρον
τὸν Πέρσην. νομίσας οὖν ὀρθῶς αὐτὸν ὑπωπτευκέναι
καὶ μεταπεμπόμενος < . . . > οὐδὲν ὤνησεν.

---

[54] ἡρώων does not belong in the text of Homer, but is more
likely a misquotation by Athenaeus than an intrusive gloss.
[55] The traditional text of Homer has οἶδας.

---

[183] I.e. Cyrus the Great (d. 530 BCE), who built the Persian
Empire, in large part by overthrowing Astyages, the king of the
Medes, around 550.   [184] In a Greek context, the word

he was singing, of course, of the famous deeds of
men who were heroes.

And as for Phemius, he says that (*Od.* 1.337–8)

he knew many stories capable of charming
mortals,
the deeds of men and of gods, tales whose fame
singers spread.

This custom was preserved among the barbarians, according to Dinon in his *History of Persia* (*FGrH* 690 F 9). The
bards knew in advance about the courage of Cyrus I,[183] for
example, and about the war that was about to take place
against Astyages. He says that when Cyrus requested permission to visit Persia—he had previously commanded
Astyages' rod-bearers,[184] and then later his armed men—
. . . and he left. Astyages was having a feast at that point
with his friends, and a man named Angares—he was the
most distinguished bard—who had been invited in, sang
the other, conventional songs, and at the end said that a
great beast, even bolder than a wild boar, had been allowed
to escape into the swamps; if it got control of the territory around there, it would soon have no difficulty fighting large numbers of men. When Astyages asked "What
kind of beast are you referring to?", the bard said that he
meant Cyrus the Persian. Although Astyages was accordingly convinced that he had been right to be suspicious of
Cyrus and tried to summon . . . it did no good.

would refer to minor local officials with police powers of some
sort; in a Roman context (too early for Dinon, who belongs to the
4th century BCE; but the interjection may not represent his actual words), it is the equivalent of "lictors."

Ἐγὼ δὲ ἔχων ἔτι πολλὰ λέγειν περὶ μουσικῆς
αὐλῶν ἀκούων βόμβου καταπαύσω τὸ πολυλογεῖν, τὰ
ἐκ Φιλαύλου Φιλεταίρου ἐπειπών·

ὦ Ζεῦ, καλόν γ' ἔστ' ἀποθανεῖν αὐλούμενον· |
f   τούτοις ἐν Ἅιδου γὰρ μόνοις ἐξουσία
ἀφροδισιάζειν ἐστίν. οἱ δὲ τοὺς τρόπους
ῥυπαροὺς ἔχοντες μουσικῆς ἀπειρίᾳ
εἰς τὸν πίθον φέρουσι τὸν τετρημένον.

Μετὰ δὲ ταῦτα ζητήσεως γενομένης περὶ σαμ-
βύκης ἔφη ὁ Μασούριος ὀξύφθογγον εἶναι μουσικὸν
ὄργανον τὴν σαμβύκην διειλέχθαι τε περὶ αὐτοῦ Εὐ-
φορίωνα τὸν ἐποποιὸν ἐν τῷ Περὶ Ἰσθμίων, χρῆσθαι
634 φήσας αὐτῷ Πάρθους καὶ Τρωγλοδύτας || τετραχόρδῳ
ὄντι· ἱστορεῖν δὲ τοῦτο Πυθαγόραν ἐν τῷ Περὶ τῆς
Ἐρυθρᾶς Θαλάσσης. καλεῖται δέ τι καὶ τῶν πολιορ-
κητικῶν ὀργάνων σαμβύκη, οὗ τό τε σχῆμα καὶ τὴν
κατασκευὴν ἀποδείκνυσι Βίτων ἐν τῷ Πρὸς Ἄτταλον
Περὶ Ὀργάνων. καὶ Ἀνδρέας ὁ Πανορμίτης ἐν τῷ
τριακοστῷ τρίτῳ τῶν Σικελικῶν τῶν Κατὰ Πόλιν, ὡς
ἀπὸ δύο νεῶν προσάγοιτο τοῖς τῶν ἐναντίων τείχεσι·
καλεῖσθαί τε σαμβύκην, ἐπειδὴ ὅταν ἐξαρθῇ γίνεται
σχῆμα νεὼς καὶ κλίμακος ἑνοποιουμένων, ὅμοιον δέ τι
b ἐστιν καὶ τὸ τῆς | σαμβύκης. Μόσχος δ' ἐν πρώτῳ

---

[185] An allusion to the punishment of the Danaids (Pl. *Grg.*
493b; *R.* 363d; X. *Oec.* 7.40).   [186] Not the philosopher but
the geographer also referred to at 4.183f–4a.

Although I have much more to say about music, I hear the roar of the pipes, and I will therefore bring this long speech to an end, after appending the following passage from Philetaerus' *The Man Who Loved the Pipes* (fr. 17):

> Zeus, it's nice to be listening to pipe-music when you
> die—
> because those are the only people allowed
> to have sex in Hades! Those who've got filthy
> manners,
> on the other hand, and don't know anything about
> music,
> fetch (water) and pour it into the jar full of holes.[185]

After this, questions arose about the *sambukê*, and Masurius said that it was a high-pitched musical instrument and had been discussed by the epic poet Euphorion in his *On the Isthmian Games* (fr. 9, *FHG* iii.73), where he claims that it has four strings and is played by Parthians and Troglodytes; also that Pythagoras[186] recorded this in his *On the Red Sea*. There is also a piece of siege-equipment known as a *sambukê*; Biton describes its appearance and construction in his *To Attalus on Machines* (paragraphs 57–61, Marsden pp. 74–6).[187] Andreas of Panormus in Book XXXIII of his *History of Sicily by City* (*FGrH* 571 F 1) (reports) that two boats brought it up against the enemy's walls; it is referred to as a *sambukê* because when it is set up, it resembles a ship and a ladder combined, and a *sambukê* looks somewhat similar. Moschus in Book I of the

---

[187] See Landels, *JHS* 86 (1966) 69–77.

Μηχανικῶν Ῥωμαϊκὸν εἶναι λέγει τὸ μηχάνημα καὶ
Ἡρακλείδην τὸν Ταραντῖνον εὑρεῖν αὐτοῦ τὸ εἶδος.
Πολύβιος δ᾽ ἐν τῇ ὀγδόῃ τῶν Ἱστοριῶν, Μάρκελλος,
φησί, δυσχρηστούμενος ἐν τῇ Συρακουσῶν πολιορκίᾳ
ὑπὸ τῶν Ἀρχιμήδους κατασκευασμάτων ἔλεγεν ταῖς
μὲν ναυσὶν αὐτοῦ κυαθίζειν ἐκ θαλάσσης Ἀρχιμήδην,
τὰς δὲ σαμβύκας ῥαπιζομένας ὥσπερ ἐκ πότου μετ᾽
αἰσχύνης ἐκπεπτωκέναι.

    Εἰπόντος δὲ ἐπὶ τούτοις Αἰμιλιανοῦ· ἀλλὰ μήν, ὦ
c ἑταῖρε | Μασούριε, πολλάκις καὶ αὐτὸς ἐν ἐννοίᾳ
γίνομαι, μουσικῆς ὢν ἐραστής, περὶ τῆς μαγάδιδος
καλουμένης, πότερον αὐλῶν εἶδος ἢ κιθάρας ἐστίν. ὁ
μὲν γὰρ ἥδιστος Ἀνακρέων λέγει που·

    ψάλλω δ᾽ εἴκοσι
       † χορδαῖσι μάγαδιν † ἔχων,
    ὦ Λεύκασπι, σὺ δ᾽ ἡβᾷς.

Ἴων δ᾽ ὁ Χῖος ἐν Ὀμφάλῃ ὡς περὶ αὐλῶν λέγει διὰ
τούτων·

    Λυδός τε μάγαδις αὐλὸς ἡγείσθω βοῆς.

ὅπερ ἐξηγούμενος ἰαμβεῖον Ἀρίσταρχος ὁ γραμμα
d τικός, ὃν μάντιν ἐκάλει Παναίτιος ὁ Ῥόδιος | φι-
λόσοφος διὰ τὸ ῥᾳδίως καταμαντεύεσθαι τῆς τῶν
ποιημάτων διανοίας, γένος αὐλοῦ φησιν εἶναι τὸν
μάγαδιν, οὔτ᾽ Ἀριστοξένου τοῦτ᾽ εἰπόντος ἐν τοῖς Περὶ

Art of Mechanics says that this is a Roman machine, and that Heracleides of Tarentum designed it. Polybius says in Book VIII (6.5–6 Buettner-Wobst) of his *History*: When Marcellus[188] was baffled during the siege of Syracuse by the devices Archimedes invented, he would say that Archimedes was ladling wine for his own ships from the sea, whereas his *sambukai* had been beaten up and ignominiously kicked out, as it were, from the party.

Aemilianus responded to these remarks: Well, my friend Masurius, since I myself am a music-lover, I often wonder whether what is referred to as a *magadis* is a type of pipe or a lyre. For the delightful Anacreon (*PMG* 374)[189] says somewhere:

> I play the harp, holding
>   a 20 † -stringed *magadis*, †
> Leucaspis, but you're young and beautiful.

Ion of Chios in *Omphale* (*TrGF* 19 F 23) refers to them as if they were pipes, in the following passage:

> And let the Lydian *magadis*-pipe initiate the noise!

In his explication of this iambic line, the grammarian Aristarchus—the philosopher Panaetius of Rhodes (fr. 93 van Straaten) used to refer to him as a *mantis* ("seer"), because he could easily divine the point of a poem—claims that the *magadis* is a type of pipe, even though Aristoxenus (fr. 100 Wehrli) does not say this in either his *On Pipe-Players* or

---

188 The Roman general Marcus Claudius Marcellus, who besieged Syracuse in 213 BCE. Archimedes (below) was killed when the city was finally sacked in 212.

189 Quoted again, in abbreviated form, at 14.635c.

Αὐλητῶν ἢ ἐν τοῖς Περὶ Αὐλῶν καὶ Ὀργάνων, ἀλλὰ
μὴν οὐδὲ Ἀρχεστράτου· πεποίηται γὰρ καὶ τούτῳ δύο
βυβλία Περὶ Αὐλητῶν. οὐκ εἶπεν δὲ τοῦτο οὐδὲ Πύρ-
ρανδρος ἐν τῷ Περὶ Αὐλητῶν, οὐδὲ Φίλλις ὁ Δήλιος·
ξυνέγραψε γὰρ καὶ οὗτος Περὶ Αὐλητῶν καὶ Εὐ-
φράνωρ. Τρύφων δ' ἐν δευτέρῳ Περὶ Ὀνομασιῶν
λέγει οὕτως· ὁ δὲ μάγαδις καλούμενος αὐλός. καὶ |
e   πάλιν· ⟨ὁ⟩[56] μάγαδις ἐν ταὐτῷ ὀξὺν καὶ βαρὺν φθόγ-
γον ἐπιδείκνυται, ὡς Ἀναξανδρίδης ἐν Ὁπλομάχῳ
φησίν·

    μαγάδι λαλήσω μικρὸν ἅμα σοι καὶ μέγα.

τὴν ἀπορίαν οὖν μοι ταύτην οὐδεὶς ἄλλος δυνήσεται
ἀπολύσασθαι, καλὲ Μασούριε, ἢ σύ.

    Καὶ ὃς ἔφη· Δίδυμος ὁ γραμματικὸς ἐν ταῖς Εἰς
Ἴωνα Ἀντεξηγήσεσιν, ἑταῖρε Αἰμιλιανέ, μάγαδιν αὐλὸν ἀκούει τὸν κιθαριστήριον· οὗ μνημονεύειν Ἀρι-
στόξενον ἐν πρώτῳ Περὶ Αὐλῶν Τρήσεως λέγοντα
f   πέντε | γένη εἶναι αὐλῶν, παρθενίους, παιδικούς, κιθα-
ριστηρίους, τελείους, ὑπερτελείους. ἢ ἐλλείπειν οὖν δεῖ
παρὰ τῷ Ἴωνι τόν τε σύνδεσμον, ἵν' ᾖ

    μάγαδις αὐλός ⟨θ'⟩[57]

[56] add. Kaibel   [57] add. Kaibel

---

[190] Otherwise unknown, but presumably not to be identified
with the gastronomic poet from Gela.
[191] For Euphranor, cf. 4.182c, 184e.

his *On Pipes and Instruments*, and neither does Archestratus;[190] the latter also produced an *On Pipe-Players* in
two Books. Pyrrhandrus also omits any mention of this instrument in his *On Pipe-Players* (*FHG* iv.486), as does
Phillis of Delos (fr. 6, *FHG* iv.476); for he too composed
an *On Pipe-Players*, as did Euphranor.[191] But Tryphon in
Book II of *On Terminology* (fr. 110 Velsen) says the following:[192] the pipe referred to as a *magadis*. And again: The
magadis produces high and low tones simultaneously, as
Anaxandrides says in *The Hoplite-Trainer* (fr. 36):

> I'll speak along with you soft and loud, like a
>   *magadis*.

No one other than you, therefore, my good Masurius, will
be able to resolve this puzzle for me.

And Masurius said: The grammarian Didymus in his
Polemical Explication of Ion (pp. 302–3 Schmidt), my
friend Aemilianus, takes a *magadis* to be a pipe played to
accompany a lyre; (he also claims that) Aristoxenus mentions the instrument in Book I of *On the Boring of Pipes* (fr.
101 Wehrli), where he asserts that there are five types of
pipes: girls' pipes, boys' pipes, pipes played to accompany
a lyre, adult-pipes, and more-than-adult pipes.[193] Alternatively, the conjunction must be missing from (the text of)
Ion (*TrGF* 19 F 23, quoted in full at 14.634c), meaning that
it ought to read:

> the magadis *and* the pipe,

[192] Virtually identical material (including Anaxandr. fr. 36) appears at 4.182c–d, but with no reference to Tryphon.

[193] A similar list appears at 4.176e–f (but with no mention of
Aristoxenus).

ὁ προσαυλούμενος τῇ μαγάδιδι. ἡ γὰρ μάγαδις ὅρ-
γανόν ἐστι ψαλτικόν, ὡς Ἀνακρέων φησί, Λυδῶν τε
εὕρημα. διὸ καὶ τὰς Λυδὰς ψαλτρίας φησὶν εἶναι ὁ
Ἴων ἐν τῇ Ὀμφάλῃ διὰ τούτων·

>   ἀλλ᾽ εἶα, Λυδαὶ ψάλτριαι, παλαιθέτων
>   ὕμνων ἀοιδοί, τὸν ξένον κοσμήσατε. ‖

635 Θεόφιλος δ᾽ ὁ κωμικὸς ἐν Νεοπτολέμῳ καὶ τὸ τῇ
μαγάδιδι ψάλλειν μαγαδίζειν λέγει ἐν τούτοις·

>   πονηρὸν υἱὸν καὶ πατέρα καὶ μητέρα
>   ἐστὶν μαγαδίζειν ἐπὶ τροχοῦ καθημένους·
>   οὐδεὶς γὰρ ἡμῶν ταὐτὸν ᾄσεται μέλος.

Εὐφορίων δὲ ἐν τῷ Περὶ Ἰσθμίων παλαιὸν μέν φησι
τὸ ὄργανον εἶναι τὴν μάγαδιν, μετασκευασθῆναι δ᾽
ὀψέ ποτε καὶ σαμβύκην μετονομασθῆναι· πλεῖστον δ᾽
εἶναι τοῦτο τὸ ὄργανον ἐν Μιτυλήνῃ, ὡς καὶ μίαν τῶν
b Μουσῶν ἔχουσαν αὐτὸ | ὑπὸ Λεσβοθέμιδος ποιηθῆναι
ἀρχαίου ἀγαλματοποιοῦ. Μέναιχμος δ᾽ ἐν τοῖς Περὶ
Τεχνιτῶν τὴν πηκτίδα, ἣν τὴν αὐτὴν εἶναι τῇ μαγάδιδι, Σαπφώ φησιν εὑρεῖν. Ἀριστόξενος δὲ τὴν
μάγαδιν καὶ τὴν πηκτίδα χωρὶς πλήκτρου διὰ ψαλμοῦ
παρέχεσθαι τὴν χρείαν. διόπερ καὶ Πίνδαρον εἰρη-

which is played along with the *magadis*. For a *magadis* is
an instrument that resembles a harp, as Anacreon (*PMG*
374, quoted at 14.634c) says, and was invented by the
Lydians. This is why Ion in his *Omphale* (*TrGF* 19 F 22) refers to the Lydian women as harp-players, in the following
passage:

> But come, Lydian women who play the harp, singers
> of ancient hymns—tend to the stranger!

The comic author Theophilus in *Neoptolemus* (fr. 7) uses
the verb *magadizein* to refer to plucking the strings of a
magadis, in the following passage:

> It's a bad idea for a son, a father, and
> a mother to sit on a wheel[194] and *magadizein*;
> because none of us is going to sing the same song.

Euphorion in his *On the Isthmian Games* (fr. 8, *FHG* iii.73)
says that the *magadis* is an ancient instrument, and that at
some late point its shape changed and it came to be referred to as a *sambukê*; this instrument was particularly
common on Mitylene, to the extent that the ancient sculptor Lesbothemis represented a Muse as holding one.[195]
Menaechmus in his *On Artists* (*FGrH* 131 F 4a)[196] claims
that Sappho (fr. 247) invented the *pêktis*, which he identifies with the *magadis*. Aristoxenus (fr. 99 Wehrli) (says)
that the *magadis* and the *pêktis* can be played without a
pick, by plucking the strings. Also that this is why Pindar, in

---

194 A torture device.

195 Very similar material appears at 4.182f. Lesbothemis'
dates are unknown.

196 Cf. 14.635e.

κέναι ἐν τῷ πρὸς Ἱέρωνα σκολίῳ, τὴν μάγαδιν ὀνο-
μάσαντα·

ψαλμὸν ἀντίφθογγον,

διὰ τὸ διὰ δύο γενῶν ἅμα καὶ διὰ πασῶν ἔχειν τὴν
c συνῳδίαν ἀνδρῶν τε καὶ παίδων. καὶ Φρύνιχος | δ' ἐν
Φοινίσσαις εἴρηκε·

ψαλμοῖσιν ἀντίσπαστ' ἀείδοντες μέλη.

καὶ Σοφοκλῆς ἐν Μυσοῖς·

πολὺς δὲ Φρὺξ τρίγωνος ἀντίσπαστά ⟨τε⟩
Λυδῆς ἐφύμνει πηκτίδος συγχορδία.

διαποροῦσι δ' ἔνιοι ὅπως τῆς μαγάδιδος οὔσης κατὰ
Ἀνακρέοντα ⟨ . . . ⟩ (ὀψὲ γάρ ποτε τὰ πολύχορδα
ὀφθῆναι) μνημονεύων αὐτῆς ὁ Ἀνακρέων λέγει·

ψάλλω δ' εἴκοσι
  † χορδαῖσι μάγαδιν † ἔχων,
ὦ Λεύκασπι.

d καὶ ὁ μὲν Ποσειδώνιός φησιν τριῶν μελῳδιῶν | αὐτὸν
μνημονεύειν, Φρυγίου τε ⟨καὶ Δωρίου⟩[58] καὶ Λυδίου·

58 add. Musurus

197 Quoted at greater length at 14.635d–e, where it is clear
that the "two types of instrument" in question (below) are the
pêktis and the *barbitos*. Another fragment of the same poem is
cited at 12.512d.

his skolion directed to Hieron (fr. 125.3),[197] says in reference to the *magadis*:

> notes that responded to its sound,

because when the two types of instrument are played simultaneously an octave apart, the men's and the boys' parts match one another. So too Phrynichus says in *Phoenician Women* (*TrGF* 3 F 11):

> singing songs that match one another in the plucking
> of their strings.

Also Sophocles in *Mysians* (fr. 412):[198]

> A Phrygian *trigônos* sounds repeatedly, and the many
> strings
> of a Lydian *pêktis* accompany it with answering notes.

Some authorities express bafflement at how it can be that, if the *magadis* was in Anacreon's time . . . [199]—for multi-stringed instruments appeared at a relatively late date— Anacreon (*PMG* 374.1–3)[200] says when he mentions it:

> I play the harp, holding
>   a 20 † -stringed *magadis*, †
> Leucaspis.

Posidonius (*FGrH* 87 F 107 = fr. 292 Edelstein–Kidd) claims that Anacreon mentions three melodic schemes, the Phrygian, the Doric, and the Lydian—these are the

---

[198] Quoted also at 4.183e.
[199] The lost portion of the text presumably included words to the effect of "only a four-stringed instrument" (cf. 14.634f–5a).
[200] Quoted at slightly greater length at 14.634c.

ταύταις γὰρ μόναις τὸν Ἀνακρέοντα κεχρῆσθαι· ὧν
ἑπτὰ χορδαῖς ἑκάστης περαινομένης εἰκότως φάναι
ψάλλειν αὐτὸν εἴκοσι χορδαῖς, τῷ ἀρτίῳ χρησάμενον
ἀριθμῷ τὴν μίαν ἀφελόντα. ἀγνοεῖ δ᾽ ὁ Ποσειδώνιος
ὅτι ἀρχαῖόν ἐστιν ὄργανον ἡ μάγαδις, σαφῶς Πιν-
δάρου λέγοντος τὸν Τέρπανδρον ἀντίφθογγον εὑρεῖν
τῇ παρὰ Λυδοῖς πηκτίδι τὸν βάρβιτον·

> τόν ῥα Τέρπανδρός ποθ᾽ ὁ Λέσβιος εὗρεν
> πρῶτος, ἐν δείπνοισι Λυδῶν
e > ψαλμὸν ἀντίφθογγον ὑψηλᾶς | ἀκούων πακτίδος.

πηκτὶς δὲ καὶ μάγαδις ταὐτόν, καθά φησιν ὁ Ἀριστόξενος καὶ Μέναιχμος ὁ Σικυώνιος ἐν τοῖς Περὶ
Τεχνιτῶν· καὶ τὴν Σαπφὼ δέ φησιν οὗτος, ἥτις ἐστὶν
Ἀνακρέοντος πρεσβυτέρα, πρώτην χρήσασθαι τῇ
πηκτίδι. ὅτι δὲ καὶ Τέρπανδρος ἀρχαιότερος Ἀνακρέοντος δῆλον ἐκ τούτων· τὰ Κάρνεια πρῶτος πάντων
Τέρπανδρος νικᾷ, ὡς Ἑλλάνικος ἱστορεῖ ἔν τε τοῖς
ἐμμέτροις Καρνεονίκαις κἀν τοῖς καταλογάδην. ἐγένετο δὲ ἡ θέσις τῶν Καρνείων κατὰ τὴν ἕκτην καὶ
f εἰκοστὴν Ὀλυμπιάδα, | ὡς Σωσίβιός φησιν ἐν τῷ
Περὶ Χρόνων. Ἱερώνυμος δ᾽ ἐν τῷ Περὶ Κιθαρῳδῶν,
ὅπερ ἐστὶ πέμπτον Περὶ Ποιητῶν, κατὰ Λυκοῦργον
τὸν νομοθέτην τὸν Τέρπανδρόν φησι γενέσθαι, ὃς ὑπὸ

---

201 Part of the third verse is quoted also at 14.635b.
202 Cf. 14.635b.

only ones he uses—and that since each requires seven strings, it makes sense that he claims to play with 20 strings, because he is subtracting one and using a round number. But Posidonius is unaware that the *magadis* is an ancient instrument, since Pindar (fr. 125) asserts unambiguously that Terpander invented the *barbitos* to respond to the sound of the Lydian *pêktis*:[201]

> which Terpander of Lesbos in fact invented
> at one point, hearing notes played on the high-
> > pitched
> *paktis* at the Lydians' dinner parties, that responded
> > to its sound.

A *pêktis* and a *magadis* are the same instrument, according to Aristoxenus (fr. 98 Wehrli) and Menaechmus of Sicyon in his *On Artists* (*FGrH* 131 F 4b);[202] the latter authority adds that Sappho, who is earlier than Anacreon, was the first person to play the *pêktis*. That Terpander as well antedates Anacreon is apparent from the following: Terpander was the first victor at the Carneia festival,[203] according to Hellanicus in both the metrical and the prose versions of his *Victories at the Carneia* (*FGrH* 4 F 85a). The Carneia was established in the 26th Olympiad,[204] according to Sosibius in his *On Chronology* (*FGrH* 595 F 3). But Hieronymus in his *On Citharodes*—that is, Book V of *On Poets* (fr. 33 Wehrli)—says that Terpander was a contemporary of the lawgiver Lycurgus,[205] who is universally and without

---

201 A major Spartan festival; cf. 4.141e–f.

204 676–672 BCE.

205 Lycurgus (Poralla #499) was the legendary founder of the Spartan state.

πάντων συμφώνως ἱστορεῖται μετὰ Ἰφίτου τοῦ Ἠλεί-
ου τὴν πρώτην ἀριθμηθεῖσαν τῶν Ὀλυμπίων θέσιν
διαθεῖναι. Εὐφορίων τε ἐν τῷ Περὶ Ἰσθμίων τὰ πολύ-
χορδά φησι τῶν ὀργάνων ὀνόμασι μόνον παρηλ-
λάχθαι, παμπάλαιον δ᾽ αὐτῶν εἶναι τὴν χρῆσιν. ‖

636   Διογένης δ᾽ ὁ τραγικὸς διαφέρειν πηκτίδα μαγάδιδος,
λέγων οὕτως ἐν τῇ Σεμέλῃ·

    καίτοι κλύω μὲν Ἀσιάδος μιτρηφόρους
    Κυβέλης γυναῖκας, παῖδας ὀλβίων Φρυγῶν,
    τυπάνοισι καὶ ῥόμβοισι καὶ χαλκοκτύπων
    βόμβοις βρεμούσας ἀντίχερσι κυμβάλων

          *   *   *

    σοφὴν θεῶν ὑμνῳδὸν ἰατρόν θ᾽ ἅμα.
    κλύω δὲ Λυδὰς Βακτρίας τε παρθένους
    ποταμῷ παροίκους Ἅλυϊ Τμωλίαν θεὸν
    δαφνόσκιον κατ᾽ ἄλσος Ἄρτεμιν σέβειν ∣
b   ψαλμοῖς τριγώνων πηκτίδων ἀντιζύγοις
    ὁλκοῖς κρεκούσας μάγαδιν, ἔνθα Περσικῷ
    νόμῳ ξενωθεὶς αὐλὸς ὁμονοεῖ χοροῖς.

καὶ Φίλλις δ᾽ ὁ Δήλιος ἐν δευτέρῳ Περὶ Μουσικῆς
διαφέρειν φησὶ πηκτίδα μαγάδιδος, λέγων οὕτως·
φοίνικες, πηκτίδες, μαγάδιδες, σαμβῦκαι, ἰαμβῦκαι,
τρίγωνα, κλεψίαμβοι, σκινδαψοί, ἐννεάχορδα. ἐν οἷς
γάρ, φησί, τοὺς ἰάμβους ᾖδον ἰαμβύκας ἐκάλουν, ἐν

---

[206] In 776 BCE.   [207] Cf. 4.182f (where the same list is
attributed to Aristoxenus) with n.

dissent reported to have joined Iphitus of Elis in establishing the first numbered Olympic Games.[206] And Euphorion in his *On the Isthmian Games* (fr. 8, *FHG* iii.73) claims that all that has changed in the case of multi-stringed instruments is the names used for them, and that they have been played for a very long time. The tragic author Diogenes (says) that a *pêktis* is different from a *magadis*, putting it as follows in his *Semele* (*TrGF* 45 F 1):

> Indeed, I hear that the headband-wearing women
> devoted to Asian Cybele, the children of the wealthy
>   Phrygians,
> producing an uproar with drums, bull-roarers, and
> the booming of bronze cymbals they hold in both
>   hands
>
>   *   *   *
>
> a wise goddess, who is celebrated in song and also a
>   healer.
> I hear too that the Lydian and Bactrian girls
> who live on the banks of the Halys River worship the
>   Tmolian
> goddess Artemis in her laurel-shaded sacred grove
> with contrasting notes played on triangular *pêktides*,
> plucking the strings of a *magadis*, where a pipe,
> treated like a guest, conspires with choruses in a
>   Persian melody.

Phillis of Delos in Book II of *On Music* (fr. 2, *FHG* iv.476) likewise claims that a *pêktis* is different from a *magadis*, putting it as follows:[207] *phoinikes, pêktides, magadides, sambukai, iambukai, trigôna, klepsiamboi, skindapsoi,* nine-strings. For they referred to the instruments played when they sang iambic poetry, he says, as *iambukes*, and to

c οἷς δὲ παρελογίζοντο τὰ ἐν | τοῖς μέτροις κλεψι-
άμβους, μαγάδιδας δὲ ‹ἐν οἷς›[59] τὰ διὰ πασῶν καὶ
πρὸς ἴσα τὰ μέρη τῶν ᾀδόντων ἡρμοσμένα. καὶ ἄλλα
δ᾽ ἦν παρὰ ταῦτα· καὶ γὰρ βάρβιτος ἢ βάρμος. καὶ
ἄλλα πλείονα τὰ μὲν ἔγχορδα, τὰ δὲ ἔνηχα κατ-
εσκεύαζον.

Ἦν γὰρ δή τινα καὶ χωρὶς τῶν ἐμφυσωμένων καὶ
χορδαῖς διειλημμένων ἕτερα ψόφου μόνον παρασκευ-
αστικά, καθάπερ τὰ κρέμβαλα. περὶ ὧν φησι Δικαίαρχος ἐν τοῖς Περὶ τοῦ τῆς Ἑλλάδος Βίου, ἐπι-
d χωριάσαι φάσκων ποτὲ καθ᾽ ὑπερβολὴν | εἰς τὸ
προσορχεῖσθαί τε καὶ προσᾴδειν ταῖς γυναιξὶν ὄρ-
γανά τινα ποιά, ὧν ὅτε τις ἅπτοιτο τοῖς δακτύλοις
ποιεῖν λιγυρὸν ψόφον· δηλοῦσθαι δὲ ἐν τῷ τῆς Ἀρτέμιδος ᾄσματι, οὗ ἐστιν ἀρχή·

> Ἄρτεμι, σοί μέ † τι φρὴν ἐφίμερον
> ὕμνον νεναιτε ὅθεν
>   αδε τις ἀλλὰ χρυσοφανια †
>   κρέμβαλα χαλκοπάραια χερσίν.

Ἕρμιππος δ᾽ ἐν Θεοῖς τὸ τούτοις κρούειν κρεμβα-
λιάζειν εἴρηκεν ἐν τούτοις·

> λεπάδας δὲ πετρῶν ἀποκόπτοντες
> κρεμβαλιάζουσιν.

Δίδυμος δέ φησιν εἰωθέναι τινὰς ἀντὶ τῆς λύρας

[59] add. Kaibel

those played when they misrepresented the metrical material as *klepsiamboi*,[208] whereas *magadides* were the ones whose octave-intervals were arranged so that all the singers had an equal share of them. There were also other instruments in addition to these, for example the *barbitos* or *barmos*.[209] They produced many others as well, some of them string instruments, others percussion instruments.

There were in fact other instruments, apart from the wind-instruments and those whose various tones are produced by strings, that merely make noise, as for example castanets. Dicaearchus discusses these in his *On the Greek Life-Style* (fr. 60 Wehrli = fr. 72 Mirhady), saying that at one point instruments of this type were extremely popular for women to dance and sing to, and that when a woman held them in her hands, they produced a high-pitched sound. Also that this is apparent from the song in honor of Artemis that begins (adesp. *PMG* 955):

> Artemis, to you me † something mind desirable
>> hymn [corrupt], whence
>>> [corrupt] someone but gold-[corrupt] †
>>>> bronze-edged castanets in her hands.

Hermippus in *Gods* (fr. 31) uses the verb *krembaliazein* to refer to clapping these together, in the following passage:

> They knock limpets off rocks and *krembaliazousin*.

Didymus (pp. 250–1 Schmidt) claims that rather than

---

208 Allegedly cognate with *kleptô* ("steal, cheat"); but the explanation of the name has the ring of desperate and unlikely etymologizing.

209 Called the *barômos* at 4.182e (citing Euphorion).

κογχύλια καὶ ὄστρακα συγκρούοντας ἔρρυθμον |
e ἠχόν τινα ἀποτελεῖν τοῖς ὀρχουμένοις, καθάπερ καὶ
Ἀριστοφάνην ἐν Βατράχοις φάναι. Ἀρτέμων δ᾽ ἐν τῷ
πρώτῳ Περὶ Διονυσιακοῦ Συστήματος Τιμόθεόν φησι
τὸν Μιλήσιον παρὰ τοῖς πολλοῖς δόξαι πολυχορ-
δοτέρῳ συστήματι χρήσασθαι τῇ μαγάδι· διὸ καὶ
παρὰ τοῖς Λάκωσιν εὐθυνόμενον ὡς παραφθείροι τὴν
ἀρχαίαν μουσικήν, καὶ μέλλοντός τινος ἐκτέμνειν
αὐτοῦ τὰς περιττὰς τῶν χορδῶν, δεῖξαι παρ᾽ αὐτοῖς
f ὑπάρχοντα | Ἀπολλωνίσκον πρὸς τὴν αὐτοῦ σύνταξιν
ἰσόχορδον λύραν ἔχοντα καὶ ἀφεθῆναι. Δοῦρις δ᾽ ἐν
τῷ Περὶ Τραγῳδίας ὠνομάσθαι φησὶ τὴν μάγαδιν
ἀπὸ Μάγδιος Θρακὸς γένος. Ἀπολλόδωρος δ᾽ ἐν τῇ
Πρὸς τὴν Ἀριστοκλέους Ἐπιστολὴν Ἀντιγραφῇ, ὃ
νῦν, φησίν, ἡμεῖς λέγομεν ψαλτήριον, τοῦτ᾽ εἶναι
μάγαδιν, ὁ δὲ κλεψίαμβος κληθείς, ἔτι δ᾽ ὁ τρίγωνος
καὶ ὁ ἔλυμος καὶ τὸ ἐννεάχορδον ἀμαυρότερα τῇ χρείᾳ
καθέστηκεν. καὶ Ἀλκμὰν δέ φησιν·

< . . . > μάγαδιν δ᾽ ἀποθέσθαι. ‖

637 Σοφοκλῆς δὲ ἐν Θαμύρᾳ·

πηκταὶ δὲ λύραι καὶ μαγαδῖδες
τά τ᾽ ἐν Ἕλλησι ξόαν᾽ ἡδυμελῆ.

Τελέστης δ᾽ ἐν Ὑμεναίῳ διθυράμβῳ πεντάχορδόν
φησιν αὐτὴν εἶναι διὰ τούτων·

playing a lyre, some people make it a practice to strike shells or potsherds against one another to produce a rhythmic sound to accompany dancers, as Aristophanes says in *Frogs* (1304–6). Artemon in Book I of *On the Dionysiac Guild* (fr. 11, *FHG* iv.342) claims that Timotheus of Miletus is widely believed to have played a *magadis* equipped with an exceptionally large number of strings. This is why, when he was being called to account in Sparta for allegedly corrupting the ancient musical style, and someone was about to cut off his excess strings, he pointed out that they had a small statue of Apollo holding a lyre with the same number of strings as his own was strung with, and was acquitted. Duris in his *On Tragedy* (*FGrH* 76 F 28) claims that the *magadis* gets its name from Magdis, whose family was from Thrace. But Apollodorus says in his *Treatise in Response to Aristocles' Letter* (*FGrH* 244 F 219): What we refer to today as a *psaltêrion* is a *magadis*, whereas what was known as a *klepsiambos* has fallen out of use, as have the *trigônos*, the *elumos*,[210] and the nine-stringer. So too Alcman (*PMG* 101) says:

> to set aside a *magadis*.

Sophocles in *Thamyra* (fr. 238):

> carefully constructed lyres and *magadides*,
> and the sweet-toned wooden instruments the Greeks
> play.

Telestes in the dithyramb *Hymenaeus* (*PMG* 808) claims that the *magadis* has five strings, in the following passage:

[210] A type of pipe; cf. 4.176f with n.

ἄλλος δ' ἄλλαν κλαγγὰν ἱεὶς
κερατόφωνον ἐρέθιζε μάγαδιν
πενταρράβδῳ χορδᾶν ἀρθμῷ
χέρα καμψιδίαυλον ἀναστρωφῶν τάχος. |

b οἶδα δὲ καὶ ἄλλο ὄργανον ᾧ τῶν Θρᾳκῶν οἱ βασιλεῖς
ἐν τοῖς δείπνοις χρῶνται, ὥς φησιν Νικομήδης ἐν τῷ
Περὶ Ὀρφέως. φοίνικα δὲ τὸ ὄργανον Ἔφορος καὶ
Σκάμων ἐν τοῖς Περὶ Εὑρημάτων ὑπὸ Φοινίκων εὑ-
ρεθὲν ταύτης τυχεῖν τῆς προσηγορίας· Σῆμος δὲ ὁ
Δήλιος ἐν πρώτῳ Δηλιάδος διὰ τὸ ἐκ τοῦ ἐν Δήλῳ
φοίνικος τοὺς ἀγκῶνας αὐτοῦ ἐξειργάσθαι. τῇ σαμ-
βύκῃ πρώτην φησὶ χρήσασθαι Σίβυλλαν, ἧς Σκάμων
c ὁ | προειρημένος < . . . > ὀνομασθῆναι δ' αὐτὴν
εὑρεθεῖσαν ὑπὸ Σάμβυκος τινός. καὶ περὶ τοῦ τρί-
ποδος δὲ καλουμένου (ὄργανον δὲ καὶ τοῦτο μουσικόν)
ὁ προειρημένος Ἀρτέμων γράφει οὕτως· ὅθεν πολλὰ
τῶν ὀργάνων οὐδ' εἰ γέγονέ ποτε γινώσκεται, καθάπερ
ὁ Πυθαγόρου τοῦ Ζακυνθίου τρίπους· ὀλιγοχρόνιον
γὰρ τὴν ἀκμὴν σχὼν ἢ διὰ τὸ δοκεῖν ἐργώδης εἶναι
κατὰ τὴν χειροθεσίαν ἢ δι' ἣν δή ποτ' οὖν αἰτίαν
συντόμως καταλυθεὶς διαλέληθε τοὺς πολλούς. ἦν δὲ
παραπλήσιος μὲν Δελφικῷ τρίποδι καὶ τοὔνομ' ἐντεῦθεν ἔσχεν, τὴν δὲ χρῆσιν τριπλῆς κιθάρας παρ-

---

211 I.e. a pick.   212 I.e. the famous palm tree to which
Leto clung when she gave birth to Apollo (h.Ap. 117 with Allen–
Halliday–Sikes ad loc.).   213 I.e. the Sibyl, Apollo's prophet-
ess/priestess, here treated as a specific historical individual.

Each of them was producing a different noise,
stirring up the *magadis*, which gets its voice from a
    bit of horn,[211]
with its set of five rod-like strings,
by rapidly moving his hand back and forth.

I also know of another instrument, which the Thracian
kings play at their dinner parties, according to Nicomedes
in his *On Orpheus* (*FGrH* 772 F 3). As for the instrument
referred to as a *phoinix*, Ephorus (*FGrH* 70 F 4) and
Scamon in his *On Inventions* (*FGrH* 476 F 4) (report that)
it got this name from the fact that the Phoenicians (*Phoinikes*) invented it, whereas Semus of Delos in Book I of
the *History of Delos* (*FGrH* 396 F 1) (claims that it was
called this) because its ribs were made from the palm tree
(*phoinix*) on Delos.[212] He says that the first person to play
the *sambukê* was Sibylla,[213] about whom the Scamon referred to above . . . ; it got its name from the fact that a certain Sambyx invented it. As for the so-called *tripous*, moreover—this is another musical instrument—the Artemon
(fr. 12, *FHG* iv.342–3) mentioned above (14.636e) writes
as follows: As a consequence of which, we do not even
know if many of the instruments ever existed, as for example the *tripous* of Pythagoras of Zacynthus; for it was important for only a short period, either because it seemed
to be difficult to play, or because it abruptly fell out of use
for one reason or another and most people forgot about it.
It resembled a Delphic tripod, hence its name, and was
played like a triple lyre. For its feet rested on a base that

εἴχετο· τῶν γὰρ ποδῶν ἑστώτων ἐπί τινος βάσεως
d εὐστρόφου, καθάπερ αἱ τῶν περιάκτων δίφρων | κατα-
σκευάζονται θέσεις, τὰς μέσας τρεῖς χώρας τὰς ἀπὸ
ποδὸς ἐπὶ πόδα διεστώσας ἐνέτεινε χορδαῖς, ὑπερθεὶς
ἑκάστῃ πῆχυν καὶ κάτω προσαρμόσας χορδοτόνια,
καὶ τὸν ἐπάνω κόσμον κοινὸν τοῦ λέβητος καὶ τῶν
παρηρτημένων † ἐνίων † ἀποδούς, ἐξ ὧν καὶ τὴν
φαντασίαν εἶχεν ἀστείαν καὶ τὸν ἦχον προσέβαλλεν
ἁδρότερον. διένειμεν δὲ τὰς τρεῖς χώρας ταῖς τρισὶν
ἁρμονίαις τῇ τε Δωριστὶ καὶ Φρυγιστὶ καὶ Λυδιστί·
καὶ καθεζόμενος αὐτὸς ἐπί τινος δίφρου περὶ ταὐτὸν
συμμέτρως ἔχοντα τῇ συστάσει, διείρας δὲ τὴν
εὐώνυμον χεῖρα πρὸς τὴν ἐπιβολήν, καὶ τῇ ἑτέρᾳ
e χρησόμενος τῷ πλήκτρῳ, | καθ᾽ ὁποίαν δὴ πρώτην
ᾑρεῖτο τῶν ἁρμονιῶν μετέστρεφε τῷ ποδὶ τὴν βάσιν
εὔτροχον⁶⁰ οὖσαν, καὶ πρὸς ἑτέραν πλευρὰν πάλιν
ἐπιβάλλων ἐχρῆτο καὶ πάλιν ἑτέραν. οὕτω δ᾽ ὀξέως
ὑπὸ τὴν χεῖρα προσῆγεν αὐτῷ τὰ συστήματα ἡ τῆς
βάσεως εὐκινησία τῷ ποδὶ ψαυομένη καὶ τὴν χειροθεσίαν ἐπὶ τοσοῦτον εἰθίσθη κατοξύνειν ὥστ᾽, εἴ τις
μὴ συνορῴη τὸ γινόμενον, ἀλλὰ διὰ τῆς ἀκοῆς μόνον
κρίνοι, νομίζειν τριῶν κιθαρῶν ἀκούειν διαφόρως ἡρ-
μοσμένων. καὶ τοῦτο τὸ ὄργανον θαυμασθὲν ἰσχυρῶς
μετὰ τὸν ἐκείνου βίον ἐξέλιπεν εὐθέως.

Τὴν δὲ ψιλὴν κιθάρισιν πρῶτόν φησιν Μέναιχμος
f εἰσαγαγεῖν | Ἀριστόνικον τὸν Ἀργεῖον, τῇ ἡλικίᾳ

⁶⁰ εὔτροχον δ᾽ A: δ᾽ del. Musurus

could be turned easily, in the same way that the seats of rotating stools are constructed; the three spaces between the legs had strings stretched across them; it had a bridge that extended over the top of each space, and was fitted on the bottom with tail-pieces that kept the strings taut; and the upper portion resembled a combination of a bowl and [corrupt] attached to it, which gave it a sophisticated appearance and made the sound more robust. He assigned each of the three spaces to one of the three scales (that is, the Doric, the Phrygian, and the Lydian); he himself would sit on a stool constructed to match its proportions, extending his left hand to hold the instrument and wielding the pick with the other, and would turn the base, which rotated easily, with his foot, depending on which scale he had chosen to begin with, and would then move on to play another side, and another one after that. The rapid movement of the base, when he touched it with his foot, brought the various sets of strings beneath his hands so quickly, and he had become accustomed to manipulating it so dazzlingly fast, that if you did not see what was going on but simply judged on the basis of what you heard, you would think that you were listening to three lyres with different tunings. Although this instrument was regarded with considerable awe, it fell out of use immediately after he died.

Menaechmus (*FGrH* 131 F 5) claims that Aristonicus of Argos,[214] who was a contemporary of Archilochus[215] and

214 Stephanis #366.
215 Archilochus belongs to the mid- to late-7th century BCE.

γενόμενον κατὰ Ἀρχίλοχον, κατοικήσαντα ἐν Κορ-
κύρᾳ. Φιλόχορος δ' ἐν τρίτῃ Ἀτθίδος, Λύσανδρος,
φησίν, ὁ Σικυώνιος κιθαριστὴς πρῶτος μετέστησε τὴν
ψιλοκιθαριστικήν, μακροὺς τοὺς τόνους ἐντείνας καὶ
τὴν φωνὴν εὔογκον ποιήσας, καὶ τὴν ἔναυλον κιθάρι-
638 σιν, ᾗ πρῶτοι οἱ περὶ Ἐπίγονον ‖ ἐχρήσαντο. καὶ
περιελὼν τὴν συντομίαν τὴν ὑπάρχουσαν ἐν τοῖς
ψιλοῖς κιθαρισταῖς χρώματά τε εὔχροα πρῶτος ἐκι-
θάρισε καὶ ἰάμβους καὶ μάγαδιν,[61] καὶ ὄργανον
μετέλαβεν μόνος τῶν πρὸ αὐτοῦ, καὶ τὸ πρᾶγμα
αὐξήσας χορὸν περιεστήσατο πρῶτος. Δίωνα δὲ τὸν
Χῖον τὸ τοῦ Διονύσου σπονδεῖον πρῶτον κιθαρίσαι
Μέναιχμος. Τιμόμαχος δ' ἐν τοῖς Κυπριακοῖς Στή-
σανδρον λέγει τὸν Σάμιον ἐπὶ πλεῖον αὐξῆσαι τὴν
b   τέχνην καὶ πρῶτον ἐν Δελφοῖς κιθαρῳδῆσαι | τὰς καθ'
Ὅμηρον μάχας, ἀρξάμενον ἀπὸ τῆς Ὀδυσσείας. ἄλλοι δὲ πρῶτόν φασιν παρ' Ἐλευθερναίοις κιθαρίσαι
τὰς ἐρωτικὰς ᾠδὰς Ἀμήτορα τὸν Ἐλευθερναῖον, οὗ
καὶ τοὺς ἀπογόνους Ἀμητορίδας καλεῖσθαι. Ἀριστόξενος δέ φησιν· ὥσπερ τῶν ἑξαμέτρων τινὲς ἐπὶ τὸ
γελοῖον παρῳδὰς εὗρον, οὕτως καὶ τῆς κιθαρῳδίας
πρῶτος Οἰνώπας· ὃν ἐζήλωσαν Πολύευκτός τε ὁ

---

[61] μάγαδιν τὸν καλούμενον συριγμόν A: τὸν καλούμενον
συριγμόν del. Olson

---

216 Stephanis #1573.   217 Or "by Epigonus and his students." Epigonus is Stephanis #855.   218 Presumably to be
identified with the *iambukai* mentioned in 14.636b.

lived on Corcyra, was the first person to play a lyre without singing along to it. But Philochorus says in Book III of the *History of Attica* (*FGrH* 328 F 23): The lyre-player Lysander of Sicyon[216] was the first person to move to a style of lyre-playing that involved no singing, by tuning the strings higher and giving them a full sound, and to one that produced something resembling pipe-music, a style Epigonus pioneered.[217] Lysander eliminated the plain style that prevailed among lyre-players who did not sing along with the music, and was the first person to introduce colorful modulations when he played *iamboi*[218] or a *magadis*. No one before him had made one instrument sound like another, and by expanding his craft he became the first musician to establish a group around him. Menaechmus (*FGrH* 131 F 6) (reports) that Dion of Chios[219] was the first person to play a libation-song in honor of Dionysus on the lyre. Timomachus in his *History of Cyprus* (*FGrH* 754 F 1) claims that Stesandrus of Samos[220] expanded the art considerably and was the first person to play the lyre while he sang the battle-scenes in Homer, beginning with the *Odyssey*, in Delphi. Other authorities report that erotic songs were first played on the lyre at Eleuthernae by Ametor of Eleuthernae,[221] whose descendants are known as the Ametoridae. Aristoxenus (fr. 136 Wehrli) says: In the same way that some people made up parodies of hexameter lines in order to be amusing,[222] so too Oenopas[223] invented parodies of citharodic performances; Polyeuctus of Achaea

---

[219] Stephanis #792.   [220] Stephanis #2301.
[221] Stephanis #152.   [222] E.g. Matro of Pitane (4.134d–7c) and Hegemon of Thasos (15.698d–9a).   [223] Stephanis #1933; cf. 1.19f–20a (where he is called Oenonas).

Ἀχαιὸς καὶ Διοκλῆς ὁ Κυναιθεύς. καὶ μοχθηρῶν δὲ
ἀσμάτων γεγόνασι ποιηταί, περὶ ὧν φησι Φαινίας ὁ
c Ἐρέσιος ἐν τοῖς Πρὸς τοὺς | Σοφιστὰς γράφων οὕτως·
Τελένικος ὁ Βυζάντιος, ἔτι δὲ Ἀργᾶς ποιηταὶ μοχθηρῶν ὄντες νόμων πρὸς μὲν τὸν ἴδιον χαρακτῆρα τῆς
ποιήσεως εὐπόρουν, τῶν δὲ Τερπάνδρου καὶ Φρύνιδος
νόμων οὐδὲ κατὰ μικρὸν ἠδύναντο ἐπιψαῦσαι. τοῦ
Ἀργᾶ μνημονεύει Ἄλεξις ἐν Ἀποβάτῃ οὕτως·

(Α.) Χορόνικος <ὁ> ποιητὴς ὁδί.
(Β.) τίνων ποιητὴς ἀσμάτων; (Α.) σεμνῶν πάνυ.
(Β.) τί πρὸς τὸν Ἀργᾶν οὗτος; (Α.) ἡμέρας
     δρόμῳ
κρείττων.

καὶ Ἀναξανδρίδης ἐν Ἡρακλεῖ· |

d ὁ μὲν γὰρ εὐφυής τις εἶναι φαίνεται·
ὡς δ' εὐρύθμως λαβὼν τὸ μελετητήριον
εἶτ' ἐσχεδίασε δριμέως † ενπαπαι †
μεστὸς γενόμενος πρὸς τὸν Ἀργᾶν βούλομαι
κωδωνίσας πέμψαι σ' ἀγωνιούμενον,
ἵνα καὶ σὺ νικᾷς τοὺς σοφιστάς, ὦ φίλε.

ὁ δὲ τοὺς εἰς Χιωνίδην ἀναφερομένους ποιήσας Πτω-

---

224 Stephanis #2095 and 702, respectively.
225 Stephanis #292; cf. 4.131b with n. Telenicus is otherwise
unknown.

and Diocles of Cynaetha[224] followed his example. There have also been poets who produced depraved songs. Phaenias of Eresus discusses them in his *Response to the Sophists* (fr. 10 Wehrli), where he writes as follows: Telenicus of Byzantium, along with Argas,[225] were poets who produced indecent tunes; although they were successful with their own type of poetry, they were unable to come anywhere near to the tunes of Terpander and Phrynis. Alexis in *The Chariot-Acrobat* (fr. 19) mentions Argas, as follows:

> (A.) This poet here's Choronicus.
> (B.) What sort of songs does he write? (A.) They're
> very distinguished.
> (B.) How does he compare to Argas? (A.) He's miles
> and miles[226]
> ahead.

Also Anaxandrides in *Heracles* (fr. 16):

> Because he looks like someone with natural talent.
> Since after he picked up his instrument gracefully,
> he then improvised piercingly [corrupt].
> I've had enough of testing you; I want
> to send you to compete against Argas,
> so that you too can defeat the sophists, my friend!

The author of the *Beggars* attributed to Chionides (fr. 4)[227]

---

[226] Literally "a day's run."

[227] Similar doubts about the play's authorship are expressed at 4.137e (contrast 3.119e).

χοὺς Γνησίππου τινὸς μνημονεύει παιγνιαγράφου τῆς
ἱλαρᾶς μούσης, λέγων οὕτως·

    ταῦτ' οὐ μὰ Δία Γνήσιππος οὐδ' ὁ Κλεομένης
e   ἐν | ἐννέ' ἂν χορδαῖς κατεγλυκάνατο.

καὶ ὁ τοὺς Εἵλωτας δὲ πεποιηκώς φησιν·

    τὰ Στησιχόρου τε καὶ Ἀλκμᾶνος Σιμωνίδου τε
    ἀρχαῖον ἀείδειν, ὁ δὲ Γνήσιππος ἔστ' ἀκούειν.
    κεῖνος νυκτερίν' ηὗρε μοιχοῖς ἀείσματ'
      ἐκκαλεῖσθαι
    γυναῖκας ἔχοντας ἰαμβύκην τε καὶ τρίγωνον.

Κρατῖνος ἐν Μαλθακοῖς·

    τίς ἄρ' ἔρωτα † μοιδεν † ὦ Γνήσιππε, ἐγὼ †
      πολλῇ χολη †;
    οἴομαι < . . . > μηδὲν οὕτως μωρὸν εἶναι καὶ
      κενόν.

σκώπτει δ' αὐτὸν εἰς τὰ ποιήματα καὶ ἐν Βουκόλοις· |

f   ὃς οὐκ ἔδωκ' αἰτοῦντι Σοφοκλέει χορόν,
    τῷ Κλεομάχου δ', ὃν οὐκ ἂν ἠξίουν ἐγὼ
    ἐμοὶ διδάσκειν οὐδ' ἂν εἰς Ἀδώνια.

---

228 Stephanis #556; *PAA* 279680. The name is rare, and this is
presumably the same man as the tragic poet (*PAA* 279690; *TrGF*
27) referred to below as the "son of Cleomachus."

229 Perhaps to be identified with the dithyrambic poet Cleomenes of Rhegium, mentioned at 9.402a.

mentions a certain Gnesippus,[228] who wrote witty little pieces of humorous poetry, saying the following:

> By Zeus—Gnesippus and Cleomenes[229] couldn't have made
> this palatable, even if they'd used nine strings!

So too the author of *Helots* (Eup. fr. 148) says:

> Singing the works of Stesichorus, Alcman,
> and Simonides is old-fashioned; but you can hear Gnesippus!
> He invented night-time songs for adulterers holding harps[230]
> to use to summon women out to them.

Cratinus in *Soft Men* (fr. 104):

> Who, then, love [corrupt], Gnesippus, I [corrupt]?
> I don't think anything . . . is so stupid and vacuous!

He also makes fun of him for his poetry in *Cowherds* (fr. 17):

> who didn't offer Sophocles a chorus when he asked for one,
> but gave one to Cleomachus' son, who *I* wouldn't have thought
> deserved to serve as my trainer even for the Adonia![231]

---

[230] Literally "an *iambukê* or a *trigônos*."   [231] The Adonia was a women's festival that involved drinking and dancing; the speaker's point is not that it actually featured state-sponsored dramatic choruses but that the poetry of Cleomachus' son is better suited to such depraved settings—if even to them.

ἐν δὲ ταῖς Ὥραις·

ἴτω δὲ καὶ τραγῳδίας
ὁ Κλεομάχου διδάσκαλος
† μετὰ τῶν † παρατιλτριῶν
ἔχων χορὸν Λυδιστὶ τιλ-
λουσῶν μέλη πονηρά. ‖

639 Τηλεκλείδης δὲ ἐν τοῖς Στερροῖς καὶ περὶ μοιχείας
ἀναστρέφεσθαί φησιν αὐτόν. Κλέαρχος δὲ ἐν δευτέρῳ
Ἐρωτικῶν τὰ ἐρωτικά φησιν ἄσματα καὶ τὰ Λοκρικὰ
καλούμενα οὐδὲν τῶν Σαπφοῦς καὶ Ἀνακρέοντος διαφέρειν. ἔτι δὲ τὰ Ἀρχιλόχου καὶ τῶν Ὁμήρου Ἐπικι-
χλίδων τὰ πολλὰ διὰ τῆς ἐμμέτρου ποιήσεως τούτων
ἔχεταί τινος τῶν παθῶν, ἀλλὰ καὶ τὰ Ἀσωποδώρου
περὶ τὸν Ἔρωτα καὶ πᾶν τὸ τῶν ἐρωτικῶν ἐπιστολῶν
γένος ἐρωτικῆς τινος διὰ λόγου ποιήσεώς ἐστιν.

b   Τοσαῦτα τοῦ Μασουρίου διεξελθόντος | περιηνέ-
χθησαν ἡμῖν καὶ αἱ δεύτεραι καλούμεναι τράπεζαι,
πολλάκις ἡμῖν διδόμεναι οὐ μόνον ταῖς τῶν Κρονίων
ἡμέραις, ἐν αἷς Ῥωμαίων παισὶν ⟨ἔθος ἐστὶν⟩[62] ἐστι-
ᾶν τοὺς οἰκέτας, αὐτοὺς τὰς τῶν οἰκετῶν ἀναδεχο-
μένους λειτουργίας. Ἑλληνικὸν δὲ τοῦτο τὸ ἔθος. ἐν
Κρήτῃ γοῦν τῇ τῶν Ἑρμαίων ἑορτῇ τὸ ὅμοιον γίνεται,

---

[62] ἔθος ἐστὶν Musurus: ἔθος ἦν CE

---

[232] Literally *didaskalos* ("trainer"); but the word is routinely
used to refer to the poet himself.

[233] *melê*, with a pun on another sense of the word, "songs."

234

And in his *Seasons* (fr. 276):

> And let the tragic poet,[232]
> Cleomachus' son, go
> † with his † along with a chorus
> of hair-pluckers, plucking their
>   nasty limbs[233] in the Lydian style.

Teleclides in his *Tough Guys* (fr. 36) claims that Gnesippus spent his time seducing women. Clearchus in Book II of the *Erotica* (fr. 33 Wehrli) says that erotic songs and the so-called *Lokrika*[234] are no different from the poems of Sappho and Anacreon. So too Archilochus' poetry and most of Homer's *For Thrushes*,[235] which are composed in meter, have some connection with these passions, while Asopodorus' essays on Eros[236] (*SH* 223) and the entire genre of erotic epistles represent a type of erotic poetry written in prose.

After Masurius completed these lengthy remarks, what are referred to as the second tables were brought around for us; we were frequently offered them, and not just during the Cronia[237] festival, when the Romans customarily provide a meal for their household slaves and take over the slaves' duties themselves. This is a Greek custom. Something similar happens, for example, during the Hermaia

---

[234] See 15.697b–c for an example of the genre (= carm. pop. *PMG* 853).

[235] Cf. 2.65b (where one ought perhaps to translate "to the boys" rather than "to the children").

[236] Cf. 10.445b (which makes it clear that Asopodorus was in fact a prose author); 14.631f.   [237] The Greek name for the Saturnalia (referred to again briefly at 14.639e, where see n.).

ὥς φησι Καρύστιος ἐν Ἱστορικοῖς Ὑπομνήμασιν·
εὐωχουμένων γὰρ τῶν οἰκετῶν οἱ δεσπόται ὑπηρε-
τοῦσιν πρὸς τὰς διακονίας. καὶ ἐν Τροιζῆνι δὲ μηνὶ
c Γεραιστίῳ· πανήγυρις | δὲ τότε γίνεται πολυήμερος,
ἧς ἐν μιᾷ οἱ δοῦλοι μετὰ τῶν πολιτῶν κοινῇ τε ἀστρα-
γαλίζουσιν καὶ οἱ κύριοι τοὺς δούλους ἑστιῶσιν, ὡς ὁ
αὐτός φησιν Καρύστιος. Βήρωσος δ᾽ ἐν πρώτῳ Βαβυ-
λωνιακῶν τῷ Λώῳ φησὶ μηνὶ ἑκκαιδεκάτῃ ἄγεσθαι
ἑορτὴν Σάκαια προσαγορευομένην ἐν Βαβυλῶνι ἐπὶ
ἡμέρας πέντε, ἐν αἷς ἔθος εἶναι ἄρχεσθαι τοὺς δεσπό-
τας ὑπὸ τῶν οἰκετῶν ἀφηγεῖσθαί τε τῆς οἰκίας ἕνα
αὐτῶν ἐνδεδυκότα στολὴν ὁμοίαν τῇ βασιλικῇ, ὃν καὶ
καλεῖσθαι ζωγάνην. μνημονεύει τῆς ἑορτῆς καὶ Κτη-
d σίας | ἐν δευτέρῳ Περσικῶν. Κῷοι δὲ τοὐναντίον
δρῶσιν, ὡς ἱστορεῖ Μακαρεὺς ἐν τρίτῳ Κωακῶν· ὅταν
γὰρ τῇ Ἥρᾳ θύωσιν, δοῦλοι οὐ παραγίνονται ἐπὶ τὴν
εὐωχίαν. διὸ καὶ Φύλαρχον εἰρηκέναι·

† σουριηι † μοῦνοι μὲν ἐλεύθεροι ἱεροεργοί,
ἀνδράσι † προσκεινοισιν † ἐλεύ‹θε›ρον ἆμαρ
      ἔχοντες·
δούλων δ᾽ οὔτις πάμπαν ἐσέρχεται οὐδ᾽ ἠβαιόν.

Βάτων δ᾽ ὁ Σινωπεὺς ὁ ῥήτωρ ἐν τῷ Περὶ Θεσσαλίας |
e καὶ Αἱμονίας σαφῶς ἐμφανίζει τὴν τῶν Σατουρναλίων
ἑορτὴν Ἑλληνικωτάτην, φάσκων αὐτὴν παρὰ τοῖς

festival on Crete, according to Carystius in the *Historical Commentaries* (fr. 13, *FHG* iv.358–9, including the description of the customs in Troezen below); for while the household slaves feast, their masters do all the work connected with the serving. So too in Troezen during the month of Geraistios: a multi-day festival takes place then, and on one day the slaves play knucklebones along with the citizens, and the masters provide their slaves with a meal, according to the same Carystius. Berosus in Book I of the *History of Babylon* (*FGrH* 680 F 2) says that a festival known as the Sakaia is celebrated in Babylon on the 16th day of the month Lôos; it lasts for five days, during which the custom is for the domestic slaves to rule their masters, and one of them has authority over the household and wears something known as a *zôganê* that resembles a king's robes. Ctesias also mentions the festival in Book II of the *History of Persia* (*FGrH* 688 F 4). The Coans do the opposite, according to Macareus in Book III of the *History of Cos* (*FGrH* 456 F 1b);[238] for when they sacrifice to Hera, no slaves attend the feast, which is why Phylarchus (*FGrH* 81 F 84 = *SH* 694A) says:

> [corrupt] free men alone carry out the rites,
> to/for men [corrupt], to whom belongs the day of
>   freedom;
> but no slave at all enters even for a moment.

The orator Bato of Sinope in his *On Thessaly and Haemonia* (*FGrH* 268 F 5) brings out the strikingly Greek character of the Saturnalia festival[239] clearly, claiming that

---

[238] Cf. 6.262c (a slightly fuller citation of the passage).
[239] Celebrated in Rome in late December.

Θεσσαλοῖς Πελώρια καλεῖσθαι, γράφων οὕτως· θυσίας κοινῆς τοῖς Πελασγοῖς γινομένης ἀπαγγεῖλαί τινα τῷ Πελασγῷ ἄνδρα, ᾧ ὄνομα ἦν Πέλωρος, διότι ἐν τῇ Αἱμονίᾳ σεισμῶν μεγάλων γενομένων ῥαγείη τὰ Τέμπη ὄρη ὀνομαζόμενα καὶ διότι διὰ τοῦ διαστήματος ὁρμήσαν τὸ τῆς λίμνης ὕδωρ ἐμβάλλοι εἰς τὸ τοῦ Πηνειοῦ ῥεῖθρον, καὶ τὴν πρότερον λιμνάζουσαν χώf ραν ἅπασαν | γεγυμνῶσθαι καὶ ἀναξηραινομένων τῶν ὑδάτων πεδία θαυμαστὰ τῷ μεγέθει καὶ τῷ κάλλει ἀναφαίνεσθαι. ἀκούσαντα οὖν τὸν Πελασγὸν τὴν τράπεζαν ἀφθόνως αὐτῷ κεκοσμημένην τῷ Πελώρῳ παραθεῖναι. καὶ τοὺς ἄλλους δὲ φιλοφρονουμένους ἕκαστον φέρειν ὅ τι ἔχοι παρ' αὐτῷ βέλτιστον καὶ παρατιθέναι ἐπὶ τὴν τράπεζαν τῷ ἀπαγγείλαντι, καὶ αὐτὸν τὸν Πελασγὸν προθύμως διακονεῖν καὶ τῶν ἄλλων τοὺς ἐν ἀξιώματι ὄντας ὑπηρετεῖν, καθότι ἑκάστῳ ὁ καιρὸς παρέπιπτεν. διόπερ, φασίν, ἐπεὶ τὴν χώραν κατέσχον, ἀπομίμημα τῆς τότε γενομένης ἑορ640 τῆς < . . . > καὶ θύοντας Διὶ Πελωρίῳ ‖ τραπέζας τε λαμπρῶς κοσμοῦντας παρατιθέναι καὶ οὕτως φιλάνθρωπον[63] τὴν πανήγυριν συντελεῖν, ὥστε καὶ τοὺς ξένους ἅπαντας ἐπὶ τὴν θοίνην παραλαμβάνειν καὶ τοὺς δεσμώτας λύειν καὶ τοὺς οἰκέτας κατακλίναντας μετὰ πάσης παρρησίας ἑστιᾶν, διακονούντων αὐτοῖς τῶν δεσποτῶν· καὶ τὸ σύνολον ἔτι καὶ νῦν Θεσσαλοὺς μεγίστην ἑορτὴν ἄγοντας προσαγορεύειν Πελώρια.

[63] φιλάνθρωπόν τε A: del. Musurus

the Thessalians refer to it as the Peloria, and writing as follows: When the Pelasgians were carrying out a public sacrifice, a man named Pelorus brought Pelasgus a message, to the effect that there had been major earthquakes in Haemonia, producing a rift in what is known as the Tempe Range; that the lake-water had rushed out through the gap and joined the course of the Peneius River, and the land that had previously been at the bottom of the lake had all been exposed; and that as the water dried up, extraordinarily large and beautiful plains were emerging. When Pelasgus heard the news, therefore, he set his table, which was covered with a large amount of food intended for him, in front of Pelorus. Everyone else similarly expressed their warm feelings by taking the finest item of food they had and setting it on the table for the man who had brought the message; and Pelasgus himself enthusiastically served him, with the other important people assisting him wherever an opportunity arose. This is why, they say, after they took control of the territory, as an imitation of the festival that occurred at that time . . . and they sacrifice to Zeus Pelorias and set out tables covered with spectacular food. They make the festival so hospitable, that they welcome all visitors to the meal, and release their prisoners; and they have their domestic slaves lie down, and then serve them a feast, during which the slaves may say anything they like, and the masters do all the serving. To sum up, even today this is the most important festival the Thessalians celebrate, and they refer to it as the Peloria.

Πολλάκις οὖν, ὡς ἔφην, τῶν τοιούτων ἡμῖν παρα-
τιθεμένων ἐπιδορπισμάτων ἔφη τις τῶν παρόντων· |

b   αἱ δεύτεραί πως φροντίδες σοφώτεραι.

τί γὰρ ποθεῖ τράπεζα; τῷ δ' οὐ βρίθεται;
πλήρης μὲν ὄψων ποντίων, πάρεισι δὲ
μόσχων τέρειναι σάρκες χηνεία τε δαὶς
καὶ πεπτὰ καὶ κροτητὰ τῆς ξουθοπτέρου
πελανῷ μελίσσης ἀφθόνως δεδευμένα,

φησὶν ὁ Εὐριπίδης ἐν Κρήσσαις. καὶ ὡς ὁ Εὔβουλος
δ' ἐν Ὀλβίᾳ ἔφη·

(Α.) ἐν τῷ γὰρ αὐτῷ πάνθ' ὁμοῦ πωλήσεται
ἐν ταῖς Ἀθήναις· σῦκα, (Β.) κλητῆρες (Α.)
βότρυς, |

c γογγυλίδες, ἄπιοι, μῆλα, (Β.) μάρτυρες (Α.)
ῥόδα,
μέσπιλα, χόρια, σχαδόνες, ἐρέβινθοι, (Β.) δίκαι
(Α.) πυός, πυριάτη, μύρτα, (Β.) κληρωτήρια
(Α.) ὑάκινθος, ἄρνες, (Β.) κλεψύδραι, νόμοι,
γραφαί.

μέλλοντος οὖν τοῦ Ποντιανοῦ λέγειν περὶ ἑκάστου τῶν
παρακειμένων, οὐ πρότερόν γε, ἔφη ὁ Οὐλπιανός,

---

240 Alluding to the "second tables" discussed in what follows.
241 Beestings (puos) is the first milk a sheep or goat produces
after giving birth, and puriatê (here translated "cottage cheese") is
beestings that have been heated and curdled.

Since, as I noted (14.639b), we were repeatedly served
after-dinner snacks (*epidorpismata*) of this sort, one of the
guests said (E. *Hipp.* 436):

Somehow second thoughts[240] are wiser.

For what does the table lack? With what is it not
    laden?
It is full of seafood; but also present is
the tender flesh of calves, and a meal that consists of
    a goose,
and baked and kneaded cakes liberally drenched
with the liquid produced by the auburn-winged
    honeybee,

as Euripides puts it in *Cretan Women* (fr. 467). And as
Eubulus said in *Olbia* (fr. 74):

(A.) Because everything will be sold all together in
    the same spot
in Athens: figs, (B.) summons-officers! (A.) grapes,
turnips, pears, apples, (B.) witnesses! (A.) roses,
medlars, after-birth pudding, honeycomb, chickpeas,
    (B.) lawsuits!
(A.) beestings, cottage cheese,[241] myrtle-berries, (B.)
    allotment machines![242]
(A.) hyacinth, lambs, (B.) waterclocks, laws,
    indictments!

As Pontianus, then, was about to begin discussing the individual items we had been served, Ulpian said: We are not

---

[242] To pick the individual jurors assigned to various law courts;
see Dow, *HSCP* 50 (1939) 1–34.

ἀκουσόμεθα περὶ τούτων, ἕως ἂν περὶ ἐπιδορπισμά-
των εἴπῃς. καὶ ὁ Ποντιανός· τραγήματα Κράτης φησὶ
Φιλιππίδην λέγειν ἐν Φιλαργύρῳ οὕτως· |

d   πλακοῦντες, ἐπιδορπίσματ᾽, ᾠά, σήσαμα·
    ὅλην λέγοντ᾽ ἄν μ᾽ ἐπιλίποι τὴν ἡμέραν.

καὶ Δίφιλος ἐν Τελεσίᾳ·

    (Α.) τράγημα, μυρτίδες, πλακοῦς, ἀμυγδαλαῖ.
    (Β.) ἐγὼ δὲ ταῦθ᾽ ἥδιστά γ᾽ ἐπιδορπίζομαι.

Σώφιλος ἐν Παρακαταθήκῃ·

    ἡδύ γε μετ᾽ ἀνδρῶν ἐστιν Ἑλλήνων ἀεὶ
    συνάγειν. τὸ πρᾶγμα χάριεν· "οὐχὶ δώδεκα
    κυάθους" ἀνεβόησέν τις, "ὑποχεῖς; κωμάσαι
    πρὸς τὴν Ταναγρικὴν δεῖ γάρ, ἵν᾽ ἐκεῖ
    κατακλιθεὶς
    ἐπιδορπίσηται τὰς ὀνείας ματτύας." |

e   Πλάτων ἐν τῷ Ἀτλαντικῷ μεταδόρπια αὐτὰ καλεῖ ἐν
τούτοις· πάντα τε εὐώδη ἔφερέ που τοῖς κατοικοῦσιν ἡ
γῆ, καὶ τὸν ἥμερον δὲ καρπὸν πλεῖστον ἔφερεν καὶ
ἀκροδρύων πλῆθος καὶ ὅσα παραμύθια ἡδονῆς μετα-

---

243 "after-dinner snacks"; cf. 14.640a.

244 Sc. of time to complete the catalogue.

245 The first verse is quoted also at 2.52f (with *trôgalia* for
tragêma, and a different form of the final word).

246 As again in Sophil. fr. 5.5 below, it is not actually the noun
but the cognate verb *epidorpizomai* that is used.

going to hear about these until you offer some remarks
about the term *epidorpismata*.[243] Pontianus (responded):
Crates (fr. 112 Broggiato) claims that Philippides in *The
Miser* (fr. 20) refers in this way to *tragêmata* ("snacks, dainties"):

> flat-cakes, *epidorpismata*, eggs, sesame-seeds;
> if I talked all day, I'd still run short.[244]

Also Diphilus in *Telesias* (fr. 80):[245]

> (A.) a snack (*tragêma*), myrtle-berries, a cake,
>   almonds.
> (B.) These are my favorite *epidorpismata!*[246]

Sophilus in *The Deposit* (fr. 5):

> It's always nice to get together with
> Greeks! It's a pleasant occasion; somebody shouts
> "Pour a dozen ladlesful! Because we've got to get
>   drunk and
> go visit the girl from Tanagra, so a person can lie
>   down there
> and have an after-dinner snack (*epidorpisma*) of
>   donkey hash!"

Plato in his *Account of Atlantis* (*Criti.* 115a–b, altered and
condensed) refers to them as *metadorpia* in the following
passage: Somehow the land produced fragrant plants of all
sorts for its inhabitants; it also produced large quantities of
domesticated crops, and a great deal of fruit and nuts, and
all the *metadorpia* that stimulate pleasure.[247] Tryphon (fr.

[247] The traditional text of Plato says "that produce satiety,
make one feel full."

243

δόρπια. Τρύφων δέ φησι τὸ παλαιὸν πρὶν εἰσελθεῖν
τοὺς δαιτυμόνας, ἐπὶ τῶν τραπεζῶν κεῖσθαι τὴν
ἑκάστου μοῖραν, ὕστερον δὲ πολλά τε καὶ ποικίλα
ἐπεισφέρεσθαι, διὸ καὶ ἐπιφορήματα κληθῆναι. Φιλύλλιος δ' ἐν Φρεωρύχῳ φησὶν περὶ τῶν δευτέρων
τραπεζῶν λέγων·

ἀμυγδάλια, καρύδι', ἐπιφορήματα.

καὶ Ἄρχιππος ἐν Ἡρακλεῖ καὶ Ἡρόδοτος ἐν πρώτῃ.
καὶ ἐπιδορπίσασθαι δ' ἔλεγον τὸ ἐντραγεῖν καὶ ἐπι-
f δειπνῆσαι.[64] ἅπερ | Ἄρχιππος ἐν Ἡρακλεῖ Γαμοῦντι
ἐπιφορήματα καλεῖ διὰ τούτων· † ἰτρίοις ἐπιφορήμασί
τ' ἄλλοις γέμουσα. † καὶ Ἡρόδοτος δὲ ἐν τῇ πρώτῃ·
σιτίοις δὲ ὀλίγοισι χρέονται, ἐπιφορήμασι δὲ πολ-
641 λοῖς. ‖ τὸ μέντοι κατὰ τὴν παροιμίαν λεγόμενον Ἀβυ-
δηνὸν ἐπιφόρημα τέλος τί ἐστιν ἐλλιμένιον,[65] ὡς
Ἀριστείδης φησὶν ἐν τρίτῳ Περὶ Παροιμιῶν. Διονύσιος δ' ὁ τοῦ Τρύφωνος· τὸ μὲν παλαιὸν πρὶν
εἰσελθεῖν τοὺς δαιτυμόνας, ἐπὶ τῶν τραπεζῶν κεῖσθαι
τὴν ἑκάστου μοῖραν, ὕστερον δὲ πολλά ‹τε καὶ›[66]
ποικίλα ἐπιφέρεσθαι, διὸ καὶ ἐπιφορήματα κληθῆναι. |

64 Kaibel deletes the entire section of text from Τρύφων δέ to
ἐπιδειπνῆσαι.   65 καὶ ἐλλιμένιον A: καὶ del. Kaibel
66 cf. 14.640e

248 The material that follows (from Tryphon, Philyllius, Archippus, and Herodotus) all appears a second time, in a different
order and a slightly expanded form, below.

136 Velsen)[248] claims that in ancient times, before the dinner guests entered the room, each man's share of the food was set on the tables, and that afterward many additional items of various sorts were brought in (*epeispheresthai*), which is why they were referred to as *epiphorêmata*. Philyllius in *The Well-Digger* (fr. 18), discussing the second tables, says:

little almonds, little nuts, *epiphorêmata*.

Also Archippus in *Heracles* (fr. 11) and Herodotus in Book I (133.2).[249] They also used the verb *epidorpisasthai* to mean "to snack" and "to eat something after dinner."[250] Archippus in *Heracles Getting Married* (fr. 11, unmetrical) refers to them as *epiphorêmata* in the following passage: † loaded with *itria*[251] and other *epiphorêmata* †. Likewise Herodotus in Book I (133.2): They do not eat much bread or cake, but consume many *epiphorêmata*. What is referred to in the proverb as an "*epiphora* from Abydos" is actually some type of harbor tax, according to Aristides in Book III of *On Proverbs*.[252] Tryphon's student Dionysius: In ancient times, before the dinner guests entered the room, each man's share of the food was set on the tables; afterward many additional items of various sorts were brought in (*epeispheresthai*), which is why they were referred to as *epiphorêmata*. Philyllius in *The Well-Digger*

[249] Quoted at 4.144a and again (at less length) below.
[250] See 14.641b n.
[251] Cakes of some sort; cf. 14.646d.
[252] Cf. Zenob. 1.1.

b Φιλύλλιος δ᾽ ἐν Φρεωρύχῳ τὰ ἐπιφερόμενα μετὰ τὸ δειπνῆσαι λέγων ὧδε·

ἀμυγδάλια, καρύδι᾽, ἐπιφορήματα.

Πλάτων δ᾽ ἐν Μενέλεῳ ἐπιτραπεζώματα αὐτὰ καλεῖ οἷον τὰ ἐπιτιθέμενα ταῖς τραπέζαις βρώματα, λέγων οὕτως·

(Α.) εἰπέ μοι,
ὡς ὀλίγα λοιπὰ τῶν ἐπιτραπεζωμάτων; |

c (Β.) ὁ γὰρ θεοῖσιν ἐχθρὸς αὐτὰ κατέφαγεν.

Ἀριστοτέλης δ᾽ ἐν τῷ Περὶ Μέθης τὰ τραγήματά φησι λέγεσθαι ὑπὸ τῶν ἀρχαίων τρωγάλια· ὡσεὶ γὰρ ἐπιδορπισμὸν εἶναι. Πίνδαρος δέ ἐστιν ὁ εἰπών·

δείπνου δὲ λήγοντος γλυκὺ τρωγάλιον
καίπερ πεδ᾽ ἄφθονον βοράν.

ὄντως γὰρ κατὰ τὸν Εὐριπίδην ἀποβλέψαντα ἔστιν εἰς τὰ παρακείμενα εἰπεῖν·

ὁρᾷς τὸν εὐτράπεζον ὡς ἡδὺς βίος.

ὅτι γὰρ ἦσαν καὶ παρὰ τοῖς ἀρχαίοις αἱ δεύτεραι τράπεζαι πολυτελῶς μεμεριμνημέναι, παρίστησιν Πίνδαρος ἐν Ὀλυμπιονίκαις περὶ τῆς Πέλοπος κρεουργίας διηγούμενος·

---

253 The second verse is quoted also at 4.171a.
254 Aristotle's comment is cited in a more complete form at 14.641d–e. *trôgalia* is cognate with *trôgô* ("nibble on, eat"), while

246

(fr. 18), discussing the food brought in after dinner was over, (puts it) thus:

little almonds, little nuts, *epiphorêmata*.

Plato in *Menelaus* (fr. 76) refers to these items as *epitrapezômata*, that is, as the foods placed upon (*epi-*) the tables (*trapezai*), putting it as follows:[253]

(A.) Tell me—
how come there's so little left of the *epitrapezômata*?
(B.) Because that bastard gobbled them down!

Aristotle in his *On Drunkenness* (fr. 674) claims that the ancients referred to *tragêmata* as *trôgalia*; for they are, as it were, an *epidorpismon*.[254] Pindar (fr. 124c)[255] is the one who said:

A *trôgalion* is tasty when dinner is coming to an end, even if it follows an immense amount of food.

For one actually can, to quote Euripides (fr. 1052.3), look at what has been served and say:

You see how pleasant life is when your table's full!

Since the fact that the ancients put considerable thought and expense into their second tables is established by Pindar in the *Olympian Victory Odes* (1.50–2), when he describes how Pelops was butchered:[256]

[254] an *epidorpismon* (cf. 14.640e *epidorpisasthai*) is literally "something eaten after (*epi*) dinner (*dorpon*)."   [255] Other portions of the fragment are preserved at 11.782d, 480c.

[256] The mythical king Tantalus butchered his son Pelops and served him to the gods, to see if they could tell what they were eating; Demeter (who was distracted by the loss of her daughter Persephone) ate Pelops' shoulder.

247

τραπέζαισι δ'⁶⁷ ἀμφὶ δεύ‹τε›ρα⁶⁸ κρεῶν |

d   σέθεν διεδάσαντο καὶ φάγον.
ἐμοὶ δ' ἄπορα γαστρίμαρ-
   γον μακάρων τιν' εἰπεῖν.

οἱ δὲ παλαιότεροι ἁπλῶς τραπέζας ἔλεγον, ὡς Ἀχαιὸς
ἐν Ἡφαίστῳ σατυρικῷ·

   (Δι.) θοίνῃ σε πρῶτον τέρψομεν· πάρεστι δέ.
   (Ηφ.) τὸ δεύτερον ‹δὲ› τῷ με κηλήσεις τρόπῳ;
   (Δι.) μύρῳ σε χρίσω πάμπαν εὐόσμῳ δέμας.
   (Ηφ.) ὕδωρ δὲ νίψαι χεῖρας οὐ πρόσθεν δίδως;
   (Δι.) ἡνίκα τράπεζά γ' ἐκποδὼν ἀπαίρεται.

Ἀριστοφάνης Σφηξίν·

   ὕδωρ κατὰ χειρός· τὰς τραπέζας εἰσφέρειν.

e Ἀριστοτέλης δ' ἐν τῷ Περὶ Μέθης | παραπλησίως
ἡμῖν δευτέρας τραπέζας προσαγορεύει διὰ τούτων· τὸ
μὲν οὖν ὅλον διαφέρειν τράγημα βρώματος νομιστέον
ὅσον ἔδεσμα τρωγαλίου. τοῦτο γὰρ πάτριον τοὔνομα
τοῖς Ἕλλησιν, ἐπεὶ ἐν τραγήμασι⁶⁹ παρατίθενται.
διόπερ οὐ κακῶς ἔοικεν εἰπεῖν ὁ πρῶτος δευτέραν
προσαγορεύσας τράπεζαν· ὄντως γὰρ ἐπιδορπισμός
τις ὁ τραγηματισμός ἐστιν, καὶ δεῖπνον ἕτερον παρα-

---

67 The traditional text of Pindar has τ'.
68 The traditional text of Pindar has δεύτατα.
69 ἐν τραγήμασι τὰ βρώματα A: τὰ βρώματα del. Kaibel

At their tables during the second course they
divided up your flesh and ate it.
But I find it impossible to describe
    any god as a glutton.

People in the more distant past referred to them simply as
"tables," for example Achaeus in the satyr play *Hephaestus*
(*TrGF* 20 F 17):

(Dionysus) First we'll treat you to a meal; here it is!
(Hephaestus) What's the second way you'll charm
    me?
(Dionysus) I'll smear sweet-smelling perfume all over
    your body.
(Hephaestus) You're not offering me water to wash
    my hands first?
(Dionysus) When the table's taken away!

Aristophanes in *Wasps* (1216):

Water over our hands! Bring in the tables!

Aristotle in his *On Drunkenness* (fr. 675)[257] refers to them
as "second tables," much as we do, in the following passage: In general, a *tragêma* should be regarded as different
from ordinary food, to the extent that what one eats differs
from what one munches on (*trôgalion*); for this is the name
the Greeks traditionally use, since these items are served
as snacks (*tragêmata*). The first person to use the term
"second table" would thus seem to have been right; for
snacking (*tragêmatismos*) is in fact eating something after
dinner (*epidorpismos*), and the *tragêmata* are served as

257 Cf. 14.641b with n.

τίθεται ⟨τὰ⟩[70] τραγήματα. Δικαίαρχος δ' ἐν πρώτῳ
τῆς Εἰς Τροφωνίου Καταβάσεώς φησιν οὕτως· ἥ γε
τὴν πολλὴν δαπάνην ἐν τοῖς δείπνοις παρέχουσα
δευτέρα τράπεζα προσεγένετο, καὶ στέφανοι καὶ μύρα |
f καὶ θυμιάματα καὶ τὰ τούτοις ἀκόλουθα πάντα.
ἐδίδοτο δὲ καὶ ᾠὸν ἐν τῇ δευτέρᾳ τραπέζῃ, ὥσπερ καὶ
λαγῷα καὶ κίχλαι κοινῇ μετὰ τῶν μελιπήκτων εἰσεφέρετο, ὡς Ἀντιφάνης ἐν Λεπτινίσκῳ φησὶν οὕτως·

    (Α.) οἶνον Θάσιον πίνοις ἄν; (Β.) εἴ τις ἐγχέοι.
    (Α.) πρὸς ἀμυγδάλας δὲ πῶς ἔχεις; (Β.)
      εἰρηνικῶς.
    † μαλακὰς σφόδρα διας † μέλιτι προσπαίζειν
      βίᾳ.
    (Α.) μελίπηκτα δ' εἴ σοι προσφέροι; (Β.)
      τρώγοιμι καὶ ‖

642 ᾠὸν δὲ καταπίνοιμ' ἄν. (Α.) ἄλλου δεῖ τινος;

ἐν δὲ Ὁμοίοις·

    εἶτ' ἐπεισῆγεν χορείαν ἢ τράπεζαν δευτέραν
    καὶ παρέθηκε γέμουσαν πέμμασι παντοδαποῖς.

Ἄμφις δὲ ἐν Γυναικομανίᾳ·

[70] add. Kaibel

what amounts to a second dinner. Dicaearchus in Book I of his *Descent into Trophonius' Shrine* (fr. 19 Wehrli = fr. 80 Mirhady) says the following: The second table, which makes dinner parties quite expensive, was also there, along with garlands, perfumes, incense, and everything that goes with them. An egg was also offered on the second table, in the same way that hare-meat and thrushes were brought in along with the honey-cakes, as Antiphanes says in *Little Leptinus* (fr. 138), as follows:

> (A.) Would you drink some Thasian wine? (B.) If
>   someone pours it in my cup!
> (A.) How do you feel about almonds? (B.) Calm.
> † extremely soft [corrupt] † to play forcefully with
>   honey.
> (A.) And if someone brought you a honey-cake? (B.)
>   I'd eat it, and
> I'd also gulp down an egg. (A.) Do you need anything
>   else?

And in *Men Who Looked Like Each Other*[258] (fr. 172.5–6):

> Then after that he'd bring in a dance or a second
>   table,
> and he'd set it beside us, loaded with pastries of all
>   kinds.

Amphis in *Crazy about Women* (fr. 9):

---

[258] Called *Women Who Looked Like Each Other* at 4.158c. Meineke combined these verses with the passage from the same play preserved at 11.471c to produce fr. 172.

(Α.) ἤδη ποτ᾽ ἤκουσας βίον
ἀληλεμένον; (Β.) ναί. (Α.) τοῦτ᾽ ἐκεῖν᾽ ἔστιν
    σαφῶς·
ἄμητες, οἶνος ἡδύς, ᾠά, σησαμαῖ,
μύρον, στέφανος, αὐλητρίς. (Β.) ὦ Διοσκόρω, |
b   ὀνόματα τῶν δώδεκα θεῶν διελήλυθας.

Ἀναξανδρίδης Ἀγροίκοις·

ὡς δ᾽ ἐστεφανώθην, ἡ τράπεζ᾽ εἰσῄρετο
τοσαῦτ᾽ ἔχουσα βρώμαθ᾽ ὅσα μὰ τοὺς θεοὺς
καὶ τὰς θεὰς οὐδ᾽ ἔνδον ὄντ᾽ ᾔδειν ἐγώ·
οὕτως παρέζων † χρηστῶς οὐκ † ἔζων τότε.

Κλέαρχος Πανδρόσῳ·

(Α.) λάβ᾽ ὕδωρ κατὰ χειρός. (Β.) μηδαμῶς·
    καλῶς ἔχει.
c   (Α.) λάβ᾽, ὠγάθ᾽· | οὐδὲν χεῖρον. ⟨ἡ⟩ παῖς,
    ἐπιτίθει
ἐπὶ τὴν τράπεζαν κάρυα καὶ τραγήματα.

Εὔβουλος Καμπυλίωνι·

(Α.) τραγημάτων δ᾽ ἔσθ᾽ ἡ τράπεζά σοι πλέα.
(Β.) οὐ φιλοτραγήμων εἰμί πως ἑκάστοτε.

Ἄλεξις Πολυκλείᾳ (ἑταίρας δ᾽ ὄνομα Πολύκλεια)·

ὁ πρῶτος εὑρὼν κομψὸς ἦν τραγήματα.

(A.) Did you ever hear about the refined[259]
life? (B.) Yes. (A.) This is certainly it:
wheat-cakes, delicious wine, eggs, sesame-bread,
perfume, a garland, a pipe-girl. (B.) Castor and
    Polydeuces!
You've listed the names of the 12 gods!

Anaxandrides in *Rustics* (fr. 2):

After a garland was put on my head, the table was
    brought in;
it had more food, by the gods and
goddesses, than I've ever seen indoors!
So I was merely living † not well † I was living then.

Clearchus in *Pandrosus* (fr. 4):

(A.) Take some water over your hands. (B.) No, no;
    it's fine.
(A.) Take it, my good sir; there's no harm done. Slave-
    girl! Put
nuts and dainties (*tragêmata*) on the table!

Eubulus in *Campulion* (fr. 44):

(A.) Your table's full of *tragêmata*.
(B.) Somehow I don't always like *tragêmata*.

Alexis in *Polycleia* (fr. 190)—Polycleia[260] is a courtesan's
name:

The guy who invented *tragêmata* was smart—

---

259 From a verb that normally refers to grinding grain.
260 *PAA* 778695.

τοῦ συμποσίου γὰρ διατριβὴν ἐξεῦρε καὶ
ἀργοὺς ἔχειν μηδέποτε τὰς σιαγόνας. |

d καὶ ἐν Ὁμοίᾳ (τὸ δ᾽ αὐτὸ δρᾶμα καὶ ὡς Ἀντιδότου
φέρεται)·

(A.) οὐδὲ φιλόδειπνός εἰμι μὰ τὸν Ἀσκληπιόν,
τραγήμασιν χαίρω δὲ μᾶλλον. (B.) εὖ πάνυ.
(A.) τραγήματ᾽ αἰσθάνομαι γὰρ ὅτι νομίζετε
τοῖς νυμφίοις μετιοῦσι τὴν νύμφην † λέγεις †
παρέχειν, ἄμητας καὶ λαγῷα καὶ κίχλας.
τούτοισι χαίρω, τοῖς δὲ κεκαρυκευμένοις
ὄψοισι καὶ ζωμοῖσιν ἥδομ᾽, ὦ θεοί.

Ἀπίων δὲ καὶ Διόδωρος, ὥς φησι Πάμφιλος, ἐπαί-
e κλειά | φησι καλεῖσθαι τὰ μετὰ τὸ δεῖπνον τραγή-
ματα. Ἔφιππος Ἐφήβοις·

χόνδρος μετὰ ταῦτ᾽ εἰσῆλθε, μύρον Αἰγύπτιον,
Φοινικικοῦ βῖκός τις ὑπανεῴγνυτο,
ἴτρια, τραγήμαθ᾽ ἧκε, πυραμοῦς, ἄμης,
ᾠῶν ἑκατόμβη. πάντα ταῦτ᾽ ἐχναύομεν.
ἐμασώμεθ᾽ οὕτως ἀνδρικῶς ὅσ᾽ εἴχομεν·
καὶ γὰρ παραμασύντας τινὰς παρεβόσκομεν[71].

---

[71] παρεβόσκομεν Olson: παράμασυλτας MSS: παρα-
βόσκομεν Casaubon

---

261 This is the only fragment preserved of a play by this title by
either poet. The title is a common one, which may be the ultimate
source of the confusion.

262 For karukê, see 4.132f n.

because he discovered how to pass the time at parties
and
never have inactive jaws!

And in *The Girl Who Looked Like Someone Else* (fr. 168)
—the same play is also assigned to Antidotus:[261]

> (A.) I don't like dinner, by Asclepius;
> I much prefer *tragêmata*. (B.) Excellent!
> (A.) Because I recognize that you think it's proper for
>   bridegrooms,
> when they go fetch the bride † you say † to supply
> *tragêmata*—wheat-cakes, and hare-meat, and
>   thrushes.
> Gods!—that's what I like; and I enjoy fancy
>   ingredients
> that've been made into *karukê*,[262] and broths.

But Apion (*FGrH* 616 F 32) and Diodorus (= Gloss. Ital.
204 K–A), according to Pamphilus (fr. IV Schmidt), claim
that the *tragêmata* served after dinner are referred to as
epaikleia.[263] Ephippus in *Ephebes* (fr. 8):[264]

> After that, wheat-pudding arrived, and Egyptian
>   perfume;
> someone opened a transport-jar of Phoenician wine;
> wafer-bread came, *tragêmata*, honey-cake, milk-cake,
> a hecatomb of eggs. We were nibbling on all these
>   items.
> That's how bravely we chewed on everything we had;
> for the fact was that we were also feeding some
>   fellow-chewers.

---

[263] Cf. 14.664e.   [264] Verse 2 is quoted also at 1.29d,
while verses 3–4 are quoted also at 2.58a.

καὶ ἐν Κύδωνι·

> καὶ μετὰ δεῖπνον κόκκος < . . . >
> ἐρέβινθος, < . . . > κύαμος,
> χόνδρος, τυρός, μέλι, σησαμίδες,
> † βράχος, βρυγμός, μνοῦς †, πυραμίδες,
> μῆλον, κάρυον, γάλα, κανναβίδες,
> κόγχαι, χυλός, Διὸς ἐγκέφαλος.

Ἄλεξις Φιλίσκῳ·

ἀρτέα

f   τράπεζ', ἀπονίψασθαι | δοτέον, προσοιστέος
> στέφανος, μύρον, σπονδή, λιβανωτός, ἐσχαρίς,
> † τραγήματα † δοτέον ἔτι, πλακοῦντος ἁπτέον.

Ἐπεὶ δὲ καὶ ὁ Κυθήριος Φιλόξενος ἐν τῷ Δείπνῳ
643 δευτέρων ‖ τραπεζῶν μνημονεύων πολλὰ καὶ τῶν ἡμῖν
παρακειμένων ὠνόμασεν, φέρε καὶ τούτων ἀπομνη-
μονεύσωμεν·

> τὰς δὲ δὴ πρόσθεν μολούσας
>   < . . . > λιπαραυγεῖς
> πορθμίδας πολ-
>   λῶν ἀγαθῶν πάλιν εἴσφε-
>   ρον γεμούσας,
> τὰς ἐφήμεροι καλέοντι
>   νῦν τραπέζας <δευτέρας>,

And in *Cydon* (fr. 13):

> And after dinner a pomegranate-seed,
> a chickpea, a bean,
> wheat-pudding, cheese, honey, sesame-cakes,
> [corrupt], wheat-and-honey-cakes,[265]
> an apple, a nut, milk, hemp-seeds,
> shellfish, barley-water, Zeus-brain.[266]

Alexis in *Philiscus* (fr. 252):

> A table
> needs to be brought; washing-water needs to be
>   offered; a garland
> has to be fetched, and perfume, a libation,
>   frankincense, and a brazier;
> † *tragêmata* † still needs to be distributed; a cake has
>   to be grabbed!

Alright—since Philoxenus of Cythera in his *Dinner Party* (*PMG* 836(e)) mentioned second tables and referred specifically to many of the items we were served, let me cite the following passage:

> As for the glistening vessels
>   . . . that came
> previously, they
>   brought them in again, loaded with
>   a great deal of good food;
> these are what mortals refer to
>   today as second tables,

---

[265] *puramides*; see 14.647b–c.
[266] An unidentified dainty; cf. 12.514e (citing Clearchus).

ἀθάνατοι δέ τ' Ἀμαλθεί-
  ας κέρας· ταῖς δ' ἐν μέσαισιν
ἐγκαθιδρύ-
  θη μέγα χάρμα βροτοῖς, λευ-
    κὸς μυελὸς γλυκερός,
λεπτᾶς ἀράχνας ἐναλιγκί-
  οισι πέπλοις
συγκαλύπτων ὄψιν αἰσχύ-
  νας ὕπο, μὴ κατίδῃς
b   μαλογενὲς † | πῶν λιπὼν
  ταῖς ἀνάγκαις †
ξηρὸν ἐν ξηραῖς Ἀρισταί-
  ου μελιρρύτοισι παγαῖς·
τῷ δ' ὄνομ' ἦς ἄμυλος.
  χερσὶν δ' ἐπέθεντο < . . . >
    < . . . > στόμιον μαλεραῖς
< . . . >
  † ταν † δεξαμέναν ὅ τι κεν
    διδῷ τις, ἃ Ζανὸς καλέοντι
τρώγματ'· ἔπειτ' ἐπένειμεν
  ἐγκατακνακομιγὲς
  πεφρυγμένον
πυρβρομολευκερεβινθο-
  † ακανθουμικτριτυαδυ †
    βρῶμα τὸ παντανάμικτον

---

267 I.e. a horn of plenty; see 11.783c n.

whereas the immortals call them Amal-
    theia's horn.[267] In the midst of them
was placed
    an enormous source of joy for mortals,
        sweet white marrow,
which was concealing its face in
    robes that resembled a
fine spider-web, out of
    shame, to keep you from seeing
its sheep-born † flock after leaving
    under compulsion †
dry among the dry, honey-flowing
    springs of Aristaeus;[268]
its name was *amulos*.[269]
    With fierce hands . . .
        . . . they placed in their mouth
. . .
    [corrupt] after it accepted whatever
        someone offered, which people call Zeus'
trôgmata. Then he began distributing
    a roasted
        mixture of entrails and safflower,
a dish that represented a thorough blending of
    wheat-oat-white-chickpea-
        † thistle-mixed-[corrupt]-

---

[268] The hero Aristaeus was a son of Apollo and the mortal
Autonoe and was associated with shepherding and the production
of honey and olive oil (e.g. [Arist.] *Mir.* 838b23–4; "Heracleides"
fr. IX.2, *FHG* ii.214). But exactly what edible substance is being
referred to is unclear.

[269] See verse 18 below; Olson on Ar. *Ach.* 1092.

† ἀμπυκικηροιδηστί-
   χας † παρεγίνετο τούτοις
σταιτινοκογχομαγὴς
   † τοξαισελαιο- †
      ξανθεπιπαγκαπύρ‹ω-
         τ›ος χοιρίνας,
ἁδέα δὲ ‹ . . . ›
   κυκλωτὰ † ομοφλωκτα † ἀνάριθμα |

c   καὶ μελίπακτα τετυγμέν᾽
      ἄφθονα σασαμόφωκτα·
τυρακίνας δὲ γάλακτι
   καὶ μέλι συγκατάφυρτος
      ἦς ἄμυλος πλαθανίτας.
σασαμοτυροπαγῆ δὲ
   καὶ ζεσελαιοπαγῆ
      πλατύνετο σασαμόπλαστα
πέμματα. κᾆτ᾽ ἐρέβινθοι
   κνακομιγεῖς ἀπαλαῖς θάλ-
      λοντες ὥραις,
ᾠά τ᾽ ἀμυγδαλίδες ‹τε›
   τᾶν μαλακοφλοΐδων
      ‹ . . . ›τετο τρωκτά τε παισὶν
† αδυιδη † κάρυ᾽ ἄλλα
   θ᾽ ὅσσα πρέπει παρὰ θοίναν
ὀλβιόπλουτον ‹ . . . ›
   πόσις δ᾽ ἐπεραίνετο κότ-
      ταβοί τε λόγοι τ᾽ ἐπὶ κοινᾶς·

headband-wax-[corrupt]-
   -[corrupt] † along with these was
a dough-shell-kneaded
   † [corrupt]-olive-oil †
      brown-all-over-crackling
        choirinas-cake,[270]
and countless . . .
   delicious, round [corrupt]
and a limitless number of honey-cakes that
   had been formed and toasted with sesame.
There was a cheese-cake kneaded together
   out of milk and honey,
      an *amulos* produced in a bread-pan.
Also pastries formed from sesame and cheese
   that had been boiled in oil
      and sprinkled with sesame-seeds
were stretched out wide. After this were chick-peas
   mixed with safflower-seeds, flourishing in
      delicate, youthful beauty;
and eggs and some soft-
   skinned almonds
      were . . . and nuts
[corrupt] that children snack on,
   and whatever else belongs at a rich,
wealthy meal . . .
   The drinking was coming to an end, along with
      games of
         cottabus[271] and general conversation;

[270] Cf. 14.647b–c.
[271] For the symposium-game cottabus, cf. 15.665d–8f.

ἔνθα τι καινὸν ἐλέχθη
d   κομψὸν | ἀθυρμάτιον, καὶ
θαύμασαν αὖτ᾽ ἐπί τ᾽ ᾔνη-
σαν.

ταῦτα καὶ ὁ Κυθήριος Φιλόξενος, ὃν ἐπαινῶν Ἀντιφάνης ἐν τῷ Τριταγωνιστῇ φησι·

πολύ γ᾽ ἐστὶ πάντων τῶν ποιητῶν διάφορος
ὁ Φιλόξενος. πρώτιστα μὲν γὰρ ὀνόμασιν
ἰδίοισι καὶ καινοῖσι χρῆται πανταχοῦ·
ἔπειτα ⟨τὰ⟩ μέλη μεταβολαῖς καὶ χρώμασιν
ὡς εὖ κέκραται. θεὸς ἐν ἀνθρώποισιν ἦν
ἐκεῖνος, εἰδὼς τὴν ἀληθῶς μουσικήν· |
e   οἱ νῦν δὲ κισσόπλεκτα καὶ κρηναῖα καὶ
ἀνθεσιπότατα μέλεα μελέοις ὀνόμασι
ποιοῦσιν ἐμπλέκοντες ἀλλότρια μέλη.

Πλακούντων δὲ ὀνόματα πολλῶν καταλεξάντων,
ὅσων μέμνημαι τούτων σοι καὶ μεταδώσω. οἶδα δὲ καὶ
Καλλίμαχον ἐν τῷ τῶν Παντοδαπῶν Συγγραμμάτων
Πίνακι ἀναγράψαντα πλακουντοποιικὰ συγγράμματα
Αἰγιμίου καὶ Ἡγησίππου καὶ Μητροβίου, ἔτι δὲ Φαί-
f   στου.[72] ἡμεῖς δὲ ἃ μετεγράψαμεν ὀνόματα | πλα-
κούντων τούτων σοι καὶ μεταδώσομεν, οὐχ ὡς τοῦ
⟨ὑπ᾽⟩[73] Ἀλκιβιάδου πεμφθέντος Σωκράτει· ὃν Ξανθίππης κατακλασάσης[74] ὁ Σωκράτης, "οὐκοῦν," ἔφη,

---

[72] Φαίστου Meineke: Φαίτου A   [73] add. Casaubon
[74] κατακλασάσης Kaibel e Aeliano: καταγελασάσης A

in the course of this a novel, clever
    little joke was made, and
        they were surprised by it and expressed
        approval.

Thus Philoxenus of Cythera; Antiphanes praises him in his
The Tritagonist (fr. 207), saying:

Philoxenus is much better than all the other
poets. Because, first of all, he uses strange
vocabulary that no one else knows everywhere;
and then, what a fine mix of modulations and
coloring in his songs (*melê*)! He was a god
among men; he knew what music really was!
Whereas today's poets produce miserable (*melea*)
ivy-woven, spring-fed, flower-flitting, bizarre
songs (*melê*), and fold miserable (*melea*) vocabulary
    into them.

Many members of the group produced lists of names of
cakes, and I will share as many of them as I can remember
with you. I am aware that Callimachus in his *Tablet of Mis-
cellaneous Treatises* (fr. 435 Pfeiffer) recorded treatises
on the art of cake-making by Aegimus, Hegesippus, and
Metrobius, as well as by Phaestus. I will share as many
names of these cakes as I copied down with you, and I will
not treat them like the one Alcibiades sent to Socrates;
for when Xanthippe[272] smashed it, Socrates said: "Well,

---

[272] Socrates' wife (*PAA* 730275), who is imagined as jealous of
Alcibiades' relationship with her husband. A more complete version of the anecdote is preserved at Ael. *VH* 11.12.

"οὐδὲ σὺ μεθέξεις τούτου." τοῦτο δὲ ἱστόρησεν Ἀντί-
644 πατρος ἐν τῷ πρώτῳ Περὶ Ὀργῆς. ‖ ἐγὼ δὲ φιλο-
πλάκουντος ὢν οὐκ ἂν περιεῖδον τὸν θεῖον ἐκεῖνον
ἐξυβριζόμενον πλακοῦντα. μνημονεύων οὖν ὁ κωμικὸς
Πλάτων εἴρηκεν ἐν τῷ Ποιητῇ οὕτως·

μόνος δ' ἄγευστος,
ἄσπλαγχνος ἐνιαυτίζομαι, ἀπλάκουντος, ἀλι-
βάνωτος.

ἀλλὰ μὴν οὐδὲ τῆς κώμης ἀμνήμων εἰμὶ ἣν Πλα-
κοῦντά φησι καλεῖσθαι Δημήτριος ὁ Σκήψιος ἐν δω-
δεκάτῳ Τρωικοῦ Διακόσμου, τῶν Ὑποπλακίων Θηβῶν
φάσκων αὐτὴν ἀπέχειν σταδίους ἕξ. περισπαστέον ‖
b δὲ λέγοντας πλακοῦς τὴν ὀνομαστικήν· συνήρηται
γὰρ ἐκ τοῦ πλακόεις, ὡς τυρόεις τυροῦς, σησαμόεις
σησαμοῦς. εἴρηται δὲ κατ' ἔλλειψιν τοῦ ἄρτος. ὅτι δὲ
καλοὺς πλακοῦντας ἐν Παρίῳ τοῦ Ἑλλησπόντου φαγεῖν ἔστιν οἱ ἐπιδημήσαντες μαρτυρήσουσιν· Ἄλεξις
γὰρ πεπλάνηται λέγων τοὺς ἐκ Πάρου. λέγει δὲ οὕτως
ἐν τῷ ἐπιγραφομένῳ Ἀρχιλόχῳ·

ὦ τὴν εὐτειχῆ[75] ναίων Πάρον, ὄλβιε πρέσβυ,
ἣ κάλλιστα φέρει χώρα δύο τῶν συναπασῶν, ‖

---

[75] ἠΰτυχῆ ("fortunate") Arnott

---

[273] Literally "Cake"; cf. *Il.* 6.396–7.
[274] Roughly three-quarters of a mile.
[275] Sc. rather than as an adjective.

you're not going to have any of it either!" Antipater told
this story in Book I of *On Anger* (fr. 65, *SVF* iii.257). I, on
the other hand, am fond of cakes, and I would not have
allowed that divine cake to be abused this way. The comic
author Plato mentions cakes in his *The Poet* (fr. 121), saying the following:

> I alone have spent a year
> without a single taste, with no entrails, no cakes, and
> no frankincense.

Nor, again, have I forgotten the village that Demetrius
of Scepsis in Book XII of the *Trojan Battle-Order* (fr. 8
Gaede) claims was known as Placous;[273] he says that it is six
stades[274] from Hypoplacian Thebes. A circumflex accent
ought to be placed on the final syllable of *plakous* when the
word is used as a substantive;[275] because it is contracted
from *plakoeis*, like *turous* from *turoeis*, and *sêsamous* from
sêsamoeis. This use involves an ellipsis of *artos* ("bread").
Anyone who spends time in Parium on the Hellespont will
attest to the fact that excellent cakes can be eaten there; for
Alexis is wrong when he refers to the cakes that come from
Paros. He puts it as follows in his play entitled *Archilochus*
(fr. 22):

> Blessed old man,[276] who inhabit Paros with its fine
>   walls!
> Your country has two products that outdo those from
>   anywhere else:

---

[276] Archilochus (the title-character of the play) was himself
from Paros, so perhaps he is the individual addressed.

c   κόσμον μὲν μακάρεσσι λίθον, θνητοῖς δὲ
      πλακοῦντας.

ὅτι δὲ καὶ οἱ Σάμιοι διαφέροντές εἰσι πλακοῦντες
Σώπατρος ὁ φλυακογράφος φησὶν ἐν Βακχίδος Μνη-
στῆρσιν·

πλακουντοποιὸν ὠνομασμένην Σάμον.

ἐγχύτων δὲ πλακούντων μνημονεύει Μένανδρος μὲν ἐν
Ψευδηρακλεῖ·

    οὐκ ἔστι κανδύλους ποεῖν οὐδ᾽ οἷα σὺ
    εἴωθας εἰς ταὐτὸν καρυκεύειν μέλι, |
d   σεμίδαλιν, ᾠά. πάντα γὰρ τἀναντία
    νῦν ἐστιν· ὁ μάγειρος γὰρ ἐγχύτους ποεῖ,
    πλακοῦντας ὀπτᾷ,[76] χόνδρον ἕψει καὶ φέρει
    μετὰ τὸ τάριχος, εἶτα θρῖον καὶ βότρυς·
    ἡ δημιουργὸς δ᾽ ἀντιπαρατεταγμένη
    κρεάδι᾽ ὀπτᾷ καὶ κίχλας.

Εὐάγγελος δὲ Ἀνακαλυπτομένῃ·

    (Α.) τέτταρας < . . . > τραπέζας τῶν γυναικῶν
      εἶπά σοι,
    ἐξ δὲ τῶν ἀνδρῶν, τὸ δεῖπνον δ᾽ ἐντελὲς καὶ
      μηδενὶ

---

[76] ὀπτούς ACE; but A has the correct reading ὀπτᾷ at 4.172b

stone that brings honor to the blessed ones,[277] and
   cakes that do the same for mortals.

The phlyax-author Sopater in *The Suitors of Bacchis* (fr. 4)
claims that Samian cakes are outstanding:

Samos, known as a cake-maker.

Menander in *The Fake Heracles* (fr. 409.6–13)[278] mentions
cakes produced in moulds:

It's not a matter of making *kanduloi*[279] or the kinds of
   dishes
you're used to, when you combine honey, flour,
and eggs in a *karukê*. Because everything's the other
   way
around nowadays: the cook makes moulded cakes,
bakes flat-cakes, and boils wheat-pudding and serves
   it
after the saltfish, followed by a fig-leaf pastry and
   grapes;
whereas the artisan-woman who's lined up opposite
   him
roasts bits of meat and thrushes.

Euangelus in *The Girl Whose Veil Was Removed*[280] (fr. 1):

(A.) I told you—four tables of women,
and six of men; and the dinner should be complete,
   with nothing

---

[277] I.e. Parian marble, used in temples, for statues, and the
like.   [278] An extract from a much longer fragment quoted
at 4.172a–c.   [279] For *kandulos* and *karukê* (below), see
4.132f nn.   [280] I.e. *The Bride*.

e ἐλλιπές. | λαμπροὺς γενέσθαι βουλόμεσθα τοὺς
γάμους.

οὐ παρ' ἑτέρου δεῖ πυθέσθαι, πάντα δ' αὐτόπτης
ἐρῶ.

† τῶν μὲν ἐλαῶν ἄφελε † πάνθ' ὅσ' ἂν βούλῃ
γένη.

εἰς δὲ τὰ κρέα μόσχον ἔλαβες, δέλφακας,
χοίρους, λαγώς,

(B.) ὡς ἀλαζὼν ὁ κατάρατος. (A.) θρῖα, τυρόν,
ἐγχύτους,

(B.) παῖ Δρόμων. (A.) κάνδυλον, ᾠά τ', ἀμύλιον
< . . . >

τὸ πέρας, ὕψος τῆς τραπέζης πήχεων ἔσται
τριῶν, |

f ὥστε τὸν δειπνοῦντ' ἐπαίρειν, ἄν τι βούληται
λαβεῖν.

Ἄμης. πλακοῦντος γένος. Ἀντιφάνης·

ἄμητες, ἄμυλοι.

Μένανδρος ἐν Ὑποβολιμαίῳ·

τὸν ἄμητα, Χαίριππ', οὐκ ἐᾷς πέττειν τινά.[77]

Ἴωνες δέ, ὥς φησι Σιληνὸς ἐν ταῖς Γλώσσαις, ἄμην
αὐτὸν καλοῦσιν. καὶ τοὺς μικροὺς ἀμητίσκους Τηλε-
κλείδης·

---

[77] A more complete version of the fragment preserved in
Photius makes it clear that τινά is in fact the interrogative τίνα,
which introduces a question by a second speaker.

missing! We want this to be a brilliant wedding feast.
You don't need to ask anyone else; I'll keep an eye on
   the situation and tell you everything.
† of the olives take away † as many types as you like,
whereas for the meat you bought a calf, pigs, piglets,
   hares,
(B.) This jerk's really full of hot air! (A.) fig-leaf
   pastries, cheese, moulded cakes,
(B.) Slave! Dromo! (A.) a *kandulos*; also eggs, a little
   amulos . . .
to cut a long story short, the table's going to be
   almost five feet[281] high,
so the guests will have to stretch, if they want to get
   anything.

Amês. A type of cake. Antiphanes (fr. 297):

amêtes, amuloi.

Menander in *The Supposititious Child* (fr. 381.1):[282]

You're not letting anyone bake the *amês*, Chaerippus!

But the Ionians, according to Silenus in his *Glossary*, refer
to it as an *amên*.[283] Teleclides (fr. 1.12)[284] refers to the
small ones as *amêtiskoi*:

---

[281] Literally "three cubits."

[282] Photius preserves a slightly longer version of the fragment,
which makes it clear that the final word in verse 1 belongs to a second speaker (Chaerippus) and that what the first speaker actually
says is "You're not letting (me) bake the *amês*, Chaerippus?"

[283] Sc. in the accusative (as opposed to the third-declension
Attic form *amêta* in the passage from Menander quoted above).

[284] An extract from a much longer fragment quoted at 6.268a–
d. Verse 12 is quoted alone also at 2.64f.

† αὐτόμαται[78] † δὲ κίχλαι μετ' ἀμητίσκων ἐς τὸν
φάρυγ' εἰσεπέτοντο.

Διακόνιον. Φερεκράτης· ||

645   ὑπὸ τῆς ἀπληστίας
διακόνιον ἐπῆσθεν, ἀμφιφῶντ' ἔχων.

Ἀμφιφῶν. πλακοῦς Ἀρτέμιδι ἀνακείμενος, ἔχει δ'
ἐν κύκλῳ καόμενα δᾴδια. Φιλήμων ἐν Πτωχῇ ἢ Ῥοδίᾳ·

Ἄρτεμι, φίλη δέσποινα, τοῦτόν σοι φέρω,
ὦ πότνι', ἀμφιφῶντα καὶ σπονδήσιμα.

μνημονεύει αὐτοῦ καὶ Δίφιλος ἐν Ἑκάτῃ. Φιλόχορος
δ' ἀμφιφῶντα αὐτὸν κληθῆναι καὶ εἰς τὰ τῆς Ἀρτέμιδος ἱερὰ φέρεσθαι ἔτι τε καὶ εἰς τὰς τριόδους, ἐπεὶ
ἐν ἐκείνῃ τῇ ἡμέρᾳ ἐπικαταλαμβάνεται ἡ σελήνη ἐπὶ
b   ταῖς δυσμαῖς ὑπὸ τῆς | τοῦ ἡλίου ἀνατολῆς καὶ ὁ
οὐρανὸς ἀμφιφῶς γίνεται.

Βασυνίας. Σῆμος ἐν δευτέρᾳ Δηλιάδος, ἐν τῇ τῆς
Ἑκάτης, φησίν, νήσῳ τῇ Ἴριδι θύουσι Δήλιοι τοὺς
βασυνίας καλουμένους· ἐστὶν δὲ ἐφθὸν πύρινον, σταῖς
σὺν μέλιτι· καὶ τὰ καλούμενα κόκκωρα, ἰσχάς, καὶ
κάρυα τρία.

---

[78] At both 2.64f and 6.268c, Athenaeus has ὀπταὶ (metrical).

† Of their own accord † thrushes accompanied by
   amêtiskoi flew into their gullets.

Diakonion. Pherecrates (fr. 167):

> Since he couldn't be satisfied,
> he ate a *diakonion* too, even though he had an
>   *amphiphôn*.

Amphiphôn. A cake dedicated to Artemis; it is sur-
rounded by burning torches. Philemon in *The Beggar-
Woman* or *The Girl from Rhodes* (fr. 70):

> Artemis, beloved mistress: I'm bringing you this
> *amphiphôn*, lady, and libation-cakes.

Diphilus also refers to it in *Hecate* (fr. 27). Philochorus
(*FGrH* 328 F 86b) (claims) that it was known as an *amphiphôn* and was taken to Artemis' shrines, as well as to the
cross-roads, because on that day the moon sets at the same
time as the sun rises, and the sky is lit up by both (*amphi-
phôs*).

Basunias.[285] Semus says in Book II of the *History of
Delos* (*FGrH* 396 F 5): The Delians sacrifice what are
known as *basuniai* to Iris on Hecate's island[286]—a *basunias*
is a wheat-dumpling made of dough mixed with honey—
along with what are known as *kokkôra*, a dried fig, and
three nuts.

---

[285] It is unclear whether this is the nominative singular or if
Athenaeus (or his source) has simply drawn the word (in the accusative plural) direct from the quotation that follows.

[286] Identified by Harpocration E 14 (citing Phanod. *FGrH* 325
F 1 and Semus *FGrH* 396 F 2) as a tiny island near Delos.

Στρεπτοὶ καὶ νεήλατα. τούτων μνημονεύει Δημοσθένης ὁ ῥήτωρ ἐν τῷ Ὑπὲρ Κτησιφῶντος Περὶ τοῦ Στεφάνου.

Ἐπίχυτον. Νικοφῶν ἐν Χειρογάστορσιν· |

c ἐγὼ μὲν ἄρτους, μᾶζαν, ἀθάρην, ἄλφιτα,
κόλλικας, ὀβελίαν, μελιτοῦτταν, ἐπιχύτους,
πτισάνην, πλακοῦντας, δενδαλίδας, ταγηνίας.

Πάμφιλος δὲ τὸν ἀττανίτην καλούμενον ἐπίχυτόν φησι καλεῖσθαι. τοῦ δὲ ἀττανίτου Ἱππῶναξ ἐν τούτοις μνημονεύει·

οὐκ ἀτταγᾶς τε καὶ λαγοὺς καταβρύκων,
οὐ τηγανίτας σησάμοισι φαρμάσσων
οὐδ' ἀττανίτας κηρίοισιν ἐμβάπτων. |

d Κηρίον[79] πλακοῦς. ἄρτος, ὃν Ἀργεῖοι παρὰ τῆς νύμφης πρὸς τὸν νυμφίον φέρουσιν. ὀπτᾶται δ' ἐν ἄνθραξιν καὶ καλοῦνται ἐπ' αὐτὸν οἱ φίλοι. παρατίθεται δὲ μετὰ μέλιτος, ὥς φησιν Φιλητᾶς ἐν Ἀτάκτοις.

Γλυκίνας. ὁ διὰ γλεύκου[80] καὶ ἐλαίου πλακοῦς παρὰ Κρησίν, ὥς φησι Σέλευκος ἐν Γλώσσαις.

Ἐμπέπτας, ὁ αὐτός φησι, πύρινος ἄρτος κοῖλος καὶ σύμμετρος, ὅμοιος ταῖς λεγομέναις κρηπῖσιν, εἰς ἃς ἐντίθεται τὰ διὰ τοῦ τυροῦ σκευαζόμενα πλακούντια. |

[79] Κηρίον Kaibel: κρηῖον A
[80] γλεύκου Olson: γλυκέος ACE

---

287 Literally "freshly rolled" (< *neos* + *elaunô*).

Streptoi ("twists") and *neêlata*.[287] The orator Demosthenes mentions these in his *On Behalf of Ctesiphon on the Crown* (18.260).

Epichutos.[288] Nicophon in *Men Who Live from Hand to Mouth* (fr. 6):

> I have loaves of bread, barley-cake, wheat-gruel,
>   barley groats,
> barley-loaves, spit-bread, honey-cake, *epichutoi*,
> barley-gruel, flat cakes, *dendalides*,[289] fried cakes.

Pamphilus (fr. II Schmidt) claims that what is known as an *attanitês* is an *epichutos*. Hipponax (fr. 37 Degani) mentions the *attanitês* in the following passage:[290]

> eating no francolins or hares,
> covering no fry-cakes with sesame seeds,
> and dipping no *attanitai* in honeycomb.

Kêrion ("honeycomb") cake. A type of bread, which the Argives take to the bridegroom from the bride; it is baked in the coals, and their friends are invited to share it. It is served with honey, according to Philetas in the *Miscellany* (fr. 9 Dettori = fr. 37 Spanoudakis).

Glukinas. A Cretan cake made with grape-must and olive oil, according to Seleucus in the *Glossary* (fr. 44 Müller).

According to the same author (Seleucus fr. 53 Müller), an *empeptas* is a hollow, symmetrical loaf of wheat-bread, which resembles what are referred to as *krêpides*, into which they stuff the small cakes made with cheese.

---

[288] The word is given in the accusative singular, as in the reference to Pamphilus that follows.   [289] A type of barley-cake.
[290] The first verse is quoted also at 9.388a–b.

e   Ἐγκρίδες. πεμμάτιον ἑψόμενον ἐν ἐλαίῳ καὶ μετὰ
τοῦτο μελιτούμενον. μνημονεύει αὐτῶν Στησίχορος
διὰ τούτων·

  χόνδρον τε καὶ ἐγκρίδας
ἄλλα τε πέμματα καὶ μέλι χλωρόν.

μνημονεύει αὐτῶν καὶ Ἐπίχαρμος καὶ ἐν τοῖς Ἐγχει-
ρογάστορσι Νικοφῶν. Ἀριστοφάνης δ᾽ ἐν Δαναΐσιν
καὶ πωλητήν φησιν αὐτῶν εἶναι ἐν τούτοις· † μητ᾽
αρμα εἶναι ἐγκριδοπώλην. † Φερεκράτης δ᾽ ἐν Κρα-
πατάλλοις·

  ταῦτ᾽ ἔχων ἐν ταῖς ὁδοῖς ἁρπαζέτω τὰς ἐγκρίδας.

f   Ἐπικύκλιος. πλακοῦς τις παρὰ | Συρακοσίοις οὕ-
τως καλούμενος. καὶ μέμνηται αὐτοῦ Ἐπίχαρμος ἐν
Γᾷ καὶ Θαλάσσᾳ.
  Γούρος. ὅτι πλακοῦντος εἶδος ὁ Σόλων ἐν τοῖς
Ἰάμβοις φησίν·

  πίνουσι· καὶ τρώγουσιν οἱ μὲν ἴτρια,
οἱ δ᾽ ἄρτον αὐτῶν, οἱ δὲ συμμεμιγμένους
γούρους φακοῖσι· κεῖθι δ᾽ οὔτε πεμμάτων
ἄπεστιν οὐδ᾽ ἕν, ἄσσ᾽ ἐν ἀνθρώποισι γῆ
φέρει μέλαινα, πάντα δ᾽ ἀφθόνως πάρα. ||

646 Κριβάνας. πλακοῦντάς τινας ὀνομαστικῶς Ἀπολ-

---

291 Quoted also, in slightly more complete form, at 4.172d–e.
292 Quoted at 3.110b (unmetrical).

Enkrides. A small pastry deep-fried in olive oil and covered with honey afterward. Stesichorus (*PMG* 179(a).1–2) mentions them in the following passage:[291]

> wheat-pudding, *enkrides*,
> and other pastries and pale honey.

Epicharmus (fr. 46)[292] also mentions them, as does Nicophon in *Men Who Live from Hand to Mouth* (fr. 10.5).[293] Aristophanes in *Danaids* (fr. 269, corrupt and unmetrical) says that there are people who sell them, in the following passage: † nor [corrupt] to be an *enkrides*-vendor. † Pherecrates in *Small Change* (fr. 99):

> Since he's got these items, let him snatch the *enkrides*
> in the streets!

Epikuklios. A type of cake the Syracusans refer to by this name. Epicharmus mentions it in *Earth and Sea* (fr. 23).

Gouros. Solon in his *Iambs* (fr. 38 West[2]) says that this is a type of cake:

> They're drinking; and some of them are eating *itria*,
> others bread, and others *gouroi* mixed up
> together with lentils. Not a single type of pastry
> is missing there, out of all those the black earth
> produces for human beings, but everything's available
> in abundance.

Kribanes.[294] Apollodorus (*FGrH* 244 F 255) (reports)

---

[293] The passage (quoted at 3.126f) actually refers to *enkrides*-vendors.   [294] The word is given in the accusative plural, as in the citation from Apollodorus that follows.

λόδωρος παρ' Ἀλκμᾶνι. ὁμοίως καὶ Σωσίβιος ἐν τρίτῳ
Περὶ Ἀλκμᾶνος, τῷ σχήματι μαστοειδεῖς εἶναι
φάσκων αὐτούς, χρῆσθαι δ' αὐτοῖς Λάκωνας πρὸς τὰς
τῶν γυναικῶν ἑστιάσεις, περιφέρειν τ' αὐτούς, ὅταν
μέλλωσιν ᾄδειν τὸ παρεσκευασμένον ἐγκώμιον τῆς
Παρθένου αἱ ἐν τῷ χορῷ ἀκόλουθοι.

Κριμνίτης. πλακοῦς ποιὸς διὰ κρίμνων γινόμενος,
ὡς Ἰατροκλῆς ἐν τῷ Περὶ Πλακούντων ἀναγράφει. |

b   Σταιτίτας. πλακοῦς ποιὸς ἐκ σταιτὸς καὶ μέλιτος.
μνημονεύει Ἐπίχαρμος ἐν Ἥβας Γάμῳ. σταῖς δ'
ἐστὶν ὑγρὸν εἰς τήγανον ὑποχεόμενον, μέλιτος ἐπι-
βαλλομένου καὶ σησάμης καὶ τυροῦ, ὡς Ἰατροκλῆς
φησίν.

Χαρίσιος. τούτου μνημονεύει Ἀριστοφάνης ἐν Δαι-
ταλεῦσιν·

ἐγὼ † δενων †
πέμψω πλακοῦντ' εἰς ἑσπέραν χαρίσιον.

Εὔβουλος δ' ἐν Ἀγκυλίωνι ὡς περὶ ἄρτου αὐτοῦ ὄντος
οὑτωσὶ λέγει·

ἐξεπήδησ' ἀρτίως
πέττουσα τὸν χαρίσιον.

c   Ἐπίδαιτρον. | πλακουντῶδες μάζιον ἐπὶ τῷ δείπνῳ
ἐσθιόμενον, ὥς φησι Φιλήμων ἐν τῷ Περὶ Ἀττικῶν
Ὀνομάτων.

that certain cakes are expressly referred to this way in Alcman (*PMG* 94).[295] So too Sosibius in Book III of *On Alcman*, claiming that they are shaped like a breast; that the Spartans use them at the feasts their women celebrate; and that they serve them when the girls participating in the chorus are about to sing the hymn of praise composed in honor of the Virgin.

Krimnitês. A type of cake made of coarse barley-meal (*krimna*), as Iatrocles records in his *On Cakes*.

Staititas. A type of cake made of spelt-flour dough (*stais*) and honey. Epicharmus mentions them in *The Wedding of Hebe* (fr. 46).[296] Moist spelt-flour dough is poured out into a frying pan, and honey, sesame-seeds, and cheese are added on top of it, according to Iatrocles.

Charisios.[297] Aristophanes mentions this in *Banqueters* (fr. 211):

> I'll [corrupt]

send a *charisios* cake in the evening.

Eubulus in *Ancylion* (fr. 1.2–3)[298] refers to it as if it were a type of bread, as follows:

> She leapt out just now,
> as she was baking the *charisios*.

Epidaitron. A small barley-cake that resembles a cake and is eaten at dinner, according to Philemon in his *On Attic Vocabulary*.

---

[295] Quoted at 3.114f.
[296] Quoted at 3.110b (unmetrical).
[297] Literally "thanksgiving," i.e. "offered to express thanks."
[298] Quoted also at 15.668d, along with another verse.

Νᾶνος. ἄρτος πλακουντώδης διὰ τυροῦ καὶ ἐλαίου σκευαζόμενος.

Ψωθία. τὰ ψαθύρια. Φερεκράτης Κραπατάλλοις·

λήψει δ' ἐν Ἅιδου κραπάταλον καὶ ψωθία.

Ἀπολλόδωρος δ' ὁ Ἀθηναῖος καὶ Θεόδωρος δ' ἐν Ἀττικαῖς Γλώσσαις τοῦ ἄρτου τὰ ἀποθραυόμενα ψωθία καλεῖσθαι, ἃ τινὰς ὀνομάζειν ἀτταράγους. |

d   Ἴτριον. πεμμάτιον λεπτὸν διὰ σησάμου καὶ μέλιτος γινόμενον. μνημονεύει αὐτοῦ Ἀνακρέων οὕτως·

ἠρίστησα μὲν ἰτρίου λεπτ⟨οῦ μικρ⟩ὸν ἀποκλάς,
οἴνου δ' ἐξέπιον κάδον.

Ἀριστοφάνης Ἀχαρνεῦσιν·

⟨ . . . ⟩ πλακοῦντες, σησαμοῦντες, ἴτρια.

Σοφοκλῆς Ἔριδι·

ἐγὼ δὲ πεινῶσ' αὖ πρὸς ἴτρια βλέπω.

Ἀμόραι. τὰ μελιτώματα Φιλητᾶς ἐν Ἀτάκτοις ἀμόρας φησὶν καλεῖσθαι. μελιτώματα δ' ἐστὶν πεπεμμένα.

e   Ταγηνίτης. πλακοῦς | ἐν ἐλαίῳ τετηγανισμένος.

---

299 According to Poll. 9.83 (= *Small Change* test. i), Pherecrates actually used *psôthia* to refer to a coin that was used in Hades and was supposedly equivalent to three obols.

Nanos. Bread that resembles a cake and is made with cheese and olive oil.

Psôthia. Crumbs. Pherecrates in *Small Change* (fr. 86):

You'll get small change and *psôthia* in Hades.[299]

Apollodorus of Athens (*FGrH* 244 F 283) and Theodorus in the *Attic Glossary* (*FGrH* 346 F 2) (claim that) bread-crumbs, referred to by some authorities as *attaragoi*, are known as *psôthia*.

Itrion. A light, thin pastry made with sesame and honey. Anacreon (*PMG* 373.1–2)[300] mentions it, as follows:

I broke off a bit of crisp *itrion* and had it for lunch,
and I drank a jar of wine.

Aristophanes in *Acharnians* (1092):

cakes, sesame-cakes, *itria*.

Sophocles in *Strife* (fr. 199):

But I'm hungry, and I've got an eye out for *itria*
again.

Amorai. Philetas in the *Miscellany* (fr. 8 Dettori) claims that *melitômata* ("honey-cakes") are referred to as *amorai*.[301] *Melitômata* are a type of baked good.

Tagênitês. A cake cooked in oil in a frying-pan

---

[300] Quoted also at 11.472e.

[301] Perhaps to be identified with the *homôron* said at 3.110b (where see n.) to have been mentioned by Epicharmus (fr. 46); see Dettori's n. on Philitas (the spelling of whose name varies in the ancient sources).

μνημονεύει Μάγνης ⟨ἢ⟩[81] ὁ ποιήσας τὰς εἰς αὐτὸν
ἀναφερομένας κωμῳδίας ἐν Διονύσῳ δευτέρῳ·

ταγηνίας ἤδη τεθέασαι χλιαροὺς
σίζοντας, ὅταν αὐτοῖσιν ἐπιχέῃς μέλι;

καὶ Κρατῖνος ἐν Νόμοις·

καὶ δρόσον βάλλων ἔωθεν χλιαρὸς ταγηνίας.

῎Ελαφος. πλακοῦς ὁ τοῖς ᾽Ελαφηβολίοις ἀναπλασ-
σόμενος διὰ σταιτὸς καὶ μέλιτος καὶ σησάμου.

Ναστός. πλακοῦντος εἶδος, ἔχων ἔνδον καρυκείας.

Χορία. βρώματα διὰ μέλιτος καὶ γάλακτος γινόμενα.

᾽Αμορβίτης. πλακοῦντος εἶδος παρὰ Σικελοῖς· οἱ δὲ
⟨ . . . ⟩

f   Παισά. | πλακούντια παρὰ Κῴοις, ὥς φησιν
᾽Ιατροκλῆς.

Σησαμίδες. ἐκ μέλιτος καὶ σησάμων πεφρυγμένων
καὶ ἐλαίου σφαιροειδῆ πέμματα. Εὔπολις Κόλαξιν·

ὃς Χαρίτων μὲν ὄζει,
καλλαβίδας δὲ βαίνει,
σησαμίδας δὲ χέζει,
μῆλα δὲ χρέμπτεται.

[81] add. Musurus

---

[302] For the *têganon/tagênon*, cf. 6.228e–9b; Olson–Sens on
Archestr. fr. 11.8–9.   [303] Literally "emitting dew."

(*têganon*).[302] Magnes—or whoever wrote the comedies attributed to him—mentions (them) in *Dionysus II* (fr. 2):

Have you ever seen hot *tagêniai*
sizzling when you pour honey on them?

Also Cratinus in *Laws* (fr. 130):

and a hot *tagênias* breathing steam[303] at dawn.

Elaphos.[304] The cake made of spelt-flour dough, honey, and sesame during Elaphebolion.[305]

Nastos. A type of cake, which is stuffed with rich food.[306]

Choria. Food made with honey and milk.[307]

Amorbitês. A Sicilian type of cake; but other authorities . . .

Paisa. Small Coan cakes, according to Iatrocles.

Sêsamides. Round pastries made of honey, roasted sesame-seeds, and olive oil. Eupolis in *Flatterers* (fr. 176):[308]

who smells like the Graces,
does *kallabides*-dances when he walks,
shits *sêsamides*,
and spits apples.

---

[304] Literally "deer."   [305] The ninth month of the Attic calendar (approximately late February/March).

[306] *karukeia*, cognate with *karukê* (a spicy, blood-based Lydian sauce; cf. 4.160b, 172b, 173d; 12.516c).

[307] More likely a dish produced by stewing ingredients of this sort within the fetal envelope (*chorion*) of a sheep or goat, meaning that the entry is out of place here. See in general Gow on Theoc. 9.19.

[308] Verses 2–3 are quoted also at 14.630a.

Ἀντιφάνης Δευκαλίωνι·

σησαμίδες ἢ μελίπηκτα † ἢ τοιοῦτό τι.

μνημονεύει αὐτῶν καὶ Ἔφιππος ἐν Κύδωνι· πρόκειται
τὸ μαρτύριον.[82] ||

647   Μύλλοι. Ἡρακλείδης ὁ Συρακόσιος ἐν τῷ Περὶ
Θεσμῶν ἐν Συρακούσαις φησὶ τοῖς Παντελείοις τῶν
Θεσμοφορίων ἐκ σησάμου καὶ μέλιτος κατασκευάζε-
σθαι ἐφήβαια γυναικεῖα, ἃ καλεῖσθαι κατὰ πᾶσαν
Σικελίαν μυλλοὺς καὶ περιφέρεσθαι ταῖς θεαῖς.

Ἐχῖνος. Λυγκεὺς ὁ Σάμιος ἐν τῇ Πρὸς Διαγόραν
Ἐπιστολῇ ἐκ παραλλήλου τιθεὶς τὰ κατὰ τὴν Ἀττικὴν
ἐξαιρέτως γινόμενα τοῖς ἐν τῇ Ῥόδῳ γράφει οὕτως· τῇ
b   δὲ | περὶ τὸν ἄμητα δόξῃ τὸν καινὸν ἀνταγωνιστὴν ἐπὶ
τῆς δευτέρας εἰσάγουσα τραπέζης ἐχῖνον. ὑπὲρ οὗ νῦν
μὲν ἐπὶ κεφαλαίου· παραγενομένου δὲ σοῦ καὶ συντε-
θέντος κατὰ τοὺς ἐν Ῥόδῳ νόμους ἀπομασησαμένου
πειράσομαι πλείω περιθεῖναι λόγον.

Κοτυλίσκος. Ἡρακλέων ὁ Ἐφέσιος πλακοῦντάς
τινάς φησιν οὕτω καλεῖσθαι τοὺς ἐκ τρίτου μέρους
τῆς χοίνικος γινομένους.

---

[82] Kaibel suggested that a lost note on the γελώνιος πλακοῦς
(attested at An.Ox. iii.168) stood originally at this point in the text.

---

[309] According to An.Ox. iii.168, Athenaeus mentioned "the
Gelonian cake" along with the *sêsamous*, and Kaibel proposed in-
serting the lost entry here (or, alternatively, at 3.114b).

Antiphanes in *Deucalion* (fr. 79):

> *sêsamides* or honey-cakes † or something like that.

Ephippus also mentions them in *Cydon* (fr. 13.3); the passage was cited earlier (14.642e).[309]

Mulloi. Heracleides of Syracuse in his *On the Customs in Syracuse* says that at the Panteleia, which is part of the Thesmophoria festival, female genitalia were manufactured out of sesame-seeds and honey, and that these are referred to everywhere in Sicily as *mulloi* and are carried in processions in honor of the goddesses.[310]

Echinos.[311] Lynceus of Samos in his *Letter to Diagoras* (fr. 15 Dalby) compares the most exceptional products of Attica with those in Rhodes, writing as follows:[312] introducing an *echinos* on the second table, as a fresh competitor to face the fine reputation attached to the *amês*. For the moment, I am offering only a summary account of it; but when you are here and chew on one prepared in the Rhodian style, I will attempt to offer a more complete description.

Kotuliskos. Heracleon of Ephesus says that certain cakes made from a third of a *choinix*[313] are referred to this way.

---

[310] Demeter and Persephone, to whom the Thesmophoria festival belonged.   [311] Normally "sea urchin," but here clearly a cake that resembles one.

[312] Probably from the same section of the letter as the fragment quoted at 14.652c–d, in which case the subject here (feminine) is the island of Rhodes itself.

[313] Sc. of wheat or barley. A *choinix* contained four *kotulai*, of which *kotuliskos* is a diminutive.

Χοιρίναι. τούτων μνημονεύει Ἰατροκλῆς ἐν τῷ Περὶ
Πλακούντων καὶ τοῦ πυραμοῦντος καλουμένου, ⟨οὐ⟩[83]

c διαφέρειν | λέγων τῆς πυραμίδος καλουμένης· γίνε-
σθαι γὰρ ταύτην ἐκ πυρῶν πεφωσμένων καὶ μέλιτι
δεδευμένων. αὗται δὲ ἆθλα τίθενται ταῖς παννυχίσι τῷ
διαγρυπνήσαντι.

Χρύσιππος δ᾽ ὁ Τυανεὺς ἐν τῷ ἐπιγραφομένῳ Ἀρ-
τοκοπικῷ εἴδη πλακούντων καὶ γένη τάδε ἀναγράφει·
Τερεντῖνον, Κρασσιανόν, Τουτιανόν, Σαβελλικὸν
κλοῦστρον, Ἰουλιανόν, Ἀπικιανόν, Κανωπικά, περ-
λούκιδον, Καππαδοκικόν, ἡδύβια, μαρυπτόν, πλίκιον,
γουττᾶτον, Μοντιανόν (τοῦτον, φησί, μάξεις ἐξ οἴνου
σκληρόν· εἰ δέ σοι τυρίον παρέσται, ἥμισυ μάξεις ἐξ

d οἴνου καὶ ἥμισυ ἐκ τυροῦ· ἡδονικώτερον | γὰρ γίνε-
ται), κλοῦστρον Κυριανόν, κλοῦστρον γουττᾶτον,
κλοῦστρον Φαβωνιανόν, μουστάκια ἐξ οἰνομέλιτος,
μουστάκια σησαμᾶτα, κλοῦστρον πούριον, † γωσλω-
ανιον †, Παυλινιανόν. ἐκ τυροῦ δέ, φησί, γίνεται
πλακουντηρὰ τάδε· ἔγχυτος, σκριβλίτης, σουβίτυλλος (γίνεται δὲ καὶ ἐξ ἅλικος σουβίτυλλος), σπῖρα
(καὶ οὗτος ἐκ τυροῦ γίνεται), λούκουντλοι, ἀργυρο-

[83] add. Kaibel

314 Cf. Philox. Cyth. PMG 836(e).15 (quoted at 14.643b).
315 An echo of Call. fr. 227.5–6 (quoted at 15.668c).
316 kloustron (as again repeatedly below) = Latin crustulum.
317 = Latin perlucidus.
318 For Cappadocian baking, cf. 3.112c.

Choirinai.[314] Iatrocles mentions these in his *On Cakes*, along with the so-called *puramous*, claiming that this is no different from the so-called *puramis*; for the latter is made from wheat that has been toasted and soaked in honey. They are offered as prizes at all-night festivals for those who stay awake the entire time.[315]

Chrysippus of Tyana in his work entitled *The Art of Baking* lists the following types and varieties of cakes: Terentine, Crassian, Tutian, Sabine pastry,[316] Julian, Apician, Canopic, *perloukidon*,[317] Cappadocian,[318] *hêdubia*,[319] *marupton*, *plikion*,[320] *gouttaton*,[321] Montian (you should knead this type, he says, with wine until the dough stiffens; if you have a bit of cheese, knead half the dough with wine, and half with cheese; this makes it tastier), Curian pastry, *gouttaton* pastry, Favonian pastry, *moustakia*[322] made with honeyed wine, *moustakia* made with sesame-seed, *pourion*[323] pastry, [corrupt], Paulinian. The following cake-like pastries, he says, are made with cheese: *enchutos*,[324] *skriblitês*,[325] *soubitullos* (a *soubitullos* is made from rice-wheat groats), *spira*[326] (this is also made with cheese), *loukountloi*,[327] *argurotruphêma*,[328] *libos*,[329] *kir-*

---

[319] Literally "life-sweeteners" *vel sim*.

[320] Probably cognate with Latin *plico* ("fold").

[321] = Latin *guttatus, guttatum*.   [322] = Latin *mustacea* ("must-cakes").   [323] Perhaps a Latinized version of a Greek adjective derived from *puros* ("wheat"); but the Latin word is attested elsewhere only in the form *purinos*).

[324] "moulded (cake)"; cf. 14.644c–f.

[325] = Latin *scriblita* or *scribilita*.

[326] = Latin *spira* ("coil").   [327] = Latin *lucunculi*.

[328] Literally "silver-luxury (cake)."

[329] = Latin *libus* or *libum*; cf. 3.125f–6a.

τρύφημα, λίβος, κίρκλος, λιξόλας, κλουστροπλακοῦς. γίνεται δέ, φησί, καὶ ὀρυζίτης πλακοῦς. ὁ δὲ φθόις οὕτω γίγνεται· τυρὸν ἐκπιέσας τρῖβε καὶ ἐμβαλὼν ἐς |

e κόσκινον χάλκεον διήθει, εἶτ᾽ ἐπίβαλε μέλι καὶ σελίγνεως ἡμίναν καὶ συμμάλαξον εἰς ἕν. κάτιλλος δὲ ὀρνᾶτος ὁ λεγόμενος παρὰ Ῥωμαίοις οὕτως γίγνεται· θρίδακας πλύνας ξέσον καὶ ἐμβαλὼν οἶνον εἰς θυίαν τρῖβε τὰς θρίδακας, εἶτα τὸν χυλὸν ἐκπιέσας σελίγνιον συμφύρασον αὐτῷ καὶ συμπεσεῖν ἐάσας μετ᾽ ὀλίγον τρῖψον εὐτόνως, προσβαλὼν ὀλίγον στέατος χοιρείου καὶ πέπερι, καὶ πάλιν τρίψας ἕλκυσον λάγανον καὶ λειάνας ἐκτεμὼν κατάτεμνε καὶ ἕψε εἰς ἔλαιον

f θερμότατον εἰς ἠθμὸν | βαλὼν τὰ κατακεκομμένα. ἄλλα πλακούντων γένη· ὀστρακίτης, ἀτταννῖται, ἄμυλον, τυροκόσκινον. τυρὸν ἐκπιάσας καλῶς θὲς εἰς ἄγγος, εἶτ᾽ ἄνω κόσκινον χαλκοῦν ἐπιθεὶς δίαγε τὸν τυρόν. ὅταν δὲ μέλλῃς προσφέρειν, βάλε μέλιτος αὔταρκες ἐπάνω. ὑποτυρίδες δὲ οὕτως γίνονται· εἰς γάλα βαλὼν μέλι ἐκπίεσον καὶ βάλε εἰς σκεῦος καὶ ἔα παγῆναι. ἐὰν δέ σοι παρῇ κοσκίνια μικρά, ἐπίβαλε εἰς αὐτὰ τὸ σκεῦος, καὶ ἔα ἐκρεῖν τὸν ὀρόν. καὶ ὅταν σοι δόξῃ πεπηγέναι, ἄρας τὸ σκεῦος μετάβαλε εἰς ἀργύρωμα, καὶ ἔσται ἡ ὄψις ἄνωθεν. ἐὰν δὲ μὴ ᾖ κοσκίνια,

---

330 = Latin *circulus* or *circlus*.

331 = Latin *lixula*.

332 "*crustulum*-cake."

333 *selignis* = Latin *siligo*. A *hêmina* is a Roman measure (Lat. *hemina*) equal to half a *sextarius*.

klos,[330] *lixolas*,[331] and *kloustroplakous*.[332] There is also a
type of cake, he says, made from rice. A *phthoïs* is made as
follows: Press a piece of cheese; mash it; and place it in a
bronze sieve and force it through. Then add honey and a
hêmina of fine flour,[333] and mix it all together. What the
Romans call a *katillos ornatos*[334] is made as follows: Wash
and grate lettuce; put some wine in a mortar, and mash the
lettuce;[335] then squeeze out the liquid and work fine flour
into it. Let it settle for a little while, then knead it vigorously. Add a bit of pork-fat and pepper; knead it again;
stretch it out into a thin sheet; smooth it; trim it; cut it into
small sections; put the pieces in a colander; and deep-
fry them in olive oil that is as hot as possible. Other types
of cakes: *ostrakitês*,[336] *attanitai*, *amulon*, *turokoskinon*.[337]
Squeeze some cheese as dry as you can, and place it in a
bowl; then place a bronze sieve on top of it, and force the
cheese through. When you are about to serve it, pour the
appropriate amount of honey on top. *Hupoturides*[338] are
made as follows: Add honey to milk; squeeze the mixture
dry; toss it in a dish; and let it curdle. If you have small
sieves, put the dish upside-down on top of them and let the
whey drain off. When it appears to have curdled, pick up
the dish and transfer it to a silver bowl;[339] the pattern[340]

---

[334] = Latin *catillus ornatus* ("elaborate dish").

[335] Sc. together with the wine.

[336] Presumably cognate with *ostrakis* ("pine seed, pine nut")
(2.57b).

[337] Literally "cheese-sieve"; the recipe apparently follows.

[338] Literally "under-cheesecakes."

[339] Sc. for serving.

[340] Produced by the sieve.

φλαβιλλίοις καινοῖς χρῶ, ἐν οἷς τὸ πῦρ ῥιπίζεται· τὴν
γὰρ αὐτὴν ποιεῖ χρείαν. κοπτοπλακοῦς. ἐν Κρήτῃ δέ,
φησίν, πλακουντάριον ποιοῦσιν, ὅπερ ὀνομάζουσι
γάστριν. γίνεται δὲ οὕτως· κάρυα Θάσια καὶ Ποντικὰ
648 καὶ ἀμύγδαλα, ἔτι δὲ ‖ μήκων, ἃ[84] φρύξας θεράπευσον
καλῶς καὶ εἰς θυΐαν καθαρὰν τρῖψον ἐπιμελῶς· συμ-
μίξας τε τὴν ὀπώραν μάλαξον μέλιτι ἡψημένῳ, προσβαλὼν πέπερι πλέον καὶ μάλαξον· γίνεται δὲ μέλαν
διὰ τὴν μήκονα. διαπλατύνας ποίησον τετράγωνον·
εἶτα σήσαμον λευκὸν τρίψας μάλαξον μέλιτι ἡψημένῳ καὶ ἕλκυσον λαγάνια δύο καὶ ἐν θὲς ὑποκάτω καὶ
τὸ ἄλλο ἐπάνω, ἵνα τὸ μέλαν εἰς μέσον γένηται, εὖ
ῥύθμισόν τε αὐτό. ταῦτα καὶ ὁ σοφὸς πεμματολόγος
b   Χρύσιππος. Ἁρποκρατίων | δὲ ὁ Μενδήσιος ἐν τῷ
Περὶ Πλακούντων τὴν παρ᾽ Ἀλεξανδρεῦσι καλουμένην παγκαρπίαν ‹ . . . › καλεῖ. ἴτρια δ᾽ ἐστὶ ταῦτα
συντεθρυμμένα μετὰ μέλιτος ἑψόμενα· καὶ μετὰ τὴν
ἕψησιν σφαιρηδὸν συντεθέντα περιδεῖται βύβλῳ
λεπτῇ ἕνεκα τοῦ συμμένειν. πολτοῦ δὲ μνημονεύει
Ἀλκμὰν οὕτως·

ἤδη παρεξεῖ πυάνιόν τε πολτὸν
χίδρον τε λευκὸν κηρίναν τ᾽ ὀπώραν.

ἐστὶ δὲ τὸ πυάνιον, ὥς φησι Σωσίβιος, πανσπερμία ἐν
γλυκεῖ ἡψημένη· χίδρον δὲ οἱ ἑφθοὶ πυροί· κηρίναν δὲ

_____
[84] μήκωνα ὂν A: corr. Kaibel

will be on top. If you have no sieves, use fresh *flabilla*[341] of the type used to fan the fire; they serve the same purpose. A *koptoplakous*.[342] On Crete, he says, they produce a small cake they call a *gastris*.[343] It is made as follows: Thasian nuts, Pontic nuts, and almonds, along with some poppy-seed; toast them, keeping a close eye on them as you do,[344] and mash the fruit in fine in a clean mortar; mix the fruit in and work it smooth along with some reduced honey; add a considerable amount of pepper and work it smooth. It turns out black because of the poppy-seed. Flatten it out into a square. Next, grate white sesame-seed; work it into a paste with reduced honey; press it into two sheets, putting one on the bottom, and the other on top of it, so that the black mixture can go in the middle; and assemble it nicely. Thus the wise pastry-expert Chrysippus. But Harpocration of Mende in his *On Cakes* refers to what the inhabitants of Alexandria call a *pankarpia*[345] as . . . These are *itria*[346] that have been ground up with honey and boiled; after being boiled, they are rolled into balls and wrapped in a thin sheet of paper to hold them together. Alcman (*PMG* 96) mentions porridge, as follows:

> Now he'll offer *puanion*-porridge,
> and white *chidron*, and waxen produce.

According to Sosibius (*FGrH* 595 F 12), *puanion* is seeds of all sorts that have been stewed in grape-must; stewed grains of wheat are *chidron*; and by "waxen produce" he

---

[341] = Latin *flabella* ("fan").   [342] Literally "pounded-cake."   [343] The word normally means "pot-belly" and thus "glutton."   [344] Sc. so as not to let them burn.
[345] Literally "all-fruit [cake]."   [346] See 14.646d.

c ὀπώραν λέγει τὸ μέλι. καὶ | Ἐπίχαρμος δὲ οὕτως λέγει
ἐν Γῇ καὶ Θαλάσσῃ·

< . . . > πολτὸν ἕψειν ὄρθριον.

καὶ τῶν καλουμένων δὲ μελικηρίδων μνημονεύει Φερεκράτης ἐν Αὐτομόλοις οὕτως·

ὥσπερ τῶν αἰγιδίων ὄζειν ἐκ τοῦ στόματος
μελικήρας.

Λεχθέντων καὶ τούτων ὁ σοφὸς Οὐλπιανὸς ἔφη·
πόθεν ὑμῖν, ὦ πολυμαθέστατοι γραμματικοί, καὶ ἐκ
ποίας βιβλιοθήκης ἀνεφάνησαν οἱ σεμνότατοι οὗτοι
συγγραφεῖς Χρύσιππος καὶ Ἁρποκρατίων, διαβάλ-
λοντες καλῶν ὀνόματα φιλοσόφων τῇ ὁμωνυμίᾳ; τίς
d δὲ καὶ ἡμίναν Ἑλλήνων ὠνόμασεν | ἢ τίς ἀμύλου
μνημονεύει; ἀπαντήσαντος δ᾽ αὐτῷ τοῦ Λαρηνσίου καὶ
εἰπόντος· τὴν μὲν ἡμίναν οἱ τὰ εἰς Ἐπίχαρμον ἀνα-
φερόμενα ποιήματα πεποιηκότες οἴδασι, κἂν τῷ Χεί-
ρωνι ἐπιγραφομένῳ οὕτως λέγεται·

καὶ πιεῖν ὕδωρ διπλάσιον χλιαρόν, ἡμίνας δύο.

τὰ δὲ ψευδεπιχάρμεια ταῦτα ὅτι πεποιήκασιν ἄνδρες
ἔνδοξοι Χρυσόγονός τε ὁ αὐλητής, ὥς φησιν Ἀριστόξενος ἐν ὀγδόῳ Πολιτικῶν Νόμων, τὴν Πολιτείαν

---

347 Referring to the Stoic Chrysippus of Soli (c.280–207 BCE)
and the Platonic philosopher Harpocration of Argos (2nd century CE).

means "honey." Epicharmus as well puts it as follows in *Earth and Sea* (fr. 20):

> to cook porridge before the sun's up.

Pherecrates in *Deserters* (fr. 30) likewise mentions what are referred to as *melikêrides*, as follows:

> to have your breath smell like a honey-cake
> (*melikêra*), as the breath of kids does.

After these remarks were complete, the wise Ulpian said: What source, my deeply learned grammarians, or what library produced these awe-inspiring essayists of yours, Chrysippus and Harpocration, who bring disgrace on the eminent philosophers whose names they share?[347] What Greek ever used the word *hêmina* or mentions an *amulon*?[348] Larensius answered him and said: The authors of the poems attributed to Epicharmus are familiar with the *hêmina*, and the following is said in the work entitled *Cheiron* ([Epich.] fr. 289):[349]

> and to drink twice as much hot water, two *hêminai*.

Well-known individuals produced these pseudepicharmic texts ([Epich.] *Pseud.* test. i), and according to Aristoxenus in Book VIII of the *Civic Laws* (fr. 45 Wehrli), the pipe-player Chrysogonus[350] wrote the one entitled *The Consti-*

---

[348] The words Ulpian asks about have been used in the quotations from Chrysippus' *The Art of Breadmaking* at 14.647e, f, respectively.
[349] Quoted also at 11.479b, along with Sophr. fr. 100.
[350] Stephanis #2637; cf. 8.350d–e.

ἐπιγραφομένην· Φιλόχορος δ' ἐν τοῖς Περὶ Μαντικῆς
e Ἀξιόπιστον τὸν εἴτε Λοκρὸν γένος ἢ Σικυώνιον | τὸν
Κανόνα καὶ τὰς Γνώμας πεποιηκέναι φησίν. ὁμοίως
δὲ ἱστορεῖ καὶ Ἀπολλόδωρος. τοῦ δὲ ἀμύλου μνημονεύει Τηλεκλείδης ἐν Στερροῖς οὑτωσὶ λέγων·

φιλῶ πλακοῦντα θερμόν, ἀχράδας οὐ φιλῶ,
χαίρω λαγῴοις ἐπ' ἀμύλῳ καθημένοις.

τούτων ἀκούσας ὁ Οὐλπιανὸς ἔφη· ἀλλ' ἐπειδὴ καὶ
κοπτήν τινα καλεῖτε, ὁρῶ δὲ ἑκάστῳ κειμένην ἐπὶ τῆς
τραπέζης, λέγετε ἡμῖν, ὦ λίχνοι, τίς τοῦ ὀνόματος
τούτου τῶν ἐνδόξων μνημονεύει; καὶ ὁ Δημόκριτος
ἔφη· τὸ μὲν θαλάσσιον πράσον κόπτην φησὶ καλεῖ-
f σθαι Διονύσιος ὁ Ἰτυκαῖος ἐν ἑβδόμῳ | Γεωργικῶν.
τοῦ δὲ ἡμῖν παρακειμένου μελιπήκτου μέμνηται Κλέαρχος ὁ Σολεὺς ἐν τῷ Περὶ Γρίφων[85] οὑτωσὶ λέγων·
σκεύων κελεύοντι λέγειν ὀνόματα[86] εἰπεῖν·

τρίπους, χύτρα, λυχνεῖον, ἀκταία, βάθρον,
σπόγγος, λέβης, σκαφεῖον, ὅλμος, λήκυθος,
σπυρίς, μάχαιρα, τρύβλιον, κρατήρ, ῥαφίς.

ἢ πάλιν ὄψων οὕτως·

[85] Γρίφων Casaubon: γράφων A   [86] σκεύων κελεύοντι
. . . ὀνόματα Kaibel: σκεύη κελεύοντα . . . ὅμοια A

351 Literally "Deserving-of-Belief"—a highly appropriate
(and thus most likely invented) name for the author of works of
gnomic wisdom.

tution. Philochorus in his *On Prophecy* (*FGrH* 328 F 79), on the other hand, claims that Axiopistus,[351] whose family was from either Locris or Sicyon, is the author of *The Rule* and *Wise Sayings*. Apollodorus (*FGrH* 244 F 226) records the same information. As for the *amulon*, Teleclides mentions it in *Tough Guys* (fr. 34), saying the following:

> I like a warm cake; I don't like wild pears;
> and I really enjoy hare-meat set on top of an *amulon*.

When he heard this, Ulpian said: Well, since you refer to something known as a *koptê*,[352] and I see one set on everyone's table—tell me, my gluttons, what reputable author mentions this word? Democritus responded: Dionysius of Utica in Book VII of *The Art of Farming* claims that the sea-leek is referred to as a *kóptê*. Whereas the honey-cake (*melipêkton*) we have been served[353] is mentioned by Clearchus of Soli in his *On Riddles* (fr. 87 Wehrli), where he says the following: When someone tells you to name furnishings,[354] say:

> table, cook-pot, lampstand, marble mortar, bench,
> sponge, basin, bowl, wooden mortar, oil-jug,
> basket, knife, cup, mixing-bowl, needle.

Or again (if he asks for the names) of prepared dishes, (say) the following:

---

[352] Presumably a reference to the mention of a *koptoplakous* in the quotation from Chrysippus at 14.647f.   [353] Sc. "and which goes by the same name" (but with the accent on the ultima); cf. the penultimate verse quoted by Clearchus at 14.649a and the fragment of Sopater that follows.   [354] Sc. as a drinking-party game; cf. 10.457c–f (citing Clearchus' *On Proverbs*).

ἔτνος, φακῆ, τάριχος, ἰχθύς, γογγυλίς,

649   σκόροδον, ‖ κρέας, θύννειον, ἅλμη, κρόμμυον,
σκόλυμος, ἐλαία, κάππαρις, βολβός, μύκης.

ἐπί τε τῶν τραγημάτων ὁμοίως·

ἄμης, πλακοῦς, ἔντιλτος, ἴτριον, ῥόα,
ὠόν, ἐρέβινθος, σησάμη, κοπτή, βότρυς,
ἰσχάς, ἄπιος, πέρσεια, μῆλ᾽, ἀμύγδαλα.

ταῦτα μὲν ὁ Κλέαρχος. ὁ δὲ φλυακογράφος Σώπατρος
ἐν τῷ ἐπιγραφομένῳ Πύλαι δράματί φησιν·

τίς δ᾽ ἀναρίθμου μήκωνος εὗρε κοπτὰς
ἢ κνηκοπύρους ἡδονὰς τραγημάτων ἔμειξεν;

ἀπέχεις, ὦ καλέ μου λογιστὰ Οὐλπιανέ, τὴν κοπτήν·
b ἧς συμβουλεύω ǀ σοι ἀπεσθίειν. καὶ ὃς οὐδὲν μελ-
λήσας ἀνελόμενος ἤσθιεν. γελασάντων δὲ πάντων
ἔφη ὁ Δημόκριτος, ἀλλ᾽ οὐκ ἐσθίειν σοι προσέταξα,
καλὲ ὀνοματοθήρα, ἀλλὰ μὴ ἐσθίειν· τὸ γὰρ ἀπεσθίειν οὕτως εἴρηκεν ἐν Φινεῖ ὁ κωμῳδιοποιὸς Θεό-
πομπος·

παῦσαι κυβεύων, μειράκιον, καὶ τοῖς βλίτοις
διαχρῶ τὸ λοιπόν. κοιλίαν σκληρὰν ἔχεις·
τὰ πετραῖα τῶν ἰχθυδίων ἀπέσθιε.

---

355 Presumably cognate with *tilton* ("scaled saltfish") (3.118e).
356 See 14.646d.

bean-soup, lentil-soup, saltfish, fish, turnip,
garlic, meat, tuna, brine-sauce, onion,
golden thistle, olive, caper, hyacinth-bulb, mushroom.

So too in the case of snacks:

amês, cake, *entiltos*,[355] *itrion*,[356] pomegranate,
egg, chickpea, sesame-seed, *koptê*, grape-cluster,
dried fig, pear, persea, apples, almonds.

Thus Clearchus. But the phlyax-author Sopater says in his play entitled *Gates* (fr. 16):

Who invented *koptai* made of countless poppy-
seeds,
or mixed together delicious snacks of wheat and
safflower-seed?

You have received full payment, my noble and precise[357] Ulpian, as far as *koptê* is concerned, and I advise you to *apesthien* it. Ulpian did not hesitate for a moment, but picked up his *koptê* and began to eat it. Everyone laughed, and Democritus said: But I did not order you to eat (*esthiein*) it, my good word-hunter; I ordered you *not* to eat it. For this is how the comic poet Theopompus uses *apesthiein* in *Phineus* (fr. 63):

Stop shooting dice, young man, and eat
blite from now on! Your guts are locked up;
don't eat (*apesthie*)[358] rock-fish!

---

[357] Ulpian is also called *logistês* at 9.401b, perhaps as a reference to supposed service at some point as an Imperial account-inspector.

[358] But the verb could just as well mean "eat" here.

ἡ τρὺξ ἄριστόν ἐστιν εἰς εὐβουλίαν.
ταῦτ' ἦν ποῆς, ῥᾴων ἔσει τὴν οὐσίαν.

c χρῶνται δὲ | τῷ ἀπεσθίειν καὶ ἀντὶ τοῦ ἀπό τινος
ἐσθίειν, ὡς Ἕρμιππος ἐν Στρατιώταις·

οἴμοι τάλας, δάκνει, δάκνει,
ἀπεσθίει μου τὴν ἀκοήν.

Ἐπὶ τούτῳ ἐλεγχθεὶς ὁ Σύρος καὶ δηχθεὶς σφόδρα,
ἀλλὰ μήν, ἔφη, παράκειται ἡμῖν ἐπὶ τῆς τραπέζης καὶ
ψιττάκια· ἅπερ ἢν εἴπῃς παρὰ τίνι κεῖται,

δώσω σοι

οὐ

χρυσέους δέκα στατῆρας

κατὰ τὸν Ποντικὸν λεσχηνευτήν, ἀλλὰ τουτὶ τὸ ἔκ-
πωμα. σιωπήσαντος δὲ τοῦ Δημοκρίτου, ἀλλ' ἐπεὶ
ἀπορεῖς, ἔφη, ἐγώ σε διδάξω. Νίκανδρος μὲν ὁ Κολο-
d φώνιος ἐν τοῖς Θηριακοῖς | μνημονεύων αὐτῶν φησιν·

φιττάκι' ἀκρεμόνεσσιν ἀμυγδαλέοισιν ὅμοια.

γράφεται δὲ καί·

βιστάκια < . . . > ἀμυγδαλόεντα πέφανται.[87]

[87] The traditional text of Nicander has πιστάκι' ἀκρεμόνεσσιν ἀμυγδαλόεντα πέφανται.

296

Unfermented wine's best for sensible behavior.
If you act like this, you'll be easier on your property.

They also use *apesthiein* to mean "to eat part of something" (*apo tinos esthiein*), for example Hermippus in *Soldiers* (fr. 51):

> Shit! He's biting me! he's biting me!
> He's eating part (*apesthiei*) of my ear!

The Syrian[359] had thus been caught in a mistake and was extremely upset, and he said: Alright—there are also pistachio nuts on our tables. If you tell me what author refers to them,

I will give you

not

ten gold staters,

to quote the chatterbox[360] from Pontus (Heraclid. Pont. Jun. *SH* 480), but this drinking vessel. When Democritus remained silent, Ulpian said: Well, since you are at a loss, I will provide you with the answer. Nicander of Colophon mentions them in his *Theriaca* (891), saying:

> pistachio nuts (*phittakia*), which resemble almonds,
> on the branches.

But there is also the reading:

> pistachio nuts (*bistakia*) that look like almonds have
> appeared.

[359] Ulpian.　　[360] *leschêneutês*, playing on the name of Heracleides' poem *Leschai*.

καὶ Ποσειδώνιος δὲ ὁ ἀπὸ τῆς στοᾶς ἐν τῇ τρίτῃ τῶν
Ἱστοριῶν γράφει οὕτως· φέρει δὲ καὶ τὸ πέρσειον ἡ
Ἀραβία καὶ ἡ Συρία καὶ τὸ καλούμενον βιστάκιον· ὃ
δὴ βοτρυώδη τὸν καρπὸν ἀφίησι λευκόφαιον ὄντα καὶ
μικρόν,[88] παρεμφερῆ τοῖς δακρύοις, ἃ δὴ ῥαγῶν τρόπον ἀλλήλοις ἐπιβάλλει, τὰ δ' ἔνδον ἔγχλωρον καὶ
τοῦ κωνίου τῶν στροβίλων ἧττον μὲν εὔχυμον, εὐώδη
e   δὲ μᾶλλον. οἱ δὲ τὰ Γεωργικὰ | συγγράψαντες ἀδελφοὶ
ἐν τῷ τρίτῳ γράφουσιν οὕτως· καὶ τὴν μελίαν καὶ τὴν
τέρμινθον, ἃ δὴ νῦν πιστάκια οἱ Σύροι καλοῦσιν. καὶ
οὗτοι μὲν διὰ τοῦ π̄ πιστάκια ταῦτα ὠνόμασαν, ὁ δὲ
Νίκανδρος δασέως φιττάκια, Ποσειδώνιος δὲ βιστάκια.

Περιβλέψας οὖν ἐπὶ τούτοις τοὺς παρόντας καὶ
τυχὼν ἐπαίνου ἔφη· ἀλλὰ μὴν καὶ περὶ τῶν ἄλλων
πάντων τῶν παρακειμένων λελέξεταί μοι, ἵνα με τῆς
πολυμαθίας ἀγασθῆτε. ἐρῶ δὲ πρότερον περὶ τῶν
παρὰ Ἀλεξανδρεῦσιν καλουμένων κοννάρων καὶ παλι-
f   ούρων. | μνημονεύει δ' αὐτῶν Ἀγαθοκλῆς ὁ Κυζικηνὸς
ἐν τρίτῃ τῶν περὶ τῆς πατρίδος λέγων οὕτως· κεραυ-
νοῦ δὲ σκήψαντος εἰς τὸν τάφον ἀνεβλάστησεν ἐκ τοῦ
σήματος δενδρίον, ὃ ἐκεῖνοι κόνναρον ἐπονομάζουσιν.
ἐστὶ δὲ τὸ δενδρίον μεγέθει μὲν πτελέης καὶ πεύκης
οὐθέν τι μεῖον, ἀκρεμόνας δὲ ἔχει θαμέας καὶ δολι-
χοὺς καὶ ἐπ' ὀλίγον ἀκανθώδεας, τὸ δὲ φύλλον τέρεν
650   καὶ χλωρόν, τῇ φυῇ περιφερές. ‖ καρποφορεῖ δὲ δὶς
τοῦ ἔτεος, ἦρός τε καὶ φθινοπώρου. γλυκὺς δὲ πάνυ ὁ

So too the Stoic Posidonius in Book III of his *History* (*FGrH* 87 F 3 = fr. 55a Edelstein–Kidd) writes as follows: Persea grows in Arabia and Syria, as does the so-called *bistakion* ("pistachio"). The latter (tree) produces clusters of small, off-white fruit that resemble tears, and that spill over on top of one another like a bunch of grapes; they are pale on the inside and not as moist as pine-nuts but more fragrant. The brothers who composed the *Art of Farming*[361] write as follows in Book III: and the manna-ash and the terebinth, which the Syrians refer to today as *pistakia*. They referred to them as *pistakia*, with a *pi*, whereas Nicander uses the aspirated form *phittakia*, while Posidonius has *bistakia*.

He glanced around at the group when he completed these remarks, and after they expressed approval, he said: Alright—I intend to discuss all the other foods we have been served, allowing you to be astonished at my wide learning. I will begin by speaking about what the inhabitants of Alexandria refer to as *konnara* and *paliouroi*. Agathocles of Cyzicus mentions these in Book III of his history of his native land (*FGrH* 472 F 4), where he says the following: After a lightning-bolt struck the tomb, a tree the locals refer to as a *konnaron* grew from the mound. This tree is at least as tall as an elm or a pine, and has long, closely-set branches that are somewhat thorny; its leaves are soft, pale-green, and round. It produces fruit twice a year, in the spring and the fall. The fruit is extremely sweet;

---

[361] Sextus Quintilius Condianus and Sextus Quintilius Valerius Maximus, who shared the consulship in 151 CE.

---

88 μικρόν Olson: μακρόν A

καρπός, μέγεθος κατὰ φαυλίην ἐλάην καὶ τὴν σάρκα
καὶ τὸ ὀστέον ταύτῃ προσείκελον, διαλλάσσον δὲ τῇ
τοῦ χυμοῦ ἡδονῇ. καὶ τρώγεται ἔτι χλωρὸς ὁ καρπός·
καὶ ἐπὴν αὐανθῇ, ποιοῦσιν ἐξ αὐτοῦ ἄλευρα, καὶ
πατέονται ταῦτα οὐ μάξαντες οὐδ᾽ ὕδατι δεύοντες,
ἀλλὰ φαύλως ὁκοῖά περ πέφυκεν. καὶ Εὐριπίδης ἐν
Κύκλωπί φησι·

< . . . > παλιούρου κλάδῳ.

Θεόπομπός τε ἐν εἰκοστῇ πρώτῃ Φιλιππικῶν μνη-
b μονεύει | αὐτῶν καὶ Δίφιλος ὁ Σίφνιος ἰατρὸς ἐν τῷ
Περὶ τῶν Προσφερομένων τοῖς Ὑγιαίνουσι καὶ τοῖς
Νοσοῦσιν. τούτων δὲ πρῶτον ἐμνήσθην, ἄνδρες φίλοι,
οὐχ ὅτι ἡμῖν παράκειται νῦν, ἀλλ᾽ ὅτι πολλάκις ἐν τῇ
καλῇ Ἀλεξανδρείᾳ ἐπὶ τῶν δευτέρων τραπεζῶν παρακείμενα ἔλαβον καὶ ζητηθέντος ἐκεῖ τοῦ ὀνόματος
ἐνθάδε τῷ βιβλίῳ ἐντυχὼν ἀνελεξάμην. ἑξῆς οὖν λέξω
περὶ τῶν παρακειμένων ἀπιῶν· ἐπεὶ ἀπ᾽ αὐτῶν καὶ ἡ
c Πελοπόννησος Ἀπία ἐκλήθη διὰ τὸ ἐπιδαψιλεύειν | ἐν
αὐτῇ τὸ φυτόν, φησὶν Ἴστρος ἐν τοῖς Ἀργολικοῖς. ὅτι
δὲ τὰς ἀπίους ἐν ὕδατι εἰσέφερον εἰς τὰ συμπόσια
Ἄλεξις ἐν Βρεττίᾳ παρίστησι διὰ τούτων·

(Α.) εἶδές ποτε
πίνουσιν ἀνθρώποις ἀπίους παρακειμένας
ἐν ὕδατι; (Β.) πολλὰ πολλάκις δήπου. τί οὖν;
(Α.) οὐκοῦν ἕκαστος ἐκλεγόμενος λαμβάνει
τῶν ἐπινεουσῶν τὴν πεπαιτάτην ἀεί;
(Β.) δηλονότι.

it is the size of a *phaulios* ("coarse") olive, which both its flesh and its pit resemble, although its juice tastes better. The fruit is eaten while still green. After it dries, they make flour out of it; when they eat this, they do not knead it or add any water, but simply consume it as is. Euripides says in *Cyclops* (394):

with a *paliouros*-branch.

Theopompus mentions *paliouroi* in Book XXI of the *History of Philip* (FGrH 115 F 133), as does the physican Diphilus of Siphnos in his *On Foods for the Healthy and the Sick*. I mentioned these items first, my friends, not because we have been served them today, but because I often had them on the second tables in beautiful Alexandria; although the question of their name came up there, I encountered them here,[362] in this book, and culled them from that source. My next topic will accordingly be the pears (*apia*) we have been served; for the Peloponnese came to be called Apia from them, since the tree flourishes there, according to Istrus in his *History of the Argolid* (FGrH 334 F 39). That they used to serve pears in water at their drinking parties is attested by Alexis in *The Girl from Bruttium* (fr. 34), in the following passage:

> (A.) Did you ever see
> pears served in water to people who were
> drinking? (B.) Of course; lots of them, all the time.
>   So what?
> (A.) Doesn't everyone always choose the ripest one
> that's floating around and take it?
> (B.) Obviously.

362 In Rome.

d αἱ δ᾽ ἀμαμηλίδες οὐκ εἰσιν ἄπιοι, | ὥς τινες οἴονται,
ἀλλ᾽ ἕτερόν τι καὶ ἥδιον καὶ ἀπύρηνον. Ἀριστομένης
ἐν Διονύσῳ φησίν·

ὁ Χῖος οὐκ οἶσθ᾽ ὡς ἀμαμηλίδας ποεῖ;

ὅτι δ᾽ ἐστὶν ἕτερον τῆς ἀπίου καὶ ἥδιον Αἰσχυλίδης
παρίστησιν ἐν τρίτῳ Γεωργικῶν. περὶ Κέω γοῦν τῆς
νήσου λέγων γράφει οὕτως· ἀπίους ἡ νῆσος φέρει
κρατίστας κατὰ τὰς ἐν Ἰωνίᾳ καλουμένας ἀμαμη-
λίδας· εἰσὶ γὰρ ἀπύρηνοί τε καὶ ἡδεῖαι καὶ γλυκεῖαι.
Ἀέθλιος δ᾽ ἐν πέμπτῳ Ὥρων Σαμίων, εἰ γνήσια τὰ
e συγγράμματα, ὁμομηλίδας αὐτὰς | καλεῖ. Πάμφιλος
δ᾽ ἐν τοῖς Περὶ Γλωσσῶν καὶ Ὀνομάτων, ἐπιμηλίς,
φησίν· ἀπίου γένος. Ἀνδροτίων δ᾽ ἐν τῷ Περὶ Γεωργικῶν φωκίδας φησὶν εἶδος ἀπίων εἶναι.

Ῥόων ⟨ . . . ⟩ δὲ σκληροκόκκων·[89] τῶν γὰρ ἀπυ-
ρήνων Ἀριστοφάνης ἐν Γεωργοῖς μνημονεύει. καὶ ἐν
Ἀναγύρῳ·

⟨ . . . ⟩ πλὴν ἀλεύρου καὶ ῥόας.

καὶ ἐν Γηρυτάδῃ. Ἕρμιππος δ᾽ ἐν Κέρκωψί φησιν·

ἤδη τεθέασαι κόκκον ἐν χιόνι ῥόας;

[89] λέγονται δέ τινες ῥόαι ἀπύρηνοι καὶ ἕτεραι σκληρό-
κοκκοι CE

Medlars (*hamamêlides*) are not pears, as some people believe, but a different type of fruit that tastes better and lacks seeds.[363] Aristomenes says in *Dionysus* (fr. 11):

Don't you know that Chios produces medlars?

Aeschylides in Book III of the *Art of Farming* establishes that this is a different fruit from a pear and tastes better. In his discussion of the island of Ceos, at any rate, he writes as follows: The island produces excellent pears that resemble what the Ionians refer to as *hamamêlides*; they lack seeds and are delicious and sweet. Aethlius in Book V of the *Annals of Samos* (*FGrH* 536 F 1b)—if the treatise is genuine—refers to them as *homomêlides*. Pamphilus says in his *On Words and Names* (fr. V Schmidt): *epimêlis*: a variety of pear.[364] Androtion in his *On the Art of Farming* (*FGrH* 324 F *78) reports that *phôkides* are a type of pear.

Pomegranates (*rhoai*) . . . while others have hard seeds; for Aristophanes mentions the type that lack stones in *Farmers* (fr. 120). Also in *Anagyrus* (fr. 52):

except for coarse-ground wheat and pomegranates.

And in *Gerytades* (fr. 188). Hermippus says in *Cercopes* (fr. 37):

Have you ever seen a pomegranate seed in the snow?

[363] But medlars have seeds, and this is presumably a bad deduction based on the passage of Aeschylides quoted below.
[364] Cited also at 3.82d.

ῥοΐδιον μέντοι ὡς βοΐδιον τὸ ὑποκοριστικόν. Ἀντιφάνης ἐν Βοιωτίᾳ·

ἐνεγκεῖν ἐξ ἀγροῦ μοι τῶν ῥοῶν
τῶν σκληροκόκκων.

Ἐπίλυκος Κωραλίσκῳ·

< . . . > μῆλα καὶ ῥόας λέγεις.

Ἄλεξις Μνηστῆρσιν·

ῥόαν γὰρ ἐκ τῆς χειρὸς αὐτῶν. |

f σίδας δ' ὅτι τὰς ῥοιὰς καλοῦσι Βοιωτοὶ Ἀγαθαρχίδης
ἐν τῇ ἐννεακαιδεκάτῃ τῶν Εὐρωπιακῶν οὕτως γράφει·
ἀμφισβητούντων Ἀθηναίων πρὸς Βοιωτοὺς περὶ τῆς
χώρας ἣν καλοῦσι Σίδας, Ἐπαμινώνδας δικαιολογού-
μενος ἐξαίφνης ἐκ τῆς ἀριστερᾶς μεταλαβὼν κεκρυμ-
μένην ῥόαν καὶ δείξας ἤρετο τί καλοῦσι τοῦτο. τῶν δ'
651 εἰπόντων ῥόαν, "ἀλλ' ἡμεῖς," εἶπε, "σίδαν" ‖ (ὁ δὲ
τόπος τοῦτ' ἔχει τὸ φυτὸν ἐν αὐτῷ πλεῖστον, ἀφ' οὗ
τὴν ἐξ ἀρχῆς εἴληφε προσηγορίαν), καὶ ἐνίκησεν.
Μένανδρος δ' ἐν Αὑτὸν Τιμωρουμένῳ ῥοίδια αὐτὰς
ὠνόμασεν διὰ τούτων·

---

365 Diminutive of *bous* ("ox, cow"). This comment appears
to belong with the quotation from Menander (fr. 83.2) below. It
is unclear whether the word ought to be printed *rhoïdion* or
rhoidion (thus Kassel–Austin in the Menander passage).

366 Referred to as *The Boeotian Woman* also at 11.474e, but as
The Boeotian at 3.84a; 9.367f.

The diminutive, moreover, is *rhoïdion*, like *boïdion*.[365] Antiphanes in *The Boeotian Woman*[366] (fr. 60):

> to bring me some of the pomegranates with hard
>   seeds
> from the countryside.

Epilycus in *Coraliscus* (fr. 2):

> You're talking about apples and pomegranates.

Alexis in *The Suitors*[367] (fr. 73):

> because a pomegranate from their hand.

As for the Boeotians referring to pomegranates (*rhoiai*) as *sidai*, Agatharchides writes as follows in Book XIX of his *History of Europe* (FGrH 86 F 8): When the Athenians were having a dispute with the Boeotians about the area they refer to as Sidai, Epaminondas,[368] in the course of arguing his side of the case, abruptly took in his right hand a pomegranate he had been keeping hidden; showed it to them; and asked what their word for it was. When they said that they called it a *rhoa*, he said: "But we call it a *sida*"— the area contains a large number of these trees, which is how it originally got its name—and won the decision. Menander in *The Masochist* (fr. 83) referred to them as *rhoidia*,[369] in the following passage:

---

[367] Sc. *"of Helen,"* as the Antiatticist (citing frr. 74–5) makes clear.

[368] Agatharcides Book XIX apparently covered events in 250 BCE, but Epaminondas died in 362; so this anecdote must have represented a bit of historical background.

[369] Or *rhoïdia*? See 14.650e n.

† μετ᾽ ἄριστον γὰρ ὡς ἀμυγδάλας ἐγὼ †
παρέθηκα καὶ τῶν ῥοιδίων ἐτρώγομεν.

λέγεται δέ τι καὶ φυτὸν σίδη ὅμοιον ῥοιᾷ, γινόμενον
ἐν τῇ περὶ Ὀρχομενὸν λίμνῃ ἐν αὐτῷ τῷ ὕδατι, οὗ τὰ
μὲν φύλλα τὰ πρόβατα ἐσθίει, τὸν δὲ βλαστὸν αἱ ὕες,
ὡς ἱστορεῖ Θεόφραστος ἐν τετάρτῳ Περὶ Φυτῶν, γίνε-
b σθαι λέγων κἂν τῷ Νείλῳ ὁμώνυμόν τι | αὐτῇ ἄνευ
ῥιζῶν.

Φοίνικες. Ξενοφῶν μὲν ἐν δευτέρῳ Ἀναβάσεώς
φησιν· ἐν‹ῆν›[90] δὲ σῖτος πολὺς καὶ οἶνος φοινίκων καὶ
ὄξος ἑψητὸν[91] ἀπὸ τῶν αὐτῶν. αὐταὶ δὲ αἱ βάλανοι τῶν
φοινίκων οἵας μὲν ἐν τοῖς Ἕλλησιν ἔστιν ἰδεῖν τοῖς
οἰκέταις ἀπέκειντο, αἱ δὲ τοῖς δεσπόταις ἀποκείμεναι
ἦσαν ἀπόλεκτοι, θαυμάσιοι τὸ κάλλος καὶ τὸ μέγεθος,
ἡ δὲ ὄψις ἠλέκτρου οὐδὲν διέφερεν. τὰς δέ τινας
ξηραίνοντες τραγήματα παρετίθεντο,[92] καὶ ἦν παρὰ
πότον ἡδὺ μέν, κεφαλαλγὲς δέ. Ἡρόδοτος δ᾽ ἐν τῇ
c πρώτῃ | περὶ Βαβυλῶνος λέγων φησίν· εἰσὶ δ᾽ αὐτόθι
φοίνικες πεφυκότες ἀνὰ πᾶν τὸ πεδίον, οἱ πλεῦνες
αὐτῶν καρποφόροι, ἐκ τῶν καὶ σιτία καὶ οἶνον καὶ
μέλι ποιέονται. τοὺς συκέων τρόπον θεραπεύουσιν·
τῶν γὰρ φοινίκων οὓς ἔρσενας καλέουσι, τούτων τὸν
καρπὸν περιδέουσι τῇσι βαλανηφόροισι τῶν φοινίκων, ἵνα τε πεπαίνῃ σφιν ὁ ψὴν τὴν βάλανον ἐνδύνων
καὶ μὴ ἀπορρείῃ ὁ καρπὸς τοῦ φοίνικος· ψῆνας γὰρ δὴ

[90] Thus Xenophon.
[91] καὶ ἑψητὸν A; the traditional text of Xenophon omits καὶ

† Because after lunch, when almonds I †
served, and we were eating some of the *rhoidia*.

There is also said to be a plant known as a *sidê* that resembles a pomegranate and is found in the marsh near Orchomenus, right in the water; the sheep and goats eat its leaves, while the pigs eat its fruit, according to Theophrastus in Book IV of *On Plants* (fr. 401 Fortenbaugh), who reports that another plant by the same name, but that lacks roots, grows in the Nile.

Date-palms. Xenophon says in Book II (3.14–15) of the *Anabasis*: A large amount of grain was available there, as well as date-wine and reduced vinegar made from the same fruit. As for the palm-fruit itself, the type one can see in Greece was reserved for the domestic slaves, whereas the select pieces were reserved for the masters; they were amazingly attractive and large, and looked exactly like electrum. The locals dried some of them and served them as snacks; they were nice to eat when you were drinking, but gave you a headache. Herodotus says in his discussion of Babylon in Book I (193.4–5, slightly condensed and modified): There are date-palms there that grow everywhere in the plain; the majority bear fruit, and are the source of their grain, wine, and honey. They care for them as one does a fig tree: they tie the fruit of what they refer to as the male palms to the fruit-bearing female palms, so that the fig-wasp can enter the fruit and make it ripen for them,[370] and to keep the fruit from falling off the tree; for

[370] For fig-wasps, see Dunbar on Ar. *Av.* 590.

---

[92] The traditional text of Xenophon has ἀπετίθεσαν.

φορέουσιν ἐν τῷ καρπῷ οἱ ἔρσενες καθάπερ οἱ ὄλον-
θοι. τὰ παραπλήσια τοῖς περὶ τὸν Ἡρόδοτον ἱστορεῖ |
d περὶ τοῦ ἐν Λιβύῃ καλουμένου λωτοῦ αὐτόπτης γενόμενος ὁ Μεγαλοπολίτης Πολύβιος ἐν τῇ δωδεκάτῃ
τῶν Ἱστοριῶν λέγων οὕτως· ἐστὶ δὲ τὸ δένδρον ὁ
λωτὸς οὐ μέγα, τραχὺ δὲ καὶ ἀκανθῶδες, ἔχει δὲ
φύλλον χλωρὸν παραπλήσιον τῇ ῥάμνῳ, μικρὸν
βαθύτερον καὶ πλατύτερον. ὁ δὲ καρπὸς τὰς μὲν ἀρχὰς ὅμοιός ἐστιν καὶ τῇ χρόᾳ καὶ τῷ μεγέθει ταῖς
λευκαῖς μυρτίσι ταῖς τετελειωμέναις, αὐξανόμενος δὲ
τῷ μὲν χρώματι γίνεται φοινικοῦς, τῷ δὲ μεγέθει ταῖς
γογγύλαις ἐλαίαις παραπλήσιος, πυρῆνα δὲ ἔχει
e τελέως | μικρόν. ἐπὰν δὲ πεπανθῇ, συνάγουσι καὶ τὸν
μὲν τοῖς οἰκέταις μετὰ χόνδρου κόψαντες σάττουσιν
εἰς ἀγγεῖα, τὸν δὲ τοῖς ἐλευθέροις ἐξελόντες τὸν πυρῆνα συντιθέασιν ὡσαύτως καὶ σιτεύονται τοῦτον. ἐστὶ
δὲ τὸ βρῶμα παραπλήσιον σύκῳ καὶ φοινικοβαλάνῳ,
τῇ δὲ εὐωδίᾳ βέλτιον. γίνεται δὲ καὶ οἶνος ἐξ αὐτοῦ
βρεχομένου καὶ τριβομένου δι' ὕδατος, κατὰ μὲν τὴν
γεῦσιν ἡδὺς καὶ ἀπολαυστικός, οἰνομέλιτι χρηστῷ
παραπλήσιος, ᾧ χρῶνται χωρὶς ὕδατος. οὐ δύναται δὲ
πλέον δέκα μένειν ἡμερῶν, διὸ καὶ ποιοῦσι κατὰ
f βραχὺ | πρὸς τὴν χρείαν. ποιοῦσι δὲ καὶ ὄξος ἐξ
αὐτῶν. Μελανιππίδης δ' ὁ Μήλιος ἐν ταῖς Δαναΐσιν
φοίνικας τὸν καρπὸν οὕτως ὀνομάζει τὸν λόγον ποιούμενος περὶ αὐτῶν τῶν Δαναΐδων·

---

[371] A prickly shrub of some sort.

the male trees produce fig-wasps in much the same way as the flowers of the wild fig do. Polybius of Megalopolis in Book XII (I.2) of his *History* offers information similar to what Herodotus has, but about what is known in Libya as the *lôtos*, which he himself saw. He says the following: The *lôtos* is a relatively small tree, and is rough and covered with thorns. Its leaves are light green and resemble those of a *rhamnos*,[371] but are slightly thicker and broader. The fruit initially resembles ripe white myrtle-berries in its color and size; but as it gets larger, it takes on a dark-red hue. It is about as big as a round olive, and has a very small pit. Once it is ripe, they harvest it, and chop up some of it with groats and pack it into jars for their slaves, whereas they first remove the pits from the portion intended for the free people, and then process it in the same way and eat it. This food is similar to figs or dates, but it smells better. Wine is also produced from the fruit when it is soaked in water and mashed. As for its taste, it is delicious and enjoyable, and resembles good *oinomeli*;[372] they drink it without adding water.[373] It cannot be stored for more than ten days, and they therefore produce it a little at a time for immediate consumption. They also make vinegar from the same ingredients. Melanippides of Melos in his *Danaids* (*PMG* 757) refers to the fruit[374] as *phoinikes* in the following passage, where he is discussing the Danaids themselves:

[372] Honey (*meli*) into which wine (*oinos*) had been mixed.

[373] Sc. in contrast to the normal Greek custom of mixing wine with water.

[374] Sc. of the date-palm, to which the discussion now returns after the brief excursus on the *lôtos*. The term *phoinix* is normally used of the tree rather than of its fruit.

οὐ γὰρ † ἀνθρώπων φόρευν μορφὰν ἐνείδος †
οὐδὲ † τὰν αὐτὰν † γυναικείαν ἔχον,
ἀλλ' ἐν ἁρμάτεσσι διφρού-
    χοις ἐγυμνάζοντ' ἀν' εὐ-
    ήλι' ἄλσεα πολλάκις
θήραις φρένα τερπόμεναι,
⟨αἱ δ'⟩ ἱερόδακρυν λίβανον εὐώ-
    δεις τε φοίνικας κασίαν τε ματεῦσαι
τέρενα Σύρια σπέρματα. ‖

652 καὶ Ἀριστοτέλης ἐν τῷ Περὶ Φυτῶν οὕτως· φοινίκων
ἀνόρχων, οὕς τινες εὐνούχους καλοῦσιν, οἱ δ' ἀπυ-
ρήνους. φοίνικα δὲ τὸν καρπὸν καὶ Ἑλλάνικος κέκλη-
κεν ἐν τῇ εἰς Ἄμμωνος Ἀναβάσει, εἰ γνήσιον τὸ
σύγγραμμα, καὶ Φόρμος ὁ κωμικὸς ἐν Ἀταλάνταις.
περὶ δὲ τῶν Νικολάων καλουμένων φοινίκων τοσοῦτον
ὑμῖν εἰπεῖν ἔχω τῶν ἀπὸ τῆς Συρίας καταγομένων, ὅτι
ταύτης τῆς προσηγορίας ἠξιώθησαν ὑπὸ τοῦ Σεβα-
στοῦ αὐτοκράτορος σφόδρα χαίροντος τῷ βρώματι,
b Νικολάου τοῦ Δαμασκηνοῦ ἑταίρου ὄντος | αὐτῷ καὶ
πέμποντος φοίνικας συνεχῶς. τῶν ἀπὸ τοῦ περιπάτου
δ' ὢν ὁ Νικόλαος καὶ ἱστορίαν συνέγραψεν πολλήν.

Ἰσχάδες. σφόδρα τῶν ἰσχάδων ἐθαυμάζοντο αἱ
Ἀττικαί. Δίνων γοῦν ἐν τοῖς Περσικοῖς φησιν· παρετίθεντο δ' ἐπὶ τῆς τραπέζης τῆς βασιλέως ὅσα ἡ γῆ
βρώματα φέρει ἧς ἄρχει βασιλεύς, ἀφ' ἑκάστου ὅσον

For not † of human beings [corrupt] shape
   [corrupt] †
and not † the same † feminine having,
but they often used to exercise
   in the sunny groves
   in chariots fitted with seats,
taking pleasure in hunting,
while others, seeking out the sacred tears of
   frankincense, fragrant *phoinikes*, and cassia,
soft Syrian seeds.

Also Aristotle in his *On Plants* (fr. 326), as follows: of cas-
trated *phoinikes*, which some authorities refer to as eunuchs, while others call them pit-less. Hellanicus in his
Journey Inland to Ammon's Shrine (*FGrH* 4 F 56)—if the
treatise is genuine—similarly calls the fruit a *phoinix*, as
does the comic author Phormus in *Atalantas* (fr. 1). As for
the so-called Nicolaus dates[375] imported from Syria, I can
tell you only that they were awarded this name by the emperor Augustus, who took great pleasure in eating them,
because Nicolaus of Damascus (*FGrH* 90 T 10a) was a
friend of his and regularly sent him dates.[376] Nicolaus was a
Peripatetic and wrote a long *History*.[377]

   Dried figs. Dried Attic figs were held in very high regard. Dinon, for example, says in his *History of Persia*
(*FGrH* 690 F 12): The king's table featured every food the
land he controlled produced, representing an offering of

[375] *phoinikes* (as again below).

[376] Very similar material is preserved at Plu. *Mor.* 723d (=
FGrH 90 T 10b).

[377] In 144 books; see 6.249a.

311

ἀπαρχήν. ξενικῷ δὲ οὐδενὶ οὔτε βρώματι οὔτε ποτῷ
ᾤετο δεῖν ὁ Ξέρξης τοὺς βασιλεῖς χρῆσθαι· ὅθεν καὶ
c νόμος τις ὕστερον ἐγένετο. εἰσενέγκαντος | γάρ ποτε
τῶν εὐνούχων τινὸς ἐν τοῖς λοιποῖς τραγήμασιν ἰσχάδας Ἀττικάς, ἐρωτῆσαι ποταπαὶ εἶεν· ἐπεὶ δὲ ἐπύθετο
ἐξ Ἀθηνῶν, τοῖς ἀγορασταῖς ἀπηγόρευεν ὠνεῖσθαι,
ἕως ἂν ἐξουσία γένηται αὐτῷ λαμβάνειν ὅταν ἐθέλῃ
καὶ μὴ ἀγοράζειν. λέγεται δὲ τὸν εὐνοῦχον ἐπίτηδες
τοῦτο ποιῆσαι, ἵνα αὐτὸν ὑπομνήσῃ τῆς ἐπὶ τὰς Ἀθή-
νας στρατείας. Ἄλεξις δ' ἐν Κυβερνήτῃ φησίν·

εἰσέβαινον ἰσχάδες,
τὸ παράσημον τῶν Ἀθηνῶν, καὶ θύμου δέσμαι
τινές.

Λυγκεὺς δὲ ἐν τῇ Πρὸς τὸν Κωμικὸν Ποσείδιππον |
d Ἐπιστολῇ, ἐν τοῖς τραγικοῖς, φησίν, πάθεσιν Εὐριπίδην νομίζω Σοφοκλέους οὐδὲν διαφέρειν· ἐν δὲ ταῖς
ἰσχάσι τὰς Ἀττικὰς τῶν ἄλλων πολὺ προέχειν. κἂν τῇ
Πρὸς Διαγόραν δὲ Ἐπιστολῇ γράφει οὕτως· ἡ δὲ γῆ
ταῖς μὲν χελιδονείοις ἰσχάσιν ἀντιπαρατιθεῖσα τὰς
Βρυγινδαρίδας καλουμένας, τῷ μὲν ὀνόματι βαρβαρι-

---

378 Xerxes I (reigned 486–465 BCE); the expedition referred
to below is the Persian invasion of mainland Greece in 480–479.
379 Plu. Mor. 173c preserves a very similar anecdote.
380 An echo of the story at Hdt. 5.105.2 about how Darius
ordered a servant to do something similar in the aftermath of the
destruction of Sardis.

first fruits, as it were, from every region. Xerxes[378] believed that the members of the royal household should not consume any foreign food or drink, as a consequence of which there was later a law to that effect. For on one occasion, when one of the eunuchs included dried Attic figs among the snacks that were served, Xerxes asked where they came from. When he heard that they were from Athens, he denied his purchasing-agents the right to buy them until he had the ability to take them whenever he wanted rather than spending money on them.[379] There is also a story to the effect that the eunuch did this deliberately, to remind Xerxes of his expedition against Athens.[380] Alexis says in *The Steersman* (fr. 122):

> Dried figs, the distinctive
> product of Athens, entered, as did some bunches of
> thyme.[381]

Lynceus says in his *Letter to the Comic Author Posidippus* (fr. 17 Dalby): In my opinion, Euripides is no better than Sophocles when it comes to tragic emotions. But as for dried figs, the Attic variety is far superior to any other. And in his *Letter to Diagoras* (fr. 13 Dalby) he writes as follows: The land counters swallow-figs[382] with what are known as Brugindarides,[383] which have a barbaric name but speak

[381] Or perhaps "some strings of bulbs" of an unidentified sort; cf. Arnott ad loc.

[382] For swallow-figs, cf. 3.75c–d; 13.582f. "The land" in question is presumably Rhodes; cf. 3.75d–e (again citing Lynceus' *Letters*).

[383] Poll. 6.81 mentions a type of Rhodian figs called *Bagindarioi*.

ζούσας, ταῖς δὲ ἡδοναῖς οὐδὲν ἧττον ἐκείνων Ἀττικι-
ζούσας. Φοινικίδης δ' ἐν Μισουμένῃ φησίν·

(Α.) μύρτων λέγουσιν καὶ μέλιτος ἐγκώμια, |
e   καὶ τῶν προπυλαίων καὶ τέταρτον ἰσχάδων·
    τούτων ἐγευσάμην καταπλεύσας εὐθέως –
(Β.) καὶ τῶν προπυλαίων; (Α.) κοὐδὲν ἦν τούτων
    ὅλως
πρὸς ἀτταγῆνα συμβαλεῖν τῶν βρωμάτων.

ἐν τούτοις τηρητέον καὶ τὴν τοῦ ἀτταγῆνος μνήμην.
Φιλήμων δ' ἐν τῷ Περὶ τῶν Ἀττικῶν Ὀνομάτων Αἰγι-
λίδας φησὶν εἶναι τὰς καλλίστας ἰσχάδας· Αἴγιλα δ'
εἶναι δῆμον τῆς Ἀττικῆς ἀπὸ Αἰγίλου τινὸς ἥρωος
ὠνομασμένον· χελιδονίας δὲ καλεῖσθαι τὰς ἐρυθρομε-
f   λαίνας ἰσχάδας. Θεόπομπος | δ' Εἰρήνῃ τὰς Τιθρα-
σίας ἐπαινῶν ἰσχάδας φησὶν οὕτως·

    μᾶζαι, πλακοῦντες, ἰσχάδες Τιθράσιαι.[93]

οὕτω δὲ ἦσαν περισπούδαστοι πᾶσιν ἀνθρώποις αἱ
ἰσχάδες – ὄντως γὰρ κατὰ τὸν Ἀριστοφάνην,

< . . . > οὐδὲν γλυκύτερον τῶν ἰσχάδων –

ὡς καὶ Ἀμιτροχάτην τὸν τῶν Ἰνδῶν βασιλέα γράψαι
Ἀντιόχῳ ἀξιοῦντα, φησὶν Ἡγήσανδρος, πέμψαι αὐτῷ
γλεῦκον[94] καὶ ἰσχάδας καὶ σοφιστὴν ἀγοράσαντα. ||

---

93 Better Τειθράσιαι (thus Kock, followed by Kassel–Austin)
94 γλεῦκον Olson: γλυκὺν ACE

Attic just as well as the other type as far as a delicious flavor
is concerned. Phoenicides says in *The Girl No One Liked*
(fr. 2):

> (A.) They offer speeches praising myrtle-berries,
>   honey,
> the Propylaia,[384] and, number four, dried figs;
> I tasted those the minute I sailed into port—
> (B.) You tasted the Propylaia? (A.) and not a single
>   one
> of these foods could compare to a francolin.

Note the mention of the francolin in this passage. Philemon in his *On Attic Vocabulary* says that the best variety of
dried figs are Aegilides—Aegila is an Attic deme that gets
its name from a hero known as Aegilus—and that reddish-
black dried figs are known as *chelidoniai* ("swallow-figs").
Theopompus in *Peace* (fr. 12) recommends Tithrasian figs,
saying the following:

> barley-cakes, cakes, dried Tithrasian figs.

There was such universal enthusiasm for dried figs—for
the fact is, to quote Aristophanes (fr. 681), that

> Nothing's sweeter than dried figs—

that, according to Hegesander (fr. 43, *FHG* iv.421), Amitrochates, the king of India,[385] wrote Antiochus asking him
to buy grape-must, dried figs, and a sophist, and send them

---

[384] The monumental entrance-way to the Athenian acropolis,
erected in the late 430s BCE.

[385] Reigned 294–269 BCE; the Antiochus in question is thus
presumably Antiochus I Soter.

653 καὶ τὸν Ἀντίοχον ἀντιγράψαι· ἰσχάδας μὲν καὶ γλεύ-
κον⁹⁵ ἀποστελοῦμέν σοι, σοφιστὴν δ' ἐν Ἕλλησιν οὐ
νόμιμον πωλεῖσθαι. ὅτι δὲ καὶ πεφωσμένας ἰσχάδας
ἤσθιον Φερεκράτης δείκνυσιν ἐν Κοριαννοῖ λέγων
οὕτως·

ἀλλ' ἰσχάδας μοι πρόελε τῶν πεφωσμένων.⁹⁶

καὶ μετ' ὀλίγα δέ·

οὐκ ἰσχάδας οἴσεις; τῶν μελαινῶν· μανθάνεις;
ἐν τοῖς Μαριανδυνοῖς ἐκείνοις βαρβάροις
χύτρας καλοῦσι τὰς μελαίνας ἰσχάδας. |

b οἶδα δὲ καὶ Πάμφιλον εἰρηκότα πρόσκνιδας⁹⁷ γένος
ἰσχάδων.

Βότρυς δὲ ὅτι μὲν κοινὸν δῆλον. σταφυλῆς δὲ
μέμνηται, καίτοι δοκοῦντος τοῦ ὀνόματος Ἀσιαγενοῦς
εἶναι, Κράτης ἐν δευτέρῳ Ἀττικῆς Διαλέκτου, ἐν τοῖς
Ὕμνοις τοῖς ἀρχαίοις φάσκων ἀντὶ τοῦ βότρυος τὴν
σταφυλὴν κεῖσθαι διὰ τούτων·

αὐτῆσι σταφυλῇσι μελαίνῃσιν κομόωντες.

ὅτι δὲ καὶ παρ' Ὁμήρῳ ἐστὶν παντὶ δῆλον. Πλάτων δὲ

⁹⁵ γλεῦκον Olson: γλυκὺν ACE
⁹⁶ Better πεφωγμένων (thus Kassel–Austin, following the lex-
icographers)
⁹⁷ Hesychius and Pollux suggest that the word ought to be
spelled πρόκνιδας.

to him. Antiochus wrote back: I'll send you dried figs and
grape-must. But trafficking in sophists is not allowed in
Greece.[386] Pherecrates in *Corianno* (fr. 74, encompassing
both quotations) shows that they used to eat toasted figs,
when he says the following:

> But pick out some of the toasted dried figs for me!

And shortly after that:

> Bring dried figs! Some of the black ones—do you
>   understand?
> In the land of those Mariandynian barbarians
> they call dried black figs *chutrai*.[387]

I am also aware that Pamphilus (fr. XXXI Schmidt) refers
to a variety of dried figs as *prosknides*.[388]

That *botrus* is a common term[389] is obvious. Crates in
Book II of the *Attic Dialect* (fr. 109 Broggiato) mentions
the word *staphulê*, even though the term appears to be of
Asian origin, and claims that *staphulê* is attested in place of
botrus in the ancient *Hymns*, in the following passage:[390]

> with long hair consisting of the black *staphulai*
>   themselves.

That the word is also found in Homer (e.g. *Il.* 18.561; *Od.*

---

[386] As if this were a dangerous commodity in which trade was
prohibited.

[387] Literally "cookpots," which the fire turned black.

[388] Hsch. π 3540 gives the word in the form *proknis*, while
Poll. 6.81 has *prokrides*.   [389] Sc. for "grape."

[390] Perhaps from the lost portion of the *Homeric Hymn to Dionysus* (= fr. B in West's Loeb).

ἐν ὀγδόῳ Νόμων καὶ βότρυς καὶ σταφυλὰς ὀνομάζει

c διὰ τούτων· ὃς ἂν ἀγροίκου | ὀπώρας γεύσηται,
βοτρύων εἴτε καὶ σύκων, πρὶν ἐλθεῖν τὴν ὥραν τὴν τοῦ
τρυγᾶν Ἀρκτούρῳ σύνδρομον, εἴτ' ἐν τοῖς αὑτοῦ χω-
ρίοις εἴτε καὶ ἐν ἄλλων, ἱερὰς μὲν ⟨πεντήκοντα⟩[98]
ὀφειλέτω τῷ Διονύσῳ δραχμάς, ἐὰν ἐκ τῶν αὑτοῦ
δρέπῃ, ἐὰν δ' ἐκ τῶν γειτόνων, μνᾶν, ἐὰν δ' ἐξ ἄλλων,
δύο μέρη τῆς μνᾶς. ὃς δ' ἂν τὴν γενναίαν νῦν λεγο-
μένην σταφυλὴν ⟨ἢ⟩[99] τὰ γενναῖα σῦκα ἐπονομα-
ζόμενα ὀπωρίζειν βούληται, ἐὰν μὲν ἐκ τῶν οἰκείων
λαμβάνῃ, ὅπως ἂν ἐθέλῃ καὶ ὁπόταν βούληται καρ-

d πούσθω, ἐὰν δ' ἐξ ἄλλων μὴ | πείσας, ἑπομένως τῷ
νόμῳ τῷ μὴ κινεῖν ὅ τι μὴ κατέθετο, ἐκείνως αἰεὶ
ζημιούσθω. ταῦτα μὲν ὁ θεῖος Πλάτων· ἐγὼ δὲ πάλιν
ζητῶ τίς ἡ γενναία σταφυλὴ καὶ τίνα τὰ γενναῖα
σῦκα. ὥρα οὖν ὑμῖν ζητεῖν, ἕως ἐγὼ περὶ τῶν ἑξῆς
παρακειμένων διεξέλθω. καὶ ὁ Μασσούριος ἔφη·

μηδ' ἀναβάλλεσθαι ἔς τ' αὔριον ἔς τ' ἔννηφι.[100]

γενναῖα λέγει τὰ εὐγενῆ ὁ φιλόσοφος, ὡς καὶ Ἀρχί-
λοχος·

⟨ . . . ⟩ πάρελθε, γενναῖος γὰρ εἶς.

[98] πεντήκοντα (i.e. νʹ) om. A   [99] Thus Plato.
[100] Better ἔς τε ἔνηφι, as at 3.100b

---

391 = 100 drachmas.
392 I.e. "I will answer your question at once!" But Masurius

5.69) is apparent to anyone. Plato in Book VIII of the *Laws* (844d–e) uses both *botrus* and *staphulê* in the following passage: Anyone who tastes wild fruit, be it *botrues* or figs, before harvest-time (coinciding with the rise of Arcturus) arrives, be it in his own fields or those of others, is to owe 50 drachmas, to be dedicated to Dionysus, if he picks them from his own field; a *mina*,[391] if he picks them from his neighbors' fields; and two-thirds of a *mina*, if he picks them from fields belonging to anyone else. And if anyone wants to harvest what is known today as a "noble *staphulê*" or what are called "noble figs," if he gets them from his own fields, he may pick them however and whenever he wishes, whereas if he gets them from someone else's field without permission, in accord with the principle that no one is to meddle with what is not his own, he is always to be punished as specified. Thus the divine Plato. But I pose the further question of what a noble *staphulê* and noble figs are. It is therefore time for you to take up this matter, while I work my way systematically through the various items we have been served. And Masurius said (Hes. *Op.* 410):

> And put nothing off until tomorrow or the next day![392]

The philosopher[393] is referring to crops that have been carefully bred (*eugenê*) as "noble" (*gennaia*), as does Archilochus (fr. 225 West²):

> Pass by; for you are noble (*gennaios*).

rapidly returns to merely cataloguing literary references to grapes generally.

[393] Plato (quoted above).

ἢ τὰ ἐπιγεγεννημένα οἷον τὰ ἐπεμβεβλημένα· ὁ γὰρ
e Ἀριστοτέλης καὶ ἐπεμβολάδας ἀπίους | ὀνομάζει τὰς
ἐγκεκεντρισμένας. Δημοσθένης ἐν τῷ Ὑπὲρ Κτησι-
φῶντος· σῦκα καὶ βότρυς καὶ ἐλαίας συλλέγων. Ξενοφῶν ἐν Οἰκονομικῷ· ὑπὸ τοῦ ἡλίου γλυκαίνεσθαι τὰς
σταφυλάς. οἴδασιν δὲ οἱ πρὸ ἡμῶν καὶ τοὺς ἐν οἴνῳ
συντιθεμένους βότρυς. Εὔβουλος γοῦν ἐν Κατακολ-
λωμένῳ φησίν·

> ἀλλὰ παραλαβὼν ἀκράτῳ κροῦε καὶ δίδου
> πυκνὰς
> καὶ βότρυς τρώγειν ἀνάγκαζ᾽ αὐτὸν ἐξ οἴνου
> συχνούς.

ὁ δὲ τὸν Χείρωνα πεποιηκὼς τὸν εἰς Φερεκράτην
f ἀναφερόμενον | φησίν·

> ἀμυγδάλας καὶ μῆλα καὶ μιμαίκυλα
> καὶ μύρτα καὶ σέλινα κἀξ οἴνου βότρυς
> καὶ μυελόν.

ὅτι δ᾽ ἐν ταῖς Ἀθήναις διηνεκεῖς ἦσαν αἱ ὀπῶραι
πᾶσαι, μαρτυρεῖ Ἀριστοφάνης ἐν Ὥραις. τί οὖν
παράδοξον ἱστορεῖν δοκεῖ Ἀέθλιος ὁ Σάμιος ἐν
πέμπτῳ Σαμίων Ὥρων λέγων· σῦκον καὶ σταφυλὴ καὶ
ὁμομηλὶς καὶ μῆλα καὶ ῥοιαὶ[101] δὶς τοῦ ἐνιαυτοῦ ἐγί-
654 νετο; ‖ Λυγκεὺς δ᾽ ἐν τῇ Πρὸς Διαγόραν Ἐπιστολῇ
ἐπαινῶν τὸν κατὰ τὴν Ἀττικὴν γινόμενον Νικο-

---

101 ῥοιαὶ Olson: ῥόδα ACE

Or else (he means) those that have been grown on something else (*epigegennêmena*), which is to say, that have been grafted; because Aristotle (fr. 327) refers to grafted pears as *epembolades*. Demosthenes in his *On Behalf of Ctesiphon*[394] (18.262): collecting figs, grapes (*botrus*), and olives. Xenophon in the *Oeconomicus* (19.19): that the grapes (*staphulai*) grow sweet in the sunlight. Our predecessors also know about grapes preserved in wine. Eubulus, for example, says in *The Man Who Was Glued to the Spot* (fr. 48):

> But take him with you and keep clobbering him with
>   unmixed wine; give him one drink after another,
> and force him to eat lots of grapes packed in wine.

The author of the *Cheiron* attributed to Pherecrates (fr. 158) says:

> almonds, apples, arbutus-fruit,
> myrtle-berries, celery, grapes packed in wine,
> and marrow.

Aristophanes in *Seasons*[395] bears witness to the fact that fruit of all types was constantly available in Athens. So what seems strange about the information provided by Aethlius of Samos in Book V of the *Samian Chronicles* (*FGrH* 536 F 1a), when he says: Figs, grapes (*staphulê*), medlars, apples, and pomegranates were produced twice a year? Lynceus in his *Letter to Diagoras* (fr. 7 Dalby) recommends the Nicostratean grape found in Attica, and

[394] Usually referred to today as the *De Corona* ("On the Crown").

[395] Cf. fr. 581.1–3, quoted at 9.372b.

321

στράτειον βότρυν καὶ ἀντιτιθεὶς αὐτῷ τοὺς Ῥοδιακούς
φησιν· τῷ δ᾽ ἐκεῖ καλουμένῳ βότρυι Νικοστρατείῳ
τὸν Ἱππώνειον ἀντεκτρέφουσι βότρυν, ὃς ἀπὸ Ἑκα-
τομβαιῶνος μηνὸς ὥσπερ ἀγαθὸς οἰκέτης διαμένει
τὴν αὐτὴν ἔχων εὔνοιαν.

Ἐπεὶ δὲ πολλάκις ὑμῖν εἴρηται περί τε κρεῶν καὶ
ὀρνίθων,[102] ἔρχομαι κἀγὼ λέξων ὅσα ἐκ πολυαναγνω-
b σίας εὑρεῖν ἠδυνήθην παρὰ τὰ προειρημένα. | περι-
στέριον οὕτως ἔστιν εὑρεῖν εἰρημένον παρὰ Μενάνδρῳ
ἐν Παλλακῇ·

           μικρὸν ἐπιμείνας προστρέχει
"ἠγόρακά σοι περιστέρια" λέγων.

ὁμοίως Νικόστρατος Ἄβρᾳ·

                      ταῦτ᾽ ἀξιῶ·
† εἰ τ᾽ ὀρνιθάριον † τὸ περιστέριον, τὸ γαστρίον.

Ἀναξανδρίδης ἐν Ἀντέρωτι·

περιστέρια γὰρ εἰσάγων καὶ στρουθία.

Φρύνιχος Τραγῳδοῖς·

περιστέριον δ᾽ αὐτῷ τι λαβὲ τριωβόλου.

Φασιανικός. Πτολεμαῖος ὁ βασιλεὺς ἐν τῷ δω-

—————

[102] καὶ ὀρνίθων καὶ περιστεριδίων A: καὶ περιστεριδίων
del. Kaibel

compares the Rhodian variety to it, saying: To match what is referred to there[396] as the Nicostratean grape, they cultivate the Hipponeian grape, which remains constantly cheerful from the month Hecatombaion[397] on, like a good domestic slave.

Since you have frequently discussed meat and birds,[398] I intend to tell you everything else I was able to find out in addition about these topics from my extensive reading. A pigeon can be found referred to as follows in Menander's *The Concubine* (fr. 280):

> Wait a bit, and then run up
> and say "I've bought you some pigeons."

Likewise Nicostratus in *Habra* (fr. 2):

> This is what I'm requesting:
> † and if a little bird † the pigeon, the stomach-
> sausage.

Anaxandrides in *The Rival in Love* (fr. 7):

> because by bringing in pigeons and sparrows.

Phrynichus in *Tragic Actors* (fr. 53):

> Buy him a pigeon for three obols!

Pheasant. King Ptolemy in Book XII of his *Commen-*

---

[396] In Attica.

[397] The first month of the Attic year, which began in midsummer.

[398] The general subject of 9.373a–403d.

δεκάτῳ τῶν Ὑπομνημάτων περὶ τῶν ἐν Ἀλεξανδρείᾳ

c βασιλείων | λέγων καὶ περὶ τῶν ἐν αὐτοῖς ζῴων
τρεφομένων φησίν· τά τε τῶν φασιανῶν, οὓς τετάρους
ὀνομάζουσιν, οὐ[103] μόνον ἐκ Μηδίας μετεπέμπετο,
ἀλλὰ καὶ νομάδας ὄρνιθας ὑποβαλὼν ἐποίησε πλῆθος, ὥστε καὶ σιτεῖσθαι· τὸ γὰρ βρῶμα πολυτελὲς
ἀποφαίνουσιν. αὕτη ⟨ἡ⟩[104] τοῦ λαμπροτάτου βασιλέως φωνή, ὃς οὐδὲ φασιανικοῦ ὄρνιθός ποτε γεύσα-
σθαι ὡμολόγησεν, ἀλλ᾽ ὥσπερ τι κειμήλιον ἀνα-
κείμενον εἶχε τούσδε τοὺς ὄρνιθας. εἰ δὲ ἑωράκει ὡς

d ἡμῶν ἑκάστῳ εἷς ἐστι παρακείμενος χωρὶς | τῶν ἤδη
κατανηλωμένων, προσαναπεπληρώκει ἂν ταῖς πολυ-
θρυλήτοις ἱστορίαις τῶν Ὑπομνημάτων τούτων ταῖς
εἰκοσιτέσσαρσιν καὶ ἄλλην μίαν. Ἀριστοτέλης δὲ ἢ
Θεόφραστος ἐν τοῖς Ὑπομνήμασι, τῶν φασιανῶν,
φησίν, οὐ κατὰ λόγον ἡ ὑπεροχὴ τῶν ἀρρένων, ἀλλὰ
πολλῷ μείζων.[105] εἰ δ᾽ ὁ προειρημένος βασιλεὺς καὶ τὸ
τῶν ταώνων πλῆθος ἑωράκει τῶν κατὰ τὴν Ῥώμην,
καταπεφεύγει ἂν ἐπὶ τὴν ἱερὰν σύγκλητον, ὡς ὑπὸ τοῦ
ἀδελφοῦ πάλιν τῆς βασιλείας ἐξεληλαμένος. τοσ-

e οῦτον | γάρ ἐστι τούτων τῶν ὀρνίθων τὸ πλῆθος ἐν τῇ
Ῥώμῃ, ὡς δοκεῖν προμεμαντευμένον τὸν κωμῳδιο-

103 οὓς οὐ A: οὓς del. Kaibel
104 add. Kaibel
105 Kaibel misguidedly proposed expelling this sentence
from the text on the ground that it is ill-integrated with what sur-
rounds it.

324

taries (*FGrH* 234 F 2a),[399] in the course of his discussion
of the royal palace in Alexandria and the animals kept
there, says: Not only did he import the variety of pheasants
known as *tetaroi* from Media, but he also bred *nomades*
birds, and produced so many of them that they could be
eaten; for they are generally regarded as expensive food.
This quotation is drawn from the illustrious king, who admitted that he had never tasted pheasant, but who instead
treated these birds like a treasure he kept stored away. If
he had seen how each of us has one sitting on the table beside him, in addition to those we have already consumed,
he would have filled another Book on top of (*FGrH* 234 T
2) the notorious 24 of those *Commentaries* of his. Aristotle
(fr. 991) or Theophrastus says in his *Commentaries*: Male
pheasants are not merely as much larger[400] as one would
expect, but far larger than that. Whereas if the king referred to above[401] had seen how many peacocks there are
in Rome, he would have run away to the sacred Senate, as
if he had been driven from the throne by his brother for a
second time. There are so many of these birds in Rome,
that the comic poet Antiphanes in *The Soldier* or *Tycho* (fr.

[399] The same passage is referred to at 9.387e, where Epaenae-
tus is also cited as claiming that another name for a pheasant is
taturas. Cf. 9.398b–9a (the *tetrax*). What follows makes it clear
that the individual to whom Ptolemy was referring was his brother
Ptolemy VI Philometor.

[400] Sc. than females.

[401] Ptolemy VI Philometor, who was driven from the Egyptian
throne in 164 BCE by Ptolemy VIII Euergetes II (the author of
the *Commentaries*) but was restored after he appealed to Rome
for support.

ποιὸν Ἀντιφάνην ἐν Στρατιώτῃ ἢ Τύχωνι εἰρηκέναι
τάδε·

>   τῶν ταῶν μὲν ὡς ἅπαξ τις ζεῦγος ἤγαγεν μόνον,
>   σπάνιον ὂν τὸ χρῆμα, πλείους εἰσὶ νῦν τῶν
>   ὀρτύγων·
>   χρηστὸν ἄνθρωπον δ᾽ ἐάν τις ἕνα μόνον ζητῶν
>   ἴδῃ,
>   ὄψετ᾽ ἐκ τούτου πονηροὺς πέντε παῖδας
>   γεγονότας. |

f Ἄλεξις δ᾽ ἐν Λαμπάδι·

>   καταφαγεῖν
>   αὐτὸς τοσοῦτ᾽ ἀργύριον; οὐδ᾽ εἰ γάλα λαγοῦ
>   εἶχον, μὰ τὴν Γῆν, καὶ ταῶς κατήσθιον.

ὅτι δὲ καὶ τιθασοὺς εἶχον αὐτοὺς ἐν ταῖς οἰκίαις
Στράττις παρίστησιν ἐν Παυσανίᾳ διὰ τούτων·

>   πολλῶν φλυάρων καὶ ταῶν ἀντάξια,
>   οὓς βόσκεθ᾽ ὑμεῖς ἕνεκα τῶν ὠκυπτέρων.

Ἀναξανδρίδης ἐν Μελιλώτῳ ||

655 >   οὐ μανικόν ἐστ᾽ ἐν οἰκίᾳ τρέφειν ταῶς,
>   ἐξὸν τοσουτουὶ δύ᾽ ἀγάλματ᾽ ἀγοράσαι;

Ἀναξίλας Ὀρνιθοκόμοις·

>   καὶ πρὸς ἐπὶ τούτοις τιθασὸς οἰμώζων ταῶς.

203)[402] would appear to have had a premonition of the situation when he said the following:

> When someone imported a single pair of peacocks
>   only once,
> they were rare. But nowadays they're more common
>   than quail.
> If someone looks for decent people, on the other
>   hand, and spots only one,
> he'll see that the guy's got five bad sons.

Alexis in *Lampas* (fr. 128):

>   that I wasted
> that much money all by myself? Not even if I'd had
>   hare's
> milk, by Earth, and ate peacocks!

Strattis in *Pausanias*[403] (fr. 28) establishes that they kept tame peacocks in their houses, in the following passage:

> worth lots of nonsense and peacocks,
> which you keep because of their tail-feathers.

Anaxandrides in *Melilot* (fr. 29):

> Isn't it crazy to raise peacocks in your house,
> when you could buy two statues for the same price?

Anaxilas in *Bird-Keepers* (fr. 24):

> And in addition, on top of that, a damned tame
>   peacock!

[402] The first two verses are quoted also at 9.397a.
[403] Referred to as *Macedonians* or *Pausanias* at 13.589a.

Μηνόδοτος δ' ὁ Σάμιος ἐν τῷ Περὶ τῶν Κατὰ τὸ Ἱερὸν τῆς Σαμίας Ἥρας φησίν· οἱ ταοὶ ἱεροί εἰσι τῆς Ἥρας. καὶ μήποτε πρώτιστοι καὶ ἐγένοντο καὶ ἐτράφησαν ἐν Σάμῳ καὶ ἐντεῦθεν εἰς τοὺς ἔξω τόπους διεδόθησαν, ὡς καὶ οἱ ἀλεκτρυόνες ἐν τῇ Περσίδι καὶ αἱ καλού-
b μεναι μελεαγρίδες ἐν τῇ Αἰτωλίᾳ. διὸ καὶ | Ἀντιφάνης ἐν τοῖς Ὁμοπατρίοις φησίν·

> ἐν Ἡλίου μέν φασι γίγνεσθαι πόλει
> φοίνικας, ἐν Ἀθήναις δὲ γλαῦκας. ἡ Κύπρος
> ἔχει πελείας διαφόρους, ἡ δ' ἐν Σάμῳ
> Ἥρα τὸ χρυσοῦν, φασίν, ὀρνίθων γένος,
> τοὺς καλλιμόρφους καὶ περιβλέπτους ταῶς.

διόπερ καὶ ἐπὶ τοῦ νομίσματος τῶν Σαμίων ταὼς ἐστιν. ἐπεὶ δὲ καὶ τῶν μελεαγρίδων Μηνόδοτος ἐμνήσθη, λέξομέν τι καὶ ἡμεῖς περὶ αὐτῶν. Κλύτος ὁ
c Μιλήσιος, Ἀριστοτέλους δὲ μαθητής, ἐν | τῷ πρώτῳ Περὶ Μιλήτου γράφει περὶ αὐτῶν οὕτως· περὶ δὲ τὸ ἱερὸν τῆς Παρθένου ἐν Λέρῳ εἰσὶν οἱ καλούμενοι ὄρνιθες μελεαγρίδες. ὁ δὲ τόπος ἐστὶν ἑλώδης ἐν ᾧ τρέφονται. ἐστὶ δὲ ἄστοργον πρὸς τὰ ἔκγονα τὸ ὄρνεον καὶ ὀλιγωρεῖ τῶν νεωτέρων, ὥστε ἀνάγκη τοῖς ἱερεῦσιν ἐπιμελεῖσθαι αὐτῶν. ἔχει δὲ τὸ μὲν μέγεθος ὄρνιθος γενναίου, τὴν δὲ κεφαλὴν μικρὰν πρὸς τὸ σῶμα καὶ ταύτην ψιλήν, ἐπ' αὐτῆς δὲ λόφον σάρκινον, σκληρόν, στρογγύλον, ἐξέχοντα τῆς κεφαλῆς ὥσπερ
d πάτταλον, καὶ τὸ χρῶμα | ξυλοειδῆ, πρὸς δὲ ταῖς γνάθοις ἀπὸ τοῦ στόματος ἀρξαμένην ἀντὶ πώγωνος

Menodotus of Samos says in his *On the Contents of the Temple of Samian Hera* (*FGrH* 541 F 2): The peacocks are sacred to Hera. And it may be that they were first bred and kept on Samos, and were dispersed from there to other regions, just as roosters originated in Persia, and the so-called *meleagrides* originated in Aetolia. This is why Antiphanes says in *Men Who Shared a Father* (fr. 173):

> People claim there are phoenixes in
> Heliopolis, and little owls in Athens. Cyprus
> has got special doves, and Samian Hera,
> they say, has her extraordinary species of birds,
> the spectacularly gorgeous peacocks.

This is why Samian coins have a peacock on them. But since Menodotus also mentioned *meleagrides*, I intend to say something on the topic. Clytus of Miletus, a student of Aristotle, writes as follows about them in Book I of *On Miletus* (*FGrH* 490 F 1): The birds known as *meleagrides* are found around the temple of the Virgin[404] in Leros. The area in which they are kept is marshy. The bird shows no concern for its offspring and neglects its chicks, and as a result the priests are forced to take care of them. It is the size of a domesticated chicken, and has a head that is disproportionately small in comparison to its body and that lacks feathers; on top of its head is a fleshy, hard, round crest, which projects from its head like a peg and is the color of wood. Attached to its jaw, beginning at its mouth, is a long

[404] Artemis.

μακρὰν σάρκα καὶ ἐρυθροτέραν τῶν ὀρνίθων. τὴν δὲ
τοῖς ὄρνισιν ἐπὶ τῷ ῥύγχει γινομένην, ἣν ἔνιοι πώ-
γωνα καλοῦσιν, οὐκ ἔχει· διὸ καὶ ταύτῃ κολοβόν
ἐστιν. ῥύγχος δὲ ὀξύτερον καὶ μεῖζον ἢ ὄρνις ἔχει.
τράχηλος μέλας, παχύτερος καὶ βραχύτερος τῶν
ὀρνίθων. τὸ δὲ σῶμα ἅπαν ποικίλον, μέλανος ὄντος
τοῦ χρώματος ὅλου, πτίλοις λευκοῖς καὶ πυκνοῖς
διειλημμένου <οὐ>¹⁰⁶ μείζοσιν φακῶν. οὗτοι δ' εἰσὶν ἐν
e ῥόμβοις | οἱ κυκλίσκοι <ἧσσον>¹⁰⁷ μέλασι τοῦ ὅλου
χρώματος· διὸ καὶ ποικιλίαν τινὰ οἱ ῥόμβοι παρ-
έχονται, τοῦ μὲν μέλανος ἔχοντες λευκότερον τὸ χρῶμα, τοῦ δὲ λευκοῦ πολὺ μελάντερον. τὸ δὲ κατὰ τὰς
πτέρυγας αὐταῖς πεποίκιλται λευκῷ πριονώδεσιν
σχήμασιν¹⁰⁸ παρ' ἄλληλα κειμένοις. σκέλη δὲ ἄκεν-
τρα ὅμοια τοῖς ὀρνιθίοις. παραπλήσιαι δ' εἰσὶν αἱ
θήλειαι τοῖς ἄρρεσιν· διὸ καὶ δυσδιάκριτόν ἐστι τὸ
τῶν μελεαγρίδων γένος. τοσαῦτα καὶ ὁ περιπατητικὸς
φιλόσοφος περὶ τῶν μελεαγρίδων ἱστόρησεν. |

f   Ὀπτῶν δελφάκων δὲ μνημονεύει Ἐπικράτης ἐν
Ἐμπόρῳ·

                    ἐπὶ τοῖσδ' ἐγὼ
μάγειρος. οὔτε Σικελία καυχήσεται
τρέφειν τοιοῦτον ἄρταμον κατ' ἰχθύων,
οὐκ Ἦλις, ἔνθα δελφάκων ἐγὼ κρέα
κάλλιστ' ὄπωπα πυρὸς ἀκμαῖς ἠνθισμένα.

Ἄλεξις δ' ἐν Πονήρᾳ·

330

bit of flesh that resembles a beard and is redder than a
rooster's wattle. But it lacks the growth found on a rooster's
beak, which some authorities refer to as a beard; it is thus
stunted in this regard. Its beak is sharper and longer than
what a rooster has. Its neck is black, and is thicker and
shorter than a rooster's. Its body is of a generally variegated
appearance: its overall color is black, interspersed with numerous white feathers the size of lentils or smaller. These
spots are set within lozenges that are not as black as the
bird's overall color; as a consequence, the lozenges produce a variegated pattern, since they are lighter in shade
than the bird's black parts but much darker than its light
parts. The portion of the body around their wings is speck-
led with white in a parallel zigzag pattern. Their legs lack
spurs like chickens'. The females resemble the males, and
meleagrides are accordingly difficult to sex. This is the information the Peripatetic philosopher has to offer about
meleagrides.

Epicrates in *The Merchant* (fr. 6) refers to roasted pigs:

> I'm their successor
> in the profession of cook. Sicily won't claim
> to produce a chef like me when it comes to handling
>   fish,
> and neither will Elis, where I've seen lovely
> pork browned by the flame's tips.

Alexis in *The Miserable Woman* (fr. 194):

---

106 add. Schweighäuser

107 add. Wilamowitz

108 σχήμασιν πυρώδεσιν καὶ A: σχήμασιν πυρώδεσιν
tantum CE: πυρώδεσιν del. Schweighäuser, καὶ del. Kaibel

τριωβόλου κρεῖσκον ἀστεῖον πάνυ
ὕειον ὀπτὸν < . . . >
656   καὶ θερμόν, ἐγχυλότερον ‖ ὅταν ᾖ, προσφέρων.

Ἀθηναῖοι δ', ὥς φησι Φιλόχορος, ταῖς Ὥραις θύοντες
οὐκ ὀπτῶσιν, ἀλλ' ἕψουσι τὰ κρέα, παραιτούμενοι τὰς
θεὰς ἀπείργειν τὰ περισκελῆ καύματα καὶ τοὺς
αὐχμούς, μετὰ δὲ τῆς συμμέτρου θερμασίας καὶ ὑδά-
των ὡραίων ἐκτελεῖν τὰ φυόμενα· τὴν μὲν γὰρ ὄπτη-
σιν ἐλάττους παρέχεσθαι ὠφελείας, τὴν δὲ ἕψησιν οὐ
μόνον τὴν ὠμότητα περιαιρεῖν, ἀλλὰ καὶ τὰ σκληρὰ
μαλάττειν δύνασθαι καὶ τὰ λοιπὰ πεπαίνειν. ἔτι δ'
εὐμενέστερον καὶ ἀκινδυνότερον πεπαίνει τὴν τροφήν,
b   διόπερ | ἑφθὸν ἐποπτᾶν οὔ φασι δεῖν οὐδ' ἐφέψειν· τὸ
μὲν γὰρ ἀνάλυσιν ἔχειν δοκεῖ τοῦ βελτίονος, ὥς
φησιν Ἀριστοτέλης, τὰ δὲ ὀπτὰ τῶν ἑφθῶν ὠμότερα
καὶ ξηρότερα. τὰ δὲ ὀπτὰ κρέα καλεῖται φλογίδες.
Στράττις γοῦν ἐν Καλλιππίδῃ ἐπὶ τοῦ Ἡρακλέους
φησίν·

αὐτίκα δ' ἥρπασε τεμάχη
θερμάς τε κάπρου φλογίδας ἔβρυχέ τε πάνθ'
ἄμα.

καὶ Ἄρχιππος ἐν Ἡρακλεῖ Γαμοῦντι·

ταδὶ δ' ἄμα χοί-
ρων ἀκροκώλια μικρῶν,

bringing a very sophisticated little piece of roasted
pork for three obols . . .
and warm, as soon as it's really juicy.

According to Philochorus (*FGrH* 328 F 173), when the
Athenians sacrifice to the Seasons, they do not roast the
meat but stew it, and they ask the goddesses to protect
them from excessive heat and droughts, and to bring the
crops to maturity with moderate temperatures and the appropriate amount of rainfall; for the process of roasting has
a less positive effect, whereas stewing not only eliminates
the rawness but is capable of softening the hard parts and
making the rest tender. In addition, (stewing) makes the
food tender in a gentler and less dangerous way, which is
why people say that food that has been stewed should not
be stewed a second time or subsequently roasted, since doing so would seem to ruin what is best about it, according
to Aristotle,[405] whereas roasted foods are rawer and dryer
than stewed foods. Bits of roasted meat are referred to as
phlogides.[406] Strattis in *Callipides* (fr. 12), for example,
says in reference to Heracles:

> He immediately grabbed fish-steaks
> and hot *phlogides* of boar-meat, and wolfed them all
> down simultaneously.

Also Archippus in *Heracles Getting Married* (fr. 10):

> And here at the same time are little
> piglets' trotters,

---

[405] Cf. *Meteor.* 380b21–3, although this is not at all what Aristotle (who is discussing the differing mechanics of boiling and
stewing) means.   [406] Cognate with *phlegô* ("to burn").

ταύρου τ' αὐξίκερω φλογίδες,

c αἱ δολιχαί τε κάπρου ǀ φλογίδες.

περὶ δὲ περδίκων τί δεῖ καὶ λέγειν ἐμέ, πλεόνων
εἰρημένων ὑφ' ὑμῶν· ἀλλ' οὐ παραλείψω τὸ ἱστορηθὲν
ὑπὸ Ἡγησάνδρου ἐν τοῖς Ὑπομνήμασιν· φησὶν γὰρ
ὅτι Σάμιοι πλεύσαντες εἰς Σύβαριν καὶ κατασχόντες
τὴν Σιρῖτιν χώραν περδίκων ἀναπτάντων καὶ ποιη-
σάντων ψόφον ἐκπλαγέντες ἔφυγον καὶ ἐμβάντες εἰς
τὰς ναῦς ἀπέπλευσαν.

Περὶ δὲ λαγῶν Χαμαιλέων φησὶν ἐν τῷ Περὶ Σιμωνίδου ὡς δειπνῶν παρὰ τῷ Ἱέρωνι ὁ Σιμωνίδης, οὐ
d παρατεθέντος αὐτῷ ἐπὶ τὴν τράπεζαν ǀ καθάπερ καὶ
τοῖς ἄλλοις λαγωοῦ, ἀλλ' ὕστερον μεταδιδόντος τοῦ
Ἱέρωνος, ἀπεσχεδίασεν·

οὐδὲ γὰρ < . . . > εὐρύς περ ἐὼν ἐξίκετο δεῦρο.

ὄντως δ' ἦν ὡς ἀληθῶς κίμβιξ ὁ Σιμωνίδης καὶ
αἰσχροκερδής, ὡς Χαμαιλέων φησίν. ἐν Συρακούσαις
γοῦν τοῦ Ἱέρωνος ἀποστέλλοντος αὐτῷ τὰ καθ'
ἡμέραν λαμπρῶς πωλῶν τὰ πλείω ὁ Σιμωνίδης τῶν
παρ' ἐκείνου πεμπομένων ἑαυτῷ μικρὸν μέρος
ἀπετίθετο. ἐρομένου δέ τινος τὴν αἰτίαν, "ὅπως," εἶπεν,
e "ἥ τε Ἱέρωνος μεγαλοπρέπεια ǀ καταφανὴς ᾖ καὶ ἡ
ἐμὴ κοσμιότης."

Οὔθατος δὲ Τηλεκλείδης ἐν Στερροῖς οὕτως μνη-
μονεύει·

---

407 Tyrant of Gela 485–478 BCE, and of Syracuse 478–466.

and *phlogides* from a high-horned bull,
and the long *phlogides* from a boar.

Why should I discuss partridges, given that you have said a
great deal about the subject (9.388e–90d)? But I will not
omit the story told by Hegesander in his *Commentaries* (fr.
44, *FHG* iv.421); for he claims that when the Samians
sailed to Sybaris and put in to shore near Siritis, some partridges flushed, producing a noise, and the Samians were
so surprised that they ran away and got into their ships and
sailed off.

As for hares, Chamaeleon in his *On Simonides* (fr. 33
Wehrli) says that Simonides was having dinner with
Hieron,[407] and that everyone else had a hare set on his table, but Simonides did not. Later on, Hieron offered him
some, and Simonides extemporized a verse to fit the occasion:

For wide though it was, it did not come this far.[408]

Simonides was in fact a true cheapskate and a money-
grubber, according to Chamaeleon. In Syracuse, for example, Hieron used to send him lavish supplies to cover his
day-to-day needs, but Simonides sold most of what he was
sent and kept only a tiny portion for himself. When someone asked him why, he said: "So that everyone can be
aware of Hieron's generosity—and also of my own sense of
propriety."

Teleclides in *Tough Guys* (fr. 33)[409] mentions udder, as
follows:

[408] A parodic echo of *Il.* 14.33.
[409] Quoted also at 9.399c, which appears to be a longer fragment of the material drawn on only in passing here.

ὡς οὖσα θῆλυς εἰκότως οὖθαρ φορῶ.

ὑπογάστριον δ᾽ αὐτὸ ὠνόμασεν Ἀντίδοτος ἐν Μεμ-
ψιμοίρῳ. σιτευτῶν δὲ ὀρνίθων μὲν μνημονεύει Μάτρων
ἐν ταῖς Παρῳδίαις οὕτως·

> ὡς ἔφαθ᾽, οἱ δ᾽ ἐγέλασσαν, ἐπήνεικάν τ᾽ ἐπὶ
> τούτῳ
> σιτευτὰς ὄρνιθας ἐπ᾽ ἀργυρέοισι πίναξιν, |
> f   ἄτριχας, οἰέτεας, λαγάνοις κατὰ νῶτον ἐίσας.

δελφάκων δὲ σιτευτῶν ὁ φλυακογράφος Σώπατρος ἐν
Βακχίδος Γάμῳ οὕτως·

> εἴ που κλίβανος ἦν, πολὺ δέλφαξ σιτευτὸς
> ἔγρυξεν.

δελφάκια δὲ Αἰσχίνης εἴρηκεν ἐν Ἀλκιβιάδῃ οὕτως·
ὥσπερ αἱ καπηλίδες τὰ δελφάκια τρέφουσιν. Ἀντι-
σθένης δ᾽ ἐν Φυσιογνωμονικῷ· καὶ γὰρ ἐκεῖναι τὰ
δελφάκια πρὸς βίαν χορτάζουσιν. καὶ ἐν Προ-
657   τρεπτικῷ δέ· ἀντὶ δελφακίων τρέφεσθαι. ‖ δέλφακα δὲ
ἀρσενικῶς εἴρηκεν Πλάτων ἐν Ποιητῇ·

> ⟨ . . . ⟩ δέλφακα δὲ ῥαιότατον.

Σοφοκλῆς Ὕβρει·

> ⟨ . . . ⟩ ἐσθίειν ἐθέλων τὸν δέλφακα.

---

410 Literally "underbelly"; cf. 9.399c–d.
411 I.e. extremely crisp. The verse is adapted from Il. 2.765.

I'm a female, so naturally I've got an udder (*outhar*).

Antidotus in *The Complainer* (fr. 1) called it a *hupogastrion*.[410] Matro in his *Parodies* (fr. 5 Olson–Sens = *SH* 538) refers to grain-fattened birds, as follows:

> Thus he spoke. But they laughed, and they brought in in addition to this
> grain-fattened birds on silver serving-platters,
> clean-plucked, all of the same age, like to pieces of wafer-bread[411] over their back.

The phlyax-author Sopater in *The Marriage of Bacchis* (fr. 5) (mentions) grain-fattened pigs, as follows:

> If there was a baking-shell anywhere, a grain-fattened pig (*delphax*) grunted loudly.

Aeschines uses the diminutive form *delphakia*[412] in *Alcibiades* (*SSR* VI A 45), as follows: in the same way that the women who run shops raise *delphakia*. Antisthenes in *The Expert in Physiognomy* (*SSR* V A 62): For those women in fact force-feed their *delphakia*. Also in the *Art of Exhortation* (*SSR* V A 63): to be raised in place of *delphakia*. Plato in *The Poet* (fr. 119) uses *delphax* as a masculine:

> an extremely easy-going (masc.) *delphax*.

Sophocles in *Outrageous Behavior* (fr. 671):

> wanting to eat the (masc.) *delphax*.

---

[412] What follows appears to be a largely separate fragment of the discussion of the use of *delphax* and its variants drawn on also at 9.374d–5b.

Κρατῖνος Ὀδυσσεῦσιν·

< . . . > δέλφακας μεγάλους.

θηλυκῶς δὲ Νικοχάρης ἔφη· † κύουσαν δέλφακα †. καὶ Εὔπολις Χρυσῷ Γένει·

οὐκ ἀλλ' ἔθυον δέλφακ' ᾠδὸν θῆστίᾳ
καὶ μάλα καλήν.

καὶ Πλάτων Ἰοῖ·

πρόσφερε δεῦρο δὴ τὴν κεφαλὴν τῆς δέλφακος.

Θεόπομπος Πηνελόπῃ·

καὶ τὴν ἱερὰν σφάττουσιν ἡμῶν δέλφακα.

b   χηνῶν δὲ σιτευτῶν | καὶ μόσχων Θεόπομπος ἐν τρίτῃ
καὶ δεκάτῃ Φιλιππικῶν καὶ ἑνδεκάτῃ Ἑλληνικῶν, ἐν
οἷς ἐμφανίζει τὸ περὶ τὴν γαστέρα τῶν Λακώνων
ἐγκρατὲς γράφων οὕτως· καὶ οἱ Θάσιοι ἔπεμψαν Ἀγη-
σιλάῳ προσιόντι πρόβατα παντοδαπὰ καὶ βοῦς εὖ
τεθραμμένους, πρὸς τούτοις δὲ καὶ πέμματα καὶ
τραγημάτων εἶδος παντοδαπῶν. ὁ δ' Ἀγησίλαος τὰ
μὲν πρόβατα καὶ τὰς βοῦς ἔλαβεν, τὰ δὲ πέμματα καὶ
τὰ τραγήματα πρῶτον μὲν οὐδ' ἔγνω· κατεκεκάλυπτο
c   γάρ. ὡς | δὲ κατεῖδεν, ἀποφέρειν αὐτοὺς ἐκέλευσεν,
εἰπὼν οὐ νόμιμον εἶναι Λακεδαιμονίοις χρῆσθαι τοι-

---

413 Cited (but not quoted) at 9.375a.
414 Quoted at 9.384a; 15.676c–d.

338

Cratinus in *Odysseuses* (fr. 155):

> big (masc.) *delphakes*.

But Nicochares (fr. 22, unmetrical) used it as a feminine:
† a pregnant (fem.) *delphax* †. Also Eupolis in *The Golden
Age* (fr. 301):[413]

> No; but they were sacrificing a singing *delphax* to
>   Hestia—
> and a very nice (fem.) one!

And Plato in *Ion* (fr. 56):

> Bring the head of the (fem.) *delphax* over here!

Theopompus in *Penelope* (fr. 49):

> And they're slaughtering our sacred (fem.) *delphax*.

Theopompus mentions grain-fattened geese and calves in
Book XIII of the *History of Philip* (*FGrH* 115 F 106)[414] and
Book XI of the *History of Greece* (*FGrH* 115 F 22), where
he calls attention to the Spartans' discipline where the
consumption of food is concerned, writing as follows: As
Agesilaus[415] was approaching, the Thasians sent him herd-
animals of all kinds and well-fed cows, as well as pastries
and every type of snack. Agesilaus accepted the sheep and
goats and the cows, but initially failed to notice the pastries
and the snacks, since they were covered up. But when he
saw them, he ordered the Thasians to take them away, saying that Spartans were not allowed to consume food of this

[415] Agesilaus II of Sparta (Poralla #9), reigned 400–360/59
BCE.

οὗτοις τοῖς ἐδέσμασι. λιπαρούντων δὲ τῶν Θασίων,
"δότε," φησί, "φέροντες ἐκείνοις," δείξας αὐτοῖς τοὺς
εἵλωτας, εἰπὼν ὅτι τούτους δέοι διαφθείρεσθαι τρώ-
γοντας αὐτὰ πολὺ μᾶλλον ἢ αὑτὸν καὶ τοὺς παρόντας
Λακεδαιμονίων. ὅτι δὲ τοῖς εἵλωσιν ὑβριστικῶς πάνυ
ἐχρῶντο Λακεδαιμόνιοι καὶ Μύρων ὁ Πριηνεὺς ἱστορεῖ ἐν δευτέρῳ Μεσσηνιακῶν γράφων οὕτως· τοῖς δ᾽

d εἵλωσι | πᾶν ὑβριστικὸν ἔργον ἐπιτάττουσι πρὸς
πᾶσαν ἄγον ἀτιμίαν· κυνῆν τε γὰρ ἕκαστον φορεῖν
ἐπάναγκες ὥρισαν καὶ διφθέραν περιβεβλῆσθαι πλη-
γάς τε τεταγμένας λαμβάνειν κατ᾽ ἐνιαυτὸν ἀδική-
ματος χωρίς, ἵνα μήποτε δουλεύειν ἀπομάθωσιν. πρὸς
δὲ τούτοις εἴ τινες ὑπερακμάζοιεν τὴν οἰκετικὴν ἐπι-
φάνειαν, ἐπέθηκαν ζημίαν θάνατον καὶ τοῖς κεκτη-
μένοις ἐπιτίμιον, εἰ μὴ ἐπικόπτοιεν τοὺς ἁδρουμένους.

e καὶ παραδόντες αὐτοῖς τὴν χώραν ἔταξαν μοῖραν | ἣν
αὐτοῖς ἀνοίσουσιν αἰεί. χηνίζειν δὲ εἴρηται ἐπὶ τῶν
αὐλούντων. Δίφιλος Συνωρίδι·

    ἐχηνίασας· ποιοῦσι τοῦτο πάντες οἱ
    παρὰ Τιμοθέῳ.

ἐπεὶ δὲ καὶ πετασῶνος μέρος ἑκάστῳ κεῖται, ἣν πέρ-
ναν καλοῦσι, φέρε τι εἴπωμεν καὶ περὶ ταύτης, εἴ τις
τοῦ ὀνόματος μνημονεύει. κάλλισται μὲν γὰρ αἱ
Γαλλικαί, οὐκ ἀπολείπονται δὲ αὐτῶν οὔτε ⟨αἱ⟩[109] ἀπὸ
Κιβύρας τῆς Ἀσιατικῆς οὔτε αἱ Λύκιαι. μνημονεύει δ᾽

[109] add. Musurus

sort. When the Thasians insisted, he said: "Take it and give it to *them*," pointing toward the helots, as a way of saying that he much preferred that the helots be ruined by eating this food than that he and the other Spartans who were there be. That the Spartans treated the helots in an extremely ugly and demeaning way is recorded by Myron of Priene in Book II of the *History of Messenia* (*FGrH* 106 F 2), where he writes as follows: They assign the helots all the ugly and demeaning jobs that bring nothing but dishonor with them. For they required each of them to wear a dog-skin cap and dress in a rough leather robe, and to be whipped a certain number of times every year, regardless of whether they did anything wrong, to keep them from forgetting that they were slaves. In addition, they imposed the death-penalty on any of them who looked healthier than a domestic slave should, and they fined their masters if they failed to take disciplinary measures against any who had too much flesh on their bones. And when they assigned the helots their land, they fixed a share of the crop that they were to bring to the Spartans in perpetuity. The verb *chênizein* ("to sound like a goose, cackle") is used to describe pipe-players. Diphilus in *Synoris* (fr. 78):

> *Echêniasas* ("You cackled"); that's typical of
> Timotheus' students!

But since each of us also has a slice of *petasôn* ("ham")[416]— also known as *perna*—well, let me say something about this as well, and in particular about whether any author uses the word. The best hams actually come from Gaul, although those from Asiatic Cibyra and Lycia are no worse

---

[416] = Latin *petaso*; *perna* (= Latin *perna*) is more common.

αὐτῶν Στράβων ἐν τρίτῃ Γεωγραφουμένων, ἀνὴρ οὐ
f πάνυ νεώτερος· | λέγει γὰρ αὐτὸς[110] ἐν τῇ ἑβδόμῃ τῆς
αὐτῆς πραγματείας ἐγνωκέναι Ποσειδώνιον τὸν ἀπὸ
τῆς στοᾶς φιλόσοφον, οὗ πολλάκις ἐμεμνήμεθα συγ-
γενομένου Σκιπίωνι τῷ τὴν Καρχηδόνα ἑλόντι. γράφει
δ᾽ οὖν ὁ Στράβων οὕτως· ἐν Σπανίᾳ πρὸς τῇ Ἀκυτανίᾳ
658 πόλις Πομπέλων, ὡς ἂν εἴποι τις Πομπηιόπολις, || ἐν
ᾗ πέρναι διάφοροι συντίθενται ταῖς Κανταβρικαῖς
ἐνάμιλλοι.

Ἁλιπάστων δὲ κρεῶν μνημονεύει ὁ τῆς κωμῳδίας
ποιητὴς Ἀριστομένης ἐν Διονύσῳ·

ἁλίπαστα ταῦτα παρατίθημί σοι.

καὶ ἐν Γόησιν·[111]

ἁλίπαστον αἰεὶ τὸν θεράποντ᾽ ἐπεσθίειν.

Ἐπεὶ δὲ καὶ Σικελίας αὔχημα τροφαλὶς ἤδ᾽ ἐστί
σοι, φίλοι, λέξωμέν τι καὶ περὶ τυρῶν. Φιλήμων μὲν
γὰρ ἐν τῷ ἐπιγραφομένῳ Σικελικῷ·

ἐγὼ πρότερον μὲν ᾤμην τὴν Σικελίαν |
b ἐν τοῦτ᾽ ἀπότακτον αὐτό, τοὺς τυροὺς ποεῖν
καλούς· ἔτι ταῦτα προσετίθην ἀκηκοώς,

---

110 αὐτὸς Schweighäuser: αὐτὸν A
111 ἐν Γόησιν ὁ Στράβων A: ὁ Στράβων del. Wilamowitz

than them. Strabo mentions them in Book III (162) of the *Geography*; he is not much earlier than our own time, given that in Book VII (fr. 60 Jones) of the same work he reports that he was personally acquainted with the Stoic philosopher Posidonius (*FGrH* 87 T 10b = test. 8 Edelstein–Kidd), to whom we have referred repeatedly, and who was a contemporary of the Scipio who captured Carthage.[417] Strabo, at any rate, writes as follows: In Spain, near Aquitania, is the city of Pompelon, that is, Pompeiopolis; outstanding hams (*pernai*), as good as those produced in Cantabria, are cured there.

The comic poet Aristomenes in *Dionysus* (fr. 12) mentions salted meat:

I'm serving you this salted (meat).

And in *Religious Quacks* (fr. 6):

that the servant always eats salted (meat) as well.

But since you also have (adesp. com. fr. *124, unmetrical) the pride of Sicily, this fresh cheese, my friends, let me offer some further comments on the topic of cheese. For Philemon (says) in his play entitled *The Sicilian* (fr. 79):

I used to think that Sicily
produced only this single specialty, first-rate
cheese. I also added these, from hearing what people
    said,

[417] In 146 BCE. The Scipio in question is P. Cornelius Scipio Aemilianus Africanus, and Athenaeus has garbled his source, confusing Posidonius and Panaetius, as also at 12.549d–e. Strabo was born *c*.64 BCE and died sometime after 21 CE.

ἱμάτια ποικίλ᾽ εἰ λέγοι τις Σικελικά.

† σκεύη μὲν οὖν καὶ κτήματ᾽ † ᾠόμην φέρειν.

καὶ ὁ Τρομιλικὸς δὲ τυρὸς ἔνδοξός ἐστι. περὶ οὗ φησιν Δημήτριος ὁ Σκήψιος ἐν δευτέρῳ Τρωικοῦ Διακόσμου οὕτως· τῆς Ἀχαίας πόλις Τρομίλεια, περὶ ἣν γίνεται τυρὸς αἴγειος ἥδιστος, οὐκ ἔχων σύγκρισιν πρὸς |

c ἕτερον, ὁ προσαγορευόμενος Τρομιλικός· οὗ καὶ Σιμωνίδης μνημονεύει ἐν Ἰάμβῳ, οὗ ἡ ἀρχή·

⟨ἣ⟩ πολλὰ μὲν δὴ προυκπονέαι, Τηλέμβροτε,

γράφων·

ἐνταῦθα μέν τοι τυρὸς ἐξ Ἀχαΐης
Τρομίλιος θαυμαστός, ὃν κατήγαγον.

Εὐριπίδης δ᾽ ἐν Κύκλωπι ὀπίαν καλεῖ τυρὸν τὸν δριμὺν τὸν πηγνύμενον τῷ τῆς συκῆς ὀπῷ·

καὶ τυρὸς ὀπίας ἔστι καὶ Διὸς[112] γάλα.

ἐπεὶ δὲ περὶ πάντων εἶπον τῶν παρακειμένων ἀποτράγημά τε πεποίημαι τὸν Τρομιλικόν, καταπαύσω |

d τὸν λόγον· τὸ γὰρ λείψανον τῶν τραγημάτων καὶ τρωξίμων ἀποτράγημα εἴρηκεν Εὔπολις· σκώπτων γὰρ Διδυμίαν τινὰ ἀποτράγημα αὐτὸν εἴρηκεν ἀλώ-

---

[112] The traditional text of Euripides has βοὸς.

if anyone mentioned embroidered Sicilian robes.
† equipment then and goods † I used to think it
yielded.

Tromilic cheese also has a good reputation. Demetrius of
Scepsis in Book II of the *Trojan Battle Order* (fr. 3 Gaede)
has the following to say about it: There is a city in Achaea
known as Tromileia, and delicious goat-cheese is produced
in the area. The cheese is incomparable, and is known as
Tromilic; Simonides mentions it in the *Iamb* that begins
(Semon. fr. 22 West²):

You certainly get a lot of work done ahead of time,
Telembrotus!

He writes (Semon. fr. 23 West²):

Here in fact is marvellous Tromilic
cheese from Achaea, which I imported.

Euripides in *Cyclops* (136) refers to sharp-flavored cheese
curdled with fig juice (*opos*) as *opias*:

and there's *opias* cheese and Zeus-milk.

Since I have discussed all the items we have been served,
and have made the Tromilic cheese a final treat (*apotragêma*), I will bring my speech to a close. For Eupolis (fr.
306) refers to what is left over from the snacks (*tragêmata*)
and dainties as an *apotragêma*; for he makes fun of a certain Didymias[418] by referring to him as a fox's *apotragêma*,[419] as a way of saying either that he is physically

---

[418] *PAA* 323582.   [419] The *Etymologicum Magnum* (p.
132.13) has *apopatêma* ("shit").

πεκος ἤτοι ὡς μικρὸν τὸ σῶμα ἢ ὡς κακοήθη καὶ
πανοῦργον, ὥς φησιν ὁ Ἀσκαλωνίτης Δωρόθεος. τοὺς
δὲ λεπτοὺς τῶν τυρῶν καὶ πλατεῖς Κρῆτες θηλείας
καλοῦσιν, ὥς φησι Σέλευκος· οὓς ἐν θυσίαις τισὶν
ἐναγίζουσιν. πυρίεφθων δὲ μνημονεύει (οὕτω δὲ κα-
λεῖται τὸ πρῶτον γάλα) Φιλιππίδης ἐν Αὐλοῖς· |

e   τὰ δὲ πυρίεφθα καὶ τὰ λάγανα ταῦτ᾽ ἔχων.

καὶ ἴσως πάντα τὰ τοιαῦτα ἐπιδειπνίδας ἔλεγον Μακε-
δόνες· κώθωνος γὰρ ἡδύσματα ταῦτα.

    Τοιαῦτά τινα ἔτι τοῦ Οὐλπιανοῦ διαλεγομένου ἐπ-
ελθὼν εἷς ἐκείνων τῶν σοφιστῶν μαγείρων ἐκήρυσσε
μῦμα. καὶ πολλῶν ξενιζομένων ἐπὶ τῷ κηρύγματι – οὐ
γὰρ ἐδείκνυεν ὁ στιγματίας ὅ τι ἦν – ἔφη· ἀγνοεῖν μοι
δοκεῖτε, ὦ ἄνδρες δαιταλῆς, ὅτι καὶ Κάδμος ὁ τοῦ
Διονύσου πάππος μάγειρος ἦν. σιωπησάντων δὲ καὶ

f ἐπὶ τούτῳ πάντων, Εὐήμερος, ἔφη, ὁ | Κῷος ἐν τῷ
τρίτῳ τῆς Ἱερᾶς Ἀναγραφῆς τοῦθ᾽ ἱστορεῖ, ὡς Σιδω-
νίων λεγόντων τοῦτο, ὅτι Κάδμος μάγειρος ὢν τοῦ
βασιλέως καὶ παραλαβὼν τὴν Ἁρμονίαν αὐλητρίδα
καὶ αὐτὴν οὖσαν τοῦ βασιλέως ἔφυγεν σὺν αὐτῇ.

    ἐγὼ δὲ φεύξομαι ⟨γ᾽⟩ ἐλεύθερος γεγώς.

---

420 Literally "fire-stewed," i.e. "heat-curdled."
421 Sc. produced by a sheep or goat after it gives birth.
422 *laganon*; cf. 3.110a; 8.363a.
423 "after-dinner dainties" *vel sim.* Cf. 14.664d–e.

unimposing or that he is nasty and treacherous, according to Dorotheus of Ascalon. The Cretans refer to thin, flat cheeses as "female," according to Seleucus (fr. 56 Müller); they offer them during certain sacrificial rites. *Puriephthoi*[420] (cheeses)—this is a term for the first milk[421]—are mentioned by Philippides in *Pipes* (fr. 10):

> having the *puriephthoi* and this wafer-bread.[422]

The Macedonians perhaps referred to all foods of this type as *epideipnides*;[423] because these are delicious items eaten in the course of a drinking party.

As Ulpian was still in the middle of remarks along these lines, one of the well-known sophist-cooks came in and announced a *muma*. When many of the guests expressed puzzlement about the announcement—because the son-of-a-bitch had not given us any indication of what this was[424]—he said: You are apparently unaware, banqueters, that Dionysus' grandfather Cadmus was a cook. This remark was met with universal silence, and he continued: Euhemerus of Cos in Book III of his *Sacred Catalogue* (*FGrH* 63 F 1) records this, citing the inhabitants of Sidon to the effect that Cadmus was the king's cook, and that he took the pipe-girl Harmonia, who was also one of the king's slaves, and ran away with her.

> But I shall escape, since I was born free.[425]

---

[424] The word is finally defined at 14.662d–e, after a long digression on cooks.

[425] An anonymous iambic trimeter line, accepted neither by Snell among the tragic adespota nor by Kassel–Austin among the comic adespota.

οὐδὲ γὰρ ἂν εὕροι τις ὑμῶν δοῦλον μάγειρόν τινα ἐν
659 κωμῳδίᾳ πλὴν παρὰ Ποσειδίππῳ μόνῳ· ‖ δοῦλοι δ'
ὀψοποιοὶ παρῆλθον ὑπὸ πρώτων Μακεδόνων τοῦτ'
ἐπιτηδευσάντων ἢ δι' ὕβριν ἢ δι' ἀτυχίαν τῶν αἰχμα-
λωτισθεισῶν πόλεων. ἐκάλουν οἱ παλαιοὶ τὸν μὲν
πολιτικὸν μάγειρον μαίσωνα, τὸν δ' ἐκτόπιον τέττιγα.
Χρύσιππος δ' ὁ φιλόσοφος τὸν μαίσωνα ἀπὸ τοῦ
μασᾶσθαι οἴεται κεκλῆσθαι, οἷον τὸν ἀμαθῆ καὶ πρὸς
γαστέρα νενευκότα, ἀγνοῶν ὅτι Μαίσων γέγονε
κωμῳδίας ὑποκριτὴς Μεγαρεὺς τὸ γένος, ὃς καὶ τὸ
προσωπεῖον εὗρε τὸ ἀπ' αὐτοῦ καλούμενον μαίσωνα, |
b ὡς Ἀριστοφάνης φησὶν ὁ Βυζάντιος ἐν τῷ Περὶ
Προσώπων, εὑρεῖν αὐτὸν φάσκων καὶ τὸ τοῦ θερά-
ποντος πρόσωπον καὶ τὸ τοῦ μαγείρου. καὶ εἰκότως
καὶ τὰ τούτοις πρέποντα σκώμματα καλεῖται μαισω-
νικά· μάλιστα γὰρ εἰσάγονται οἱ μάγειροι σκωπτικοί
τινες, ὡς παρὰ Μενάνδρῳ ἐν Ἐπιτρέπουσιν. καὶ Φιλήμων δέ πού φησιν·

σφίγγ' ἄρρεν', οὐ μάγειρον, εἰς τὴν οἰκίαν
εἴληφ'. ἁπλῶς γὰρ οὐδὲ ἕν, μὰ τοὺς θεούς,
ὧν ⟨ἂν⟩ λέγῃ συνίημι· καινὰ ῥήματα |
c πεπορισμένος γάρ ἐστι[113].

113 πάρεστιν (rightly) 9.382b and the papyrus

426 Cf. Posidipp. Com. fr. 2, cited at 14.659c.
427 Literally "cicada."

For none of you could name a single slave cook in any comedy, except in Posidippus.[426] Slave chefs were first introduced by the Macedonians, who made this a practice as a consequence either of their insolence or of the bad luck of the cities they captured. The ancients referred to a cook who had citizen-status as a *maisôn*, and to a cook from abroad as a *tettix*.[427] The philosopher Chrysippus (xxviii fr. 13, *SVF* iii.200) believes that the term *maisôn* is derived from *masasthai* ("to chew") and refers to someone who is uneducated and fixated on his belly. He is unaware that Maison[428] was a comic actor, whose family was from Megara and who invented the *maisôn*-mask, which gets its name from him; thus Aristophanes of Byzantium in his *On Masks* (fr. 363 Slater), who claims that the same individual also invented the servant-mask and the cook-mask. It comes as no surprise that the jokes appropriate to such characters are referred to as *maisônika*; for some cooks are brought onstage for comic relief in particular, for example in Menander's *Men at Arbitration*.[429] Philemon as well says somewhere:[430]

> I've taken a male Sphinx into my house,
> not a cook! By the gods, I don't understand
> a single word he says. He's here with a full supply
> of strange vocabulary.

[428] Stephanis #1594.
[429] Presumably a reference to the (largely lost) opening scene of the play, which featured the cook Cario.
[430] At 9.382b–c, in another long section on cooks, these lines are attributed instead to Strato Comicus (= fr. 1.1–4).

τὸν δὲ Μαίσωνα Πολέμων ἐν τοῖς Πρὸς Τίμαιον ἐκ
τῶν ἐν Σικελίᾳ φησὶν εἶναι Μεγάρων καὶ οὐκ ἐκ τῶν
Νισαίων. ἀλλ' ὅ γε Ποσείδιππος περὶ δούλων μαγείρων ἐν Ἀποκλειομένῃ φησίν·

> ταυτὶ μὲν οὖν τοιαῦτα. συμβαίνει δέ τι
> νῦν μοι διακονοῦντι παρὰ τῷ δεσπότῃ
> ἀστεῖον· οὐχ ἁλώσομ' ἐκφέρων κρέας.

καὶ ἐν Συντρόφοις·

> (Α.) ἐβάδιζες ἔξω τῶν πυλῶν μάγειρος ὤν; |
> d (Β.) ἐντὸς πυλῶν γὰρ ⟨ἂν⟩ μένων ἄδειπνος ἦν.
> (Α.) πότερ' οὖν ἀφεῖσαι; (Β.) κατ' ἀγορὰν
>   ἐργάζομαι·
> ἐπρίατο γάρ τις ὁμότεχνός με γνώριμος.

οὐδὲν οὖν ἦν παράδοξον εἰ καὶ θυτικῆς ἦσαν ἔμπειροι
οἱ παλαίτεροι μάγειροι· προΐσταντο γοῦν καὶ γάμων
καὶ θυσιῶν. διόπερ Μένανδρος ἐν Κόλακι τὸν τοῖς
τετραδισταῖς διακονούμενον μάγειρον ἐν τῇ τῆς Παν-
δήμου Ἀφροδίτης ἑορτῇ ποιεῖ ταυτὶ λέγοντα· |

> e σπονδή· δίδου σὺ σπλάγχν' ἀκολουθῶν. ποῖ
> βλέπεις;

---

431 Nisaea was the port of the mainland city of Megara (as opposed to Megara Hyblaea, in Sicily). This comment belongs with
the citation from Aristophanes of Byzantium above, suggesting
that two source-documents have been crudely spliced together.

432 I.e. a group of people who gathered on the fourth day of

Polemon in his *Response to Timaeus* (fr. 46 Preller), on the other hand, claims that Maison was a Megarian from Sicily rather than from Nisaea.[431] But Posidippus in *The Girl Who Was Locked Out* (fr. 2) says on the subject of slave cooks:

> So much for that. But something funny's
> happening for me today, as I work in my master's
> house—I'm not going to get caught when I swipe
> meat!

And in *Foster-Brothers* (fr. 25):

> (A.) You left the courtyard, even though you're a
>   cook?
> (B.) Sure—if I'd stayed inside it, I wouldn't have had
>   any dinner.
> (A.) Were you set free? (B.) I work in the
>   marketplace;
> because another cook I know bought me.

It was not unusual, therefore, for ancient cooks to be familiar with sacrificial procedure; at any rate, they were in charge of both wedding feasts and sacrifices. This is why Menander in *The Flatterer* (*Kol.* fr. 1 Sandbach) represents the cook who is working for the fourth-day group[432] at the festival of Aphrodite Pandêmos as saying the following:

> Libation! Follow me, and hand me the entrails!
>   What're you gawking at?

every month (often identified as the birthday of Hermes or Heracles) to have a party; see Arnott on Alex. fr. 260.

σπονδή. φέρ᾽ ὦ παῖ Σωσία. σπονδή. καλῶς
ἔχει. θεοῖς Ὀλυμπίοις εὐχώμεθα
Ὀλυμπίαισι, πᾶσι πάσαις – λάμβανε
τὴν γλῶτταν ἐν τούτῳ – διδόναι σωτηρίαν,
ὑγίειαν, ἀγαθὰ πολλά, τῶν ὄντων τε νῦν
ἀγαθῶν ὄνησιν πᾶσι. ταῦτ᾽ εὐχώμεθα.

καὶ παρὰ Σιμωνίδῃ δέ φησιν ἕτερος·

f   κῶς | ⟨ὗν⟩ ἀπεῦσα κῶς ἐμίστυλα κρέα
ἱρωστί· καὶ γὰρ οὐ κακῶς ἐπίσταμαι.

ἐμφαίνει δ᾽ αὐτῶν τὴν ἐμπειρίαν καὶ ἡ Πρὸς Ἀλέξανδρον Ὀλυμπιάδος Ἐπιστολή. προτρεπομένη μάγειρον αὐτῇ πρίασθαι θυσιῶν ἔμπειρον ἡ μήτηρ φησί·
Πελίγναν τὸν μάγειρον λαβὲ παρὰ τῆς μητρός. οὗτος
γὰρ οἶδε τὰ ἱερά σου τὰ πατρῷα πάντα ὃν τρόπον
θύεται καὶ τὰ Ἀργαδιστικὰ καὶ τὰ Βακχικά, ὅσα τε
660   Ὀλυμπιὰς προθύεται οὗτος οἶδεν. ‖ μὴ οὖν ἀμελήσῃς,
ἀλλὰ λαβέ, καὶ ἀπόστειλον πρὸς ἐμὲ τὴν ταχίστην.
ὅτι δὲ σεμνὸν ἦν ἡ μαγειρικὴ μαθεῖν ἔστιν ἐκ τῶν
Ἀθήνησι Κηρύκων· οἶδε γὰρ μαγείρων καὶ βουτύπων
ἐπεῖχον τάξιν, ὥς φησιν Κλείδημος ἐν Πρωτογονίας
πρώτῳ. Ὅμηρός τε τὸ ῥέζειν ἐπὶ τοῦ θύειν τάσσει, τὸ

---

433 Sc. to remove the bristles.

434 In fact, the letter appears to be by someone other than
Olympias (Alexander's mother; Berve i #581) and merely refers to
her in the third person.

435 Berve i #625.

Libation! Slave! Sosias! Come on! Libation! It's
okay. Let us pray to all the Olympian
gods and Olympian goddesses—put
the tongue in here!—that they grant us all
safety, health, everything good, and enjoyment of
whatever property we possess at the moment. Let us
   make this our prayer!

So too in Simonides (Semon. fr. 24 West²) another (cook)
says:

and how I singed a pig[433] and stuck the meat on spits,
as the ritual requires. Because I understand it quite
well.

Olympias' *Letter to Alexander*[434] brings out their range of
expertise. In the course of encouraging him to buy her a
cook familiar with making sacrifices, his mother says: Buy
the cook Pelignas[435] from your mother. For he knows how
all your ancestral sacrifices, including the Argadistica and
the Bacchica, are made; he also knows about all the pre-
liminary sacrifices Olympias makes. Don't miss this opportunity; purchase him and send him to me as rapidly as possible! That cooking was a respectable occupation can be
gathered from the case of the Athenian Kêrukes;[436] for
they occupied the position of cooks and slaughterers, according to Cleidemus in Book I of *Early Origins* (*FGrH*
323 F 5a).[437] Homer as well uses the verb *rhezein* in the

---

[436] An old aristocratic family with a hereditary right to carry
out certain official duties associated with the mysteries at Eleusis.

[437] Cf. below (after the intrusive comments on verbs meaning
"to sacrifice"); 10.425e; 14.660d–e.

δὲ θύειν ἐπὶ τοῦ ψαιστὰ μεταδόρπια θυμιᾶν. καὶ οἱ
παλαιοὶ τὸ θύειν δρᾶν ὠνόμαζον. ἔδρων δ᾽ οἱ Κήρυκες
ἄχρι πολλοῦ βουθυτοῦντες, φησί, καὶ σκευάζοντες καὶ
b μιστύλλοντες, ἔτι δ᾽ οἰνοχοοῦντες· | Κήρυκας δ᾽ αὐ-
τοὺς ἀπὸ τοῦ κρείττονος ὠνόμαζον. ἀναγέγραπταί τε
οὐδαμοῦ μαγείρῳ μισθός, ἀλλὰ κήρυκι. καὶ Ἀγαμέμνων δὲ παρ᾽ Ὁμήρῳ θύει βασιλεύων. φησὶ γὰρ ὁ
ποιητής·

ἦ, καὶ ἀπὸ στομάχους ἀρνῶν τάμε νηλέι χαλκῷ.
καὶ τοὺς μὲν κατέθηκεν ἐπὶ χθονὸς ἀσπαίροντας,
θυμοῦ δευομένους, ἀπὸ γὰρ μένος εἵλετο χαλκός.

καὶ Θρασυμήδης ὁ τοῦ Νέστορος υἱὸς ἀναλαβὼν |
c πέλεκυν κόπτει τὸν βοῦν, ἐπεὶ διὰ τὸ γῆρας ὁ Νέστωρ
οὐκ ἠδύνατο· συνεπόνουν δ᾽ αὐτῷ καὶ οἱ ἄλλοι ἀδελ-
φοί. οὕτως ἔνδοξον ἦν καὶ μέγιστον τὸ τῆς μαγειρικῆς
τέχνης ἀξίωμα. καὶ παρὰ Ῥωμαίοις δ᾽ οἱ τιμηταί –
μεγίστη δ᾽ αὕτη ἀρχή – τὴν περιπόρφυρον ἐνδεδυ-
κότες καὶ ἐστεφανωμένοι πελέκει τὰ ἱερεῖα κατέβαλ-
λον. οὐ παρέργως δὲ παρὰ τῷ Ὁμήρῳ καὶ τὰ ὅρκια

---

438 E.g. *Il.* 1.147; *Od.* 1.61.

439 Cakes made of ground (*psaistos*) barley; perhaps a reference to *Od.* 14.446, where the word used is, however, *argmata*.

440 Literally "to do, accomplish (rites)"; used in the description of the Kêrukes that follows.

441 "better, stronger"; a nonsensical etymology. Harp. K 52,
Hsch. κ 2560, and Suda κ 1542 all derive the name from "Kêrux
the son of Hermes," suggesting that the etymology proposed in
Athenaeus merely reflects a manuscript error.

sense *thuein* ("to make sacrifice"),[438] and *thuein* to refer to burning the after-dinner *psaista*.[439] The ancients also referred to making sacrifice (*thuein*) with the word *dran*.[440] The Kêrukes acted (*edrôn*) as slaughterers for a long time, says (Cleidemus), and prepared and spitted meat, and also poured wine; the name Kêrukes was derived from *kreittôn*.[441] There is no record anywhere of a cook having been paid a wage, although a *kêrux* is.[442] So too Homer's Agamemnon carries out a sacrifice, despite being a king; for the poet says (*Il.* 3.292–4):

> He spoke; and he slit the lambs' throats with pitiless bronze.
> And he set them down on the ground, gasping
> and stripped of life; for the bronze took away their vigor.

Nestor's son Thrasymedes also picks up an ax and strikes the cow (*Od.* 3.439–44), since Nestor was unable to do this on account of his advanced age;[443] the rest of his brothers assisted him. This is how respectable and important was the esteem in which the cook's craft was held. So too the Roman censors—this is an extremely important office—used an ax to fell the sacrificial victims, wearing togas with purple borders, and with garlands on their heads. When Homeric heralds (*kêrukes*) fetch the objects needed for

---

[442] Presumably an observation offered by Cleidemus as further evidence that Athens' Kêrukids functioned originally as cooks and slaughterers, since animals had to be butchered as part of public cult from the very earliest times.

[443] The explanation of Thrasymedes' behavior does not appear in Homer, but has been added by Athenaeus (or his source).

καὶ τὰ ἱερόθυτα κήρυκες κομίζουσιν, ὡς παλαιᾶς
οὔσης καὶ προσηκούσης αὐτοῖς τῆς λειτουργίας· |

d   Ἕκτωρ δὲ προτὶ ἄστυ δύο[114] κήρυκας ἔπεμπεν
καρπαλίμως, ἄρνάς τε φέρειν Πρίαμόν τε
        καλέσσαι.

καὶ πάλιν·

αὐτὰρ ὃ Ταλθύβιον προΐει κρείων Ἀγαμέμνων
νῆας ἔπι γλαφυρὰς ἰέναι, ἠδ' ἄρν' ἐκέλευσεν
οἰσέμεναι.

καί·

        Ταλθύβιος δὲ θεῷ ἐναλίγκιος αὐδὴν
κάπρον ἔχων ἐν χερσὶ παρίστατο ποιμένι λαῶν.

ἐν δὲ τῷ πρώτῳ τῆς Ἀτθίδος Κλείδημος φῦλον |
e ἀποφαίνει μαγείρων ἐχόντων δημιουργικὰς τιμάς, οἷς
† καὶ τὸ πλῆθος ἐνεργεῖν † ἔργον ἦν. οὐκ ἀπεικότως δὲ
καὶ Ἀθηνίων ἐν Σαμόθραξιν, ὥς φησιν Ἰόβας, μάγειρον εἰσάγει φυσιολογοῦντα διὰ τούτων·

    (Α.) οὐκ οἶσθ' ὅτι πάντων ἡ μαγειρικὴ τέχνη
    πρὸς εὐσέβειαν πλεῖστα προσενήνεχθ' ὅλως;
    (Β.) τοιοῦτόν ἐστι τοῦτο; (Α.) πάνυ γε, βάρβαρε.
    τοῦ θηριώδους καὶ παρασπόνδου βίου

114 The traditional text of Homer has the dual δύω (necessary
for the meter).

356

oath-ceremonies and sacrifices, this is not merely an inci-
dental service, since the duty is an ancient one with which
they are closely associated (*Il.* 3.116–17):

> Hector swiftly dispatched two heralds
> to the city, to fetch lambs and to summon Priam.

And again (*Il.* 3.118–20):

> But King Agamemnon sent Talthybius off, to go
> to the hollow ships, and ordered him to bring
> lambs.

And (*Il.* 19.250–1):

> Talthybius, whose voice resembled a god's,
> stood beside the shepherd of the people, holding a
> boar in his hands.

In Book I of his *History of Attica* (*FGrH* 323 F 5b),[444]
Cleidemus makes it clear that there was a guild of cooks
who held public office; their job was † and the masses to
carry out †. It is quite understandable, according to Juba
(*FGrH* 275 F 86), that Athenio in *Samothracians* (fr. 1)
brings a cook onstage discussing natural phenomena in the
following passage:

> (A.) Don't you realize that the art of cooking has
> contributed more to pious practice than all the others
>   combined?
> (B.) It's that type of business? (A.) Absolutely, you
>   barbarian!
> Because it liberated us from a savage existence,

---

[444] Cf. 14.660a–b with n.

ἡμᾶς γὰρ ἀπολύσασα καὶ τῆς δυσχεροῦς |

f ἀλληλοφαγίας ἤγαγ' εἰς τάξιν τινὰ
καὶ τουτονὶ περιῆψεν ὃν νυνὶ βίον
ζῶμεν. (Β.) τίνα τρόπον; (Α.) πρόσεχε, κἀγώ σοι
    φράσω.
ἀλληλοφαγίας καὶ κακῶν ὄντων συχνῶν
γενόμενος ἄνθρωπός τις οὐκ ἀβέλτερος
ἔθυσ' ἱερεῖον πρῶτος, ὤπτησεν κρέας.
ὡς δ' ἦν τὸ κρέας ἥδιον ἀνθρώπου κρεῶν,
αὑτοὺς μὲν οὐκ ἐμασῶντο, τὰ δὲ βοσκήματα
θύοντες ὤπτων. ὡς δ' ἅπαξ τῆς ἡδονῆς ‖

661 ἐμπειρίαν τιν' ἔλαβον, ἀρχῆς γενομένης
ἐπὶ πλεῖον ηὖξον τὴν μαγειρικὴν τέχνην.
ὅθεν ἔτι καὶ νῦν τῶν πρότερον μεμνημένοι
τὰ σπλάγχνα τοῖς θεοῖσιν ὀπτῶσιν φλογὶ
ἅλας οὐ προσάγοντες· οὐ γὰρ ἦσαν οὐδέπω
εἰς τὴν τοιαύτην χρῆσιν ἐξευρημένοι.
ὡς δ' ἤρεσ' αὐτοῖς ὕστερον, καὶ τοὺς ἅλας
προσάγουσιν ἤδη τῶν ἱερῶν † γεγραμμένων †
τὰ πάτρια διατηροῦντες. ἅπερ ἡμῖν μόνα
ἅπασιν ἀρχὴ γέγονε τῆς σωτηρίας, |

b τὸ προσφιλοτεχνεῖν διά τε τῶν ἡδυσμάτων
ἐπὶ πλεῖον αὔξειν τὴν μαγειρικὴν τέχνην.

in which no covenants are possible, and from harsh
cannibalism; provided us with some order;
and bestowed this life we live today
upon us. (B.) How? (A.) Pay attention, and I'll tell
    you!
There was cannibalism and trouble of all kinds.
But someone who was no fool
made the first sacrifice and roasted meat;
and because this meat tasted better than human
    flesh,
they stopped chewing on one another, and began
    sacrificing
domestic animals and roasting them. Once they got
    some
experience with how delicious this was, that was the
    beginning,
and they developed the art of cooking further and
    further.
As a consequence, even today people recall life in the
    old days
by roasting the entrails on the fire for the gods
but not adding salt; because they hadn't yet
discovered using it for such purposes.
Since they got to like it later on, however, nowadays
they include salt in the ceremony too † having been
    written †
preserving the traditional practices. This was the sole
origin of the security we all enjoy:
the pleasure we take in improving our skills, and our
    continual
upgrading of the art of cooking through the use of
    spices.

(Β.) καινὸς γάρ ἐστιν οὑτοσὶ Παλαίφατος.
(Α.) μετὰ ταῦτα γαστρίον τις ὠνθυλευμένον
προϊόντος εἰσηνέγκατ' ἤδη τοῦ χρόνου·
ἐρίφιον ἐτακέρωσε, πνικτῷ διέλαβεν
περικομματίῳ, διεγίγγρασ' ὑποκρούσας γλυκεῖ,
ἰχθὺν παρεισεκύκλησεν οὐδ' ὁρώμενον, |

c   λάχανον, τάριχος πολυτελές, χόνδρον, μέλι.
† ὡς πολὺ † διὰ τὰς ἡδονὰς ἃς νῦν λέγω
ἀπεῖχ' ἕκαστος τοῦ φαγεῖν ἂν ἔτι νεκροῦ·
αὐτοῖς ἅπαντες ἠξίουν συζῆν, ὄχλος
ἠθροίζετ', ἐγένονθ' αἱ πόλεις οἰκούμεναι
διὰ τὴν τέχνην, ὅπερ εἶπα, τὴν μαγειρικήν.
(Β.) ἄνθρωπε χαῖρε, περὶ πόδ' εἶ τῷ δεσπότῃ.
(Α.) καταρχόμεθ' ἡμεῖς οἱ μάγειροι, θύομεν,
σπονδὰς ποοῦμεν, τῷ μάλιστα τοὺς θεοὺς
ἡμῖν ὑπακούειν διὰ τὸ ταῦθ' εὑρηκέναι |

d   τὰ μάλιστα συντείνοντα πρὸς τὸ ζῆν καλῶς.
(Β.) ὑπὲρ εὐσεβείας οὖν ἀφεὶς παῦσαι λέγων·
ἥμαρτον. ἀλλὰ δεῦρο ⟨νῦν⟩ συνείσιθι
ἐμοί, τά τ' ἔνδον εὐτρεπῆ ποίει λαβών.

καὶ Ἄλεξις δ' ἐν Λεβητίῳ δηλοῖ ὅτι ἡ μαγειρικὴ τέχνη

---

445 Palaephatus is variously described as a historian, epic poet, and grammarian (*FGrH* 44 T 1–4); almost none of his work survives.

446 Referred to elsewhere as *The Cauldron* (e.g. 6.226a; 9.383c).

(B.) This guy's a new Palaephatus![445]
(A.) After this, as time continually moved forward,
someone introduced a stuffed stomach-sausage:
he stewed kid-meat until it was tender, wrapped it in
    casseroled
hash, hit the right note by drizzling grape-must on
    top,
and smuggled in a fish no one had ever seen before,
plus vegetables, expensive saltfish, wheat-pudding,
    and honey.
† How much † because of the delicious flavors I'm
    describing now,
they would all have given up eating corpses after that.
They all began to like the idea of living together; a
    crowd
began to form; and cities came to be inhabited—
on account of the art of cooking, as I said!
(B.) Greetings, sir! You're exactly what your master
    needs!
(A.) We cooks take care of the preliminaries, make
    the sacrifice,
and perform the libations—because the gods pay
    particular
attention to us, since we invented these practices
that are intimately connected to living a good life.
(B.) Drop the issue, then, and stop defending your
    piety;
I was wrong. Come inside here now with
me, and take charge of everything there and make it
    right.

So too Alexis in *The Little Cauldron*[446] (fr. 134) makes it

ἐπιτήδευμα ἦν ἐλευθέρων· πολίτης γάρ τις οὐκ ἀγενὴς
ἐν αὐτῷ δείκνυται ὁ μάγειρος. καὶ οἱ τὰ Ὀψαρτυτικὰ
e δὲ συγγράψαντες | Ἡρακλείδης τε καὶ Γλαῦκος ὁ
Λοκρὸς οὐχ ἁρμόττειν φασὶ <δούλοισι>[115] τὴν μαγειρικήν, ἀλλ' οὐδὲ τοῖς τυχοῦσι τῶν ἐλευθέρων. ἐκ-
σεμνύνει δὲ τὴν τέχνην καὶ ὁ νεώτερος Κρατῖνος ἐν
τοῖς Γίγασι λέγων·

(Α.) ἐνθυμεῖ δὲ τῆς γῆς ὡς γλυκὺ
ὄζει καπνός τ' ἐξέρχετ' εὐωδέστατος;
οἰκεῖ τις, ὡς ἔοικεν, <ἐν> τῷ χάσματι
λιβανωτοπώλης ἢ μάγειρος Σικελικός. |

f (Β.) παραπλησίαν ὀσμὴν λέγεις ἀμφοῖν γλυκύς;

καὶ Ἀντιφάνης δ' ἐν Δυσπράτῳ ἐπαινῶν τοὺς Σικε-
λικοὺς μαγείρους λέγει·

Σικελῶν δὲ τέχναις ἡδυνθεῖσαι
δαιτὸς διαθρυμματίδες.

καὶ Μένανδρος ἐν Φάσματι·

ἐπισημαίνεσθ' ἐὰν
ἡ σκευασία καθάρειος ᾖ καὶ ποικίλη.

Ποσείδιππος ἐν Ἀναβλέποντι·

ἐγὼ μάγειρον ἀναλαβὼν ἀκήκοα ‖

115 add. Kaibel

clear that the art of cooking was practiced by free people;
for in the course of the play the cook is revealed to be a citizen from a good family. The cookbook-authors Heracleides and Glaucus of Locris also deny that the art of cooking
is appropriate for slaves, or even for the average free person.[447] Cratinus Junior in his *Giants* (fr. 1) stresses the
majesty of the profession, saying:

> (A.) Do you realize how sweet the earth
> smells, and what delectable smoke is emerging from
>   it?
> Apparently a frankincense-dealer lives
> in the chasm—or a Sicilian cook!
> (B.) You're saying they both produce a similar scent,
>   my sweet?

So too Antiphanes in *Hard to Sell* (fr. 90) praises Sicilian
cooks, saying:

> banquet-*diathrummatides*, seasoned
> with Sicilian arts.

Also Menander in *The Ghost* (*Phasma* 73–4):

> Indicate whether
> your style of cooking's decent or elaborate.

Posidippus in *The Man Who Tried To Recover His Sight*
(fr. 1):

> In the course of hiring a cook, I've heard

[447] Dindorf interpreted these words as fragments of two anonymous comic iambic trimeters (not accepted among the adespota
by Kassel–Austin).

662 τὰ τῶν μαγείρων πάνθ᾽ ἃ καθ᾽ ἑκάστου κακὰ
ἀντεργολαβοῦντος ἔλεγον· ὁ μὲν ὡς οὐκ ἔχει
ῥῖνα κριτικὴν πρὸς τοὔψον, ὁ δ᾽ ὅτι ⟨τὸ⟩ στόμα
πονηρόν, ὁ δὲ τὴν γλῶτταν εἰς ἀσχήμονας
ἐπιθυμίας ἔνιά τε τῶν ἡδυσμάτων,
κάθαλος, κάτοξος, χναυστικός, προσκαυστικός,
καπνὸν οὐ φέρων, πῦρ οὐ φέρων. ἐκ τοῦ πυρὸς
εἰς τὰς μαχαίρας ἦλθον· ὧν εἷς οὑτοσὶ |

b   διὰ τῶν μαχαιρῶν τοῦ πυρός τ᾽ ἐλήλυθεν.

Ἀντιφάνης δ᾽ ἐν Φιλώτιδι τὴν σοφίαν τῶν μαγείρων
ἐμφανίζων φησίν·

(A.) οὐκοῦν τὸ μὲν γλαυκίδιον, ὥσπερ ἄλλοτε,
ἕψειν ἐν ἄλμῃ φημί. (B.) τὸ δὲ λαβράκιον;
(A.) ὀπτᾶν ὅλον. (B.) τὸν γαλεόν; (A.) ἐν
     ὑποτρίμματι
ζέσαι. (B.) τὸ δ᾽ ἐγχέλειον; (A.) ἅλες, ὀρίγανον,
ὕδωρ. (B.) ὁ γόγγρος; (A.) ταὐτόν. (B.) ἡ βατίς;
     (A.) χλόη.
(B.) πρόσεστι θύννου τέμαχος. (A.) ὀπτήσεις.
     (B.) κρέας
ἐρίφειον; (A.) ὀπτόν. (B.) θάτερον; (A.) τἀναντία. |
c   (B.) ὁ σπλήν; (A.) σεσάχθω. (B.) νῆστις; (B.)
     ἀπολεῖ μ᾽ οὑτοσί.

---

448 Clearly proverbial, like the English "Out of the frying pan,
into the fire!"

449 Quoted also, in slightly less complete form, at 7.295d.

364

all the abusive remarks the cooks made against
each competitor—how one guy doesn't have
a discriminating nose, when it comes to fish; and
    another one's mouth
is no good; and as for a third, that he's ruined his
    tastebuds,
so that he prefers overly heavy seasonings,
or uses too much salt or vinegar, or nibbles the food,
    or burns it,
or can't stand the smoke or the fire. I've gone
from the fire to the butchers' knives![448] But this one
    here
made his way through the knives and the fire.

Antiphanes in *Philotis* (fr. 221)[449] brings out how clever
cooks are, when he says:

(A.) So then, as for the *glaukidion*, I'm ordering you
    to stew it
in brine, like the other times. (B.) What about the
    little sea-bass?
(A.) Roast it whole. (B.) The thresher shark?
    (A.) Stew it
in a sauce. (B.) The eel? (A.) Salt, marjoram,
and water. (B.) The conger eel? (A.) Ditto! (B.) The
    ray? (A.) Green herbs.
(B.) There's a tuna steak. (A.) Roast it.
    (B.) The kid-meat?
(A.) Roasted. (B.) The other meat? (A.) The opposite.
(B.) The spleen? (A.) Let's have it stuffed. (B.) The
    jejunum? (A.) This guy's gonna be the death of
    me!

ἀοιδίμων δ' ὀψαρτυτῶν ὀνόματα καταλέγει Βάτων ἐν
Εὐεργέταις οὕτως·

   (A.) εὖ γ', ὦ Σιβύνη, τὰς νύκτας οὐ καθεύδομεν
   οὐδ' ἀνατετράμμεθ', ἀλλὰ καίεται λύχνος,
   καὶ βιβλί᾿ <ἐν> ταῖς χερσί, καὶ φροντίζομεν
   τί Σόφων καταλέλοιπ' ἢ τί Σημωνακτίδης |
d   ὁ Χῖος ἢ Τυνδάριχος ὁ Σικυώνιος
   ἢ Ζωπυρῖνος. (B.) αὐτὸς εὕρηκας δὲ τί;
   (A.) τὰ μέγιστα. (B.) ποῖα ταῦτα;
   (A.) τοὺς τεθνηκότας.

ἐγὼ δὲ τοιουτονὶ βρῶμα ὑμῖν, ἄνδρες φίλοι, τὸ μῦμα
φέρω. περὶ οὗ Ἀρτεμίδωρος μὲν ὁ Ἀριστοφάνειος ἐν
Ὀψαρτυτικαῖς Γλώσσαις φησὶν ὅτι σκευάζεται ἐκ
κρεῶν καὶ αἵματος, πολλῶν ἀρτυμάτων συνεμβαλλο-
μένων. Ἐπαίνετος δ' ἐν Ὀψαρτυτικῷ λέγει ταῦτα·
μῦμα δὲ παντὸς ἱερείου, καὶ ὄρνιθος δὲ χρὴ ποιεῖν τὰ |
e   ἁπαλὰ τῶν κρεῶν μικρὰ συντεμόντα καὶ τὰ σπλάγχνα
καὶ τὸ ἔντερον καὶ τὸ αἷμα διαθρύψαντα καὶ ἀρτύ-
σαντα ὄξει, τυρῷ ὀπτῷ, σιλφίῳ, κυμίνῳ, θύμῳ χλωρῷ
καὶ ξηρῷ, θύμβρᾳ, κοριάννῳ χλωρῷ τε καὶ ξηρῷ καὶ
γητίῳ καὶ κρομμύῳ καθαριῷ[116] πεφωσμένῳ ἢ μήκωνι
καὶ σταφίδι ἢ μέλιτι καὶ ῥόας ὀξείας κόκκοις. εἶναι δέ
σοι τὸ αὐτὸ μῦμα καὶ ὄψου.[117]

116 καθαριῷ Olson: καθαρῷ A
117 ὄψου Schweighäuser: ὄψον A

450 Presumably a reference to the Sophon of Acarnania men-

Bato in *Benefactors* (fr. 4) lists the names of well-known chefs, as follows:

(A.) Good for us, Sibyne, that we don't sleep at night
or even lie down. Instead, a lamp stays lit,
and there are books in our hands, and we puzzle over
what Sophon's[450] left behind, or Semonactides
of Chios, or Tyndarichus of Sicyon,
or Zopyrinus. (B.) Have you invented anything
yourself?
(A.) The greatest invention ever. (B.) What's that?
(A.) Dead people![451]

As for me, my friends, the type of food I am serving you here is a *muma*.[452] Aristophanes' student Artemidorus[453] in *Culinary Vocabulary* claims that the dish is made of bits of meat and blood, with numerous spices added. But Epaenetus in *The Chef's Art* says the following: A *muma* of any sort of meat, including chicken, should be made by dicing up the soft portions of the meat; stirring them in with the entrails, the guts, and the blood; and seasoning the dish with vinegar, roasted cheese, silphium, cumin, fresh and dried coriander, a bulb-less onion,[454] some nice toasted onion or poppy-seeds, raisins or honey, and seeds from an acidic pomegranate. You can make the same *muma* from fish as well.

tioned in Anaxipp. fr. 1.1 (quoted at 9.403e); cf. 14.622e n.; Poll. 6.70–1 (probably drawing *inter alia* on this passage).

[451] Doubtless what Speaker B actually said was "I bring dead people back to life with it!" (cf. Philem. fr. 82.25–6, quoted at 7.290a). [452] Cf. 14.658e (before the extended digression on cooks). [453] Cf. 1.5b with n.

[454] See Arnott, *Alexis*, p. 388 n. 2.

ATHENAEUS

Τοσαῦτα καὶ τούτου κατακόψαντος οὐ μόνον τὰ
προειρημένα ἀλλὰ καὶ ἡμᾶς, ἄλλος ἐπεισῆλθεν τὴν
f ματτύην | κομίζων. ὑπὲρ ἧς καὶ ζητήσεως γενομένης
καὶ τοῦ Οὐλπιανοῦ εἰπόντος τὰ ἐκ τῶν Ὀψαρτυτικῶν
Γλωσσῶν τοῦ προειρημένου Ἀρτεμιδώρου, Αἰμιλι-
ανὸς Δωροθέῳ ἔφη τῷ Ἀσκαλωνίτῃ σύγγραμμα ἐκδε-
δόσθαι ἐπιγραφόμενον Περὶ Ἀντιφάνους καὶ Περὶ τῆς
Παρὰ τοῖς Νεωτέροις Κωμικοῖς Ματτύης· ἦν Θεττα-
λῶν φησιν εἶναι εὕρημα, ἐπιχωριάσαι δὲ κἂν ταῖς
663 Ἀθήναις κατὰ τὴν Μακεδόνων ‖ ἐπικράτειαν. ὁμολο-
γοῦνται δ' οἱ Θετταλοὶ πολυτελέστατοι τῶν Ἑλλήνων
γεγενῆσθαι περί τε τὰς ἐσθῆτας καὶ τὴν δίαιταν· ὅπερ
αὐτοῖς αἴτιον ἐγένετο καὶ τοῦ κατὰ τῆς Ἑλλάδος
ἐπαγαγεῖν τοὺς Πέρσας, ἐζηλωκόσι τὴν τούτων τρυ-
φὴν καὶ πολυτέλειαν. ἱστορεῖ δὲ περὶ τῆς πολυτελείας
αὐτῶν καὶ Κριτίας ἐν τῇ Πολιτείᾳ αὐτῶν. ὠνομάσθη
δὲ ἡ ματτύη, ὡς μὲν ὁ Ἀθηναῖος Ἀπολλόδωρός φησιν
ἐν τῷ πρώτῳ τῶν Ἐτυμολογουμένων, ἀπὸ τοῦ μα-
b σᾶσθαι, ὥσπερ καὶ ἡ μαστίχη καὶ ἡ μάσταξ· | ἡμεῖς
δέ φαμεν ἀπὸ τοῦ μάττειν, ἀφ' οὗ καὶ ἡ μᾶζα αὐτὴ
ὠνομάσθη καὶ ἡ παρὰ Κυπρίοις καλουμένη μαγίς, καὶ
τὸ τρυφᾶν καθ' ὑπερβολὴν ὑπερμαζᾶν. κατ' ἀρχὰς

---

455 I.e. in the aftermath of the Battle of Chaeronea in 338
BCE.

456 Sc. in 480–479 BCE.

457 Cited also at 12.527a–b (which makes it clear that the
material immediately before this was drawn direct from Critias
rather than from some anonymous source).

After this fellow reduced not just the topics mentioned above but us as well to hash with these extended remarks, another cook came in after him, bringing us a *mattuê*. There was some discussion of it, and after Ulpian quoted the relevant passage from the *Culinary Vocabulary* of the Artemidorus referred to above (14.662d), Aemilianus noted that Dorotheus of Ascalon had published a treatise entitled *On Antiphanes and On the Mattuê Mentioned by the New Comic Poets* (= Antiph. test. 7); Dorotheus claims that the Thessalians invented the dish, which was a local delicacy in Athens during the period when the Macedonians were in control.[455] The Thessalians are generally agreed to have been the most extravagant Greeks when it came to their clothing and their life-style. This is why they convinced the Persians to invade Greece,[456] because they were eager to adopt their luxurious and expensive habits. Critias in his *Constitution of the Thessalians* (88 B 31 D–K)[457] describes their extravagance. According to Apollodorus of Athens in Book I of his *Etymologies* (*FGrH* 244 F 222), the word *mattuê* is derived from *masasthai* ("to chew"), just as *mastichê* ("mastich") and *mastax* ("jaw; mouthful") are.[458] In my judgment, however, it comes from *mattein* ("to knead"), which is also the source of the word *maza*[459] ("barley-cake") and the Cyprian term *magis*,[460] as well as of *hupermazan*, meaning "to live in ex-

---

[458] *mastax* is in fact derived from *masasthai*, and *mastichê* may be as well. But *mattuê* is more likely a Macedonian loan-word (e.g. Hsch. μ 412; Poll. 6.70, where it is given in the form *matullê*).

[459] A correct etymology.

[460] Glossed *mazai* ("barley-cakes") by Phot. μ 9, citing Ar. fr. 851 (cf. S. fr. 734).

μὲν οὖν τὴν δημοτικὴν καὶ κοινὴν ταύτην τροφὴν τὴν
ἐκ τῶν ἀλφίτων μᾶζαν ὠνόμαζον καὶ μάττειν τὸ παρα-
σκευάζειν αὐτήν. ὕστερον δὲ ποικίλλοντες τὴν ἀναγ-
καίαν τροφὴν ἀκολάστως καὶ περιέργως μικρὸν παρ-
αγαγόντες τοὔνομα τῆς μάζης ματτύην ὠνόμαζον πᾶν
c   τὸ πολυτελὲς ἔδεσμα, τὸ δὲ ματτυάζειν | τὸ παρα-
σκευάζειν αὐτά, εἴτε ἰχθὺς εἴη εἴτε ὄρνις εἴτε λάχανον
εἴτε ἱερεῖον εἴτε πεμμάτιον. τοῦτο δὲ δῆλόν ἐστιν ἐξ οὗ
καὶ ὁ Ἀρτεμίδωρος παρέθετο μαρτυρίου Ἀλέξιδος·
συνεμφῆναι γὰρ βουλόμενος ὁ Ἄλεξις τὴν ἀκολασίαν
τῆς παρασκευῆς προσέθηκε τὸ λέπεσθαι. ἔχει δ'
⟨οὕτως⟩[118] ἡ σύμπασα ἐκλογὴ οὖσα ἐκ τοῦ διεσκευ-
ασμένου δράματος ὃ ἐπιγράφεται Δημήτριος·

> τοὖψον λαβοῦσαι τοῦτο τἀπεσταλμένον
> σκευάζετ', εὐωχεῖσθε, προπόσεις πίνετε, |
d   λέπεσθε, ματτυάζετε.

τῷ δὲ λέπεσθαι χρῶνται οἱ Ἀθηναῖοι ἐπ' ἀσελγοῦς καὶ
φορτικῆς δι' ἀφροδισίων ἡδονῆς. καὶ ὁ Ἀρτεμίδωρος
ἐν ταῖς Ὀψαρτυτικαῖς Γλώσσαις τὴν ματτύην ἀποφαίνει κοινὸν εἶναι πάντων ὄνομα τῶν πολυτελῶν
ἐδεσμάτων, γράφων οὕτως· ἔστι τις ὄρνιθος ματτύης.
ἐσφάχθω μὲν διὰ τοῦ στόματος εἰς τὴν κεφαλήν, ἔστω

[118] add. Kaibel

---

[461] Properly "to be peeled"; cf. Latin *glubo*.
[462] The discussion above suggests that this means "make a
mattuê." But that would be a flat and unsatisfying final element in

370

traordinary luxury." They referred originally to this ordinary food eaten by average people and made of barley
groats as a *maza*, and to the process of preparing it as
mattein. But later they began to make their most basic
food more elaborate in a reckless, fussy manner, and they
lengthened the word *maza* slightly and began to refer to
expensive food of any kind as a *mattuê*, and to preparing it,
whether it was a fish, a bird, a vegetable, an animal, or a
pastry, as *mattuazein*. This is apparent from the evidence
Artemidorus cited from Alexis; for when Alexis wanted
to emphasize the excessive character of the preparations,
he appended the verb *lepesthai*.[461] The complete excerpt,
which is drawn from the revised version of the play entitled *Demetrius*, runs as follows (fr. 50):

> After you get this fish we've been sent,
> prepare it; have a feast; drink toasts;
> act dirty (*lepesthe*); and *mattuazete*.[462]

The Athenians use *lepesthai* to refer to crude, low-class
sexual pleasure.[463] Artemidorus in his *Culinary Vocabulary* makes it clear that *mattuê* is a general term for expensive food of all kinds. He writes as follows: There is a
type of *mattuês*[464] made with chicken. The bird should be
slaughtered by thrusting the knife through its mouth into

this catalogue of increasingly wild behavior, and Arnott *ad loc.*
suggests that the word may have had a colloquial sense (unknown
to the lexicographer quoted here) that referred to debauchery of
some sort.

[463] Cf. Mnesim. fr. 4.18 (quoted at 9.403a).

[464] A variant (masculine first-declension) form of the word,
used again below.

δὲ ἕωλος καθάπερ ὁ πέρδιξ· ἐὰν δὲ θέλῃς, ὡς ἔχει
αὐτοῖς πτεροῖς ἐὰν ⟨μὴ⟩[119] τετιλμένην. εἶτα τὸν τρό-
e πον ἐκθεὶς τῆς ἀρτύσεως καὶ | τῆς ἑψήσεως ἐπιφέρει
εὐθύς· καὶ νομάδα παχεῖαν ἕψε καὶ νεοσσοὺς τῶν ἤδη
κοκκυζόντων, ἐὰν θέλῃς παρὰ πότον χρῆσθαι. εἶτ᾽
ἐξελὼν τὰ λάχανα εἰς τρυβλίον καὶ τῆς ὄρνιθος τῶν
κρεῶν ἐπιθεὶς παρατίθει, τοῦ θέρους ἀντὶ τοῦ ὄξους
τῆς ὄμφακος ἐμβαλὼν εἰς τὸν ζωμὸν ὡς ἔχει τοὺς
βότρυς. ἐπειδὰν δὲ ἑφθὴ γένηται, ἔξελε μετὰ τοῦ
βοτρυδίου πρὸ τοῦ τὸ γίγαρτον ἐξαφεῖναι, εἶθ᾽ οὕτως
τὸ λάγανον κατάθρυπτε. οὗτος ⟨ὁ⟩[120] ματτύης ἐν τοῖς
ἡδίστοις. ὅτι μὲν οὖν κοινὸν ἦν τοὔνομα τῶν πολυτε-
λεστάτων ἐδεσμάτων φανερόν, ὅτι δὲ καὶ ὁ τρόπος τῆς |
f τοιαύτης εὐωχίας ὁμοίως ἐλέγετο Φιλήμων φησὶν ἐν
Ἁρπαζομένῳ·

γυμνῷ φυλακὴν ἐπίταττε ⟨ . . . ⟩ καὶ διὰ τριῶν
ποτηρίων με ματτύης εὐφραινέτω.

καὶ ἐν Ἀνδροφόνῳ·

πιεῖν τις ἡμῖν ἐγχεάτω καὶ ματτύην
ποιεῖτε θᾶττον.

Ἄλεξις δ᾽ ἐν Πυραύνῳ ἀμφιβόλως εἴρηκεν· ‖

119 add. Dalechamp
120 add. Kaibel

its head, and allowed to sit for a day, just as a partridge is; if you like, leave it as is, feathers and all, unplucked. After describing next how it should be seasoned and stewed, he continues immediately thereafter: Also stew a plump guinea-hen or some young roosters, if you want to eat them while you're drinking. Then remove the vegetables and put them in a bowl; set the chicken meat on top; and serve the dish. In the summer, add unripe grapes, just as they are, to the broth in place of the vinegar. Once the chicken is stewed, remove it (from the broth), along with the grapes, before the grape-seeds dissolve, and then at this point crumble up the wafer-bread[465] (over it). This is one of the most delicious *mattuai*. That the word was commonly used to refer to the most expensive foods is apparent; that the same term was applied to the manner in which a feast of this kind was celebrated is asserted by Philemon in *The Man Who Was Kidnapped* (fr. 11):

> "Put an unarmed man on guard"[466]—and let a
>   *mattuês*
> cheer me up along with every three cups!

And in *The Murderer* (Philem. fr. 8):

> Somebody pour us a drink! Hurry up
> and make us a *mattuês*!

Alexis uses the word ambiguously in *The Pan of Coals* (fr. 208):

[465] *laganon*; cf. 3.110a; 8.363a.
[466] A proverb that referred to giving a person orders he would obviously be unable to carry out (Zenob. 2.98).

664 ἐγὼ δ᾽ ἐπειδὰν ἀσχολουμένους λάβω,
ἀνέκραγον "οὐ δώσει τις ἡμῖν ματτύην;",

ὥσπερ ἂν εἰ τὸ δεῖπνον ἔλεγεν· πιθανὸν δὲ καὶ ἰδίως
ἐπὶ <τι>[121] τῶν ἐδεσμάτων ἀναφέρειν. Μάχων δ᾽ ὁ
Σικυώνιος τῶν μὲν κατὰ Ἀπολλόδωρον τὸν Καρύστιον
κωμῳδιοποιῶν εἷς ἐστι καὶ αὐτός· οὐκ ἐδίδαξεν δ᾽
Ἀθήνησι τὰς κωμῳδίας τὰς ἑαυτοῦ, ἀλλ᾽ ἐν Ἀλεξανδρείᾳ. ἦν δ᾽ ἀγαθὸς ποιητὴς εἴ τις ἄλλος τῶν μετὰ
τοὺς ἑπτά· διόπερ ὁ γραμματικὸς Ἀριστοφάνης
b ἐσπούδασε συσχολάσαι αὐτῷ νέος ὤν. | ἐποίησε δὲ
καὶ οὗτος ἐν δράματι Ἀγνοίᾳ ταυτί·

ἥδιον οὐδέν ἐστί μοι τῆς ματτύης.
τοῦτ᾽ εἴτε πρῶτοι Μακεδόνες τοῖς Ἀττικοῖς
κατέδειξαν ἡμῖν, εἴτε πάντες οἱ θεοί,
οὐκ οἶδα πλήν † ἐστίν γε μουσικωτάτου τινός †.

ὅτι δὲ ὕστατον καὶ ἐπὶ πᾶσιν εἰσεφέρετο Νικόστρατός
φησιν ἐν Ἀπελαυνομένῳ. μάγειρος δ᾽ ἐστὶν ὁ διηγούμενος ὡς λαμπρὰν καὶ εὔτακτον παρεσκεύασεν
εὐωχίαν· προδιηγησάμενός τε οἷον ἦν τὸ ἄριστον καὶ
c τὸ δεῖπνον καὶ τρίτης μνησθεὶς παραθέσεως | ἐπι-
φέρει·

[121] add. Kaibel

467 It is unclear whether Alexis used the feminine form *mattuê*
or the masculine *mattuês* (like Artemidorus and Philemon in fr.
11, and thus presumably in fr. 8 as well), since both would yield the
accusative singular *mattuên*.

As for me, whenever I caught them busy,
  I started shouting "Somebody give us a *mattuês*!",[467]

as if he were referring to the dinner, although it is possible
that he is referring specifically to an individual dish. Macho of Sicyon (test. 1) is also one of the comic poets contemporary with Apollodorus of Carystus (test. 1);[468] he did
not stage his comedies in Athens but in Alexandria. He was
as good a poet as anyone outside of the Seven,[469] which is
why the grammarian Aristophanes (Ar. Byz. test. 13B Slater) was eager to study with him as a young man.[470] He
wrote the following in his play *Ignorance* (fr. 1):

  I don't think there's anything more delicious than a
    mattuê.
  Whether it was the Macedonians who introduced it
    to us in Attica, or all the gods,
  all I know † it is in fact of someone extremely
    ingenious †.

That it was served last, after everything else, is asserted
by Nicostratus in *The Man Who Was Being Driven Away*
(fr. 7). A cook is describing what a brilliant, well-organized
feast he prepared. He first offers a description of what the
lunch and the dinner were like, and then continues, giving
an account of the third course:

[468] Macho and Apollodorus both belong to the middle of the
3rd century BCE.
[469] I.e. the Alexandrian Pleiad of tragic poets, although eight
names rather than seven are generally given: Alexander Aetolus,
Homerus of Byzantium, Sosiphanes of Syracuse, Sositheus of Alexandria Troas, Lycophron, Philicus, Dionysiades of Tarsus, and
Aeantides.
[470] Cf. 6.241f.

εὖ γ', ἄνδρες, εὖ σφόδρ'· ἀλλὰ μὴν τῇ ματτύῃ
οὕτω διαθήσω τὰ μετὰ ταῦθ' ὥστ', οἴομαι,
οὐδ' αὐτὸν ἡμῖν τοῦτον ἀντερεῖν ἔτι.

καὶ ἐν Μαγείρῳ·

θρῖον δὲ καὶ κάνδαυλον ἢ τούτων τι τῶν
εἰς ματτύην οὐδέτερον εἶδε πώποτε.

ἄλλος δέ τίς φησιν·

περιφέρειν ματτύην ⟨καὶ⟩ ποδάριον, |
d   καὶ γαστρίον τακερόν τι καὶ μήτρας ἴσως.

Διονύσιος δ' ἐν Ἀκοντιζομένῳ· μάγειρος δ' ἐστὶν ὁ
λέγων·

ὥστ' ἐνίοτ' ἂν τούτοισι ποιῶν ματτύην
σπεύδων ἅμ' εἰσήνεγκα διαμαρτὼν μίαν
ἄκων περιφορὰν τῶν νεκρῶν ὡς τὸν νεκρόν.

Φιλήμων ἐν Πτωχῇ·

ἐξὸν ἀποσάττεσθαι δ' ὅλην τὴν ἡμέραν,
ποιοῦντα καὶ διδόντα ματτύας ἐκεῖ.

Μόλπις δ' ὁ Λάκων τὰ παρὰ τοῖς Σπαρτιάταις |
e   ἐπαίκλεια, ⟨ἃ⟩ σημαίνει τὰς ἐπιδειπνίδας, ματτύας

---

471 The first verse and part of the second are quoted at
12.517a.   472 The sense of the final two verses is obscure.
473 Called *The Beggar-Woman* or *The Girl from Rhodes* at
14.645a.   474 Cf. 4.141d–e.

Excellent, gentlemen, really excellent! But I'll
     arrange what
comes next with the *mattuê* in a way that, I imagine,
will keep even this guy himself from arguing with us
     any more.

And in *The Cook* (fr. 16.2–3):[471]

but as for a fig-leaf pastry or a *kandaulos*, or any of
     these ingredients
that go into a *mattuê*—he's never seen a single one!

And someone else says (adesp. com. fr. 125):

to serve a *mattuê* and a pig's foot,
and perhaps a tender little stomach-sausage and sows'
     wombs.

Dionysius in *The Man Who Was Hit by a Javelin* (fr. 1); a
cook is speaking:

So that sometimes, if I was making a *mattuê* for these
     guys
and was in a hurry, I made a mistake and
     unintentionally served
the dead man a single course of corpses at the same
     time.[472]

Philemon in *The Beggar-Woman*[473] (fr. 71):

when he could have kept stuffing himself all day long,
producing and handing out *mattuai* there.

Molpis of Sparta (*FGrH* 590 F *2a)[474] claims that other
people refer to what the Spartans call *epaikleia*—that is to

φησὶ λέγεσθαι παρὰ τοῖς ἄλλοις. ὁ δὲ κυνικὸς Μένιππος ἐν τῷ ἐπιγραφομένῳ Ἀρκεσιλάῳ γράφει οὕτως· πότος ἦν ἐπικωμασάντων τινῶν καὶ ματτύην ἐκέλευσεν εἰσφέρειν Λάκαινάν τις· καὶ εὐθέως περιεφέρετο περδίκεια ὀλίγα καὶ χήνεια ὀπτὰ καὶ τρύφη πλακούντων. τὸ δὲ τοιοῦτον δεῖπνον οἱ μὲν Ἀττικοὶ προσηγόρευον ἐπιδόρπισμα, οἱ δὲ Δωριεῖς ἐπαῖκλον, τῶν δ' ἄλλων Ἑλλήνων οἱ πλεῖστοι ἐπιδειπνίδα.

f   Τοσούτων καὶ περὶ | τῆς ματτύης λεχθέντων ἔδοξεν ἀπιέναι· καὶ γὰρ ἑσπέρα ἦν ἤδη. διελύθημεν οὖν οὕτως.

say, *epideipnides*[475]—as *mattuai*. Menippus the Cynic in his work entitled *Arcesilaus* (fr. II, p. 245 Riese) writes as follows: There was a party that included some people who had barged in already drunk, and someone called for a Spartan *mattuê* to be served. Immediately a few small partridges were brought around, along with roasted geese and some fancy cakes. The Athenians referred to a dinner like this as an *epidorpisma*, whereas the Dorians called it an *epaiklon*,[476] and most other Greeks called it an *epideipnis*.

After these lengthy remarks had been made about the *mattuê*, we decided to leave; for it was now evening. So at this point we went our separate ways.

[475] Cf. 14.658e with n.
[476] Cf. 14.642d–e.

INDEX

Achaeus, *tragic poet* (*TrGF* 20),
F 17: 14.641d

Achilleus, *Homeric hero,*
13.601b; 14.624a, 627f, 633c

Adaeus of Mitylene, *author of
treatise on sculptors,* 13.606a

adespota, comic (K–A), fr. *124:
14.658; fr. 125: 14.664c–d

adespota, epigrams (*FGE*),
1482–3: 13.609d; 1844–7:
14.629a

adespota, lyric (*PMG*), 953:
13.599d; 954a: 14.633a; 954b:
14.633a; 955: 14.636d

Adon, *Phrygian pipe-player*
(Stephanis #53), 14.624b

Aegilus, *Attic hero,* 14.652e

Aegimus, *author of treatise on
cake-making,* 14.643e

Aemilianus, *grammarian and
deipnosophist,* 14.634b, 662f

Aeneas, *prince of Troy,* 14.632e

Aeschines Socraticus of Athens,
philosopher (*PAA* 321970),
13.611d–12f; (*SSR* VI.A), F
45: 14.656f

Aeschylides, *author of treatise
on farming,* 14.650d

Aeschylus of Alexandria, *epic
and tragic poet* (*TrGF* 179), F
1: 13.599e; (*FGrH* 488), T 1:
13.599e

Aeschylus of Athens, *tragic
poet,* 13.601a–b; (Radt ed.),
fr. 44: 13.600a–b; (fr. 79:
14.629f; fr. 135: 13.602e; fr.
314: 14.632c; (Radt ed. =
FGE), test. 162 = 478–9:
14.627c–d

Aethlius of Samos, *historian*
(*FGrH* 536), F 1a: 14.653f; F
1b: 14.650d–e

Agamemnon, *Homeric hero,*
13.603d; 14.660b, d

Agatharchides of Cnidus, *historian* (*FGrH* 86), F 8:
14.650f–1a

Agathocles of Cyzicus, *historian*
(*FGrH* 472), F 4: 14.649f–
50a

Agesilaus II, *king of Sparta*
(Poralla #9), 13.609b;
14.613c, 616d–e, 657b–c

Agias, *author of treatise on music* (*FHG*), fr. 4, iv.293:
14.626f

INDEX

Agias of Argos, *epic poet*
(Bernabé ed.), test. 3:
13.610c

Ahura Mazda, 13.603c

Alcaeus of Lesbos, *lyric poet,*
13.598b; (Voigt ed.), fr. 140:
14.627a–b

Alcibiades of Athens, *politician
and general,* 14.643f

Alcman of Sparta, *lyric poet,*
14.638e; (*PMG*), 59(a):
13.600f; 59(b): 13.601a; 94:
14.646a; 96: 14.648b; 101:
14.636f; 109: 14.624b

Alexander II of Macedon,
brother of Philip II, 14.629d

Alexander Aetolus, *elegiac poet*
(Powell ed. = Magnelli ed.),
fr. 21, p. 129 = fr. 18:
14.620e–f

Alexander "the Great," *king of
Macedon,* 13.594d, 603a–c,
606c–d, 607f

Alexas, *Ionicologos* (*SH*), 41:
14.620e–f

Alexis, *comic poet,* 14.663c; (K–
A), fr. 19: 14.638c; fr. 22:
14.644b–c; fr. 34: 14.650c; fr.
41: 13.605f–6a; fr. 50:
14.663c–d; fr. 64: 14.613c; fr.
73: 14.650e; fr. 99: 13.610e;
fr. 122: 14.652c; fr. 128:
14.654f; fr. 134: 14.661d; fr.
143: 13.595d; fr. 146:
14.621d–e; fr. 168: 14.642d;
fr. 190: 14.641c; fr. 194:
14.655f–6a; fr. 208: 14.663f–
4a; fr. 252: 14.642e–f

Alyattes, *king of Lydia,* 13.599c

Amaltheia, *goat that nursed
Zeus,* 14.643a

Ametor of Eleuthernae, *musician* (Stephanis #152),
14.638b

Amitrochates, *king of India,*
14.652f–3a

Amoebeus, *citharode*
(Stephanis #159; *PAA*
124327), 14.623d

Amoebeus, *citharode and deipnosophist* (Stephanis #160),
14.622d–3d

Amphilochus of Olene, *boy
loved by goose,* 13.606c

Amphion of Thespiae, *historian*
(*FGrH* 387), F 1: 14.629a

Amphis, *comic poet* (K–A), fr. 9:
14.642a–b

Anacharsis of Scythia, *sage*
(Kindstrand ed.), fr. A11A:
14.613d

Anacreon of Teos, *lyric poet,*
13.598c, 599c–d, 600d–e;
14.635c–e, 639a; (*PMG*),
373.1–2: 14.646d; 374:
14.634c, 634f; 374.1–3:
14.635c

Anacus of Phigaleia, *pipe-player*
(Stephanis #172), 14.629a

Ananius, *iambic poet* (West[2]
ed.), fr. 2: 14.625c

Anaxandrides, *comic poet* (K–
A), fr. 2: 14.642b; fr. 7:
14.654b; fr. 10: 14.614b–c; fr.
16: 14.638c–d; fr. 29:
14.654f–5a; fr. 36: 14.634e

382

Anaxilas, *comic poet* (K–A), fr. 24: 14.655a; fr. 27: 14.623e–f

Anaxippus, *comic poet* (K–A), fr. 4: 13.610f–11a

Anchises, *Trojan elder and father of Aeneas,* 14.632e

Andreas of Panormus, *historian* (*FGrH* 571), F 1: 14.634a–b

Androtion, *historian* (*FGrH* 324), F *78: 14.650e

Angares, *bard of Astyages,* 14.633d–e

Anoutis, *wife of Bagabyzus and sister of Xerxes,* 13.609a

Anticleides of Athens, *author of Returns* (*FGrH* 140), F 6: 13.609c–d

Antidotus, *comic poet,* 14.642d; (K–A), fr. 1: 14.656e

Antigeneidas, *pipe-player* (Stephanis #196), 14.631f

Antigonus Gonatas, *king of Macedon,* 13.603d–e, 607c

Antigonus of Carystus, *biographer* (Wilamowitz ed. = Dorandi ed.), p. 117 = fr. 34A: 13.607e–f; p. 117 = fr. 35A: 13.603e

Antimachus of Colophon, *poet,* 13.596f–7a, 598a–b

Antiochus I Soter, 14.652f–3a

Antiope, *lover of Musaeus,* 13.597d

Antipater (*SVF*), fr. 65, iii.257: 14.643f

Antiphanes, *comic poet,* 14.671d; (K–A), test. 7: 14.662f–3a; fr. 49: 14.618b; fr. 60: 14.650e; fr. 79: 14.646f; fr. 90: 14.661f; fr. 138: 14.641f–2a; fr. 172.5–6: 14.642a; fr. 173: 14.655a–b; fr. 203: 14.654e; fr. 207: 14.643d–e; fr. 216: 14.622f–3c; fr. 221: 14.661b–c; fr. 297: 14.644f

Antisthenes (*SSR* VA), F 62: 14.656f; F 63: 14.656f

Aphrodite, 13.599e–600c, 601d; 14.619d–e, 631d; *as Aphrodite Argynnis,* 13.603d; *as Aphrodite Pandêmos,* 14.659d; *as Cypris,* 13.599a, 600f, 601c, 608f; *as Pythionice Aphrodite,* 13.595c

Apion of Alexandria, *historian* (*FGrH* 616), F 32: 14.642d–e

Apollo, 13.599a, 602b, 604b; 14.614b, 619b, 627f, 628a–b, 632c, 636e–f

Apollodorus of Athens, *grammarian* (*FGrH* 244), F 219: 14.636f; F 222: 14.663a; F 226: 14.648e; F 255: 14.646a; F 283: 14.646c

Apollodorus of Carystus, *comic poet* (K–A), test. 1: 14.664a

Apollonius, *son of Sotades of Maroneia,* 14.620f

Archedice of Naucratis, *courtesan,* 13.596e

Archestratus, *author of treatise on pipe-players,* 14.634d

Archilochus, 13.599d; 14.620c, 637e–f, 639a, 644b; (West[2] ed.), fr. 1: 14.627c; fr. 120:

14.628b; fr. 225: 14.653d; (West² = *FGE*), fr. spur. 331 = 540–1: 13.594c–d

Archimedes of Syracuse, *engineer,* 14.634b

Archippus, *comic poet* (K–A), fr. 10: 14.656b–c; fr. 11: 14.640e–f

Archytas, *music-theorist,* 13.600f

Ares, 14.627a; *as Lord Enyalius,* 14.627c

Argas, *indecent poet* (Stephanis #292), 14.638b–d

Argiope of Thrace, *lover of Orpheus,* 13.597b–c

Argynnus, *beloved of Agamemnon,* 13.603d

Ariadne, *daughter of Minos,* 13.601f

Aristaeus, *shepherd and beekeeper, son of Apollo,* 14.643b

Aristarchus, *tragic poet* (*TrGF* 14), F 4: 13.612f

Aristarchus of Samothrace, *grammarian,* 14.634c–d

Aristeas, *author of treatise on citharodes,* 14.623d

Aristeas of Proconnesus, *wanderer and sage* (Bolton ed.), fr. 18: 13.605c–d

Aristides, *author of treatise on proverbs,* 14.641a

Aristippus of Cyrene, *philosopher,* 13.599b

Aristocles, *author of treatises on music and choruses* (*FHG*), fr. 7, iv.331: 14.620d–e; fr. 8,

iv.331: 14.621b–c; fr. 9, iv.331: 14.630b; fr. 10, iv.331: 14.620b

Aristocles, *citharode* (Stephanis #340), 13.603d–e

Aristodemus, *lover of Cratinus of Athens* (*PAA* [168580]), 13.602d–f

Aristogiton of Athens, *creditor* (*PAA* 168110), 13.611f

Aristogiton of Athens, *tyrannicide* (*PAA* 168195), 13.602a

Aristomenes of Athens, *comic poet* (K–A), fr. 6: 14.658a; fr. 11: 14.650d; fr. 12: 14.658a

Aristonicus of Argos, *lyre-player* (Stephanis #366), 14.637e–f

Aristophanes of Athens, *comic poet,* 14.653f; *Ach.* 1092: 14.646d; *V.* 1216: 14.641d; *Ra.* 1304–6: 14.636d–e; (K–A), fr. 52: 14.650e; fr. 120: 14.650e; fr. 188: 14.650e; fr. 211: 14.646b; fr. 269: 14.645e; fr. 287: 14.629c; fr. 352: 14.619a; fr. 681: 14.652f

Aristophanes of Byzantium, *grammarian,* 14.662d; (Slater ed.), test. 13B: 14.664a; fr. 340: 14.619b; fr. 363: 14.659b

Aristotle of Stagira, *natural scientist and philosopher,* 14.655b, 656a–b; (Gigon ed.), fr. 326: 14.652a; fr. 327: 14.653d–e; fr. 520.1: 14.618e–19a; fr. 674: 14.641c; fr. 675: 14.641d–e; fr. 991: 14.654d

Aristoxenus of Tarentum, *Peripatetic philosopher* (Wehrli ed.), fr. 45: 14.648d; fr. 78: 14.624b; fr. 89: 14.619d–e; fr. 98: 14.635e; fr. 99: 14.635b; fr. 100: 14.634d; fr. 101: 14.634e–f; fr. 103: 14.630e; fr. 107: 14.630b; fr. 108: 14.631c; fr. 109: 14.631d–e; fr. 110: 14.621c–d; fr. 111: 14.620e; fr. 124: 14.632a–b; fr. 129: 14.619e; fr. 136: 14.638b

Arsinoe II Philadelphus, *wife of Lysimachus and queen of Egypt*, 14.616c, 621a

Artemidorus, *author of treatise on cooking*, 14.662d, f, 663c, d–e

Artemis, 13.600c; 14.619b, 636a–b, d, 645a; *as Artemis Chitônea*, 14.629e; *as the Virgin*, 14.658c

Artemon of Cassandreia (*FHG*), fr. 11, iv.342: 14.636e–f; fr. 12, iv.342–3: 14.637c–e

Asclepius, 14.632e

Asopichus, *boyfriend of Epaminondas of Thebes*, 13.605a

Asopodorus of Phlius, *pipe-player* (Stephanis #468; *SH*), 223: 14.639a; 224: 14.631f

Aspasia of Miletus, *beloved of Socrates*, 13.599b

Astyages, *king of the Medes*, 14.633d–e

Athena, 13.594f, 609e; 14.616e–17a

Athenio, *comic poet* (K–A), fr. 1: 14.660e–1d

Atlas, 13.600c

Augustus, *Roman emperor*, 14.652a–b

Axiopistus of Locris or Sicyon, *purported author of pseudepicharmic texts*, 14.648d–e

Babys, *Phrygian pipe-player* (Stephanis #506), 14.624b

Bacchiades of Sicyon, *dancer and choreographer* (Stephanis #510), 14.629a

Bacchis, *pipe-girl and owner of Pythionice* (PAA 261090), 13.595a

Bacchis, *rival turned friend of Plangon of Miletus*, 13.594b–c

Bacchylides, *epinician poet* (Snell–Maehler ed.), fr. 15.1: 14.631c

Bagoas, *eunuch loved by Alexander "the Great"* (Berve i #195), 13.603a–b

Bato, *comic poet* (K–A), fr. 4: 14.661c–d

Bato of Sinope, *orator* (FGrH 268), F 5: 14.639d–40a

Berosus, *historian* (FGrH 680), F 2: 14.639f

Bilistiche of Argos, *courtesan*, 13.596e

Bithys, *favorite of Lysimachus*, 14.614f

Biton, *author of treatise on siege-machines* (Marsden

ed.), §57–61, pp. 74–6:
14.634a

Bittis, *object of song for Philetas,* 13.598f

Bormus, *young man abducted by nymphs,* 14.619e–20a

Bromias, *pipe-girl* (Stephanis #535), 13.605b

Bromius. *See* Dionysus

Cadmus, *king of Thebes,* 14.658e–f

Callimachus of Cyrene, *scholar and poet* (Pfeiffer ed.), fr. 435: 14.643e

Callimedon "the Crayfish," *notorious wit* (Stephanis #1343; PAA 558185), 14.614e–e

Calycê, *tragic lover,* 14.619d–e

Caphisias, *pipe-player* (Stephanis #1387), 14.629a–b

carmina popularia (PMG), 849: 14.618e; 850: 14.619d; 851a: 14.622b–c; 851b: 14.622c–d; 852: 14.629e

Carystius of Pergamum, *historian* (FHG), fr. 5, iv.357: 13.603b–c; fr. 8, iv.358: 14.620b; fr. 9, iv.358: 13.610d–e; fr. 13, iv.358–9: 14.639b–c; fr. 19, iv.359: 14.620f

Cassander, *king of Macedon* (Berve i #414), 14.620b

Cassiepeia, *woman praised in adespota epic line,* 14.632f

Cephisodorus, *comic poet* (K–A), fr. 2: 14.629c

Cephisodorus, *wandering show-man* (Stephanis #1395; PAA 568055), 14.615e–f

Cerberus, *guard-dog of Underworld,* 13.597c

Chaeremon, *tragic poet* (TrGF 71), F 1: 13.608d; F 5: 13.608e; F 8: 13.608f; F 9: 13.608d–e; F 10: 13.608e; F 12: 13.608f; F 13: 13.608e; F 14: 13.608a–c

Chamaeleon of Pontus, *Peripatetic philosopher* (Wehrli ed.), fr. 4: 14.623f–4a; fr. 25: 13.600f; fr. 26: 13.599c–d; fr. 28: 14.620b–c; fr. 33: 14.656c–e; fr. 35: 13.611a; fr. 42: 14.628e

Charaxus, *brother of Sappho,* 13.596b, e

Chariton of Acragas, *unsuccessful tyrannicide,* 13.602a–c

Charmus, *Athenian polemarch* (PAA 988430), 13.609d

Charon of Chalcis, *friend of Alexander "the Great"* (Berve i #827), 13.603b–c

Charondas, *lawgiver of Catana in Sicily,* 14.619b

Chionides, *comic poet* (K–A), fr. 4: 14.638d–e

Choronicus, *poet,* 14.638c

Chryse of Sparta, *sister of Xenopeitheia* (Poralla #769), 13.609b

Chrysippus, *son of Pelops,* 13.602f–3a

Chrysippus of Soli, *Stoic philosopher* (SVF), xxviii fr. 7, iii.199: 14.616a–b; xxviii fr. 8,

INDEX

iii.199: 14.616b; xxviii fr. 13, iii.200: 14.659a

Chrysippus of Tyana, *author of treatise on bread-making,* 14.647c–8a, 648c

Chrysogonus, *pipe-player* (Stephanis #2637), 14.648d

Cimon, *Athenian politician* (*PAA* 569795), 13.594f

Cion, *Phrygian pipe-player* (Stephanis #1404), 14.624b

Clearchus, *comic poet* (K–A), fr. 2: 14.623c; fr. 3: 14.613b; fr. 4: 14.642b–c

Clearchus of Soli, *Peripatetic philosopher* (Wehrli ed.), fr. 16: 13.611b–d; fr. 23: 13.605d; fr. 26: 13.605e–f; fr. 27: 13.606c; fr. 28: 13.606c; fr. 32: 14.619c–d; fr. 33: 14.639a; fr. 34: 13.597a; fr. 87: 14.648f–9a; fr. 92: 14.620c

Cleidemus of Athens, *historian* (*FGrH* 323), F 5a: 14.660a–b; F 5b: 14.660d–e

Cleinias, *Pythagorean philosopher,* 14.623f–4a

Cleisophus of Selymbria, *fell in love with statue,* 13.605f–6b

Cleomenes, *rhapsode* (Stephanis #1445), 14.620c–d

Cleomenes of Rhegium, *erotic poet,* 13.605e; 14.638d–e

Cleonymus of Sparta, *general* (Bradford pp. 246–7), 13.605d–e

Cleosthenes, *tyrant of Sicyon,* 14.628c–d

Clotho, *one of Fates,* 14.617a

Clytus of Miletus, *Peripatetic philosopher* (*FGrH* 490), F 1: 14.655b–e

Cocytus, *Underworld river personified,* 13.597c

Codalus, *Phrygian pipe-player* (Stephanis #1523), 14.624b

Coiranus of Miletus, *befriended dolphin,* 13.606d–f

Craterus of Macedon, *companion of Alexander "the Great"* (Berve i #446), 13.603b

Crates, *comic poet* (K–A), fr. 42: 14.619a

Crates of Mallos, *grammarian* (Broggiato ed.), fr. 109: 14.653b; fr. 112: 14.640c–d

Cratinus, *comic poet* (K–A), fr. 17: 14.638e–f; fr. 104: 14.638e; fr. 127: 14.629c; fr. 130: 14.646e; fr. 155: 14.657a; fr. 276: 14.638f; fr. 369: 13.596c

Cratinus Junior, *comic poet* (K–A), fr. 1: 14.661e–f

Cratinus of Athens, *sacrificed himself for city* (*PAA* 584305), 13.602c–f

Critias of Athens, *associate of Socrates* (88 D–K), B 1: 13.600d–e; B 31: 14.663a

Ctesias, *historian* (*FGrH* 688), F 4: 14.639c–d

Ctesicles, *sculptor,* 13.606a

Cybele, 14.636a; *as Mother of the Gods,* 14.618c; *as Mountain Mother,* 14.626a

Cyclops, 13.610d

387

INDEX

Cynulcus, *cynic deipnosophist,* 13.599e, 602f, 610b, d, 612f

Cypselus, *tyrant of Corinth,* 13.609e–f

Cyrus I ("the Great"), *king of Persia,* 13.599c; 14.633d–e

Damippus son of Epilycus of Amphipolis, *boyfriend of Onomarchus,* 13.605c

Damon of Athens, *musicologist* (*PAA* 301540; 37 D–K), B 6: 14.628c

Danaids, 14.651f

Darius III, *king of Persia,* 13.603c, 607f

Deiniades, *owner of the pipe-girl Bromias,* 13.605b

Deinias of Athens, *notorious wit* (Stephanis #587; *PAA* 302175), 14.614d–e

Delphic Oracles (Fontenrose ed.), Q85: 13.602c; Q101.3: 14.630d; Q185: 14.614a–b

Demeter, 13.597d, 600b; 14.618d–e, 619b, 624e–f, 647a; *as Chloê or Ioulô,* 14.618d; *as Eleusinian Demeter,* 13.609f

Demetrius I Poliorcetes, *son of Antigonus I,* 13.610e; 14.614e–15a

Demetrius of Byzantium, *historian* (*FHG*), ii.624: 14.633a–b

Demetrius of Magnesia (Mejer ed.), fr. 7: 13.611b

Demetrius of Phaleron, *Peripatetic philosopher* (*PAA* 312150; Wehrli ed. = Fortenbaugh–Schütrumpf eds.), fr. 33 = fr. 55A: 14.620b

Demochares of Athens, *orator* (*PAA* 321970; Baiter–Sauppe ed.), ii.341–2, I: 13.610e–f

Democritus of Nicomedia, *philosopher and deipnosophist,* 14.648e, 649b

Demosthenes of Athens, *orator,* 13.610e; 2.19: 14.614e; 18.260: 14.645b; 18.262: 14.653e

Diagoras of Melos ("the Atheist"), *lyric poet,* 13.611a–b

Dicaearchus of Messene, *Peripatetic philosopher* (Wehrli ed. = Mirhady ed.), fr. 19 = fr. 80: 14.641e–f; fr. 21 = fr. 81: 13.594e–5a; fr. 23 = fr. 83: 13.603a–b; fr. 60 = fr. 72: 14.636c–d; fr. 87 = fr. 85: 14.620c–d

Didymias, *mocked as "fox-shit"* (*PAA* 323582), 14.658d

Didymus of Alexandria, *grammarian* (Schmidt ed.), pp. 250–1: 14.636d–e; pp. 302–3: 14.634e–f

Dinon of Colophon, *historian* (*FGrH* 690), F 1: 13.609a; F 9: 14.633d–e; F 12: 14.652b–c

Diocles of Cynaetha, *parodist* (Stephanis #702), 14.638b

INDEX

Diodorus, *grammarian,*
14.642d–e

Diogenes, *tragic poet (TrGF*
45), F 1: 14.636a–b

Diomus, *Sicilian cowherd and
inventor of boukoliasmos,*
14.619a–b

Dion of Chios, *musician*
(Stephanis #792), 14.638a

Dionysius, *grammarian and student of Tryphon,* 14.641a

Dionysius Chalcous, *poet and
orator (PAA* 336985), 13.602c

Dionysius of Iasus, *boy befriended
by dolphin,* 13.606c–d

Dionysius of Leuctra, *author of
treatise on Elean festivals,*
13.609f–10a

Dionysius of Sinope, *comic poet*
(K–A), fr. 1: 14.664d; fr. 4:
14.615e–f

Dionysius of Utica, *author of
treatise on farming,* 14.648e–f

Dionysus, 13.595e; 14.613a,
628a–b, 631a–b, d, 638a,
641d, 653c, 658e; *as Bacchus,*
13.598e; 14.622c; *as Bromius,*
13.599e; 14.617a, c; *as
Dithyrambos,* 14.617f; *as
Thriambos,* 14.617f

Diotimus, *author of epic poem
about Heracles (SH),* 393:
13.603d

Diotimus, *enemy of Epicurus,*
13.611b

Diphilus, *comic poet* (K–A), fr.
27: 14.645a; fr. 71: 13.599d;
fr. 78: 14.657e; fr. 80: 14.640d

Diphilus of Siphnos, *physician,*
14.650b

Doriche, *courtesan associated
with Charaxus,* 13.596b–e

Dorotheus of Ascalon, *grammarian,* 14.658d, 662f–3a

Duris of Samos, *tyrant of
Samos and historian (FGrH*
76), F 7: 13.606c–d; F 16:
14.618b–c; F 18: 13.605d–e;
F 28: 14.636f

Empedocles of Agrigentum,
philosopher (31 D–K), A 12:
14.620c–d

Enyalius, *Ares-like deity,*
14.627c

Eoie, *lover of Hesiod,* 13.597d–f

Epaenetus, *cookbook author,*
14.662d–e

Epaminondas of Thebes, *general,* 13.602a, 605a; 14.650f–
1a

Ephippus, *comic poet* (K–A), fr.
7: 14.617f–18a; fr. 8: 14.642e;
fr. 13: 14.642e; fr. 13.3:
14.646f

Ephorus of Aeolian Cumae, *historian (FGrH* 70), F 4:
14.637b; F 8: 14.626a

[Epicharmus],
Pseudepicharmeia (K–A),
test. i: 14.648d; fr. 289:
14.648d

Epicharmus of Syracuse, *comic
poet and philosopher* (K–A),
fr. 4: 14.619a–b; fr. 14:
14.618d; fr. 20: 14.648c; fr.

389

23: 14.645e–f; fr. 46: 14.645e, 646b; fr. 104: 14.619a–b; fr. 131: 14.628b

Epicrates of Ambracia, *comic poet* (K–A), fr. 4: 13.605e; fr. 6: 14.655f

Epicurus, *hedonist philosopher*, 13.611b

Epigonus, *lyre-player* (Stephanis #855), 14.637f–8a

Epilycus, *comic poet* (K–A), fr. 2: 14.650e

Epimenides of Crete, *holy man* (*FGrH* 457; D–K 3; *PAA* 396032), 13.602c

Erigone, *daughter of Icarius*, 14.618e

Eriphanis, *lyric poetess*, 14.619c–d

Eros, 13.599c, e–f, 600d, f, 604f, 609d; 14.639a

Euangelus, *comic poet* (K–A), fr. 1: 14.644d–f

Euathlus, *love interest of Calycê*, 14.619d–e

Eubulus, *comic poet* (K–A), fr. 1.2–3: 14.646b; fr. 14: 14.622e–f; fr. 44: 14.642c; fr. 48: 14.653e; fr. 74: 14.640b–c

Euchemenes, *historian* (*FGrH* 459), F 1: 13.601e–f

Euhemerus of Cos, *historian* (*FGrH* 63), F 1: 14.658e–f

Euphorion, *scholar and poet* (*FHG*), fr. 8, iii.73: 14.635a–b, f; fr. 9, iii.73: 14.633f–4a

Euphranor, *author of treatise on pipe-players*, 14.634d

Eupolis, *comic poet* (K–A), fr.

176: 14.646f; fr. 176.2–3: 14.630a; fr. 301: 14.657a; fr. 306: 14.658c–d; fr. 366: 14.623e

Euripides of Athens, *tragic poet*, 13.598d–e, 603e, 604e–f; 14.652d; *Cyc.* 136: 14.658c; 394: 14.650a; *Hipp.* 3–6: 13.600b–c; 436: 14.640b; *HF* 348–9: 14.619b–c; 678–9: 13.608f; (Kannicht ed.), fr. 148: 14.638e; fr. 269: 13.600c–d; fr. 467: 14.640b; fr. 492: 14.613d–14a; fr. 494.9–10: 14.614a; fr. 898: 13.599f–600a; fr. 1052.3: 14.641c

Eurystheus, *as lover of Heracles*, 13.603d

Eurytion, *centaur*, 14.613a–b

Examue, *companion of Mimnermus*, 13.598a

Galateia, *beloved of Philoxenus*, 13.598e

Ganymede, *Trojan prince*, 13.601e–f, 602e

Genthius, *king of Illyria*, 14.615a

Glaucus of Locris, *cookbook author*, 14.661d–e

Glycera, *courtesan* (Berve i #231, *PAA* 277490), 13.595d–6b, 605d

Glycera, *lover of Menander* (*PAA* 277495), 13.594d

Gnesippus, *erotic poet* (Stephanis #556; *PAA* 279680), 14.638d–9a

Gorgias of Athens, *grammarian or historian* (*FGrH* 351), F 1: 13.596f

Grace(s), *personified*, 13.597d, 601e; 14.646f

Hades, 13.597b, d; *as Clymenus,* 14.624e–f

Hagnon of the Academy, *philosopher,* 13.602d–e

Harmodius of Athens, *tyrannicide* (*PAA* 203425), 13.596f, 602a

Harmonia, *queen of Thebes,* 14.658f

Harpalus of Macedon, *treasurer of Alexander "the Great"* (Berve i #143, *PAA* 204010), 13.594d–6b

Harpalycê, *doomed lover,* 14.619e

Harpocration of Mende, *author of treatise on cake-making,* 14.648a–b, c

Hecate, 14.645b

Hector, *prince of Troy,* 14.660d

Hegesander of Delphi, *historian* (*FHG*), fr. 12, iv.415–16: 14.620f–1b; fr. 43, iv.421: 14.652f–3a; fr. 44, iv.421: 14.656c

Hegesias, *comic actor* (O'Connor #209; Stephanis #1055), 14.620d

Hegesippus, *author of treatise on cake-making,* 14.643e

Hellanicus of Lesbos, *historian* (*FGrH* 4), F 56: 14.652a; F 85a: 14.635e

Hephaestus, 14.641d

Hera, 14.639d, 655a–b

Heracleides, *cookbook author,* 14.661d–e

Heracleides of Pontus, *Peripatetic philosopher* (*SH*), 480: 14.649c; (Wehrli ed. = Schütrumpf ed.), fr. 65 = fr. 37: 13.602b; fr. 163 = fr. 114: 14.624c–e

Heracleides of Syracuse, *author of treatise on Syracusan institutions,* 14.647a

Heracleides of Tarentum, *engineer,* 14.634b

Heracleon of Ephesus, *grammarian,* 14.647b

Heracles, 13.603d; 14.614d, 656b–c

Heraclitus, *philosopher* (40 D–K), B 22: 13.610b

Hermaeus, *perfume-maker* (*PAA* 401965), 13.612e

Hermeias son of Hermodorus, *author of treatise on sexual attraction,* 13.606c

Hermesianax of Colophon, *elegiac poet,* 13.597a, 599c–d; (Powell ed.), fr. 7, pp. 98–100: 13.597a–9b; fr. 7.35–7, p. 99: 13.597a; fr. 7.41–6, p. 99: 13.597a

Hermesilaus of Chios, *friend of Sophocles and Athenian proxenos,* 13.603f

Hermippus, *comic and iambic poet* (K–A), fr. 31: 14.636d; fr. 37: 14.650f; fr. 51: 14.649c

Hermippus, *pipe-player* (Stephanis #898), 14.615b

INDEX

Hermippus of Smyrna, *Peripatetic philosopher* (Wehrli ed.), fr. 88: 14.619b

Hermobius, *rival of Mimnermus,* 13.598a

Hermophantus, *comic actor* (Stephanis #908), 14.620d

Herodice, *wife of Cypselus,* 13.609f

Herodotus of Halicarnassus, *historian,* 1.17.1: 14.627d; 1.133.2: 14.640e–f; 1.135: 13.603a; 1.193.4–5: 14.651b–d; 1.212.2: 14.613b; 2.135.1, 4: 13.596b–c; 2.135.5: 13.596e

Hesiod, *didactic poet,* 13.597d–f; 14.620c–d; *Op.* 410: 14.653d; (Merkelbach–West eds.), fr. 277: 13.609e

Hestia, 14.657a

Hieron, *tyrant of Gela and Syracuse,* 14.635b, 656c–e

Hieronymus of Rhodes, *Peripatetic philosopher* (Wehrli ed.), fr. 33: 14.635f; fr. 34: 13.602a; fr. 35: 13.604d–f

Hippagoras, *historian* (*FGrH* 743), F 1: 14.630a

Hipparchus, *tyrant and son of Pisistratus* (*PAA* 537615), 13.609c–d

Hippias of Athens, *tyrant and son of Pisistratus* (*PAA* 537810), 13.596f, 609d

Hippias of Elis, *sophist* (*FGrH* 6), F 3: 13.608f–9a

Hippocleides of Athens, *suitor of Cleosthenes' daughter* (*PAA* 538230), 14.628c–d

Hippolochus of Macedon, *correspondent of Lynceus of Samos,* 14.614d

Hippolytus, *Euripidean hero,* 13.599c

Hippon "the Atheist," *philosopher* (3 D–K), B 38: 13.610b

Hipponax of Ephesus, *iambic poet,* 13.599d; (Degani ed.), fr. 37: 14.645c; fr. 153: 14.624b; fr. spur. 218: 14.625c

History of Argos (*FGrH* 311), F 1: 13.596e

Homer, *epic poet,* 13.597e–f; 14.620b–d, 624a, 632c–d, 638a–b, 639a, 653b, 660a; *Il.* 1.603–4: 14.627f; 2.731: 14.632e; 3.116–17: 14.660c–d; 3.118–20: 14.660d; 3.292–4: 14.660b; 3.375: 14.632e; 9.189: 14.633c; 12.208: 14.632e–f; 19.250–1: 14.660d; 23.2: 14.632e; *Od.* 1.337–8: 14.633c; 2.1: 13.604b; 3.439–44: 14.660b–c; 8.99: 14.627e; 9.212: 14.632e–f; 12.423: 14.632e; 17.270–1: 14.627e; 21.293–8: 14.613a–b

Hyagnis of Phrygia, *credited with the invention of Phrygian scale,* 14.624b

Hymenaeus, *beloved of Argynnus,* 13.603d

Hyperides of Athens, *orator* (Jensen ed.), fr. 34: 14.616c–d

Iason, *historian* (*FGrH* 632), F 1: 14.620d

392

Iatrocles, *author of treatise on cakes*, 14.646a, b, e–f, 647b–c

Ibycus of Rhegium, *lyric poet (PMG)*, 286: 13.601b–c; 309: 13.603c–d

Icarius, *father of Penelope*, 13.597f

Idomeneus (*FGrH* 338), F 17c: 13.611d–e

Io, *lover of Zeus*, 14.619c

Ion of Chios, *tragic, lyric, and elegiac poet and memoirist*: (*TrGF* 19), T 4b: 13.603e; F 22: 14.634f; F 23: 14.634c, f; (*FGrH* 392), F 6: 13.603e–f

Iphiclus, *love interest of Harpalycê*, 14.619e

Iphitus of Elis, *cofounder of Olympic games*, 14.635f

Iris, 14.645b

Istrus, *historian (FGrH* 334), F 39: 14.650b–c

Juba, *king of Mauretania (FGrH* 275), F 86: 14.660e

Kêrukês, *Athenian priestly family*, 14.660a–b

Lacydes, *philosopher*, 13.606c

Laius, *king of Thebes*, 13.602f–3a

Lamia, *pipe-girl of Demetrius Poliorcetes* (Stephanis #1527; *PAA* 601325), 14.614f–15a

Lamynthius of Miletus, *poet*, 13.597a, 605e; (*PMG*), 839: 13.597a

Larensius, *host of the dinner party*, 14.613c–d, 620b, 648d

Lasus of Hermione, *lyric poet (PMG)*, 702: 14.624e–f

Leaena, *courtesan (PAA* 602683), 13.596e–f

Lêmê, *courtesan (PAA* 607353), 13.596f

Leontion, *courtesan and lover of Hermesianax of Colophon*, 13.597a

Lesbothemis, *sculptor*, 14.635a–b

Leto, 14.614b

Leucaspis, *addressee of Anacreon*, 14.634c, 635c

Licymnius of Chios, *dithyrambic poet (PMG)*, 768: 13.603d

Lucius Anicius, *Roman general*, 14.615a–e

Lyceas of Naucratis, *historian (FGrH* 613), F 2: 14.616d–e

Lycurgus of Sparta, *lawgiver* (Poralla #499), 14.635f

Lyde, *courtesan associated with Antimachus of Colophon*, 13.596f–7a, 598a–b

Lyde, *courtesan associated with Lamynthius of Miletus*, 13.597a

Lynceus of Samos, *comic poet and memoirist* (Dalby ed.), fr. 7: 14.654a; fr. 13: 14.652d; fr. 15: 14.647a–b; fr. 17: 14.652c–d

Lysander of Sicyon, *lyre-player* (Stephanis #1573), 14.637f–8a

Lysandridas, *enemy of King Agesilaus of Sparta* (Poralla #503), 13.609b

Lysanias, *author of treatise on iambic poets*, 14.620c

INDEX

Lysias of Athens, *speech-writer* (Carey ed.), fr. 1: 13.611d–f, 612b–f

Lysimachus, *pipe-player* (Stephanis #1582), 14.615b

Lysimachus, *successor of Alexander "the Great,"* 13.610d–e; 14.614e–15a, 616b–c, 620f

Macareus, *historian (FGrH 456)*, F 1b: 14.639d

Macho of Sicyon, *comic poet and anecdotalist* (K–A), test. 1: 14.664a; fr. 1: 14.664b

Magdis of Thrace, *lyre-player*, 14.636f

Magnes, *comic poet* (K–A), fr. 2: 14.646d–e

Magnes, *deipnosophist*, 14.615e

Maison of Megara, *comic actor* (Stephanis #1594), 14.659a–c

Mandrogenes of Athens, *notorious wit* (Stephanis #1600; PAA 632020), 14.614d

Marcellus, *Roman general*, 14.634b

Marsyas, *satyr musician*, 14.616f–17a

Marsyas of Philippi, *historian (FGrH 135)*, F 11: 14.629d

Masurius, *deipnosophist*, 14.623e, 633f, 634b–c, e, 639a, 653d

Matro of Pitane, *parodist* (Olson–Sens = SH), fr. 5 = 538: 14.656e–f

Megalostrate, *beloved of Alcman*, 13.600f–1a

Melanippides of Melos, *lyric poet*, 14.616f; (PMG), 757: 14.651f; 758: 14.616e

Melanippus of Acragas, *unsuccessful tyrannicide*, 13.602a–c

Meletus, *tragic poet (PAA 639320 = 639322; TrGF 47)*, 13.605e

Memory, *personified. See* Mnemosyne

Menaechmus of Athens, *notorious wit* (Stephanis #1640; PAA 650910), 14.614d–e

Menaechmus of Sicyon, *historian (FGrH 131)*, F 4a: 14.635b; F 4b: 14.635e; F 5: 14.637e–f; F 6: 14.638a

Menalces, *beloved of Eriphanis*, 14.619c–d

Menander of Athens, *comic poet*, 14.659b; (K–A), test. 17: 13.594d; fr. 83: 14.651a; fr. 280: 14.654b; fr. 381.1: 14.644f; fr. 409.6–13: 14.644c–d; (Sandbach ed.), *Kol.* fr. 1: 14.659d–e

Mene, *father of Musaeus*, 13.597c; *Phasma* 73–4: 14.661f

Menelaus, *member of court of Demetrius Poliorcetes* (perhaps Berve i #505), 14.614f

Menetor, historian *(FHG)*, iv.452: 13.594c

Menippus, *Cynic philosopher* (Riese ed.), fr. II, p. 245: 14.664e; fr. IV, p. 246: 14.629e

Menodotus of Samos, *historian*, 14.655b; (FGrH 541), F 2: 14.655a

394

INDEX

Metrobius, *author of treatise on cake-making,* 14.643e

Miltiades of Athens, *politician* (*PAA* 653815), 13.594f

Mimnermus of Colophon, *elegiac poet,* 13.597a, 597f–8a; 14.620c

Minos, *king of Crete,* 13.601e–f

Mnasigiton of Athens, *notorious wit* (Stephanis #1714; *PAA* 654660), 14.614d–e

Mnasion, *rhapsode* (Stephanis #1721), 14.620c

Mnemosyne, 13.608f

Molpis of Sparta, *historian* (*FGrH* 590), F *2a: 14.661d–e

Monimus, *ruler of Pella,* 13.609b–c

Moschus, *author of treatise on mechanics,* 14.634b

Musaeus, *mythical epic singer,* 13.597d

Muse(s), 13.597e, 598c, 599d, 601a; 14.624f, 627c, f, 629a, 633a, 635a–b

Myron of Priene, *historian* (*FGrH* 106), F 2: 14.657c–e

Myrsilus, *historian* (*FHG*), fr. 16, iv.460: 13.610a

Myrtilus, *deipnosophist,* 13.596f, 610b, d; 14.616b–c

Nanno, *pipe-girl associated with Mimnermus* (Stephanis #1770), 13.597a, 598a

Neanthes of Cyzicus, *historian* (*FGrH* 84), F 16: 13.602c–d

Nestor, *king of Pylos,* 14.660b–c

Nicander of Calchedon, *historian* (*FGrH* 700), fr. 2: 13.606b–c

Nicander of Colophon, *didactic poet and grammarian,* 14.649e; *Th.* 891: 14.649c–d

Nicarete of Megara, *courtesan,* 13.596e

Nicias of Nicaea, *historian* (*FGrH* 318), F 1: 13.609e–f

Nicochares, *comic poet* (K–A), fr. 9: 14.619a; fr. 22: 14.657a

Nicolaus of Damascus, *Peripatetic philosopher and historian* (*FGrH* 90), T 10a: 14.652a–b

Nicomedes II, *king of Bithynia,* 13.606b–c

Nicomedes of Acanthus, *historian* (*FGrH* 722), F 3: 14.636b

Nicophon, *comic poet* (K–A), fr. 6: 14.645b–c; fr. 10.5: 14.645e

Nicostratus, *comic poet* (K–A), fr. 2: 14.654b; fr. 7: 14.664b–c; fr. 16.2–3: 14.664c; fr. 25: 14.615f

North Wind, *personified,* 13.604f

Nymphis of Heracleia, *historian* (*FGrH* 432), F 5b: 14.619e–20a

Nymphodorus of Syracuse, *historian* (*FGrH* 572), F 6: 13.596e; F 7: 13.609e

Odysseus, *Homeric hero,* 13.610c–d

Oeagrus, *father of Orpheus,* 13.597b

395

INDEX

Oenopas, *parodist* (Stephanis #1933), 14.638d

Oineus, *son of Dionysus and king of Calydon*, 13.608a–c

Olympias, *mother of Alexander "the Great"* (Berve i #581), 13.609b–c; 14.659f–60a

Onomarchus, *Phocian tyrant*, 13.605a–c

Orpheus, *mythical epic singer*, 13.597b–c; 14.632c

Oxythemis, *member of court of Demetrius Poliorcetes* (Billows #86), 14.614f

Palaephatus, *historian, epic poet, and grammarian* (FGrH 44), T 1–4: 14.661b

Palamedes, *epic hero and enemy of Odysseus*, 14.614b–c

Pamphilus of Alexandria, *grammarian* (Schmidt ed.), fr. II: 14.645c; fr. IV: 14.642d–e; fr. V: 14.650e; fr. XXXI: 14.653b

Panaetius of Rhodes, *Stoic philosopher* (van Straaten ed.), 14.634c–d, 657f n.

Pantaleon, *wandering showman* (Stephanis #1996; PAA 764430), 14.616a–b

Pantica of Cyprus, *wife of Monimus the son of Pythion*, 13.609b–c

Paris, *favorite of Lysimachus*, 14.614f

Parmenion, *general of Philip II and companion of Alexander "the Great"* (Berve i #606), 13.607f–8a

Parmeniscus of Metapontum, *devotee of Leto*, 14.614a–b

Patroclus, *companion of Achilleus*, 13.601b

Patroclus, *general of Ptolemy II*, 14.621a–b

Pelasgus, *king of Thessaly*, 14.639e–f

Pelignas, *cook for Olympias and Alexander "the Great"* (Berve i #625), 14.659f–60a

Pelops, *early Greek king*, 13.602f–3a; 14.625e–6a, 641c–d

Pelorus, *messenger to Pelasgus*, 14.639e–f

Penelope, *wife of Odysseus*, 13.597e–f

Pentheus, *king of Thebes*, 14.631b

Periander of Corinth, *elegiac poet*, 14.632d

Pericles, *Athenian politician* (PAA 772645), 13.594f, 604d

Perithous, *king of the Lapiths*, 14.613a–b

Persaeus of Citium, *Stoic philosopher*, 13.607e–f; (FGrH 584 = SVF), F 4 = fr. 451, i.100: 13.607a–e

Persephonê, 14.619b, 647a; *as Cora*, 14.624e–f

Persuasion, *personified*, 13.601e

Peucestas, *member of court of Demetrius Poliorcetes* (Berve i #634; Billows #90), 14.614f

Phaenias of Eresus, *Peripatetic philosopher* (Wehrli ed.), fr. 10: 14.638b–c

396

INDEX

Phaestus, *author of treatise on cake-making*, 14.643e

Phalaris, *tyrant of Acragas*, 13.602b

Phaon, *beloved of Sappho*, 13.596e

Pharsalia, *dancing-girl favored by Philomelus of Thebes* (Stephanis #2462), 13.605c–d

Phayllus of Phocis, *tyrant*, 13.605a–b

Phemius, *Phaecian singer*, 14.633c

Pherecles, *enemy of Mimnermus*, 13.598a

Pherecrates, *comic poet* (K–A), fr. 30: 14.648c; fr. 48: 14.653e–f; fr. 70: 13.612a–b; fr. 74: 14.653a; fr. 86: 14.646c; fr. 99: 14.645e; fr. 167: 14.644f–5a

Philemon of Athens, *grammarian*, 14.646c, 652e

Philemon of Syracuse, *comic poet*, 14.659b–c; (K–A), fr. 8: 14.663f; fr. 11: 14.663e–f; fr. 15: 13.595c; fr. 70: 14.644a; fr. 71: 14.664d; fr. 79: 14.658a–b; fr. 127: 13.606a; fr. dub. 198: 13.594d

Philetaerus, *comic poet* (K–A), fr. 17: 14.633e–f

Philetas (Philitas) of Cos, *poet and grammarian*, 13.598e–f; (Dettori ed.), fr. 8: 14.646d; (Dettori ed. = Spanoudakis ed.), fr. 9 = fr. 37: 14.645d

Philinus, *father of Theodorus the pipe-player*, 14.621b

Philip, *comedian* (Stephanis #2498; *PAA* 929295), 14.614c–d

Philip II, *king of Macedon*, 13.605b; 14.614e, 629d

Philippides, *comic poet* (K–A), fr. 10: 14.658d–e; fr. 20: 14.640c–d

Phillis of Delos, *historian* (*FHG*), fr. 2, iv.476: 14.636b–c; fr. 6, iv.476: 14.634d

Philo, *student of Aristotle* (*PAA* 953760), 13.610e–f

Philochorus, *historian* (*FGrH* 328), F 23: 14.637f–8a; F 79: 14.648d–e; F 86b: 14.645a–b; F 172: 14.628a–b; F 173: 14.656a; F 216: 14.630f

Philomelus of Thebes, 13.605c

Philoxenus of Cythera, *dithyrambic poet*, 13.598e; 14.626b, 642d–e; (*PMG*), 836(e): 14.642f–3d

Philyllius, *comic poet* (K–A), fr. 18: 14.640e, 641b

Phocylides, *gnomic poet*, 14.620c, 632d

Phoenicides, *comic poet* (K–A), fr. 2: 14.652d–e

Phormus, *Syracusan comic poet* (K–A), fr. 1: 14.652a

Phrynichus, *comic poet* (K–A), fr. 53: 14.654b

Phrynichus, *tragic poet*, 13.604a; (*TrGF* 3), F 11: 14.635b–c; F 13: 13.603f–4a

Phrynis, *poet*, 14.638c

Phye daughter of Socrates, *wife of Hipparchus the son of*

397

Pisistratus (*PAA* 966190), 13.609c–d

Phylarchus of Athens or Naucratis, *historian* (*FGrH* 81), F 12: 14.614e–15a; F 21: 13.609b–c; F 26: 13.606d–f; F 34: 13.609a–b; F 36: 13.606f–7a; F 42: 13.610d; (*FGrH* 81 = *SH*), F 84 = 694A: 14.639d

Physcidas son of Lycolas of Trichonium, *boyfriend of Onomarchus*, 13.605b–c

Pieris, *Muse-like figure*, 14.617d

Pindar, *epinician poet*, 14.625e; *O.* 1.50–2: 14.641c–d; 6.41: 13.604b; (Snell–Maehler eds.), fr. 112: 14.631c; fr. 123: 13.601d–e; fr. 124c: 14.641c; fr. 125: 14.635d–e; fr. 125.3: 14.635b; fr. 127: 13.601c

Pisistratus, *tyrant of Athens* (*PAA* 771760), 13.609c–d

Plangon of Miletus, *notorious courtesan*, 13.594b–d

Plato, *comic poet* (K–A), fr. 56: 14.657a; fr. 76: 14.641b–c; fr. 119: 14.657a; fr. 121: 14.644a; fr. 138: 14.628e

Plato, *philosopher*, 14.653e; *Criti.* 115a–b: 14.640e; *Lg.* 844d–e: 14.653b–d

Pleisthenes, *dedicant at Delphi*, 13.605c

Polemon, *travel writer* (Preller ed.), fr. 28: 13.606a–b; fr. 46: 14.659c; fr. 53: 13.602e–f

Polybius of Megalopolis, 4.20.5–21.9: 14.626a–f; 8.6.5–

6: 14.634b; 12.1.2: 14.651c–f; 30.22: 14.615a–f

Polycleia, *courtesan* (*PAA* 778695), 14.642c

Polycrates of Samos, *tyrant*, 13.599c, 602d

Polyeuctus of Achaea, *parodist* (Stephanis #2095), 14.638b

Polystratus of Athens ("the Etruscan"), *student of Theophrastus* (*PAA* 780975), 13.607f

Pontianus of Nicomedia, *philosopher and deipnosophist*, 14.640c

Posidippus of Cassandreia, *comic poet*, 14.658f; (K–A), fr. 1: 14.661f–2b; fr. 2: 14.659c; fr. 25: 14.659c–d

Posidippus of Pela, *epigrammatic poet* (Austin–Bastianini eds.), 146: 13.596c; (Austin–Bastianini eds. = *HE*), 122 = 3142–9: 13.596c–e

Posidonius of Apamea, *Stoic philosopher*, 14.635d, 649e; (*FGrH* 87 = Edelstein–Kidd eds.), T 10b = test. 8: 14.657f; F 3 = fr. 55a: 14.649d; F 14 = fr. 66: 13.594e; F 107 = fr. 292: 14.635c–d

Pratinas of Phlius, *lyric and tragic poet* (*PMG*), 708: 14.617c–f; 709: 14.633a; 712a: 14.624f

Praxilla of Sicyon, *lyric poet* (*PMG*), 751: 13.603a

Priam, *king of Troy*, 14.660d

INDEX

Pronomus of Thebes, *pipe-player* (Stephanis #2149; *PAA* 789605), 14.631e

Ptolemy II Philadelphus, *king of Egypt*, 14.620f–1a

Ptolemy III Euergetes, *king of Egypt and memoirist* (*FGrH* 234), T 2: 14.654c–d; F 2a: 14.654b–d

Ptolemy IV Philomator, *king of Egypt*, 14.654c–d

Ptolemy of Alorus, *king of Macedon*, 14.629d

Pyretus of Miletus, *Ionokologos* (*SH*), 714: 14.620e–f

Pyrrhandrus, *author of treatise on pipe-players*, (*FHG*), iv.486: 14.634d

Pyrrhichus of Sparta, *dancer* (Poralla #653), 14.630e

Pythagoras, *geographer*, 14.634a

Pythagoras of Samos, *mystic philosopher*, 13.599a; 14.632b–c

Pythagoras of Zacynthus, *musician*, 14.637c–e

Pythermus of Teos, *lyric poet*, 14.625c–d; (*PMG*), 910: 14.625c

Pythionice, *courtesan loved by Harpalus*, 13.594e–6a

Pythodorus of Sicyon, 13.605a

Python of Catana, *tragic poet* (*TrGF* 91), F 1: 13.595e–6b

Rhadamanthys "the Just," 13.603c–d; 14.614b–c

Rhodopis, *Herodotean courtesan*, 13.596b–c

Sambas, *Phrygian pipe-player* (Stephanis #2209), 14.624b

Sambyx, *musician*, 14.637c

Sappho of Eresus, *courtesan*, 13.596e

Sappho of Lesbos, *lyric poet*, 13.596e, 599c–d, 605e; 14.635e, 639a; (Voigt ed.), fr. 15: 13.596b; fr. 247: 14.635b; fr. 250: 13.599c; fr. 254c: 13.596b

Scamon, *historian* (*FGrH* 476), F 2: 14.630b; F 4: 14.637b–c

Scipio Africanus, *Roman general*, 14.657f

Seasons, *personified*, 14.656a

Secundus, *wine-steward of Nicomedes II*, 13.606b–c

Seleucus, *grammarian* (Müller ed.), fr. 44: 14.645d; fr. 53: 14.645d; fr. 56: 14.658d

Semonactides of Chios, *cook*, 14.661c–d

Semonides of Amorgos, *elegiac poet* (West[2] ed.), fr. 22: 14.658c; fr. 23: 14.658c; fr. 24: 14.659e–f

Semus of Delos, *historian* (*FGrH* 396), F 1: 14.637b–c; F 5: 14.645b; F 10: 14.614a–b; F 11: 14.618a; F 23: 14.618d–e; F 24: 14.622a–d

Sextus Quintilius Condianus and Sextus Quintilius Valerius Maximus, *consuls and coauthors of book on farming*, 14.649d–e

Sibylla, *Apollo's Sibyl treated as individual*, 14.637b–c

399

Sicinnus, *barbarian who invented satyr-dance*, 14.630b

Silenus, *grammarian*, 14.644f

Simonides of Ceos, *lyric and epigrammatic poet*, 14.620c, 625e, 638e, 656c–e; (*PMG*), 585: 13.604b

Simonides of Zacynthus, *rhapsode* (Stephanis #2281), 14.620c

Simus of Magnesia, *hilarodic poet*, 14.620d

Sinope of Thrace, *owner of Bacchis* (*PAA* 823250), 13.595a

Sirites, *Libyan nomad credited with inventing pipe-playing*, 14.618b–c

Socrates of Athens, *sage and poet*, 13.599a–b, 611a, d, 612a–b; 14.643f; (West² ed.), fr. 3: 14.628e–f

Solon of Athens, *lawgiver, elegiac poet, and sage*, 14.632d; (Ruschenbusch ed.), fr. 73b: 13.612a; (West² ed.), fr. 25.2: 13.602a; fr. 38: 14.645f

Sopater of Paphos, *comic poet* (K–A), fr. 4: 14.644c; fr. 5: 14.656f; fr. 16: 14.649a

Sophilus, *comic poet* (K–A), fr. 5: 14.640d

Sophocles of Athens, *opponent of philosophers* (*PAA* 829235), 13.610e–f

Sophocles of Athens, *tragic poet*, 13.598c–d, 601a–b, 603e–4f, 638f; 14.652d; (Radt ed.), test. 75: 13.603e; fr. 199:

14.646d; fr. 238: 14.637a; fr. 345: 13.602e; fr. 412: 14.635c; fr. 671: 14.657a; (*FGE*), 1040–3: 13.604f

Sophon, *cook in Larensius' house*, 14.622e–3c

Sophon of Acarnania, *comic cook*, 14.662c

Sosibius, *author of treatise on Alcman*, 14.646a

Sosibius of Sparta, *historian* (*FGrH* 595), F 3: 14.635e–f; F *7 = test. 2: 14.621d; F 12: 14.648b

Sosinomus, *banker* (*PAA* 862820), 13.611f

Sotades of Maroneia, *Ionikologos*, 14.620e–1b; (Powell ed.), fr. 1, p. 238: 14.621a; fr. 2, p. 238: 14.621b

Statira, *wife of Persian king*, 13.609a–b

Stesandrus of Samos, *citharode* (Stephanis #2301), 14.638a–b

Stesichorus of Himera, *lyric poet*, 13.601a; 14.638e; (*PMG*), 179(a).1–2: 14.645e; 199: 13.610c; 277: 14.619d–e

Stilpo of Megara, *philosopher* (Döring ed. = *SSR* II), fr. 156 = O 17: 13.596e

Strabo, 3.162: 14.657e–8a; (Jones ed.), fr. 60: 14.657e–f

Stratocles, *orator* (*PAA* 837400), 13.596f

Straton of Athens, *notorious wit* (Stephanis #2314; *PAA* 839370), 14.614d

Strattis, *comic poet* (K–A), fr.

12: 14.656b; fr. 28: 14.654f;
fr. 49: 14.621f–2a

Sulla, *Roman general,* 14.615a–e

Sun, *personified,* 13.604f. *See
also* Ahura Mazda

Tachos, *Egyptian king,*
14.616d–e

Talthybius, *Homeric herald,*
14.660d

Talus, *lover of Rhadamanthys
"the Just,"* 13.603c–d

Tantalus, *king of Sipylus and father of Pelops,* 14.625f

Teleclides, *comic poet* (K–A), fr.
1.12: 14.644f; fr. 8: 14.619a;
fr. 33: 14.656e; fr. 34:
14.648e; fr. 36: 14.639a

Telembrotus, *addressee of
Semonides,* 14.658c

Telenicus of Byzantium, *indecent poet,* 14.638b–c

Telephanes, *historian* (FHG),
iv.507: 14.614d–e

Telesias, *dancer* (Stephanis
#2387), 14.630a

Telesilla of Argos, *lyric poet*
(PMG), 718: 14.619b

Telesphorus, *chief official of
Lysimachus,* 14.616c

Telestes of Selinus, *dithyrambic
poet* (PMG), 805a: 14.616f–
17a; 805b: 14.617a; 805c:
14.617a–b; 806: 14.617b; 808:
14.637a; 810: 14.625f–6a

Telus, *Phrygian pipe-player*
(Stephanis #2409), 14.624b

Terpander, *musician and poet,*
14.635d–f, 638c

Thargelia of Miletus, *beautiful
and wise woman,* 13.608f–9a

Theano, *beloved of Pythagoras,*
13.599a

Theodorus, *grammarian* (FGrH
346), F 2: 14.646c

Theodorus of Boeotia, *pipe-player*
(Stephanis #1159), 14.615b–d

Theodorus of Colophon, *poet*
(SH), 753: 14.618e–19a

Theodorus son of Philinus,
pipe-player (Stephanis
#1173), 14.621b

Theodorus "the Atheist," *philosopher* (SSR IV H), F 11:
13.611a–b

Theognetus, *comic poet* (K–A),
fr. 2: 14.616a

Theognis of Megara, *elegiac
poet,* 14.632d

Theophilus, *comic poet* (K–A),
fr. 5: 14.623f; fr. 7: 14.635a

Theophrastus of Eresus, *philosopher and naturalist,* 13.607f;
14.654d; (Fortenbaugh ed.),
fr. 401: 14.651a–b; fr. 562:
13.609e; fr. 563: 13.609f; fr.
564: 13.610a–b; fr. 567A:
13.606c; fr. 726B: 14.624a–b

Theopompus, *comic poet* (K–
A), fr. 12: 14.652e–f; fr. 49:
14.657a; fr. 63: 14.649b

Theopompus, *pipe-player*
(Stephanis #1180), 14.615b

Theopompus of Chios, *historian*
(FGrH 115), F 22: 14.657a–c;
F 106: 14.657a–c; F 108:
14.616d–e; F 133: 14.650a–b;
F 216: 14.627d–e; F 240:

13.609b; F 247: 13.604f–5a;
F 248: 13.605a–c; F 253:
13.595a–c; F 254b: 13.595d–e
Theoxenus of Tenedos, *beloved
of Pindar*, 13.601d–e
Thersippus, *inventor of satyr-
dance* (Stephanis #1196),
14.630b
Theseus, *king of Athens*,
13.601f
Thrasymedes, *son of Nestor*,
14.660b–c
Timaeus of Taureomenium, *historian* (*FGrH* 566), F 144:
13.602f
Timo of Phlius, *invective poet*
(*SH*), 791.1: 13.601c–d;
791.2: 13.601c; 794: 13.610b
Timocrates, *Athenaeus' interlocutor*, 14.613a
Timomachus, *historian* (*FGrH*
754), F 1: 14.638a–b
Timosa, *concubine associated
with Oxyartis*, 13.609a–b
Timotheus of Miletus, *citharode
and dithyrambic poet*,
14.626b, 636e–f, 657e
Trophonius, *oracular god*,
14.614a, 641e
Tryphon of Alexandria, *grammarian*, 14.641f; (Velsen ed.),
fr. 109: 14.618c; fr. 110:
14.634d–e; fr. 113: 14.618c–
d; fr. 136: 14.640e
Tyndarichus of Sicyon, *cook*,
14.661d
Tyrtaeus of Sparta, *elegiac poet
and general* (Poralla #709),
14.630f

Ulpian, *grammarian and symposiarch*, 14.613c, 615e,
616c–d, 640c, 648c, e, 649a–
c, 658e, 662e–f

Xanthippe, *wife of Socrates*
(*PAA* 730275), 13.611d–e;
14.643f
Xenocrates of Chalcedon, *philosopher*, 13.610e
Xenopeitheia, *mother of
Lysandridas* (Poralla #570),
13.609b
Xenophanes of Colophon, *poet
and philosopher*, 14.632d
Xenophon of Athens, *philosopher and soldier*, *Ages*. 5.1:
14.613c; *An*. 2.314–15:
14.651b; *Oec*. 19.19: 14.653e;
Smp. 1.11: 14.614c–d; 2.3–4:
13.612a
Xerxes I, *king of Persia*,
14.652b–c

Zenis (or Zeneus) of Chios, *historian* (*FGrH* 393), F 1:
13.601f
Zeno of Citium, *Stoic philosopher*, 13.603e, 607e–f
Zeno of Sidon, *Epicurean philosopher*, 13.611b
Zenobius, *paroemiographer*,
4.81: 14.624b
Zeus, 13.597e, 601e–f, 602e;
14.633e, 643b; *as Zeus
Pelorias*, 14.639f–40a
Zopyrinus, *cook*, 14.661d